Theory and Cultural Value

Theory and Cultural Value

Steven Connor

BLACKWELL
Oxford UK & Cambridge USA

First published 1992

Blackwell Publishers
108 Cowley Road
Oxford OX4 1JF
UK

Three Cambridge Center
Cambridge, Massachusetts 02142
USA

British Library Cataloguing in Publication Data

A CIP catalogue record for this book is available from
the British Library.

Library of Congress Cataloging-in-Publication Data

Connor, Steven.
Theory and cultural value / Steven Connor.
p.   cm.
Includes bibliographical references and index.
ISBN 0–631–18281–0 (acid-free paper). – ISBN 0–631–18282–9 (pbk.:
acid-free paper)
1. Literature – Philosophy.   2. Value in literature.
3. Literature, Modern – 20th century – History and criticism – Theory,
etc.   I. Title.
PN49.C63   1992
801'.3 – dc20   91–47108
                                                          CIP

Typeset in 10½ on 12pt Garamond
by Graphicraft Typesetters Ltd, Hong Kong
Printed in Great Britain by T.J. Press Ltd, Padstow, Cornwall

This book is printed on acid-free paper

Contents

Acknowledgements

Early versions of sections from chapters 2 and 4 have appeared in *Textual Practice* and *Paragraph*; I am grateful in both cases for permission to reprint. The figure on p. 254 is reprinted by permission of the publishers from *The Predicament of Culture: Twentieth-Century Ethnography, Literature, and Art* by James Clifford, Cambridge, Mass.: Harvard University Press, Copyright © 1988 by the President and Fellows of Harvard College. Most of the ideas in this book have been formed, corrected and renewed in discussions with colleagues and students in my own institution and elsewhere. I first thought of writing this book while organizing the conference on 'Cultural Value' at Birkbeck College in 1988, and I want to thank very much indeed my co-organizers, Lynda Nead and Claire Buck, and all the participants in that conference, especially Barbara Herrnstein Smith, Gayatri Spivak and Terry Eagleton. I also want to thank the organizers of and participants in the following, for helping me to think through, and often forcing me to come up with, the arguments in this book: the graduate seminars in political theory at the universities of Sussex and Oxford, the graduate seminar in twentieth-century literature in the University of Oxford, the conference on 'Modernism from the Viewpoint of Modernity' and the English department graduate seminar at the University of Southampton, the seminar on critical theory of the French department of Birkbeck College and the conference on 'Literary Studies in a Postmodern World' at Lancaster University. I wish to thank, in particular, William Outhwaite, Peter Middleton, Christopher Butler and Tony Pinkney. I am grateful to the Department of English of the University of Alberta, Edmonton and the Falmouth School of Art, who invited me to lecture on aspects of the question of value. The arguments about intercultural value developed in chapter 9 were formed during the International Symposium of the English Literature and Language Association of Korea in 1990; I want to record my thanks to the organizers of ELLAK for inviting me to and making me feel so very welcome at this conference, as well as to the British Council for making it possible for me to attend. I have benefited hugely from the energy, wisdom and generosity, collective and individual, of colleagues working in the Department of English and the Centre for Interdisciplinary Research in Culture and the Humanities at Birkbeck, and especially Laura Marcus, Annie Coombes, Jo Labanyi, Eddie Hughes, Lynda Nead, Tom Healy and Isobel Armstrong. Barbara Hardy provided in a number of conversations the spark from which the whole book took light. Jacqueline Harvey read the text with an acute and perspicacious eye, thus saving me from innumerable follies. Perhaps the greatest value of intellectual work of this kind is that it leaves one sunk in a condition of ethical ruin, having run up social and intellectual debts that can never be discharged. The largest and most unpayable of these is to my beloved Lynda Nead. The book is dedicated to our little boy Sam, who was born during the course of its writing.

Abbreviations

ATVM	Jacques Derrida, 'At This Very Moment in This Work Here I Am'
BPP	Sigmund Freud, *Beyond the Pleasure Principle*
CI	Terry Eagleton, *Criticism and Ideology*
CIS	Richard Rorty, *Contingency, Irony, and Solidarity*
CP	David Harvey, *The Condition of Postmodernity*
CPES	Jean Baudrillard, *For a Critique of the Political Economy of the Sign*
CV	Barbara Herrnstein Smith, *Contingencies of Value*
D	Jean-François Lyotard, *The Differend*
DE	Theodor Adorno and Max Horkheimer, *Dialectic of Enlightenment*
DP	Clifford Geertz, 'Deep Play: Notes on a Balinese Cockfight'
EDS	Luce Irigaray, *Ethique de la différence sexuelle*
FC	Seyla Benhabib and Drucilla Cornell (eds), *Feminism as Critique*
FW	Kate Fullbrook, *Free Women*
G/E	Mary Daly, *Gyn/Ecology*
HD	Vincent Crapanzano, 'Hermes' Dilemma: The Masking of Subversion in Ethnographic Description'
IA	Terry Eagleton, *The Ideology of the Aesthetic*
IE	Georges Bataille, *Inner Experience*
JL	Sigmund Freud, *Jenseits des Lustprinzips*
LE	Georges Bataille, *Literature and Evil*
LK	Clifford Geertz, *Local Knowledge*
PA	Christine Delphy, 'Protofeminism and Antifeminism'
PC	James Clifford, *The Predicament of Culture*
PDM	Jürgen Habermas, *The Philosophical Discourse of Modernity*
'Pleasure'	Fredric Jameson, 'Pleasure: A Political Issue'
PT	Roland Barthes, *The Pleasure of the Text*

PU	Fredric Jameson, *The Political Unconscious*
QLV	Antony Easthope, 'The Question of Literary Value'
TS	Luce Irigaray, *This Sex which is Not One*
TSF	Jacques Derrida, 'To Speculate – on "Freud"', in *The Post-Card*
TWJ	Jacques Derrida, 'Two Words for Joyce'
U	James Joyce, *Ulysses*
UP	Jürgen Habermas, 'What is Universal Pragmatics?'
VE	Georges Bataille, *Visions of Excess*
VM	Jacques Derrida, 'Violence and Metaphysics: An Essay on the Thought of Emmanuel Levinas'
WH	Samuel Beckett, *Worstward Ho*
WL	Clifford Geertz, *Works and Lives*

1

Introduction

No serious discussion of the question of value can proceed very far without encountering one form or another of the conflict between absolute and relative value, a conflict traditionally polarized by those who, on the one hand, believe in the need for, and possibility of, norms and values which are unconditional, objective and absolute, and those who, on the other, accept the unmasterable historicity, heterogeneity and cultural relativity of all values. One of the features of this opposition between the absolute and the relative is that it provides no common frame within which to assess both claims, since each position derives its identity from its repudiative characterization of the other. Any attempt to synthesize the rival claims of the absolutist and the relativist is always liable to be construed and condemned by one side as itself tyrannically absolutist, or by the other as insufficiently armed against the corruptive force of relativism. This might seem to qualify the opposition as a 'differend', as defined by Jean-François Lyotard in *The Differend: Phrases in Dispute* (1988), a disagreement that cannot be brought to the bar of any higher argumentative authority.

Unpromising though it may seem, the proposal of this book is that we should attempt the difficult feat of thinking absolutism and relativism together rather than as apart and antagonistic. The account of value that I offer, simply, is that one should refuse to surrender either the orientation towards universal, absolute and transcendent value, or the commitment to plurality, relativity and contingency. The motivation for this is not a desire to have it every way, or the disinclination to make a stand, for I do not in the least underestimate the absolute antagonism between these opposed accounts of things. Rather it arises from the apprehension of the mutual implication of the various versions of the absolutist and relativist cases, the fact that, as well as contradicting each other, each side of the argument also requires, confirms and regenerates the other.

So in what follows I offer no sort of reconciling vision or splitting of a difference. Rather, I recommend the acceptance of the radical self-contradiction and unabatable paradox of value. Where traditional accounts of value abhor inconsistency and aporia, and attempt to resolve them wherever they arise, I suggest that such resolutions of evaluative questions are always inauthentic, partial and perhaps even violent. If such an account of value seems initially to be overtheoretical and cerebrally remote from the practicalities of social and political life, I want to suggest that it is both the desire for an absolute grounding of political practice, and the attempt to imagine a political practice entirely without grounding, which are hopelessly impractical and unresponsive to the practical complexity attaching to questions of value. Almost every actual circumstance of contemporary political life that one could imagine implies the need to sustain, rather than prematurely to resolve, the absolutism/relativism opposition, in any of its many different allotropes, as for example: universalism/particularism, essentialism/historicism, intrinsic value/contingency, intransitive value/transitive value, use-value/exchange-value. All these contradictory pairs must be thought together, rather than resolved, either in favour of one or other alternative, or in favour of some imagined synthesis of the two.

I hold the imperative that governs this is to be the necessity, or value, of value itself. It is easier to feel the force of this imperative than to give it a local habitation and a name. Value, in this imperative sense, is the irreducible orientation towards the better, and revulsion from the worse; or it is what will be described in chapter 4 as the irreducible principle of generalized positivity, the inescapable pressure to identify and identify with whatever is valuable rather than what is not valuable. The imperative to value might be identified with the pleasure principle, which seeks always to increase the yield of pleasure and to avoid all forms of unpleasure; or it might be identified with the biological basis of our beings, in our seemingly inbuilt need to preserve life and to resist death. But both of these drives are in fact themselves mere secondary manifestations of the imperative to value, since they can themselves be subject to evaluation and resisted or inverted. Neither the suicide who believes that individual annihilation is preferable to continued existence, nor the philosopher who argues that it would have been better for the human race, even life itself, never to have existed, can resist the imperative of value, even in the apparent denial of all values in particular, since they both depend upon the affirmation of and preference for the *better*, even if, as in writers such as Freud, Bataille and Beckett, the route to the better may seem to lie through the worse.

The imperative dimension of value is not only distinct from the operation of particular values, it is opposed to it. This is because the imperative dimension commands that we continue evaluating in the face of every apparently stable and encompassing value in particular. The desirability of universal freedom may seem hard to dispute, but universal freedom (like universal anything) must include within it the freedom to question and criticize its own nature. Could a form of freedom that forbade the willed choosing of slavery really be freedom? The values that we prize come into being because of acts of energetic, painful appraisal; values are the sedimental deposits of the imperative to value. But all values must remain continually vulnerable to appraisal. The imperative to value therefore turns out to involve an extreme reflexivity, since it is an imperative not only to continue valuing, but to continue evaluating values themselves, or value itself. It is also, necessarily, an imperative to continue evaluating the imperative to value.

Described in this way, the imperative of value is clearly not to be thought of as generating a set of objective essences; such that what I have been calling the imperative of value does not equal absolute or intrinsic value. Indeed, it would never be possible to give a name to this imperative, or isolate it reliably for inspection, without freezing it into objecthood. The imperative of value may therefore be thought of as the Derridean *différance* of value, not only because it defers the arrival of ultimate value (though it is always necessarily orientated towards it), as *différance* defers the arrival of meaning, but because of the reflexive structure which I have just specified, in which every value is itself subject to the force of evaluation.

We live, we tell ourselves constantly, in a pluralizing world. Much recent work in critical theory has tended to assume that value lies entirely on the side of opening, expansion, alterity and invention, and not on the side of fixity, conservation, tradition and repetition. This book assumes that these are not clear or continuous opposites. The paradoxical structure of value enacts itself in avant-garde art, which can be truly new only by means of its refusal to abandon what it aims to leave behind in its past, or in a deconstructive philosophy that can avoid re-enacting tradition only by a repetitive working through of that tradition. Only an institution can dissolve itself, only an identity can know plurality, only the same is vulnerable to alterity, only a kind of consciousness can embrace the unthought, only tradition can beget newness; in sum, only the commitment or imperative to value can effect any kind of transvaluation.

This institutionalization of value is, in the end, not in the interest or on the side of the institution, but on the side of its opposite, which is to say, on the side of exchange and relativity. As I suggest in my discussion of Marxist theories of value in chapter 6, the evil of economic exchange-value is not that it melts away the fixity of use-value, but precisely that it subordinates all forms of exchange to the force of one form alone – the economic. The general corruption of an era of exchange-value lies in the fact that it makes everything exchangeable according to this one standard or register. Joining together the iron constriction of the law of the market-place with the ghostly indeterminacy of all value under market conditions, the realm of economic exchange-value represents the bad or negative version of the paradox of value, in denying the possibility of value while seeming to multiply it. Seen from this point of view, the principal imperative is not to rescue values or value in general from 'corruption', but to bring about an even more general or encompassing corruption, by the multiplication not only of values, but also of the standards or registers of value. The utopia towards which this theory of value is orientated is not a utopia of incomparables, incommensurables or absolute loss, all versions of an escape from exchange, but rather a utopia of *maximized* exchange, dominated by the theoretically infinite productivity not only of values, but of forms of the exchange of value. A utopia, therefore, not of incommensurability, but of infinitely multiple commensurabilities. But this can come about only by a positive intensification of the paradox of value, in which various kinds of institution enable the anti-institutional diversification of value, as opposed to the bad paradox of the era of exchange-value, in which diversity acts in the service of uniformity.

The principle of the maximal multiplication of forms and registers of value expresses itself through the imperative to self-reflexivity mentioned a moment ago, the imperative, in the interests of maximizing value, of submitting every form of value to continuous evaluation. This principle of value-reflexivity is paradoxical in the way that forms of reflexivity usually are, because the very imperative to continue and extend the investigation of value is continually vulnerable to its own force. In practical terms, the institutions and procedures which we employ to actualize the evaluation of values – schools, universities, local and national government, political organizations of all kinds – are always likely to become fixated by the desire to conserve and reproduce particular values. The forms of plurality must therefore be both protected and themselves pluralized; and we need to think and institute ways in which the protection of pluralism is enacted precisely through its pluralization, rather than instituting limits. But no pluralism is entirely without limits, forms and institutions, since these are precisely what is necessary to make pluralism possible and actual.

This is why the imperative to submit value to continuous question is not opposed to, or a distraction from, a political discourse of emancipation. In fact, it is itself, in its essence, such a discourse of emancipation. For, in the first place – a first place that looks to be a long way off for most of the world – it is only through emancipation from hunger, poverty, exploitation, autonomization, degradation and exclusion of all kinds that anyone can be in any position to begin the questioning of value that I recommend. Furthermore, denied the possibility of rational interchange with the greatest plurality of emancipated subjects, no singular individual, however apparently unconstrained, can have access to maximally free transaction of value. But, at the same time, it is important not to allow an infinite deferral of the questioning of value, but rather, now, strategically, institutionally, politically, as well as in dreams, desires, writing and philosophy, to begin bringing about instances of such valuing of value, to begin instantiating the 'community of the question about the possibility of the question' (VM, 80).

I argue in different ways in the chapters that follow for the necessary and inescapable intertwining of (what have been known as) ethical and aesthetic value in this process. Traditionally, accounts of the relationship between the ethical and the aesthetic have tended to subordinate or assimilate one to the other, either aestheticizing ethics, as in Nietzsche's call for a ceaseless aesthetic transvaluation of all the falsely and repressively fixated values of ethics, or, as in many current critiques of Nietzsche and Nietzschean poststructuralism coming from the political left, in the demonstration of the repressive or ideological nature of the aesthetic, in its capacity to distort and disguise political facts and values. Typically, the choice of whether to assimilate the ethical to the aesthetic, or vice versa, has presented itself as a choice between stability and turmoil; though we must also recognize that, at different moments, the relative values attached to the domains opened up under the names of the ethical and the aesthetic may shift and invert. We should remember, for example, that the aesthetic can and does appear historically both as the guarantee of certain forms of absolute and eternal value and as the very force of Becoming itself, the very name of relativity. So if the ethical and the aesthetic embody the opposition of stable value and shifting relativity, they do so only as the effects of a historically dynamic process which works out the stability and flux of value itself precisely through the shifting and unstable forms of ethical and aesthetic value. The divisions and exchanges between ethics and aesthetics therefore not only regulate the play of value, they are also produced by and out of it.

It is for these reasons that I argue in the following pages, not for any forms of reconciliation of the ethical and the aesthetic, or any kind of choice between them, but rather for an active engagement with the ways in which the ethical and the aesthetic endlessly transact with and against each other, endlessly produce and enlarge each other's form through their very antagonism. Sometimes this will mean arguing, as in my discussion of Habermasian discourse ethics in chapter 5, for the authentic ethical purpose of those forms of poetic or non-serious discourse commonly constituted as marginal or excessive to serious rational and political discourse. Sometimes, as in the discussion of the ethics of deconstruction in chapter 8, it will involve stressing the ways in which ethics itself must be imagined and constituted not in the constancy of fundamental, self-identical value, but through the dynamic self-estrangement which can be enacted through the forms of the literary and the aesthetic.

But it will be necessary quite as often to submit those forms of value exchange and transaction known as the aesthetic to ethical critique, asking hard questions about the idealizing, reifying or displacing purposes of the aesthetic, and insisting on the social and political equivalences of every form of aesthetic value. It will be necessary to be suspicious of every attempt to project oneself outside or beyond the field of socially constituted value through the various theories of the aesthetic, from the fraudulent disinterestedness of the aesthetic in Kant, to the claims for the transcendence of the accumulative logic of the economic by processes of aesthetic squandering in Bataille, or the aesthetic ideal of wholeness which underlies some forms of Marxist utopia. And certainly, it will involve refusing, or questioning the value of, any kind of aesthetic experience or form that does not implicitly begin the work of subjecting the ideal and identity of the aesthetic to self-reflexive critique.

This study explores the forms in which the question of value has been shrouded or silenced in much contemporary theory, arguing the necessity for this question to be brought back to theoretical consciousness. But there is a danger here. For is it not the case that in the past the question of value has been too much, too emphatically, in the conscious grip of theory? Is it not the case that the academic theory and discourse of value which has in fact become so developed in the twentieth century – with its history of debates, genealogy of concepts, glossary of terms, its insti-tutional embodiments and network of tensions and affiliations – consti-tute a single mechanism or medium of exchange, a method of talking about value which, like the money-form in the sphere of the economic, in fact flattens and serializes value rather than actualizing it? Seen in this way, the institutionalization of value theory is a deterrence of value. If this is the case, then what is regretted in the following pages as the apparent failure of some (perhaps most) areas of contemporary critical theory to articulate the question of value may in fact be a reflex away from this system of exchange, a negativity designed to enlarge the field of value, or to draw into exchange the very medium of exchange in which academic discussions of value have been conducted. This apparent turning away from value would then be seen as a turning back (out) towards value, and the account that this book offers of such a turn would represent an impoverishment, a translation of what is already a process of creative mistranslation into a generalized system of equivalence, the Esperanto of value.

But the metaphor of translation cuts in several directions. For if contemporary cultural and philosophical critique is dedicated to thinking out forms of incommensurability, to articulating what has preciously been lost in translation, whether it be the incoherence of thought or the *logos*, or in the experience and identity of women or those others dispossessed by (and of) the knowledges of the West, then it can only be by an act of translation, with all the imperfection and contamination that it brings with it, that such untranslatability can be known or shown. My final chapter suggests that in a world in which the question of culture is pre-eminently a question of translation, another form of the paradox of value is to be discovered. To adapt the words of Clifford Geertz, the value that is always lost in translation can only ever be found in translation. Value and culture must know themselves in order to begin to know what escapes them. If twentieth-century theory has valuably enforced the awareness of the excessiveness of value, the endless surpassing, in fact and possibility, of the values and thematics of value dominant in Western culture, then it is also necessary to try to constitute a political discourse which could secure and nurture the permanent possibility of this reflexive surpassing of value.

2

The Necessity of Value

Value is inescapable. This is not to be taken as a claim for the objective existence or categorical force of any values or imperatives in particular; but rather as a claim that the processes of estimating, ascribing, modifying, affirming and even denying value, in short, the processes of *evaluation*, can never be avoided. We are claimed always and everywhere by the necessity of value in this active, transactional sense. The argument of this book will be that we should acknowledge that value and evaluation are necessary as a kind of law of human nature and being, such that we cannot help but enter the play of value, even when we would wish to withdraw from or suspend it. The necessity of value is in this sense more like the necessity of breathing than, say, the necessity of earning one's living. There are ways of continuing to exist as a human being without the latter, but not without the former.

Evaluation and the play of value here involve every actual or conceivable action or condition of estimation, comparison, praising or relative preference. Seen in this way, the play of value is bound up intimately with motivation and purpose of every kind. No one has put this point more emphatically in recent years than John Fekete, so I will gratefully borrow his words:

> Not to put too fine a point on it, we live, breathe, and excrete values. No aspect of human life is unrelated to values, valuations, and validations. Value orientations and value relations saturate our experiences and life practices from the smallest established microstructures of feeling, thought, and behavior to the largest established macrostructures of organizations and institutions. The history of cultures and social formations is unintelligible except in relation to a history of value orientations, value ideals, goods values, value responses, and value judgements, and their objectivations, interplay, and transformations.[1]

Traditionally, questions of value have been central to the disciplines designated as the humanities and social sciences rather than to the scientific disciplines. It is often assumed that this division reflects a certain division in terms of subject matter and its conditions of knowability. Where the scientist seeks knowledge about objects and processes which are held to be independent of his or her procedures of observation, the enquiries of the humanities and social sciences are directed towards cultural objects and processes which are not to be understood otherwise than in social and cultural terms. Such a distinction has traditionally been used to distinguish between evaluative and non-evaluative enquiry, though, with the increasing awareness of the ways in which scientific enquiry is always culturally conditioned and conditional, this distinction has lately come to seem very fragile. But the real force of this objection to the idea of scientific objectivity comes not from the descriptive force of its characterization of the way in which science is inevitably affected by evaluative choices and assumptions – for such an account of things might still conceal an aspiration towards objectivity beneath its melancholy acknowledgement that such objectivity may be difficult to achieve. The force of the objection lies rather in the paradoxical principle that the very notion of freedom from evaluation must always itself embody an evaluative force; as we know, for scientists and others, a very high value is attached to work that can be seen to be fully value-free. In fact, any and every claim to escape the necessity of value must end up demonstrating that necessity, simply by being a claim. The non-evaluative or value-free will always be a particular suburb of the domain of value, never a space outside it.[2]

However, even if one rejects the idea of a distinction between disciplines that are saturated with value and disciplines that are free of value, one might still find a use for such a distinction in terms of the self-designations of such disciplines. Clearly, there is a usable, if still only provisional, distinction to be made between disciplines that are orientated towards an ideal of value-freedom and disciplines that are consciously orientated towards the positing or affirmation of values. And these are indeed the terms under which one might want to distinguish the natural, physical and life sciences from the social sciences and the humanities. Where the former seeks to minimize the force of value choices, the latter has sought to deepen this force. This is not to say that the humanities and social sciences have always accepted their saturation with questions of value willingly. On the contrary, many of the best efforts of sociologists, economists, historians and literary critics have been directed towards the establishment of theories, rules and procedures which will allow them to speak in a value-free way of the operations and effects of evaluative choice (in the philosophy of moral choice, for example, or the attempts to found a scientific theory of literature). But it seems important to acknowledge that such disciplines can never hope finally to escape the necessity of value; since they are defined partly in terms of the fact that they never merely take the field of value as their object, but always also participate in, which is to say, extend or prolong, the play of value.

Traditionally, of course – by which I mean up to about the middle of this century – the disciplines of the humanities have been only too willing to acknowledge the priority of evaluative questions. If cultural modernism takes the form of an extreme differentiation of the value of culture and the arts, along with the gradually consolidated (and increasingly implausible) claim that artistic value is identical with value *as such*, then the academic study of cultural and artistic practices has provided an institutional embodiment of this differentiation. If the Kantian claim was that art and literature possessed a special and intrinsic kind of value which was not to be measured in anything but its own terms, then the claim of progressively more specialized disciplines such as literature, art history and even philosophy was that they alone could provide the competence to recognize and reproduce these forms of intrinsic value. There is something paradoxical about the idea of such institutionalized access to the differentiated sphere of the aesthetic, for it represents the particularization and interested putting into social and economic exchange of values that are held to be disinterested and radically non-transferable. The inculcation of sensitivity and evaluative tact which were the professed aims of Leavisite and New Critical peda-gogy may have had transferable forms of value in social life generally – for the ethical claims made for the value of formalism are always very marked – but the claim was always paradoxically that it was only by close attention to the specifics of the text's value in itself, and the rigorous disallowing of more general forms of ethical evaluation, that these general or transferable qualities could be guaranteed. The doctrine of close reading did not allow one to enquire what a text was good *for*, only what it was good *as*. Of course, the natural consequence of such an organization was the fixing of canons and criteria of quality and evalu-ation, such that the activity of evaluation became identical with the ritualized acknowledgement and reproduction of the value of particular predetermined texts and cultural forms.

Gradually since the 1960s and increasingly since the 1970s, the disciplines of the humanities have detached themselves from this relation-ship. During this period a practice and sometimes a theory of cultural value and evaluation have given way to a concern with interpretation. It would be inaccurate to suggest that this switch of emphasis was entirely without precedent in this century since, of course, the disciplines of the humanities, and perhaps especially of literature, throughout the twentieth century have tried to negotiate the rival claims of scholarship and judgement, fact and value. But the rise of literary and critical theory since the 1970s has brought about a decisive swing away from a concern with judgement and towards a concern with meaning and interpretation. It is this concern that holds together and provides an institutional identity for the otherwise striking diversity of the forms of contemporary critical theory. What hermeneutics, reader-centred criticism, semiotic analysis, discourse theory, psychoanalytic theory, new historicism, deconstruction and all the varieties of politically accented criticism which draw on the former perspectives, Marxism, feminism, gay and ethnic critical discourse have in common is their focus on the activities of knowing, understanding, decoding and interpreting. Even forms of criticism which might be expected to ask other kinds of question instead of, or alongside, the questions 'what does it mean?' or 'how do we know what it means?', and indeed proclaim their independence from such questions, are drawn in by the force of the interpretative paradigm.

Reader-centred theory, for example, as it is demonstrated in the work of Stanley Fish or Wolfgang Iser, has tended to focus only on a narrow strip of the spectrum of things that readers do to texts and texts do to readers, in the attention it pays to the reader's attempts to make sense of the text, testing assumptions, reconciling contradictions, filling in gaps and so on. Psychoanalytic theory, although it promises a heightened attention to the affective structures and relationships of identification, absorption, splitting, subordination and the ethical concerns which they embody, has in fact fixated upon the hermeneutics rather than upon the ethics of the self, focusing as a consequence on what might be called 'psychotextual' processes such as concealment, displacement, encrypting, decoding and discovery. The various accents of poststructuralist theory and criticism might have seemed to open up a move beyond, or, in Susan Sontag's phrase, 'against' interpretation, but the extreme and usually cheerful scepticism about the possibility of fixing or assigning meaning which characterizes much poststructuralist critical theory has the effect again of focusing attention exclusively on matters of meaning, reading and interpretation. The most representative form of poststructuralist thought in this respect is deconstruction. Although the work of Jacques Derrida is shot through with questions of value and ethics, it is striking that the deconstructive critical practices that have been developed in his name draw almost entirely upon his work on linguistic and interpretative matters, and appear to be largely ignorant of the concern with the ethical shown from the beginning of his career in his work on Levinas, Heidegger and Nietzsche. Even the current interest in the question of discourse and the relationships of power which it embodies and enacts, an interest deriving largely from the work of Bakhtin and Foucault, has centred on the business of codifying, classifying and regularizing the workings of power and the concentrations and distributions of value which it brings about, contenting itself therefore with activities of mapping which mimic the 'neutral' processes of mapping in which power and value are dissimulated in the modern world, rather than with evaluating (or considering the question of how one might or should evaluate) those concentrations of value themselves.

Barbara Herrnstein Smith ascribes this 'exile of evaluation' within the literary academy especially to the predominance of linguistic models and a lack of familiarity with those disciplines such as sociology and economics in which questions of value continue to occupy a central place (*CV*, 17–18). But, quite apart from the dubious accuracy of this assessment (the association between literature and sociology has been strong, if intermittent, over the last few decades), this does not adequately account for the exile of evaluation in the disciplines of the humanities, since it does not really explain why linguistic models and theories have come to exercise their dominance. The reason for this lies, I believe, in the increasing professionalization and institutionalization of the disciplines of the humanities and, more generally, the consolidation and multiplication of the forms by which culture is socially managed and mediated. In the universities and institutions of learning, this professionalization was first encouraged by the expansion of higher education in the societies of the developed West during the 1960s and subsequently reinforced and, surprisingly, even accelerated by the assaults on the humanities mounted by successive governments in Britain and the USA during the 1980s.[3] For what these assaults amounted to was a rejection of the concept of an evaluative discipline in favour of a positivist and instrumentalist model of education as training, a model which was itself derived from a narrowly idealized version of scientific and technical education, in which facts, knowledge and interpretation have an ascendancy over values and the processes of value judgement. Seen in this way, the retreat from evaluation in the disciplines of the humanities is a kind of protective colouring, an attempt to conform to a newly dominant paradigm of research and education. And, of course, in line with the paradoxical principle set out a moment ago, this denigration of evaluation and preference for the positive and apparently more demonstrable forms of knowledge and competence is itself not a retreat from evaluation, but a powerful and influential evaluative action itself.

But this is far from being the most striking paradox about the situation. For if the dominance of interpretative critical theory during the last two decades has been achieved at the cost of exiling evaluation, then it is also conspicuously the case that this has been a period in which the force of value in the humanities has been felt unmissably and ubiquitously, a period in which Fredric Jameson can declare with justice that the prevailing mode of criticism is in fact the ethical (*PU*, 59). Indeed, when one considers the kinds of question which have driven critical theory and practice through the 1970s and the decade that has followed Jameson's judgement – the concern with the politics of interpretation and representation, the prejudiced representation of minority groups in literature and art, the violent effects of discourse and the question of the social effects and functions of cultural practices of all kinds – one does seem forced to acknowledge an intensification rather than a waning of ethical and evaluative concerns.

How, then, are we to reconcile this with Smith's uncompromising judgement that 'the entire problematic of value and evaluation has been evaded and explicitly exiled' in contemporary theory (*CV*, 17)? One explanation of what is happening here might be that critical theory, especially of the politically adversary kind such as feminism, Marxism or the varieties of politically accented deconstruction, has turned away from what had been newly experienced as unacceptably narrow and implausible views of the value of literary and cultural works, and especially that view associated with artistic modernism which suggests that the only true value of art is a value intrinsic to itself. On this view, critical theory would have rejected not the idea of value as such, but the notion of aesthetic value as autotelic and self-determining. The most sophisticated and convincing political objections to this notion of aesthetic value argue not so much that this notion is inaccurate as that it masks and perpetuates certain very definite relations of power, that the notion of pure and non-negotiable aesthetic value always has a non-aesthetic exchange-value in political and economic terms. The resulting critique of aesthetic ideology is therefore, strictly speaking, not a critique of the notion of value, or a denial of the possibility of evaluation in general, but a rejection of the unjustly limiting forms which aesthetic evaluation has taken.[4] In returning the aesthetic to the political, such critics are restoring the authority of the question 'what is this text/artefact/practice good *for*?' against the modernist question 'what is it good *as*?', and allowing the question '*what* good is it?' to be added to the question '*how* good is it?'

But, if we accept that the rise of postmodern theory involves such a shift from a restricted to an expanded economy of value, we have still to account for a reluctance on the part of much theory to speak of or to theorize the question of value itself. There is no paucity of evaluations and evaluative positions and commitments in such theory, but there continues to be a failure to open out the question of value to theory on its own terms, or to address the question of value other than implicitly or indirectly. Given the everywhere-detectable force of ethical and evaluative motivations in contemporary theory, the frailty of attempts to subject this force to enquiry is truly striking. In the light of this, we might offer a refinement of Smith's judgement and suggest that value and evaluation have not so much been exiled as driven into the critical unconscious, where they continue to exercise force but without being available for analytic scrutiny.

The evidence of this is to be found in the shape and form of many of the recurrent debates within adversary critical theory. For feminism, the most complex and recurrent problem in recent years has surely been how to reconcile an oppositional politics grounded in the idea of a distinctive and victimized female identity with a politics that criticizes the fetishistic and oppressive notion of identity as traditionally constituted. A similar problem recurs in contemporary Marxist debates, in which the critique of false totalizations and absolutisms must find a way to stop short of dissolving its own claims to provide a total or encompassing narrative of oppression and emancipation. The various forms of cultural study, especially ethnic and postcolonial critical theory, which draw on Foucault's critique of universalist notions of the human, must similarly find a way of balancing a liberal and progressive antihumanism against the regressive forms of antihumanism so rife in the world today. All of these problems involve an interesting unwillingness or failure to engage theoretically with the problem of value, and this may be said partly to account for the recalcitrance of the problems. In each of them, the ethico-evaluative impulse is to be found in a practice of *negative interpretation*, in the impulse to liquefy certain violent or oppressive coagulations of value (the mistaking of white or male culture for culture in general, the priority of elite culture over popular culture, the centring of history around narrowly reductive categories and subjects and so on), which leads to a suspicion of value and evaluation in general, as though the operations associated with the transaction of value were always destined to lead to (unjust) hierarchy and (violent) exclusion. The notion of value in this situation can become the object of a superstitious dread and induce a state of neurotic dependency, in which the feared or despised object, whatever, it may be (intentionality, the unified subject, the notion of fixed meaning, metaphysics, the grand narrative), is repeatedly and obsessively invoked in order to be revoked. When such processes begin to pale in affect and to become mere superstitious routines, they have begun to install just such a dangerous fixation of value as was reacted against in the first place.

The problem is, then, that for a theory that depends on negative interpretation or the hermeneutics of suspicion, on an essentially hygienic practice of extricating itself from error, delusion and ideology, the category of value along with the practices of evaluation may seem to be contaminated from top to bottom. But value, like the unconscious, tolerates no negativity, since every negative evaluation, even of the practice of evaluation itself, must always constitute a kind of evaluation on its own terms, even if it implies or states no positive alternative value. Theory of any kind, but perhaps especially a theory driven by an ethic of extrication and embodied in negative interpretation, is always steeped in value, and always asks the question of value in a particularly intense form. A period in which values are profoundly in question is always equally and correlatively a period of energetic value-formation. But a situation in which the energy of ethical disidentification is unmatched by an attention to the nature of ethics and value themselves, in which it has become difficult to be explicit about the question of value, is a strange and dangerous one indeed.

One response to this might be that it is neither necessary nor desirable to be explicit about the question of value; that such explicitness belongs not to the critic, but to the legislator. Indeed, the critique of rationality and all its associated psychopolitical apparatuses offered by contemporary theory might seem to compromise precisely the possibility of a rational grasping of the nature of value implied by the ideal of such explicitness. The various versions of such a critique need to be taken very seriously indeed, but it is precisely their force and seriousness, which is to say, the rational and ethical claims that they exercise, that reveals their own evaluative and prescriptive nature, in such a way as to loop back to the question of value that strategies of reticence seem designed to evade.

This recursive entanglement of theory with value has been characterized by Jürgen Habermas in *The Philosophical Discourse of Modernity* as 'performative self-contradiction' (*PDM*, 185–6). For Habermas, to enter into critical discourse at all is to accede to the orientation towards consensus implicit in all rational exchange. To attempt to undermine these norms and values within one's own discourse, as thinkers such as Foucault and Derrida do in Habermas's view, is to place oneself in a condition of intolerable and enfeebling self-refutation. It will become clear that, while accepting Habermas's characterization of the self-reflexive problems arising from all contemporary varieties of the hermeneutics of suspicion, I believe that performative self-contradiction is not an accidental or historically contingent fact, but rather a recurrent feature of all debates about value. Under such circumstances, the point is not to purge the paradox, either by reining back one's sceptical critique, or by leaping into some magical sublation beyond the antagonism of suspicion and affirmation, but rather to find productive ways of living and thinking within and through this paradox; not, in other words, to constrain or, in the eighteenth-century sense of the word, to ascertain the question of value, but to define that condition which would produce its very productivity.

We have seen that the replacement of evaluation with interpretation is one way of enacting such a constraint on and of value. There are also two others, which, depressingly enough, seem to be characteristic of most of the attempts to return to the question in recent years. The first is the impulse to uphold, return to or orientate oneself towards stable or absolute forms of value. The second (and it may seem surprising to characterize this as a constraint rather than an expansion of the question of value) is the relativizing desire to recognize and tolerate the maximum of competing values. Insofar as the first attitude depends upon the idea of absolute values, which lie above and beyond the play of transaction and relativity, it may be said to favour values as objects over evaluative processes, or, in terms of a distinction once offered by John Dewey, to favour 'prizing' over 'appraising'.[5] Such a view of value will typically regard it as the object of evaluation to escape from or get beyond evaluative processes, to 'arrive' at evaluative outcomes. The second, more pluralistic, attitude will tend, on the contrary, to favour the continuation or enabling of evaluative processes, as against the attempt to preserve, discover or derive particular values. This second attitude may be embodied, for example, in Jean-François Lyotard's notion that justice consists in 'the possibility of continuing to play the game of the just', and is that which allows 'that the question of the just and the unjust be, and remain, raised'.[6] A familiar version of the opposition between the two attitudes is the stand-off between metaphysics versus *différance*, as presented by Kate Soper: there is, on the one hand, 'a fierce and burly crew, stalwartly defending various bedrocks and foundations by means of an assortment of trusty but clankingly mechanical concepts such as "class", "materialism", "humanism", "literary merit", "transcendence" and so forth' and, on the other, 'the feline ironists and revellers in relativism, dancing lightheartedly upon the waters of *différance*, deflecting all foundationalist blows with an adroitly directed ludic laser beam'.[7] This is a self-confessed caricature; but, as we shall see later on, it is hard to characterize the opposition between these two modes, the fixation and the relativizing of value, in any way that does not implicitly confirm one or other account or evaluation of value, the metaphysical or the relativist.

Almost more of an ethical curtailment than these two forms of constraint in themselves, therefore, is the limiting exclusiveness of the binarism they form together, in which it proves impossible to imagine a theory of value which does not propose either some absolute closure or some absolute openness, fixation or difference. But there is in fact no choice, or possibility of choice, between these two alternatives, between the role of legislator and critic. No negative critique, even in the most svelte, most ironic form, is imaginable without investment in or assumption of alternative values; while, on the other hand, the assertion of absolute value always brings with it a vulnerability to critique in terms of the value proposed. Scepticism about metanarratives is impossible except as instructed by the hypothesis of some more just, more inclusive metanarrative, in terms of which the suspected metanarrative falls short; the assertion of a metanarrative must always leave open, in the name of its very claim to total inclusiveness, the possibility of its discrediting, its failure justly to narrate the totality. The structure of value is therefore paradoxical, involving the simultaneous desire and necessity to affirm unconditional values and the desire and necessity to subject such values to continuous, corrosive scrutiny.

To date, discussions of value in critical theory have simplified this paradoxical structure into an *either/or*: *either* absolute value *or* relativism; *either* fixity *or* play. The attempt to fix the play of value may be instanced in contrasting ways in two recent studies which otherwise contrast markedly in critical style, Wayne C. Booth's *The Company We Keep: An Ethics of Fiction* (1988), which may be described without caricature as a liberal-pragmatist account of value, and J. Hillis Miller's *The Ethics of Reading* (1987), which is an avowedly deconstructive account of its subject. Booth's aim in *The Company We Keep* is not so much to determine *a priori* grounds of ethical possibility or legitimacy as to examine the operation of such questions in practice, and in particular in the workings of narrative. Narrative is a very capacious generic category for Booth, which can encompass without strain films, dreams and even metaphors, as well as fictional stories. The definitions of ethical value that Booth offers in the course of his roaming, restless enquiry are characteristically open and undogmatic; as we are reminded, questions of value and evaluation are inherently complex, since they invariably involve us in acts of self-reflexion, as we inspect and evaluate our own acts of evaluation. Booth's account is at once committedly pluralist and uncertainly pragmatist. His conviction of the irreducible plurality of human experience and of ways of understanding it lead him throughout to be suspicious of definitions that prematurely generalize or fixate upon falsely universal principles. We should learn, he says, to stop worrying about *the* value of literary texts, and to respond to and articulate their multiple ethical effects. His pragmatism seems to follow sweetly from this pluralism. If we cannot know the single and absolute ground of an artefact's value, it is because there are no such absolute grounds to be had, no values which are not formed and legitimated by the needs and norms of particular communities. Booth's starting point, therefore, is that value neither needs to be proved, in the strong logical sense, nor is susceptible of disproof. That something seems to us to be valuable is sufficient ground for assuming that it is so indeed.

Here, notoriously, yawns an abyss, and its name is relativism. Booth recoils from this abyss, wanting to assert that, despite the conditions he describes, real values are susceptible of being formed and sustained collectively, and of surviving, and even being refined, through time. Value is generated, he argues, through acts of continuing conversation, in which judgements about literary texts are tested by and against other judgements, and judgements of other texts. The useful term which Booth has coined for this participatory process of ethical reasoning is 'coduction'. Obviously, such a procedure is open to the objection that the values thus derived remain entirely contingent upon continuing agreement, or agreement to continue discussing, among the company of coducers. Booth protects his argument against this radical contingency by some odd manoeuvres. Frankly, not everybody's opinion *counts* in this process of communal coduction. Booth seems to regard it as self-evident that the only persons who might legitimately be consulted and coduced with on questions of value are those who are already by training and selection saturated by the values in question. You could not take seriously, for example, anybody who was sceptical about the value of Shakespeare, since this value is something 'that every person who undergoes a proper apprenticeship and comes to understand enough about Shakespeare's culture can discern'.[8] The reasoning here is immaculately self-confirming: but one wants to ask, could any 'apprenticeship' which didn't yield a sense of Shakespeare's value ever count for Booth as 'proper'?

Booth also attempts to defend the idea that certain works possess more value, or, what seems to come to the same thing, more potential to become valuable, than certain other works, regardless of their audiences or receiving cultures – that *King Lear*, for example, simply possesses more value than a group of couplets such as 'To love and hate – / This is my fate. / Stanley Fish / Is my dish. / Reading Terry / Makes me merry' (p. 87). 'No conceivable circumstances,' he declares, 'no conceivable community of interpretation, could produce a range and depth of criticism on "To love and hate – / This is my fate" equaling what we already have on *King Lear*, to say nothing of what is yet to come in the history of that infinitely fecund work' (p. 89). Now, there may not be many who would want to quarrel with Booth's actual prediction here, but this need not imply at all what he claims it does, that this has something to do with the intrinsic qualities of *King Lear*, or be a proof of 'how much is, after all, in the work itself' (p. 89). Booth's inability to conceive a culture or interpretative community who would not prefer *King Lear* to improvised doggerel is proof rather of his own, no doubt culture-specific, notion of what cultures are or must be, for it seems that, for Booth, conceivable cultures are those which are already constituted such that they are predisposed to value texts like *King Lear*.

A similar impulse to check the implications of a pragmatic definition of value characterizes the rest of the argument in *The Company We Keep*. This argument may be said to be sustained throughout by an ethic of otherness, of responsible *Sorge* or caring. For Booth, the experience of reading, and especially of reading narrative, involves an ethical opening of the bounded individual ego on to other lives, experiences and languages. However, this openness to the other is circumscribed in two ways. Firstly, the fact that Booth's ethic is based upon and finally referable to the individual person rather than the community means that, in the end, he asserts a parochial ideal of self-culture as opposed to any kind of collective or more properly political ideal. Secondly, and perhaps more seriously, this ethic of otherness is conceived of as primarily an assimilative rather than a disintegrative process, in which the self meets its other(s) only by becoming more energetically versatile in its capacity for imaginative identification, rather than ever being susceptible to radical transformation. 'It is not the degree of otherness that distinguishes fiction of the highest ethical kind', he suggests, 'but the depth of education it yields in *dealing with* the "other"' (p. 195). This will to assimilate can also make itself felt in uncomfortably coercive ways in Booth's argument. All the way through his book he appeals to the 'evidence' of various informal surveys and referendums in lecture halls and classrooms to show the kinds of consensus that allegedly exist about such things as technical virtues in poetry, and to suggest that it is impossible to disagree about these shared values without losing the right to be considered a serious coductive companion – 'If you as reader really disagree with the judgement, I know not quite what to do with you', he confesses in one winningly bewildered footnote (p. 103).

J. Hillis Miller, who would probably be one of the others who lie beyond the reach of Wayne Booth's companionability, has a narrower focus in *The Ethics of Reading*, but aims to take a much deeper bite into questions of first principle. Actually, his aim is nothing less than to forge with the equipment of deconstructive analysis a form of ethical imperative. Despite the otherwise huge differences in style between them, there is an interesting continuity between Miller's outlook and Booth's, for both see ethical questions as inescapably bound up with forms of narrative. Miller's work takes its impetus from a paradox at the heart of Kant's ethics, that in order to assert or even imagine any kind of transcendent moral law, unconditioned by the contingencies of time, circumstance and self-interest, it is always necessary in the end to resort to some kind of narrative or figural exemplification, with the attendant risk of introducing contingency back into the categorical. In the readings of Paul de Man, George Eliot, Anthony Trollope, Henry James and Walter Benjamin that make up Miller's book, the focus remains on this necessary return of contingency into every projected moral absolute via the actions of figural exemplification.

So far so good. Any devoted reader of Paul de Man, as Miller obviously is, might follow this far without demur. The surprise comes in the move that Miller makes next. For the ethical imperative, which is seemingly thus annulled by deconstructive reading, mysteriously crosses over to that act of reading itself. This reading, says Miller, is governed by an 'implacable law' which insists that we read texts in such a manner as to remain faithful not to their apparent coherence, but to their inner principles of self-contradiction.[9] Reading, for Miller, is a curious mixture of obedience and dissidence, in the general compulsion to follow through the unique and idiomatic ways in which a given text exemplifies, but also deviates from, the compulsion of its inner law. We are consequently under an absolute ('ethical') obligation to carry through the undermining of all absolute coherences:

> It is subjection to this power, as to an implacable law, that determines both the ethics of writing and then the ethics of reading that writing. Reading is not of the text as such but of the thing that is latent and gathered within it as a force to determine in me a re-vision of what has been the latent law of the text I read.[10]

So the ethics of reading for Miller are not a matter of simply deriving patterns of behaviour from texts which may then be put to account in the real world; rather, they are an ethics of interpretation, since the ethical requirements proper to and characteristic of the act of reading are paradigmatic for ethical behaviour in the real world, insofar as that behaviour always necessitates forms of interpretation, judgement and narrative.

As always, Miller's analyses impress his reader deeply with a sense of an unswerving respect for the singularity of the texts he reads; in this, they richly exemplify his ethic of absolute critical attention. But it is odd nevertheless to find him so dogmatic and portentous in his assertion of the compelling ethical force of deconstruction; time and again, the sky darkens with the evocation of implacable laws, unconditioned absolutes and irresistible necessities. It is true that, for Miller, there is some constitutive uncertainty about the nature of the imperative involved in reading, partly, one supposes, because the imperative is an imperative to incite rather than to excoriate contradiction and uncertainty. So Miller confesses: 'I am unable to know whether in this experience I am subject to a linguistic necessity or an ontological one. Or, rather, I am unable to avoid making the linguistic mistake of responding to a necessity of language as though it had ontological force and authority.'[11] But if the logical compulsion of such absolutes is carefully and publicly compromised by Miller's argument, the psychic compulsion to such necessity seems to loom in him too hugely to be accessible to analysis.

There are many obvious and important differences between the accounts of the ethics of reading offered by Booth and Miller, and I have to acknowledge a preference for the paradoxical compulsion to freedom argued for in Miller's work over Booth's more amiable, but in the end more coercive notion of coduction. (Indeed, as will become apparent, my own case about the paradoxical nature of value and evaluation owes much to Miller's.) But, despite their many differences, both writers have in common a certain reluctance to push what is an otherwise sceptically unconstrained enquiry beyond the point where it threatens what stands as non-negotiable for each writer: the possibility, even the necessity, of coductive consensus for Booth, and the irresistible law of fidelity to the text for Miller. It is as though value can be affirmed only in some cavity of rationality, in some *epoché* of the theoretical.

The second form which I have said the constraint of value takes is in the pluralizing of value. How can this be? If the pluralizing of value is exemplified in the rupturing of the canon, the widespread discrediting of the idea of universal value and of the autotelism of the aesthetic artefact, with a corresponding sensitivity to and tolerance of difference and diversity, then how can this mean anything other than the simultaneous loosening and motivation of the question of value? To understand how this might be so, it may be useful to consider some contrasting versions of the pluralist position.

In his essay 'The Question of Literary Value', Antony Easthope attempts to argue what may seem like a version of the argument suggested in this present discussion, namely that arguments about the existence of literary value (and, by extension, cultural value more generally) are unhelpfully constricted by the terms of a binarism (QLV, 376–89). Most rejections of the concept of literary value, argues Easthope, have rested on the rejection of the idea of literature as an absolute category, encompassing a body of texts sharing objectively verifiable characteristics and possessing certain stable and transhistorical forms of value. But the suspicion of the category of literature and the idea of literary value derives its energy from the brutal simplicity of two alternatives: either literary value exists (in absolute terms) or it does not (again, in absolute terms). Easthope usefully recommends that we breach the essentialism/anti-essentialism binarism involved here and acknowledge the contingency of the category of literature, attending to 'the multiplicity of ways in which literary value has entered discourse, both in our century and across history' (QLV, 386). If we want a definition of literature or good literature, then it is to be found simply and sufficiently in the fact of historical success, in texts that have been read and reread in different ways in different periods: 'literature', Easthope tells us, 'consists merely of texts that are more functionally polysemous than some others' (QLV, 387).

Now one of the problems with Easthope's account is his unhappy choice of the work of Terry Eagleton and Stanley Fish to exemplify the binary constriction between the *either* and the *or* of literary value. For, in fact, in their different ways, both Eagleton and Fish are arguing for what turns out to be Easthope's own modest proposal, namely that, while literature and literary value cannot be said to exist *in themselves*, intransitively and unconditionally, nevertheless they have a contingent or historical existence. This is to say that 'literature' is the same kind of category as the categories 'weeds', 'vermin' or 'aliens' – the occupants of such categories being defined not by the intrinsic qualities they possess but by their meaning and value for the particular speakers, groups ('interpretive communities') or societies for whom the categories have force.

But Easthope persists in his view that if Eagleton and Fish reject literature as an absolute category, and say that it has no essential value, then they must be saying that literature neither exists nor has any value at all. The *tertium quid* here is what Easthope begins by calling the 'literature-as-construction analysis' (QLV, 377), which means not that the idea of literature is just whistled up out of thin air, but that literature has a historically relative nature and is defined according to the needs, beliefs and values of specific communities and social formations in specific times. This is Easthope's version of the claim:

> Literary value is a matter of functional polysemy, a function of the reader/text relation, and cannot be defined outside the known ways in which texts – some more than others – demonstrably have worked transhistorically and polysemically. Although most of the terms of analysis used to define literary value in greater detail make some sense in relation to the period in which they were variously deployed – typicality, representing general nature, organic unity, imaginative vision, defamiliarization, foregrounding, capacity to excite pleasurable fantasy, and so on – not much more can be said about it unless it is assumed as an essence. And not much more needs to be said for I think we can live with this. (QLV, 386)

On the view set out here, value is historically contingent. Even works which appear not to be limited to any particular historical period but are found to be valuable in many such periods cannot be held to be universally or essentially valuable in themselves; rather, they are perennially valued because of the specific and specifiable historical circumstances which condition or facilitate their transhistoricality. The persistence of certain texts in Western culture (Easthope instances those of Homer) could never provide grounds for a prediction that such texts would necessarily be found valuable by all or even some other cultures. Transhistorical persistence means simply that, for various reasons, certain texts turn out to have had a perennial adaptability within a particular culture or in different cultures in different periods. And, of course, among these reasons is the inertial force of a text's very persistence and the resulting circle of confirmation, in which Homer, for example, persists in Western culture partly because one of the defining features of Western culture is the centrality of Homer to it.

But this is precisely what Eagleton and Fish, among others, have argued about the contingency and transitivity of literary value. To arrive at this view of things, as I believe Easthope does at the end of his essay, is to restore the excluded middle to arguments that appear to lack it only because Easthope has himself excluded it in the first place. In condemning the Eagleton/Fish position for its brutal binarism of *either* essential value *or* no value at all, Easthope actually prolongs rather than dissolves the binarism, precisely by confining Eagleton and Fish so tightly within it. Indeed there is an interesting relapse at the end of Easthope's essay into the very binarism he has been abhorring, when he writes that 'since the magic of essence was the main reason why literature was preferred to the high cultural forms, and the texts of popular culture correspondingly denigrated, literary value in my account loses its value' (QLV, 387).

Easthope's description of the historical contingency of literary value resembles that of Smith's *Contingencies of Value* (1988), one of the most toughly combative expositions of what might be called the 'radical-pragmatist' case about value. Smith's powerful argument is simply stated: everything participates in value, but nowhere in the world or out of it are there to be found any unfalsifiable use-values, transcendent aesthetic values or ultimate moral goods. She cheerfully accepts the principle which has been so horrifying to most moral philosophers, that there are no statements of value, or evaluations, which are not statements of particular needs, desires or preferences, whether of individuals or of groups. This means that it makes no sense to speak of the truth or not of moral or evaluative statements. *This is good* is always in fact a variant of the statement *I like this*, or *I value this*. All values are entirely contingent, always in the process of being transacted in the multiple, overlapping economies of needs, desires and wants which make up human life and history. Although there are certain limited forms of regularity in the patterns of social evaluation in particular cultural groups, Smith urges a view of the fundamental 'scrappiness' or heterogeneity of human needs, interests and goals, which can consequently never be concentrated or simplified into any single principle of value:

> There is ... no way for individual or collective choices, practices, activities, or acts, 'economic' or otherwise, to be ultimately summed-up, compared, and evaluated: neither by the single-parameter hedonic calculus of classic utilitarianism, nor by the most elaborate multiple-parameter formulas of contemporary mathematical economics, nor by any mere inversion or presumptive transcendence of either. There is no way to give a reckoning that is simultaneously total and final. There is no Judgement Day. There is no *bottom* bottom line anywhere, for anyone or for 'man.' (*CV*, 149)

One of the most striking manoeuvres employed by Smith is her assault on what she incisively calls the 'Egalitarian Fallacy', the belief that in a system in which no values can be shown to have final or absolute authority, in which no values can be shown to be finally and objectively true, all values must therefore be equivalent, rather than merely powerfully or widely believed. But to acknowledge 'that no value judgement can be more "valid" than another *in the sense of* an objectively truer statement of the objective value of an object' in no way disallows the possibility of making meaningful value judgements. It is just that the value of these value judgements 'must be understood, evaluated, and compared *otherwise*, that is, as something other than "truth-value" or "validity" in the objectivist, essentialist sense' (*CV*, 98). The Egalitarian Fallacy is therefore for Smith simply the bad dream of an objectivism which is unable to imagine a world other than its own; the lack of absolute values no more makes all other values interchangeable than the absence of an agreed gold standard makes all world currencies worth the same.

One ought to be able to recognize in Smith's Egalitarian Fallacy the binarism between absolute value or no value at all that is condemned by Easthope. In arguing for a sense of the contingency of value, Easthope is surely recommending a version of the pragmatism urged by Smith, which neither gives absolute status to value judgements, nor accepts that this dissolves all possibility of meaningful evaluation. Smith devotes the last chapter of *Contingencies of Value* to an energetic defence of relativism against the two principal objections which are usually made against it. The first of these is that it is self-refuting, since, if all truth is relative, then this must be true of the statement about all truth being relative, which must therefore suicidally grant its own relativity. As Smith argues, this is really another effect of the inability of objectivist or absolutist thought to conceive any other view of the world but its own. The relativist position, she argues, is not self-refuting, because it is not a logical deduction, or statement of the fundamental truth of things in the objectivist's strong sense. If Smith's kind of relativism 'cannot found, ground, or prove itself, cannot deduce or demonstrate its own rightness' (*CV*, 183), in other words, cannot prove itself in principle, then it is equally not susceptible of any refutation in principle. For this reason, if the relativist's view of the world seems to require adjustment or modification, this is not to be taken as evidence of its untruth, in the strong sense. Rather, its self-consistency is demonstrated in the fact that 'it conceives of itself as continuously changing, of all conceptions of the irreducibly various as irreducibly various, and of the multiply configurable as always configurable otherwise'. (ibid.).

The second charge that Smith is concerned to rebut is that, since it discourages commitment to absolute principles and to the programmes of action that are usually founded upon them, relativism encourages at best 'a condition of genial, torpid philosophical que-serà-seràism' and at worst a complete moral paralysis. Her answer to this charge is, firstly,

that it places far too much faith in the power of moral absolutism, which
has hardly had conspicuous success in keeping away 'the jackals, the
Gulag and the death camps' (*CV*, 154); and secondly, and more importantly, that it drastically caricatures the nature of the relativist:

> Someone's distaste for or inability to grasp notions such as 'absolute value'
> and 'objective truth' does not in itself deprive her of such other human
> characteristics, relevant to moral action, as memory, imagination, early
> training and example, conditioned loyalties, instinctive sympathies and
> antipathies, and so forth. Nor does it deprive her of all interest in the
> subtler, more diffuse, and longer-range consequences of her actions and
> the actions of others, or oblige her, more than anyone else, to be
> motivated only by immediate self-interest. (*CV*, 161)

The problem with Smith's account is that, while it constitutes a
powerful and fiercely precise description from the outside of the
conditions and contingencies of value choices, it appears not to be able
to theorize the force of value from the inside. Most remarkably, it
appears to be unaware of the powerful evaluative force which its own
argument exercises and which apparently contradicts elements of that
argument. In the terms borrowed from Habermas a little earlier, Smith is
caught within, but apparently insufficiently able to speak of, a performative self-contradiction. It will become plain that I believe this to be the
problem with all such attempts to assert the absolute absence of
absolutes, the regulation of the field of value by a rule of non-regulation.

Strikingly, although she is concerned to demonstrate that relativists
are perfectly capable of vigorous evaluative activity, Smith avoids
explicitly characterizing the value of a relativist view of value. Indeed,
she quite emphatically insists that 'given only that denial of objectivism
which is sufficient to evoke the quietist objection, *no particular moral
positions or types or modes of moral action follow from it at all*, neither those
typically attributed to "relativism," such as liberalism, egalitarian tolerance, and passivity, or any others' (*CV*, 161). Although her point here is
to demonstrate that relativists are not necessarily morally quietistic, her
reply to the specimen question 'how would you (as a relativist) answer
the Nazi?' is rather alarming. As one might expect, she tells us that, like
everything else under the moon, '*it depends*' (*CV*, 154) – depends, that is,
on the relative circumstances and dispositions of power between the Nazi
and the relativist. What is said to the Nazi, or done in response to the
Nazi, depends, in other words, on what pragmatic possibilities present
themselves; and, she says, this is in fact what has tended to happen in all
cases anyway. But there has been a dramatic narrowing of the force of

the question here, which surely means not only 'how would you be likely to answer the Nazi?' but also 'how *should* you answer the Nazi?' – not, of course, under all or any circumstances, but in circumstances that did not constrain your evaluative possibilities. Smith here seems to see no possibility of any distinction between contingent circumstances and imperatives which transcend them, no possibility that one might indeed, under some circumstances, say nothing to the Nazi, and yet regret it profoundly, or judge it to be an error or failure.

Smith goes on to suggest that anyway we are mistaken in thinking that answering the Nazi is a matter primarily of 'getting one's ethical/epistemological arguments in good axiological order', and suggests that what is really required is 'a theoretically subtle and powerful analysis of the conditions and, even more important, *dynamics* of the Nazi's emergence and access to power and, accordingly, a specification of political and other actions that might make that emergence and access less likely, both in one's own neighborhood and elsewhere' (*CV*, 154–5). Here, again, the question of value has been collapsed into the strategic and predominantly interpretative question of how to make sense of the contingent factors that have encouraged and sustained Nazism. The question of how to describe Nazism has here replaced the question of how to evaluate it (in the strong sense that would encompass, for example, the question of how, if at all, to justify attempting to suppress or destroy it). Evaluation has mysteriously dropped out of Smith's account, or, to be more precise, it is not exposed to analysis, not itself subject to evaluation. For of course there is a form of evaluative assumption present here – we seek to understand Nazism, Smith says, in order to make its emergence in our neighbourhood less likely. Why, one wants to ask, should one want in the first place to make Nazism less likely in one's neighbourhood? Smith's answer, or failure to develop an answer, seems to indicate that this is not the sort of question a relativist can cope with, and that we perhaps just have to accept that there never is a 'first place' any more than a last analysis, and that the contingencies of 'where the Nazi and I – given, of course, my particular identity – each are' will determine entirely whether or not we embrace Nazism. But the relativist position must be taken in itself to be an argument against the Nazi, insofar as Nazism stood (and stands) for the violent and mystificatory constraining of the processes of free, participatory evaluation. If the reluctance to articulate this evaluative position is in one sense precisely in accord with the relativist disinclination to pin her faith in absolutes, it is in another profoundly self-contradictory, in that it threatens the basis on which she could continue to be or act as a relativist.

The principal objection I want to make about this revealing passage of exemplification is not the one that Smith is concerned to defend herself against, that this kind of relativism does not allow one to make judgements or evaluations. Rather, it makes evaluative choices (usually the choices of others) seem either entirely determined, entirely the product of their contingent circumstances, or (usually when they are one's own acknowledged or unacknowledged values) entirely spontaneous, and beyond the reach of evaluative scrutiny of any kind that could be called rational. As we have seen, one of the most serious consequences of this is that Smith's subtle analysis remains alienated from its own powerful evaluative force. This force can be detected at certain moments in her critique of the objectivist thought that holds to the idea of absolute values existing in the world rather than as a result of human transactions with and upon it. Objectivist thought, she argues, typically not only accords an absolute value and distinction to what are in fact the contingent values of particular powerful groups, it also operates to devalue the pleasures and values of others. This she calls the 'The-Other's-Poison-Effect', explaining that it means 'not only that one man's meat is sometimes the other's poison but that one man sometimes gets sick just *watching* the other fellow eat his meat and, moreover, that if one of them is a cultural theorist (left-wing or conservative as otherwise measured), he or she may be expected to generate an account of how the other fellow is himself actually being poisoned by the meat he likes and eats' (*CV*, 26). This joins with a more generalized sensitivity throughout *Contingencies of Value* to the forms of exclusion and violence practised as a consequence of objectivist notions of absolute value, as well as to the 'securing of authority from interrogation and risk' (*CV*, 161) that the upholding of absolute standards may seem to bring with it. Against these effects, Smith suggests that 'it might be thought that there was some communal value to ensuring that authority was *always* subject to interrogation and *always* at risk. *All* authority: which must mean that of parent, teacher, and missionary as well as that of tyrant, pope, and state flunky' (*CV*, 161).

There is a surprising imperative force here ('*all* authority', she insists), even though the reason that Smith offers may seem modest and pragmatic ('it might be thought that there was some communal value' in this). But elsewhere in her argument she is deeply suspicious of the notion that community either in the narrow or large sense could provide ultimate moral justification, and criticizes, for example, the residues of teleology and idealism in Richard Rorty's recent arguments that we should prefer solidarity to truth (*CV*, 166–73). However, Smith's suspicion of the values of community leads her not into moral atomism, a sense of the impossibility of any communitarian horizon in the face of the irreducible diversity and incommensurability of patterns of allegiance, identification and investment, but rather to an articulation of the need, *in the light of* this diversity, for 'the continuous development and refinement of more richly articulated, broadly responsive, and subtly differentiated nonobjectivist accounts of, among other things, "truth," "belief," "choice," "justification," and "community"' (*CV*, 172). But the scepticism about community and solidarity here can never be total, if only because it seems based on a desire not to do violence to the irreducible diversity of human beings and their forms of social organization and interaction – in other words, based on some form of communal value. The more Smith insists on the necessity not to impose universalist accounts falsely or prematurely, the more commitment she displays to the ideal of an expanded, more richly diversified sense of community. This value appears to be absolute rather than relative, since it is the expression of the principle of the desirability of general improvement. In order to demonstrate that the relativist can indeed make meaningful value choices, Smith must display her commitment to such general improvement, aimed not at any form of positive utopia, but rather at the best that can be achieved, that 'general optimum' which consists of 'that set of conditions that permits and encourages, precisely, *evaluation*, and specifically that continuous process described here in relation to both scientific and artistic activity: that is, the local figuring/working out, as well as we, heterogeneously, can, of what seems to work better rather than worse' (*CV*, 179).

It is hard to see how one could conceive of, or recommend the achievement of, a 'general optimum' based entirely on case-by-case reasoning, or 'local figuring/working out', since this must involve the projection and orientation towards some general moral and evaluative perspective, even if the force of this orientation is expressed in a conscious and vigilant refraining from absolutist intervention in local dispute. For the kind of evaluation that Smith is recommending here is not the simple abandonment or unconsciousness of the horizon of absolute value, but rather a knowledgeable, sensitive and principled holding off from the violence of objectivism, educated by her own richly diversified, and therefore powerfully inclusive, account of value.

The commitment to the achievement of a general optimum implies a commitment to another form of non-negotiable value. For, we might want to ask, why should 'we', heterogeneously or not (and it is hard to imagine what a completely heterogeneous 'we' could possibly be), bother? Why not actually recommend conflict, tyranny or degeneration rather than the encouraging prospects set out here? It may be replied, because these things are less desirable to most people, and it is not only more sensible, but also better to go for what seems better rather than worse. But then, surely one non-contingent value is being asserted here, even if it is of a rather abstract kind, namely, the value of evaluative choice and action, in fact, the irreducible value of value itself.

There seems, therefore, to be no possibility for Smith to admit and examine the contingency of her own view of the contingency of all value. Between contingency and absolutism, as she emphasizes at many points through *Contingencies of Value*, there can only be stand-off, with no possibility of negotiation, or 'local figuring/working out'. For the most part, Smith presents this as the fault of the absolutist, who refuses to believe in the possibility of value aside from absolute value and therefore can only caricature the relativist case. For an absolutist to understand the claims of a relativist, she would have to have already abandoned absolutism. But there is intractability on the other side too, since, for the relativist, there is equally no possibility of limited accommodation to absolutist thought. Absolutism must be absolutely rejected, since the idea of a limited or partial absolutism is, of course, ludicrous; you can be partly absolutist only in the sense that you can be slightly pregnant. To be fair, Smith does try at one point to demonstrate just such a partial adjustment to absolutism, when she suggests that 'it would be no more logically inconsistent for a nonobjectivist to speak, under *some* conditions, of fundamental rights and objective facts than for a Hungarian ordering his lunch in Paris to speak French' (*CV*, 158). But the flexible relativist could not be said here to be really speaking of fundamental truths and objective facts, except as a kind of strategy or imposture. Of course, Smith's remark here might be interpreted as meaning that all fundamentalist and objectivist thought is really strategic in this manner, whether consciously or not, but this again demonstrates not the mutual accommodation of relativism and absolutism, but precisely the (absolute) triumph of the relativist case. Once again, we arrive at an impasse, in the 'game of pure non-engagement, ending in a draw by default' (*CV*, 156).

Smith argues that this very impasse, or the perception of it as an impasse, is further evidence of the inflexibility of the objectivist, since 'the idea that conceptualizations are radically contingent, and that conceptual/discursive impasses may be intractable will be, to the objectivist, a mark of relativism' (*CV*, 156). But is not such a situation also 'a mark of relativism' for the relativist and, in some sense, a demonstration of the preferability of a relativist case to an absolutist one? And is this not a mirror image of the absolutist's aggressive annexation to the terms of his world-view of everything that opposes it? The absolutist says, 'the fact that we cannot agree is proof of the chaos that results from abandoning faith in absolutes', while the relativist says, 'the fact that we cannot agree is proof of the untenability of absolutist positions', each side proving its case by the very fact that the other side disagrees with them, and by its interpretation of that disagreement. The impasse results, in other words, from the intractability of both sides of the argument, not just from the absolutist's refusal to understand the point of view of the relativist. There seems no way for the relativist to tolerate absolutism as a mere difference of conceptual style or philosophical idiom, since this very toleration is lethal to the absolutist case. The situation is nicely illustrated by the joke about the new arrival in heaven who is shown the adherents of the various denominations and religions of the world enjoying their posthumous bliss; noticing the absence of any Catholics, the new recruit to felicity is told that they have to be kept in a separate compartment since, as St Peter explains, 'they think they're the only ones here'. It is a joke that can be told to the discredit of any absolutist creed, since its point is to show that the toleration of an absolutism is in fact its intellectual confounding.

My point here is that, in all these respects, in its unswerving commitment to the notion of general betterment, the collective value of value, and its absolute commitment to the contingency of all absolutes, Smith's account is paradoxical and deficient. It may appear that my objection is really only a version of the classical argument of self-refutation which is often directed against relativism, and which Smith claims can be answered by the counter-argument that relativism does not make truth-claims that are strong enough to make it vulnerable to self-refutation. But I am not concerned to argue here that Smith's relativism refutes itself, or that her argument is deficient *because* it is paradoxical. Its deficiency lies not in any failure to expunge paradox or self-contradiction, but in its failure to recognize its own paradoxical structure (indeed, the paradoxical nature of all value systems) and to seek to articulate and explore it.

I believe that it would be possible to show in a similar way that any of the current relativisms or alleged relativisms in fact relies upon certain values that are not held to be relative. The point of doing so, however, would not be to re-establish the authority of the absolutist case, in the quasi-Kantian 'critique of pure value' suggested by Kate Soper which is designed 'to acquire a better sense of the minimal value-commitments essential to the critical power of social and cultural theory'.[12] The point would be to demonstrate that there is really no absolute choice possible between the retrieval and critique of values, minimal or otherwise: no choice possible between absolutism and relativism, between transcendent and contingent values, between essences and history. For it is impossible to choose plurality without making a non-contingent commitment to the value of plurality; just as it is impossible to imagine any absolute value – absolute beauty, universal freedom, equality, justice – which would not have in principle to be vulnerable to the kind of relativizing critique with which the last couple of decades have made us familiar. If the critique of absolute forms of value seems to assert the principles of relativity or contingency against them, then such critique may also be seen as determined and compelled by the theoretical desire for the total dominion of absolute concepts which it attempts to thwart. Absolutes, by their nature, are paranoid as well as imperialist, and ceaselessly provoke the dread of the unassimilably particular which they deny.

The question of value cannot be seized all at once or all together, since absolute value and relative value are not the sundered halves of a totality. Nor is it a matter of prudently splitting the difference between absolutism and relativism, since prudential optimizations of this kind are always governed precisely by the desire to maximize value and therefore simply reinstall the paradoxical question of value at a higher level (would there be an absolute imperative to the pragmatic middle way, or only a pragmatic imperative?). As in all paradoxes (rather than contradictions), the absolute opposites of absolutism and relativism both follow from and are implied by each other. Even to acknowledge this paradoxical structure of value, though it is very far from being nothing, is not to make the question of value knowable or masterable as a whole or entire structure. If this is very far from the assertion of the possibility of fixed values, then neither is it anything as simple as an assertion of 'play' or pure relativity against such fixity; perhaps it is best thought of as a claim that what seems to us like fixity is coiled closely together with what seems like play. These peculiar torsions in the question of value make for a strange kind of claim upon us, for we can never be entirely separate from the question of value, never fully escape its gravitational pull, nor ever fully inhabit it as our home or ethos. The question of value will always exert an imperative force which disturbs us from our safe inhabitation of ourselves, impelling us to question beliefs, certainties and values with a view not only to their potential betterment, but to the revaluation of the very notions of better and worse. The necessity of value is thus endlessly to value and revalue our values themselves. But it is absurd to think of this imperative as coming from outside ourselves, even if its force is to evict us from our complacent tenure of that first-person plural. The paradoxical structure of value as immanent transcendence is what enables and requires us to recognize that it is only in the absolute putting of the 'we' at risk that we realize the possibilities of our humanity. Neither side of the paradox, the side of risk or the side of realization, is definitive, or can diminish the necessity of the other.

NOTES

1   John Fekete, 'Introductory Notes for a Postmodern Value Agenda', in *Life after Postmodernism: Essays on Value and Culture*, ed. John Fekete (London: Macmillan, 1988), p. i.
2   We will meet another version of this necessity of value in the discussion in chapter 4 of the principle of generalized positivity which contradicts every claim to negate value.
3   I have a little more to say about this process of institutionalization and its effects on theory in my *Postmodernist Culture: An Introduction to Theories of the Contemporary* (Oxford: Basil Blackwell, 1989), pp. 14–21.
4   Two important carriers of the critique of aesthetic ideology are Pierre Bourdieu's *Distinction: A Social Critique of the Judgement of Taste* (1979), trans. Richard Nice (London and New York: Routledge & Kegan Paul, 1984), which urges a reintegration of the aesthetic and sociopolitical with a reading of the social and cultural capital constituted by cultural and aesthetic competence, and Terry Eagleton's *The Ideology of Aesthetic* (Oxford: Basil Blackwell, 1990), which sees the category of the aesthetic as a means simultaneously to displace and to consolidate relations of political power.
5   John Dewey, *Theory of Valuation*, in *John Dewey: The Later Works, 1925–1953*, ed. Jo Ann Boyditon and Barbara Levine (Carbondale and Edwardsville: Southern Illinois University Press, 1988), vol. 13, p. 195.
6   Jean-François Lyotard and Jean-Loup Thébaud, *Just Gaming*, trans. Brian Massumi (Manchester: Manchester University Press, 1985), pp. 66, 67.
7   Kate Soper, 'Postmodernism, Subjectivity and the Question of Value', *New Left Review*, 186 (1991), p. 122.
8   Wayne C. Booth, *The Company We Keep: An Ethics of Fiction* (Berkeley, Los Angeles and London: University of California Press, 1988) p. 99. References hereafter incorporated in the text.
9   J. Hillis Miller, *The Ethics of Reading: Kant, de Man, Eliot, Trollope, James, and Benjamin* (New York: Columbia University Press, 1987), p. 120.
10 Ibid., p. 120.
11 Ibid., p. 127.
12 Soper, 'Postmodernism, Subjectivity and the Question of Value', p. 128.

3

Value of Pleasure, Pleasure of Value

Just as the question of value has required of economic and philosophical theory a periodic reversion to the question of needs, the various attempts through the nineteenth and twentieth centuries to construe the objective and universal conditions of aesthetic value have been related closely, if also differentially, to the question of pleasure. For Kant, if the aesthetic were to be characterized entirely and exclusively in terms of pleasure, then this would inevitably be to reduce it to a matter of purely private interest or indulgence. For aesthetic pleasure to be valuable, therefore, it must be disinterested and, consequently, universal pleasure; this is to say, pleasure without individual profit, advantage or gratification. One contemporary current of anti-Kantian thought would view this account of aesthetic pleasure as a simple denial or abolition of sensual pleasure in favour of an aesthetic 'pleasure purified of pleasure', as Pierre Bourdieu puts it, that is no longer really pleasure at all.[1] Another, perhaps more nuanced view is that suggested by Terry Eagleton in *The Ideology of the Aesthetic* (1990), which sees the emergence of the self-legitimating realm of the aesthetic after Kant as instructed by the political necessity of mediating experience and authority; the self-governing artefact, which blends together desire and law, sensuous pleasure and abstract structure, submits to no external principle of restraint or regulation, but is all the more effective for that as a model of the interiorization of authority in bourgeois society. The aesthetic blending of pleasure and value is necessary precisely because of the sense of the new autonomy of the body and the whole realm of the affective, which threatened to tear apart from the realm of moral judgement. Of course, this account requires one to accept that such a bond between the libidinal and the legislative existed in the first place, or at least prior to the rise of the aesthetic in the modern sense, to accept, for instance, the rather dubious claim that 'for Samuel Johnson, there was absolutely no problem about "aesthetically" enjoying a work which morally disgusted you. It simply couldn't be done. Johnson would have been incapable of reaping pleasure from a text with the moral ideology of which he was fundamentally at odds.'[2]

Eagleton suggests valuably the doubleness of autotelic aesthetic pleasure, the fact that it can represent a challenge to dominative and instrumentalist modes of thinking even as it brings about a soothing and reactionary resolution of political tensions and problems. In holding to this duality, Eagleton's work is unusual. Accounts of the issue of pleasure both in nineteenth- and twentieth-century aesthetic theory and in contemporary cultural practice tend to be more strictly bifurcated, between the disapproval of pleasure on the one hand and the assertion that pleasure is all on the other. This is by no means a question that is confined to aesthetics alone. Recent Anglo-American moral philosophy has also been exercised by the problem of whether value is reducible in the end purely to the satisfaction of needs and desires or whether it is possible to change or create desires in the light of rational reflection.[3] This bifurcation is related to a more fundamental division regarding the relation of pleasure and value; a division between a hedonic or utilitarian view that, in the end, every form of value must be grounded in and reflect human needs and desires, and a moralist view that, even though pleasure can or should conduce to or be educated to conform with moral or ethical value, pleasure and value are distinct. Put simply, for the hedonist, pleasure and value are identical; for the moralist, they are distinct. Where the moralist will characteristically attempt to measure the value of pleasure by exchanging it for some other currency, such as 'good' or 'justice', the hedonist takes pleasure to be the very medium of exchange, as it were, the money-form of value; the moralist aims to convert pleasure into value, the hedonist to convert all value back into pleasure. As in the impasse between the absolutist and the relativist discussed in chapter 2, to whose positions the moralist and the hedonic views of pleasure are respectively analogous, there seems no way to negotiate the disagreement without in effect settling the question in favour of one or the other side.

But, in fact, it is also only by a ruthless logical shrinkage that this problem can be presented according to the alternatives set out above: either pleasure and value are distinct, or they are identical. As with the absolutist/relativist impasse, the very enquiry into the relationship and opposition of pleasure and value induces splittings, displacements and transferences in their respective meanings; such that, for example, attempts to distinguish value from pleasure tend to end up with a distinction between fundamentally different forms of pleasure; while attempts to identify value and pleasure may depend on a similar distinction between different forms of value in pleasure. In most cases too, the move to concentrate, generalize and hypostatize the alternatives of value and pleasure will be undercut by the very mobility of the terms as employed in the argument. Nowhere is this more so than in political versions of aesthetic theory, which bring about a particularly intense conjunction of questions of pleasure with questions of value; and, as a consequence, nowhere is it more important to resist the reductive binarism of pleasure or value.

Sublimation: Value against Pleasure

Most people would agree, wrote Roger Fry confidently in 1909, 'that the pleasures derived from art were of an altogether different character and more fundamental than merely sensual pleasure'.[4] The separation of different forms of pleasure effected here is in fact the commonest form in which pleasure is distinguished from value. According to this view, pleasure can be valuable, or lead to value, only as a result of being concentrated, purified, sublimated or otherwise transformed from itself. It might seem odd to associate I. A. Richards with this separation of pleasure and value, since, in his *Principles of Literary Criticism* (1924), he argues against the aestheticist view, held by Fry and others, that the experience of art is utterly *sui generis* and distinct from any other kind of experience. Arguing, as he does, for the identity of pleasure and value – 'anything is valuable which will satisfy an appetency without involving the frustration of some equal or *more important* appetency' – Richards is therefore opposed to any objectification or universalization of principles of value, the consequence of this view being 'that morals become purely prudential, and ethical codes merely the expression of the most general scheme of expediency to which an individual or a race has attained'.[5] So Richards identifies value not with individual desires which are to be satisfied at the expense of others, but with the systems by which competing desires are balanced, co-ordinated and organized to yield the most productive results, which is to say, the most satisfaction. The work of art is life-giving and valuable insofar as it produces such states of 'intricately wrought composure' and the 'equilibrium of opposed impulses'.[6] Literature and the arts are justified on these economic grounds, as the organizing of tensions and the maintaining of civilization, which Richards glosses as 'free, varied and unwasteful life'.[7]

But if Richards's argument suggests an unbroken continuum between disorganized and organized pleasure (or value), it also tends to concentrate dualistically on the two extremes of that continuum, producing the effect of a sharp and absolute division between pleasure and value. Bad art, says Richards, is characterized by its tendency to provide instant gratification and to encourage fixation upon stock responses and received ideas, rather than to encourage the ironic, impersonal play of judgement. In the way of such arguments, Richards's relative scale of evaluation for good and bad art quickly turns into a way of distinguishing art from non-art, this latter identified paranoically in the forms of mass culture and especially the cinema. The distinctions between immediacy and complexity, childishness and maturity, culture and art, all enforce an absolute distinction between pleasure and value:

> At present bad literature, bad art, the cinema, etc. are an influence of the first importance in fixing immature and actually inapplicable attitudes to most things ... The losses incurred by these artificial fixations of attitude are evident. Through them the average adult is worse, not better adjusted to the possibilities of his existence than the child.[8]

When adapted to the purposes of the New Criticism, the model of value that Richards here proposes will have hardened into a critical technology of tensions, ambiguities and resolutions, having apparently purged itself of the rather awkward questions of affectivity and response that here bulk so large. But, awkward as it is, the synthesis that Richards offers between the aesthetic, the subjective and the social is also usefully revealing. For it is plain that the stress on the ironic equilibrium of contending forces provides a model not only of the well-adjusted person, but also of the well-balanced liberal state. But it is equally plain that the model is also contradicted by the implicit social divide between those who have access to the affective complexity of the cultured classes, and those who are abandoned to the cretinous gratifications of mass culture. There seems to be no way of effecting an aesthetic resolution of the contradiction between different forms of aesthetic response, of imagining a sociocultural co-ordination of those who are co-ordinated and those who are not. By allowing pleasure to precipitate into brutish gratification, and determining value as the transcendence of such gratification, Richards's model here settles into the kind of fixation that it condemns.

Richards's argument has proved adaptable to many forms of twentieth-century aesthetic and cultural theory. An essay by Leonard B. Meyer of 1959 entitled 'Some Remarks on Value and Greatness in Music' shows just how easily this account of pleasure, along with its neurotic politics, can be transferred to another cultural realm. Here, as in Richards, the

establishment of a criterion of aesthetic value depends upon a differentiation of pleasures that hardens into an absolute duality between pleasure and value. Meyer distinguishes the pleasure experienced in listening
to 'primitive' music (by which he means, mostly, not non-Western native
music but Western pop music), which 'operates with such conventional
clichés that gratification is almost immediate' and the more complex
pleasure offered by sophisticated music (by which he means classical
music and modern jazz) which 'consists in the willingness to forgo
immediate, and perhaps lesser gratification, for the sake of future ultimate gratification'.[9] Where primitive listeners must be content with
'sensuous-associative pleasure', sophisticated listeners, who are able to
tolerate the uncertainties and formal resistances proposed by musical
works, harvest the rewards of 'syntactical-associative' pleasure. Like
Richards, Meyer seems to acknowledge that both of these are forms of
pleasure and are both valuable (though to different degrees). Nevertheless, Meyer surrenders progressively to the irresistible urge to reify the
artistic extremes of banality and greatness, and to personify the extremes
of response. It never occurs to him, for example, to wonder whether the
listener to primitive music must always and necessarily be a 'primitive
listener'. This produces something like an absolute distinction between,
on the one hand, the primitive or mass-cultural response, which leads to
'the degradation and dissolution of the self', in its merging, violent and
inert at once, with 'the primordial impulses of the group which, as Freud
has pointed out, "cannot tolerate any delay between its desires and the
fulfillment of what it desires"', and, on the other hand, that mature,
civilized self which has achieved individuation through its assimilation
and tempering of opposed impulses and resistances to gratification.[10] The
cultured adult knows what the tantrum-prone consumer of mass culture
does not – that you can't have your pudding before you've eaten your
greens.

Meyer's split between mass and individual pleasures seems to derive
quite closely from Richards. For Richards too, mass culture is life-
denying because its instantaneous gratifications, its immediate discharges
of unpleasurable tension, seem to produce a kind of entropy, a running
down towards death. High culture is life-affirming, on the other hand,
because the forms of equilibrium it achieves take longer, and involve
more delay and resistance. But it is exactly this Freudian sense of the
economic basis of pleasure (which Richards may actually derive not so
much from Freud as from Freud's own partial source, G. T. Fechner)
that undermines the value distinction Richards wants to maintain. For
Freud identifies pleasure not with stimulation, but with the lessening or

controlling of stimulation to achieve equilibrium. Richards seems to adopt this idea in *Principles of Literary Criticism*, suggesting that 'the pleasure–unpleasure attaching to the impulse may be no character of the impulse itself, but of its fate, its success or failure in restoring equilibrium'.[11] But there is an uncertainty in the very notion of equilibrium which crucially complicates the Freudian economic model of pleasure that is at work here. Does the achievement of equilibrium involve the maintenance of a balance between opposing forces or appetencies, or the gradual lowering of all tensions to zero? Freud was never able to give a definite answer to this question and, as we shall see in chapter 4, this uncertainty means that it is difficult for him to maintain an absolute distinction between life and death, pleasure and unpleasure, value and non-value. This uncertainty is reproduced in Richards's distinction between vital pleasure and deathly pleasure. The pleasures of art are valuable, Richards says, insofar as they maintain a flexed balance of opposed forces, in a muscular tension which does not cancel out, but binds and conserves energies; the instantaneous gratifications of mass culture are dangerous because they can be seen as pure discharge. But the distinction between the gainful and affluent pleasure of art and the entropic or effluent pleasures of mass culture are both derived from the same economic or differential structure, in which threatening or disabling levels of stimulus are mastered, displaced or discharged, in which more becomes less, in the interests of preserving the ego. So Richards can never entirely avert the danger of 'the degradation, the lowering of a response',[12] which he takes to be characteristic of mass culture or mere gratification, since all pleasure is of this kind in that it always involves an economy between the raising *and* lowering of a response.

Theodor Adorno and Max Horkheimer have a thoroughly different political outlook on contemporary culture; but they nevertheless share some of Richards's disdain and suspicion of mass culture. For Adorno and Horkheimer, pleasure is also associated unequivocally with the deathliness of mass culture, or, as they gloss it repeatedly, the 'pleasure industry'. Their *Dialectic of Enlightenment* (1944) presents the pleasures of popular music, of the radio and of that 'bloated pleasure apparatus', the cinema, as simply the extension of the rhythms and structures of work, for both work and leisure consist of nothing more than 'the automatic succession of standardized operations' (*DE*, 137). Like Richards, Adorno and Horkheimer inherit from Freud a notion of pleasure which is related closely to the idea of resistance. The mass pleasure induced by the culture industry 'hardens into boredom because, if it is to remain pleasure, it must not demand any effort and therefore moves rigorously in the worn

grooves of association' (*DE*, 137). The terms of this metaphor are striking. Mass pleasure is both soft and hard; soft because it involves no
resistance from the reality principle, no effort of self-distantiation, so that
even the grooves it runs along are softened and worn; hard precisely
because, encountering no resistance on its path, pleasure becomes
calcified into fixed and invariable patterns. A similar idea recurs a little
later on when Adorno and Horkheimer are discussing the omnipresence
of laughter in mass culture as 'the instrument of the fraud practised on
happiness' (*DE*, 140). Where Bergson had conceived of laughter as life
bursting through the rigid carapace of the inorganic or the mechanical,
Adorno and Horkheimer see the laughter induced by the culture industry as an 'invading barbaric life, self-assertion prepared to parade its
liberation from every scruple' (*DE*, 141). Meeting no resistance from
anything, the 'life which ... breaks through the barrier' (*DE*, 141) here is
inhumanly liberated from any constraint, a pure and unopposable
gratification which therefore hardens into a kind of mechanization, or
barrier to flexible response.

For Adorno and Horkheimer, mass pleasure displays a strange blending of vigour and inertness. Mass pleasure is a peculiarly exacting sort
of dissipation, an absolute relaxation of attention which, because it is
routinized and disciplinary, actually requires a continued effort of attention. Distraction becomes exertion in the watching of cartoon films in
which 'nothing that the experts have devised as a stimulant must escape
the weary eye; no stupidity is allowed in the face of all the trickery: one
has to follow everything and even display the smart responses shown and
recommended in the film' (*DE*, 139).

There are two alternatives to this regularized distraction. One is the
'pure nonsense' of popular art, of clowning, farce and the circus, whose
traces are to be seen in Charlie Chaplin and the Marx Brothers (*DE*, 137);
the other is the authentic work of art. Adorno and Horkheimer follow a
dominant tradition in setting the sublimated pleasures of art against the
unsublimated pleasures of the popular. But the sublimation they imagine
is of an extreme kind. In the model employed by Richards, the negativity
of art, its more or less complex deferral of pleasure, is in the interests of a
higher pleasure, a more abundant form of satisfaction in the long run.
For Adorno and Horkheimer, the value of the aesthetic lies precisely
in its refusal or permanent deferral of pleasure and its stimulation of
suspicion as to every form of gratification: 'The secret of aesthetic sublimation is its representation of fulfillment as a broken promise' (*DE*, 140).
But there turns out to be no absolute distinction between authentic art
and mass culture here, because, by refusing to gratify desire, authentic

art draws attention to that failure of gratification which in fact also characterizes mass culture. Like most severe moralists of pleasure, Adorno and Horkheimer see the lower pleasures as both dangerously intense and indifferently vacuous; the unsublimated or desublimated energies of mass pleasure are in fact insubstantial and unsatisfying:

> The culture industry perpetually cheats its consumers of what it perpetually promises. The promissory note which, with its plots and staging, it draws on pleasure is endlessly prolonged; the promise which is actually all the spectacle consists of, is illusory: all it actually confirms is that the real point will never be reached, that the diner must be satisfied with the menu. (*DE*, 139)

Strikingly, then, art and mass culture are here distinguished not in terms of value as opposed to pleasure, or even as sublimated pleasure as opposed to brute gratification, but in terms of a higher as opposed to a lower form of frustration. This goes further than most in the imposition of a split between pleasure and value, suggesting that under the debased conditions of modern capitalism, value inheres only in the more or less intense refusal or negation of pleasure. Where mass culture produces a state of addiction, a desire for more and more of the pleasure that brings no satisfaction, authentic art provides a higher form of disappointment altogether, which points to the emptiness of all corrupted pleasures. Though the negations of authentic art allow the reconstitution of a certain masochistic pleasure in the severe rapture of the mystic ('Delight is austere: *res severa verum gaudium*', write Adorno and Horkheimer (*DE*, 141)), their real value lies in their very refusal of the possibility of pleasure; for it is the very absoluteness of this absolute refusal which opens up a chink of utopian possibility, the purely negative hope of a transcendence in the form of a happiness in which desire and gratification would no longer be alienated.

The notion of the value of a negative transcendence of pleasure is also to be found, unpredictably enough, perhaps, in the work of Lionel Trilling. In his essay 'The Fate of Pleasure' (1963), Trilling argues that post-Romantic literature is characterized by its fierce opposition to the eighteenth-century identification of art with luxury, which is to say 'with the pleasure or at least the comfort of the consumer, or with the quite direct flattery of his ego'.[13] Trilling suggests that this hostility to pleasure is brought about by the steady marginalization of art in an increasingly commodified economic system and under a political rationality based with increasing explicitness on affluence and the extension of the pleasure principle. Against this is set the adversary morality of art and literature which 'regards with a stern and even minatory gaze all that is implied by affluence, and ... takes a dim or at best a very complicated view of the principle of pleasure'.[14] This develops from the work of Keats, with its ambivalent relish of and suspicion of sensual pleasure, into an aristocratic disdain for the acquisitive compulsions of the market-place and the desire for the 'negative transcendence of the human, a condition which is to be achieved by freeing the self from its thralldom to pleasure'.[15] Though Trilling regrets the separation of art from the world of rational politics which is brought about by this rejection of pleasure, his solution is not, as one might anticipate, a call for a more moderate and concessive view of pleasure on the part of artists, but a call for an enlargement of the sphere of politics to take account of the adversary 'election of unpleasure' in modern art.[16]

In its unsystematic way, this account of the value and function of art resembles that proposed by Adorno and Horkheimer, for Trilling too sees the value of art as lying principally in the negation of the dominance of pleasure. Where these accounts differ is in the nature of the transcendence which is negatively adumbrated. For Adorno and Horkheimer, as we have just seen, the negation of pleasure in art opens up the possibility of a non-alienated form of pleasure, a pleasure produced otherwise than under the debased conditions of commodity production and exchange. For Trilling, the utopia towards which the oppositional unpleasure of art gestures is an aristocratic utopia, centred on the aspirations of 'the extruded high segment' of society to escape society itself, rather than the desire to reconstitute social life in general. In the case of Trilling, pleasure is resisted because of the cloying threat it offers to the freely self-determining individual in 'the complex fullness of its appropriate life', while in the case of Adorno and Horkheimer, pleasure is resisted because of its desiccation of the complex relationship between the individual and the social totality.

The suspicion of pleasure and the segregation of pleasure from value which are to be found in Richards, Adorno and Horkheimer and Trilling alike undergoes some interesting mutations among some more recent critical accounts. Laura Mulvey has perhaps been the most radical antagonist of pleasure in recent years. In her influential 'Visual Pleasure and Narrative Cinema' (1975), Mulvey argues that it is the job of theory, and feminist theory in particular, to resist the 'skilled and satisfying manipulation of visual pleasure' in Hollywood cinema. For that visual pleasure is primarily the pleasure of the male viewer, or the female viewer constituted *as* the male viewer, and the object of that pleasure (and so its objectified victim) is primarily the woman. Most of the work that has followed on from this article has emphasized the structure of power-relations between the male gaze and the female object of that gaze; but the force of Mulvey's argument lies in her rejection of the pleasure involved in this relation:

> It is said that analysing pleasure, or beauty, destroys it. That is the intention of this article. The satisfaction and reinforcement of the ego that represent the high point of film history must be attacked. Not in favour of a reconstructed new pleasure, which cannot exist in the abstract, nor of intellectualised unpleasure, but to make for a total negation of the ease and plenitude of the narrative fiction film. The alternative is the thrill that comes from leaving the past behind without rejecting it, transcending outworn or oppressive forms, or daring to break with normal pleasurable expectations in order to conceive a new language of desire.[17]

The account of pleasure that is at work in Mulvey's essay is a psychoanalytic one that has certain resemblances to that assumed by I. A. Richards. Here too there is an identification of pleasure with an infantile gratification, in which no delay or interruption to the quest for pleasure can be tolerated. But the mobile and multiple appetencies which provoke the quest for pleasure in Richards have here broadened and simplified at once, into a general condition of lack or alienation. In the Lacanian account which lies behind Mulvey's argument, and many other recent accounts of visual pleasure, the ego seems to be conceived not as the source or origin of pleasure, but as its result. The gaining of pleasure is what defines and endlessly confirms the ego in an imaginary oneness and plenitude. But since the entry into sociolinguistic being, with all the enlarged possibilities for gathering pleasure that it brings, is also, necessarily, the abandonment of narcissistic pleasure, of the possibility of the coincidence of the subject and the object of its desire, this pleasure must always be temporary and vulnerable to disruption. The possibility of substitution which protects pleasure is precisely what makes all pleasure in the end unsatisfactory.

But it is for this very reason that the fragile and temporary pleasures gained by the ego are violent and conservative pleasures. It is not just that pleasure soothes or gratifies the ego, or even that the ego depends on pleasure as the junkie depends on his needle; in Freud's concept of the 'pleasure-ego', the individual self is *made up* of pleasure, since everything that is unpleasurable is violently expelled from it. But, of course, this results not in a weakly insubstantial ego, made up of shifting and phantasmal substitutions, but in a violent and aggressive ego, determined to preserve its illusory identity at all costs. For the adherents of this account of the ego, pleasure of any kind is likely to be suspected, and therefore dissociated from value. As we have just seen, value for Mulvey consists in the breaching or suspension of pleasure rather than the surrender to it.

It might seem, then, as though the distinction between higher and lower pleasures that is found in Richards has given way to a much simpler picture, in which all forms of pleasure, insofar as they involve a structure of return to the ego, are to be suspected. No matter how subtle and extended the excursions of the ego outside itself may be, in alternative identifications, in enlarging perceptions and sympathies, those experiences are always snapped back to the benefit of the ego on the elastic of the pleasure principle. To put it another way: though it may seem as if the reality principle is opposed to the violent primitive energies of the pleasure principle, the very delays, postponements and blockages of gratification demanded by the reality principle result not in the relinquishment of pleasure, but in a qualitative if not quantitative increase in pleasurable yield. The reality principle therefore proves to be in the grip of the pleasure principle. In cultural and aesthetic terms, we could say that the softening of the ego's demands, and the growth into tempered and co-ordinated pleasure demanded alike of the mature work of art and the liberal self by I. A. Richards may have come to seem like the dominative exercise of pleasure through greater complexity, rather than its ethical relinquishment.

One may see the tenacious persistence of pleasure in the above passage from Mulvey. If she counsels a careful and absolute 'total negation of the ease and plenitude' of pleasure in all its forms, including the relinquishment of the various reconstructions of pleasure, perhaps especially in the displaced or sublimated form of 'intellectualised unpleasure', it is plain that the value of this negation must itself be pleasurable, though perhaps in an alternative way. Mulvey's austere call for a 'total negation' of pleasure is instantly qualified by an assertion of the value of such a negation in terms of a distinctly pleasurable transgression. 'The alternative', she writes, 'is the thrill that comes from leaving the past behind without rejecting it, transcending outworn or oppressive forms, or daring to break with normal pleasurable expectations in order to conceive a new language of desire.' So what is being abandoned here is not pleasure *per se*, but a certain assimilative model of pleasure, pleasure as the profit of the ego. The affective language switches from terms that suggest inertia to terms suggesting dynamism, from 'ease' and 'plenitude' to 'thrill' and 'daring', in a way that appears to reinstate the vitalism of Richards's model, where the rejection of pleasure in the interests of value or ethics becomes a promotion of certain ethical pleasures which promise life rather than death, novelty rather than the recursion to the same, risk to the self rather than its reinforcement.

Desublimation: Pleasure against Value

This reconfiguration of pleasure is to be found elsewhere in contemporary theory, and perhaps most notably and influentially in Jacques Lacan's promotion of the principle of *jouissance*. Lacan reacts against the Freudian pleasure principle on the grounds of its conservatism and homeostatic inertia, and finds a true 'beyond' of the pleasure principle not in death (for the drive of pleasure to keep the level of tension in the organism as low as possible is itself a kind of death instinct) but in *jouissance* or desire, which tends insatiably towards unattainable limits:

> Pleasure limits the scope of human possibility – the pleasure principle is a principle of homeostasis. Desire on the other hand finds its boundary, its strict relation, its limit, and it is in relation to this limit that it is sustained as such, crossing the threshold imposed by the pleasure principle.[18]

Lacan's distinction between pleasure and *jouissance* is taken over and given a particularly aesthetic resonance in Roland Barthes's *The Pleasure of the Text*. Barthes suggests, like Lacan, that there are in fact two kinds of pleasure and two kinds of text to go with them, the text of pleasure and the text of bliss. Plainly, the text of pleasure is rooted in the conservative, homeostatic pleasure principle as defined by Lacan, for it is 'the text that contents, fills, grants euphoria; the text that comes from culture and does not break with it, is linked to a *comfortable* practice of reading'. The text of bliss (Barthes uses the same word *jouissance* in the original) is 'the text that imposes a state of loss, the text that discomforts (perhaps to the point of a certain boredom), unsettles the reader's historical, cultural, psychological assumptions, the consistency of his tastes, values, memories, brings to a crisis his relation with language' (*PT*, 14). Like Lacan's *jouissance*, Barthes's text of bliss is orientated towards extremity rather than containment, but it is a paradoxical, non-teleological extremity, an extremity of non-finality. As opposed to the centred, genital finality of texts governed by the pleasure principle and the sense of an ending, the text of bliss perversely resists or turns aside from centred pleasure. But this is not enough; for Barthes, even perversion presupposes a certain predictable curriculum or outcome of pleasure, and so the text of bliss must be polymorphously, unpredictably, *perversely* perverse:

> Such texts are perverse in that they are outside any imaginable finality – *even that of pleasure* (bliss does not constrain to pleasure: it can even apparently inflict boredom). No alibi stands up, nothing is reconstituted, nothing recuperated. The text of bliss is absolutely intransitive. However perversion does not suffice to define bliss; it is the extreme of perversion which defines it: an extreme constantly shifted, an empty, mobile, unpredictable extreme. The extreme guarantees bliss: an average perversion quickly loads itself up with a play of subordinate finalities: prestige, ostentation, rivalry, lecturing, self-serving, etc. (*PT*, 51–2)

Obviously, this is a claim for the absolute value of bliss over mere pleasure. The problem with all such assertions of absolute value, of course, is that they continuously draw on the structures of exchange they attempt to transcend; the demonstration of their absolute status requires, paradoxically, that they be estimated relative to other forms of profit or advantageous outcome. This is true even and especially of Barthes's own text, which constitutes such a relative evaluation in the very fact of offering a theory or thesis about the bliss that is unrecuperable for the pleasurable coherence of theory. This theory must therefore reject its own status as theory, remaining content merely to gesture at its own unsatisfactoriness (its failure to give pleasure) in this respect: 'No "thesis" on the pleasure of the text is possible; barely an inspection (an introspection) that falls short' (*PT*, 34). In order to promote or make visible the absolute value of the text of bliss, it is better to resist assigning it any value in particular, 'better to renounce the passage from *value*, the basis of the assertion, to *values*, which are the effects of culture' (*PT*, 34). And this means in turn that, in order to preserve the exchange-value of his own demonstration of the value of bliss, Barthes must withhold it from exchange, refusing to allow it the standing of a model or exemplar.

Barthes's account of pleasure, along with his account of the account of pleasure, involves an irreducible complexity. For, as in the austere account of valuable non-pleasure offered by Adorno and Horkheimer, the extreme pleasure of bliss can take the form of a frustration of pleasure, of the closed, homeostatic gratifications to which the ego is so addicted.[19] This is a version of the aesthetics of the sublime as they are to be found in Kant, especially as interpreted recently by Jean-François Lyotard. The pleasure of the sublime is an anxious mingling of pleasure and unpleasure, a thrilling apprehension of some awesome largeness or grandeur which nevertheless frustrates all our attempts to conceive it, to draw it together in the form of a concept. Kant distinguishes between an aesthetic of beauty and an aesthetic of the sublime in terms of the different kinds of pleasure they invoke, the one a pleasure of conformity between the stimulus and human capacities, the other an anxious pleasure in the disruption of that conformity: 'Whereas natural beauty ... conveys a finality in its form making the object appear, as it were preadapted to our power of judgement ... that which ... excites the feelings of the sublime, may appear, indeed, in point of form to contravene the ends of our power of judgement, to be ill-adapted to our faculty of presentation, and to be, as it were, an outrage on the imagination.'[20] This is why, for Lyotard, the postmodern aesthetics of the sublime are to be distinguished in a certain refusal of simply ego-based pleasure, the 'solace of good forms, the consensus of a taste which would make it possible to share collectively the nostalgia for the unattainable',[21] and why, indeed, the sublime might just as well be thought of in terms of melancholy and despair rather than in terms of pleasure: for Kant and Burke, Lyotard points out, 'sorrow (*der Kummer*) also counts among the "vigorous emotions," if it is grounded in moral Ideas. The despair of never being able to present something within reality on the scale of the Idea then overrides the joy of being nonetheless called upon to do so' (*D*, 179).

The sublime in this account is always liminal, neither entirely above nor entirely below the threshold of human capacities. Indeed, the word 'sublime' illustrates in its history the crossing of the threshold it designates; it derives apparently from Latin *sublimis*, i.e. *sub* up to and *limen* the lintel. The notion, perhaps originally architectural, that height is to be measured in terms of proximity to or distance from the lintel, the point of division between upper and lower, becomes simplified in a use of 'sublime' to mean simply high or elevated. Usage therefore pushes the idea of going *up to* the lintel over the top into pure transcendence, so that 'the sublime' comes to mean that which *goes beyond* the threshold. But for Burke, Kant and, recently, Lyotard, the sublime always opens up or inhabits a gap between experience on the one hand and consciousness/ conceptuality on the other. The sublime names neither the experience, lying *above* or *beyond* the capacities of the mind, nor the conceptualization, lying *beneath* the intensities of the experience, but the (incomplete) relation and movement between them. It is therefore not surprising that the notion of *sublimis* also yields in 1824 the word 'subliminal', to represent psychological states or sensations that are *below* the threshold of conscious experience.[22] Here the ideas of ultimate pleasure as an impingement upon a limit and of ultimate pleasure as a transgression of that limit combine and alternate. The effort to imagine this ultimate pleasure is an anxiety of loss (the desolate *fort* of Freud's fort:da game) which can always yield pleasure in being mastered or bound by the concept of the sublime itself, a concept which simultaneously lets itself go into otherness and, in naming that process, gathers itself back to itself.

This is why Barthes's bliss is not simply a heightened pleasure. Bliss does not lie beyond the pleasure principle, but, as it were, on the very boundary between the pleasure principle and its beyond. In *The Pleasure of the Text*, bliss is promoted not so much as the pure value of a transcendence of mere pleasure, as the state between pleasure and its transcendence, between the consolidation of the ego and its dissolution:

> Whence, perhaps, a means of evaluating the works of our modernity: their value would proceed from their duplicity. By which it must be understood that they always have two edges. The subversive edge may seem privileged because it is the edge of violence; but it is not violence which affects pleasure, nor is it destruction which interests it; what pleasure wants is the site of a loss, the seam, the cut, the deflation, the *dissolve* which seizes the subject in the midst of bliss. Culture thus recurs as an edge: in no matter what form. (*PT*, 7)

Whether applauded or decried, as liberating or repressive, Barthes's *Pleasure of the Text* is usually taken to be a hedonist text, a text which identifies value with pleasure rather than separating them. But, oddly, despite the structure of the sublime that is enacted in the text, Barthes's hedonism may be said to be desublimating in effect; that is to say, it resists the attempt to raise up, educate or otherwise transform pleasure upwards into value, in the manner specified by Freud. In this, it joins with some other influential writing, including that of Bourdieu and Lyotard, in the effort to resist sublimation, whether in culture generally, or in cultural theory, and to affirm the value of unsublimated pleasures. This effort is nowhere more visible than in the study of popular culture, where the influence of the rather aristocratic writing of Barthes has been if anything stronger than in the cultural mainstream to which his work belonged. Cultural studies have tended to take the negative definitions of mass culture offered by modernism and reverse its valencies; if mass culture is characterized by the formless intensities of its pleasures, an unmasterable energy of particularity which refuses the centring, channelling force of sublimation, then this may be affirmed as its value. Such accounts may draw energy from Mikhail Bakhtin's idea of carnival, in which categories slide, high and low interchange, energy overflows structure, desire masters law. In its opposition to theory, to the capturing force of conceptuality, and, above all, in the fact that it constitutes not an inversion, the world turned merely upside-down, but a topographic disruption, a dissolution of the threshold between high and low, Bakhtin's carnival is surely a kind of 'sublimity from below', and therefore potentially a populist, democratic version of the textual erotics evoked by Barthes.

The question of pleasure has been central in feminist rereadings of popular culture, since it is the theory of the irredeemable sensuality and triviality of unsublimated pleasure which has ensured the regular homology between woman and mass culture for two centuries. Recent work has tended to concentrate in particular upon women's experience of popular forms such as romance, attending to the complex specificities of their reading and generally attempting to repudiate the open stigmatization of reactionary popular pleasure such as is found in Mulvey's essay. As we have seen, negative accounts of popular pleasure like I. A. Richards's tend to stress the dominance of identification, or structures of infantile ego-gratification, in the watching of films, reading of romance and so on, as opposed to the more developed, delayed and complex pleasures of the mature, civic self, and some feminist writers have found it hard to resist this evaluation. As Cora Kaplan has pointed out, such condemnations begin as early as the rationalist attack mounted by Mary Wollstonecraft on the excess of sensibility and the debilitating effects of pleasure in women, particularly in those who read romances. Such habits only confirm the passive dependency of women, their identification with the primitive or infantile desire for pleasure alone, rather than the capacity for reasoned, independent critique. For Wollstonecraft, as for Jane Austen, romance-reading prevents the formation of a rationally autonomous self by the premature fixations of reader-identification, or by the abandonment of the ego in escapism; in either case, writes Kaplan, 'pleasure of fantasy numbs the nerve of resistance to oppression'.[23] This suspicion of pleasure survives in certain moralist forms of feminist critique. Sabina Lovibond, for example, has recently regretted feminism's too precipitate turning away from the critical and reconstructive analysis of social conditions in favour of an ethics of immediate pleasure. Lovibond believes that, in promoting fluid, self-creating subjectivity, this may mistake consolatory or enforced pleasures for more authentic forms of fulfilment, and thus leave structures of oppression and alienation (which often work precisely through pleasure rather than against it) intact.[24]

But Kaplan argues that the problem for Wollstonecraft, as it is for contemporary theory of pleasure in popular culture, is that it accepts too readily what is an ideological construction of femininity, and female response as an actual psychological and sociological fact. Indeed, she argues, the stress on the narrowing narcissism of identification in fantasy is itself mistaken, and ignores the complexity of the processes of pleasure. Drawing on the work of J. Laplanche and J.-B. Pontalis, Kaplan argues that the pleasure of fantasy involves not a fixing of the subject in identification, but rather a mobile plurality of identifications, an identification with the syntax of the fantasy rather than with the central protagonist.[25] It is for this reason that she would want to distinguish in romance a certain heterogeneity of pleasure, or a pleasure in heterogeneity itself. Though novels like Colleen MacCullough's *The Thorn Birds* do indeed centre the (female) reader in ways that are ultimately reactionary, they 'confirm not a conventional femininity but women's contradictory and ambiguous place within sexual difference', and they do this by 'reworking the contradictory elements that make female subjectivity such a vertiginous social and psychic experience'.[26]

Kaplan's argument for the complexity of the pleasures involved in the popular stops far short of the libidinal politics proposed by Barthes, but the stress on the irreducible complexity of these pleasures constitutes an exemplary resistance to the sublimations practised in aesthetics and in contemporary cultural politics. On this account, the value of popular pleasure lies in its disruption of the processes whereby identity is fixed and sustained, in the mobility of *jouissance* rather than the greedy egoism of the pleasure principle in its baser forms. We should note the congruences between this account of the value of pleasure and that of Barthes in *The Pleasure of the Text*. For what is being claimed about the value of pleasure depends upon a moral discrimination between two different kinds of pleasure, with preference being accorded to the open and productive pleasure of mobile identifications, rather than the closed and narcissistic gratification of fixed identification. Claims for the force of desire, or polymorphous pleasure in the popular, tend, like Kaplan's, to be more modulated, less extreme than Barthes's evocation of the fugitive intensities of *jouissance*. Characteristically, they may suggest not that popular pleasure provides a pure revolutionary dissolution of authority and identity, but a certain disruptive force within or alongside settings or frames of a more conservative kind, as when Kaplan suggests that in *The Thorn Birds* 'the reactionary political and social setting secures, in some fashion, a privileged space where the most disruptive female fantasy can be "safely" indulged'.[27] The uncertainty of Kaplan's judgement here is signalled in the inverted commas around the word 'safely': do these signify that the reactionary frame in fact constrains the disruption of mobile pleasure, or only appears to? This uncertainty about the value of pleasure comes close to Barthes's characterization of the value of uncertainty in pleasure; Barthes too, we remember, characterizes *jouissance* as liminal, as lying between the two edges of conformity and disruption. These are 'an obedient, conformist, plagiarizing edge (the language is to be copied in its canonical state, as it has been established by schooling, good usage, literature, culture), and *another edge*, mobile, blank (ready to assume any contours), which is never anything but the site of its effect: the place where the death of language is glimpsed' (*PT*, 6).

Accounts of the value of unsublimated pleasure, or claims for what I have called 'sublimity from below', must struggle with the same problem that Barthes does. This is the problem of resisting sublimation or reification, the problem of maintaining the resistant force of pleasure's pure unruliness without either abstracting it into a principle or surrendering its political value as resistance; the problem of maintaining it as a value in itself, rather than subordinating it to some higher value to which it may then in its turn be elevated. Fredric Jameson confronts just this problem in 'Pleasure: A Political Issue' (1983), a discussion of Barthes's *Pleasure of the Text*. Characteristically, Jameson attempts to hold together without prematurely resolving the two terms of the antinomy set up by Barthes's essay, the hedonism of *jouissance* – 'the consent of life in the body' – with the puritanism of political commitment – 'that very different relationship between myself or my body and other people – or in other words, with History, with the political in the stricter sense' ('Pleasure', 10, 11). The answer to this problem lies in the broad lines of Jameson's argument in *The Political Unconscious* (1981) that a purely sensuous pleasure, a pleasure of extreme and autonomous physicality, is always political, even and especially in its apparent refusal or liquidation of the political realm. It is for this reason that Jameson can perceive that 'the immense merit of Barthes' essay is to restore a certain politically symbolic value to the experience of *jouissance*, and to make it impossible to read the latter except as a response to a political and historical dilemma, whatever position one chooses (puritanism/hedonism) to take about that response itself' ('Pleasure', 9). If Barthes's pure pleasure is alienated from the political world, then that alienation must be read symptomatically, as a critical gesture pointing away from itself and back to the very political dimension that is absent from it.

Jameson achieves this conciliation of pleasure and the political via a characterization of Barthes's pleasure as sublime, in the sense of the term offered by Edmund Burke's *Philosophical Enquiry into the Origin of our Ideas of the Sublime and the Beautiful* (1757). Jameson argues that the particular

mixture of pleasure and unpleasure, rapture and fear, which constitutes
the experience of the sublime for Burke, is founded on 'the apprehension
through a given aesthetic object of what in its awesome magnitude
shrinks, threatens, diminishes, rebukes individual human life' ('Pleasure',
12). If the threatened object is the individual body for Burke, it is the
fragile bourgeois ego for Barthes. In both cases, the fear is provoked by
a sense of what lies beyond, what painfully transcends, the capacities of
the human. As we have seen, this last crucially includes the capacity to
represent the experience of the sublime. For this reason, Jameson calls the
experience of the sublime an 'allegorical' one, in that the sublime as
represented must always point beyond itself to some absent never-to-
be-named referent, that 'sheer unfigurable force itself, sheer power ...
[which] stuns the imagination in the most literal sense' ('Pleasure', 12–
13). But Jameson is perfectly confident that he can give a name to that
repressed referent of Barthesian pleasure. Here it is:

> The immense culture of the simulacrum whose experience, whether we
> like it or not, constitutes a whole series of daily ecstasies and punctual fits
> of *jouissance* or schizophrenic dissolutions ... may appropriately, one would
> think, be interpreted as so many unconscious points of contact with that
> equally unfigurable and unimaginable thing, the multinational apparatus,
> the great suprapersonal *system* of a late capitalist 'technology'. ('Pleasure',
> 13)

So, if the missing referent of the Burkean sublime is 'God', the missing referent or political unconscious of Barthesian pleasure is late capitalism. But there is something very odd here. For Jameson is designating
as allegorical an experience that is the very frustration or untenability
of allegory – that is, if we take allegory in the traditional sense of an
embodiment of hidden rather than inaccessible meaning, of reference
deferred rather than simply denied. Even if it is true that the sublime can
never in fact achieve the immaculately self-refuting status that it seems to
claim, in that it must always in some wise make representable and
conceivable what it suggests is beyond the power of human beings to
represent and conceive, nevertheless, the sublime can be allegorical only
in a very specialized sense, as the allegory of the non-allegoricality of its
experience, as the very figure of non-figurability. Indeed, Jameson's
identification of late capitalism as the missing referent of Barthesian
pleasure is itself really only a repetition or *mis en abîme* of the problematic
of the sublime, since the figured object here functions in a sense as a kind
of unfigurability, as a thing that can no longer be easily conceived or
constituted as an object by theory. Nevertheless, by insisting that what

assails the defenceless ego in the experience of the sublime is something hidden or repressed, rather than something permanently unnameable and unrepresentable, Jameson is in fact maintaining the dominion of the pleasure principle in the narrow sense decried by Barthes, the principle that gathers in and puts to its own service the experience of self-abandonment or dissolution. Jameson is completing the circuit of the fort:da of the pleasure principle, reclaiming for the pleasure of theory the unpleasure of bliss.

Jameson here may be according to pleasure, which is aesthetic only in that it belongs to the wholesale aestheticization of cultural experience in postmodernity, the conversion of experience into style by advertising and the marketing of pleasure more generally, something of the ambivalent value of the aesthetic which Adorno accords to authentic and autonomous art. The fluxes of intensity, the skidding mobility of pleasures in postmodern subjectivity may therefore be seen as a form of the sublimity from below that I characterized earlier, which resists every traditional, Kantian sublimation of pleasure into higher pleasure, affirming the value of unsublimated pleasure against the sublimation (abstraction, narrowing, conservation, recuperation) of pleasure into 'higher' civilized values. But, where others might wish to maintain the sublime resistance to the sublimation of pleasure on its own terms, either by the hypertheorization of pleasure evidenced in Barthes's *Pleasure of the Text*, or by a kind of cultivated and strategic empiricism, a refusal to allow the irrecuperable energy and particularity of pleasure to be swallowed up by political theory and strategy, Jameson attempts the virtuoso feat of sublimating the very desublimating energy of pleasure, deriving a political value from its very refusal of sublimated value.

> [T]he thematizing of a particular 'pleasure' as a political issue ... must always involve a dual focus, in which the local issue is meaningful and desirable in and of itself, but is also *at one and the same time* taken as the figure for Utopia in general, and for the systemic revolutionary transformation of society as a whole. ('Pleasure', 13)

This is an impossible and self-contradictory project in precisely the same way as Barthes's theoretical refusal to totalize pleasure in theory; for, in both cases, the hedonic and the moralist positions imply and inhabit each other. To assert the value of pleasure in itself, which is the only way in which it can be rescued from the false sublimation of bourgeois aesthetics, is always to moralize, to reduce to a principle its unprincipled refusal of sublimation. The hedonic position that pleasure is value always becomes a version of the moralist position that pleasure only conceals, implies or figures a value, which must, by some exterior or supplementary operation of theory, be spelled out of it. It might seem as though things were simpler for the kind of moralist critic of pleasure that Jameson is in the end. But such a critic will predictably encounter sooner or later the objection of the hedonist that abstract systems of moral value can apparently always be desublimated, which is to say, unmasked as forms of pleasure or gratification, as in the critique of a Freud or a Bourdieu.

These contradictions work against every attempt to hypostatize pleasure, whether in the good form of pleasure valued positively by the hedonist, or the bad form of pleasure suspected and rejected by the moralist. Pleasure resists this hypostatization, refusing to lie unambiguously either on the side of value or against value. A politics of pleasure must accordingly resist both the hedonist and the moralist temptations insofar as they rely on or tend towards notions of 'pure' (unsublimated) pleasure and 'pure' (sublimated) value. This will involve paying close attention to the complex instabilities of pleasure, aesthetic and otherwise, and the complex exchanges between pleasure and value. More than this, a politics of pleasure must also aim to participate in this dynamic process whereby pleasure and value endlessly produce and reproduce each other. The experience of pleasure in art and culture may be a useful place to start, not because art and culture offer access to any kind of pure or disinterested pleasure, but precisely because of the uncertain and impure nature of pleasure in these areas, poised between the interested and the disinterested, between use-value and exchange-value, between homeostatic ego-gratification and the indefiniteness of sublime pleasure. If the aesthetic has hitherto been constituted as a conceptual mechanism for separating pleasure and value out from each other, and for fixing their differential values, then it is conceivable that the aesthetic, in the enlarged form of a politics of culture, may yet become a realm in which the pleasurable renegotiation of the political value of pleasure may take place.

NOTES

1 Bourdieu, *Distinction*, p. 6.
2 Terry Eagleton, 'Poetry, Pleasure and Politics', in *Against the Grain: Selected Essays 1975–1985* (London: Verso, 1986), p. 179.
3 The first position is held by Bernard Williams, in *Ethics and the Limits of Philosophy* (Cambridge, Mass.: Harvard University Press, 1985), the second

exemplified by E. J. Bond, who tries to show in his *Reason and Value* (Cambridge: Cambridge University Press, 1983) that it is possible to conceive of objective forms of value which are not marked by 'the shadow of desire'.

4 Roger Fry, 'An Essay in Aesthetics' (1909), repr. in *Modern Art and Modernism: A Critical Anthology*, ed. Francis Frascina and Charles Harrison (London: Harper & Row, 1982), p. 81.

5 I. A. Richards, *Principles of Literary Criticism* (1924, repr. London: Routledge & Kegan Paul, 1983), p. 36.

6 Ibid., p. 197.

7 Ibid., p. 43.

8 Ibid., p. 159.

9 Leonard B. Meyer, 'Some Remarks on Value and Greatness in Music' (1959), repr. in *Aesthetics Today*, ed. Morris Philipson and Paul J. Gudel, rev. edn (New York and Scarborough, Ont.: Meridian, 1980), p. 277.

10 Ibid., p. 283.

11 Richards, *Principles of Literary Criticism*, p. 72.

12 Ibid., p. 186.

13 Lionel Trilling, 'The Fate of Pleasure' (1963), repr. in *Beyond Culture: Essays on Literature and Learning* (London: Secker & Warburg, 1966), p. 69.

14 Ibid., p. 67.

15 Ibid., p. 81.

16 Ibid., p. 85.

17 Laura Mulvey, 'Visual Pleasure and Narrative Cinema', *Screen*, 16 (1975), p. 87.

18 Jacques Lacan, 'On the Subject of Certainty', in *The Four Fundamental Concepts of Psycho-Analysis*, trans. Alan Sheridan (Harmondsworth: Penguin, 1979), p. 31.

19 The closeness of the ecstatic and the austere accounts of pleasure may be obliquely suggested by a student essay I once read which suggested that 'the interminable self-reflexions of modernist texts can bring about a feeling of boredom in the reader, a feeling which Barthes describes as "bliss" '.

20 Immanuel Kant, *The Critique of Judgement* (1790), trans. James Creed Meredith (Oxford: Clarendon Press, 1952), p. 91.

21 Jean-François Lyotard, 'Answering the Question: What is Postmodernism?', in *The Postmodern Condition: A Report on Knowledge* (1979), trans. Geoff Bennington and Brian Massumi (Manchester: Manchester University Press, 1984), p. 81.

22 The *OED* gives J. G. Herbart's *Psychologie als Wissenschaft* as the first appearance of this word, to denote that which remains 'unter der Schwelle des Bewußtseins'.

23 Cora Kaplan, '*The Thorn Birds*: Fiction, Fantasy, Femininity', in *Sea Changes: Essays on Culture and Feminism* (London: Verso, 1986), p. 122. Kaplan expands her critique of Wollstonecraft in the essay 'Wild Nights: Pleasure/Sexuality/Feminism' in the same volume, pp. 31–50.

24 Sabina Lovibond, 'Feminism and Postmodernism', *New Left Review*, 178 (1989), pp. 25–8.
25 Kaplan, '*The Thorn Birds*', pp. 127–31.
26 Ibid., pp. 120–1.
27 Ibid., p. 145.

4

Absolute Rubbish: *Cultural Economies of Loss in Freud, Bataille and Beckett*

The metaphor of economy has proved in recent years to have had a very great binding and explanatory power in philosophy and literary and cultural theory. The claim that the cultural itself functions by means of structures that must be seen as economic in the widest sense is a simultaneous intensification and inversion of the vulgar Marxist model of base and superstructure, which enacted the determination of the cultural by the economic along with the absolute ontological separation of the two realms, while it also represents a profound challenge to the traditional liberal conception of the autonomy of the cultural sphere from the economic. (One should note, of course, that it has been largely in Marxist attempts to grasp the materiality of the sign that the expanded importance of the principle of economy has been most amply demonstrated.) It has now become possible to construe languages, texts, images, social structures and practices, cultural and discursive relationships, even (especially) the structure of the psyche and its intersubjective relations in the dynamic terms made available by the metaphor of economy (and, we should therefore specify, the economy of metaphor), and conditions indeed seem propitious for the establishment of a general theory of symbolic practice, of which the economic, in the more usual financial and commercial sense, would be only a particular and limited form and would lose thereby its explanatory privilege.[1]

If the move towards economy may be seen as a move away from the domination of the concept of structure, what shift of values and analytic advantage does this bestow? One answer would seem to be that an economy is a *dynamic* structure, which allows and obliges the critic not only to order and distribute the elements of his field of study in inert relationships of equivalence and distinction, but also to show the processes of exchange, circulation and interested negotiation which bring these relationships dynamically into being. Seen in this way, economy can be described as the purposive activity which precipitates structure as its outcome. The metaphor of economy may allow one, therefore, to escape some of the closure or reductiveness of the metaphor of structure, to seize, for instance, the formless but intense pulsions of the 'libidinal economy' in its transactions between the self and the social other.[2]

However, the metaphor of economy is not without its own (necessary) forms of binding effect. Any economy, to the degree that it *is* an economy and not just a set of exchanges reduced diagrammatically to a structure, must be orientated towards some goal, which we may call the law of value; though economies allow for the production of many different kinds of value, the concept of an economy in which the principle of value was absent, allowing for no regular possibility of gain or gainful outcome, would seem to be an entirely empty one. It is this principle, and especially the necessity that it brings with it of being able to measure and rationally predict forms of gain, which seems to exert a narrowing or reductive influence.

The coming into being of a distinctively modern sense of the nature of culture and cultural value involves various kinds of refusal of these principles of calculation, profit and instrumentality. For Kant and Arnold in the nineteenth century, cultural and aesthetic value had to be set definitively against the values of the narrowly contingent or economic world, and was therefore constituted as absolute value in itself, which could not in principle be captured by or reduced to the processes of the economic. There is a certain congruity between such accounts and the early Marxist division between the authenticity of lived 'use-value' and the alienated inauthenticity of 'exchange-value'; if use-value appears to be the very opposite of disinterested aesthetic contemplation in one sense, it is equivalent to it in the sense that it is held to be irreducible and non-exchangeable.

A sharp division of this kind between economic value and non-economic value proves increasingly difficult to sustain during the twentieth century, as the rise of the mass-cultural market and increasing commodification of the cultural sphere threatens more and more to contaminate its autonomy. One extreme but characteristic response in avant-garde cultural practice has been to reaffirm the distinction between the cultural and the economic not in terms of different *kinds* of value, but in terms of a distinction between value and an absolute non-value; such practice aims for forms of activity and product that would not only resist inclusion within narrow profit/loss structures of accounting, but constitute a realm which would be *in principle* unassimilable to any form of economic relationship. The difference between Kantian and, for instance, Dadaist aesthetics is therefore a difference between two equivalent attempts to escape economy, one in the overdetermined form of absolute or autotelic value, the other in the underdetermined form of non-value, disposability, or the ready-made. Not the least of the complexities attaching to this is the fact that the dynamic relationship of these attempts to thwart economy is precisely an economic one, of surplus to shortfall, concentration as opposed to expenditure.

The problem with all such attempts to escape the contingency of economic exchange is the fact that they are all vulnerable to recuperation by the law of value or profit. In the obvious case of Duchamp's ready-mades, for example, the refusal of aesthetic aura has presented absolutely no obstacle to the processes of cultural sanctification and museumification; and, indeed, these objects are now as much part of the universe of artistic exchange-value as any other artistic icon. Even when such strategies are pursued further, to the point of refusing to provide any durable artwork at all, as in the performance art of the 1960s onwards, the processes of commodification can continue unabated (and may have an even more intense power), since such performances can always be represented in the market in terms of their documentary residues. Such practices will, in fact, always be vulnerable to the charge that, insofar as their very challenges to the structures of artistic value and value in general will themselves constitute forms of value, they will be promptly restored to the fields of exchange and transaction which they had attempted to transcend.

Such attempts to escape the determination of value seem to illustrate two co-operating features of the general economy of social and symbolic practice; these are the principles of ineliminable exchange and general positivity. First of all, the system of general economy disallows any form of absolute or self-grounding value, or absolute non-value, since such apparent transcendings or transgressions of the general economy can exist only relative to it. The second principle, which derives from the first, asserts the possibility for any and every negation of value itself to be construed or function as a positive value. This general positivity has recently been identified by Barbara Herrnstein Smith as the axiomatic principle of 'the good' (here with a structural rather than a moral valence):

> As the recurrent tautologies, circularities and infinite regresses that mark the discourses of value suggest, the concept of 'good' operates axiomatically within them: its radical positivity cannot be dispensed with nor can it be defined, explained, or analyzed without recursion to another concept of radical positivity, whether by the name of 'good' or one of its virtual equivalents, such as 'benefit,' 'profit,' 'gain,' 'pay-off,' 'reward,' 'positive reinforcement,' or, of course, 'value' itself used as a (valenced) positive

term. Indeed, it appears that 'good' operates within the discourse of value
as does money in a cash economy: *good* is the universal value-form of value
and its standard 'measure'; it is that 'in terms of which' all forms of value
must be 'expressed' for their commensurability to be calculated; and *good* is
that *for* which and *into* which any other name or form of value can – 'on
demand' we might say – be (ex)changed. (*CV*, 146)

All claims to escape the government of the general positivity of 'the
good' must therefore fail insofar as they claim or imply any kind of
value: '*anything* that is indicated, predicated, or otherwise constituted
either as a positivity within some economy or as the object of a need,
desire, or interest (individual or collective) is measured, in the very
moment that it is put forward as such, as so much "good"; and this
anything includes expenditure, consumption, sacrifice, self-annihilation,
death, universal destruction, and even "absolute loss"' (*CV*, 147). This
diagnosis has the effect of deflating some of the more glamorous claims
made in different forms of aesthetic and cultural theory and practice
throughout this century, and seems to require us to read the various
negations of value by writers and artists as various as Nietzsche,
Duchamp, Bataille and Beckett as in fact refusals of the limitations of
particular value systems alone, and therefore arguments for the widening
rather than the abolition of economies of value.

Powerful though Smith's argument is, however, it runs the risk of
homogenizing the field of value; like the money-form to which she
compares it, the principle of general positivity tends to flatten into mere
operational equivalence the terms of any kind of competition, conflict or
incommensurability. In particular, by immediately cashing every posited
negative in for its positive equivalent, she may move too rapidly away
from the complex processes of resistance and transaction between negative value and positive value, in the interval between negotiation and the
positive return of value. This chapter considers three different attempts
to transact negative value; Freud's discovery of the death instinct in
Beyond the Pleasure Principle (and elsewhere), Bataille's economics of
expenditure and Beckett's negative aesthetics, especially in *Worstward Ho*.
In each case, the analysis will attempt to resist telescoping the process
whereby negativity is recuperated as positive value, and will try to
suggest some (inescapably positive) implications of this act of delay. The
final aim of the discussion is to examine the relationship between such
attempts to refuse or elude the law of positive value and the constitution
of forms of cultural value. That this aim will be reached by what Freud
in *Beyond the Pleasure Principle* calls 'ever more complicated *détours*' (*BPP*,

39) may itself suggest some of the (necessarily) problematic value of retarding positive exchange.

Beyond the Pleasure Principle

Throughout his work Freud insists time and again on the importance and usefulness of the metaphor of economy for understanding the workings of the human psyche. Usually, this term suggests all the processes whereby fixed (and, as Freud believed, ultimately *measurable*) quantities of psychic energy were concentrated, displaced, circulated, invested, expended and brought into equivalence within any psychic dynamism. Many problems arise from this hydraulics of the self, not least the problem of knowing precisely what this 'psychic energy' might consist of and where it might come from. However, the particular problem that I want to focus on here is of a more abstract but no less consequent kind. Up until the early 1920s, Freud was able to maintain his belief that this economy was governed by a single principle – the pleasure principle. In general, we may say that Freud identifies pleasure with the discharge or avoidance of unpleasurable excitation, and unpleasure with the increase of such excitation. As J. Laplanche and J.-B. Pontalis point out, there is a great uncertainty in Freud's account as to whether the aim of the psychic apparatus is to keep the level of excitation at a constant level, or to reduce it to zero.[3]

We may note straight away an oddity in Freud's account of quantity and value here, in its suggestion that pleasure is derived, or positively procured (Freud will often speak explicitly of the 'yield' of pleasure), from a form of diminution; the lessening of the total amount of tension seems to create a surplus value of pleasure (though the surplus is not identical with what has been discharged, but a reaction from it). This might look at first sight like an instance of Smith's principle of general positivity; but here the co-presence of a quantitative economy and a qualitative one is puzzling. For what does the 'yield' of pleasure from the reduction of tension consist of? Or, to put it differently, by what process of exchange does the lessening of psychic energy produce a qualitative surplus of pleasure? Furthermore, how does this surplus of pleasure relate to the psychic economy of conservation and expenditure? Does it not work against the conservation or lowering of levels of tension by its continual, unwelcome increase? This is to have identified usefully an ambiguity in Freud's use of the term 'economy'. Sometimes he uses the word to denote the movement of finite quantities of energy; at other times he uses it to denote a system which is productive of value in the form of pleasure.

So it is clear that the pleasure principle will prove hard to understand precisely in economic terms. Indeed, by the time of *Beyond the Pleasure Principle*, Freud had already perceived the many difficulties attaching to the theory of the economy of pleasure, noting that pleasure and unpleasure are not to be consistently identified with high or low levels of excitation, and surmising that pleasure may actually be crucially determined by the rate of increase or decrease of excitation over time (*BPP*, 8).

But even worse problems are thrown up by the more substantial claim that Freud has to make in *Beyond the Pleasure Principle*, which is, of course, that the pleasure principle is neither dominant nor even primary in governing the behaviour of individual organisms. Freud's argument is that the compulsion to repeat reveals *'an urge inherent in organic life to restore an earlier state of things'*(*BPP*, 36). Repetition acts in the service of this urge by resisting and, as it were, giving as little ground as possible to the contrary urges 'which push forward towards progress and the production of new forms' (*BPP*, 37). Throughout the essay, therefore, repetition is identified with the process whereby energies and excitations are 'bound' – organized, focused, given coherence. This instinct to bind energies is distinct from and prior to the pleasure principle:

> A failure to effect this binding would provoke a disturbance analogous to a traumatic neurosis; and only after the binding has been accomplished would it be possible for the dominance of the pleasure principle (and of its modification, the reality principle) to proceed unhindered. Till then the old task of the mental apparatus, the task of mastering or binding excitations, would have precedence – not, indeed, in *opposition* to the pleasure principle, but independently of it and to some extent in disregard of it. (*BPP*, 39)

Freud sees the famous fort:da game as being orientated towards the production of pleasure, but attempts to distinguish this kind of positive gain from the primary uses of a principle independent of the principle of pleasurable gain. Freud's difficulty throughout the essay is in bringing forward convincing examples of repetition compulsion which do not have the possibility of some sort of gain, if only the gain of temporary mastery over a situation otherwise experienced as unrelieved trauma or loss. The pleasure principle may then be identified as the general positivity in the value system of the human psyche. In his attempts to read back through the pleasure principle, Freud is forced, in the fifth section of *Beyond the Pleasure Principle*, to leave behind the particular problems of battle trauma and the repetition-compulsion of patients under analysis, and to speculate about the most primary dynamics of human biological life. 'The elementary living entity', Freud writes, 'would from its very beginning have had no wish to change; if conditions remained the same, it would do no more than constantly repeat the same course of life' (*BPP*, 38). However, this contented, minimal existence is broken in upon by the forces of life, inducing in the organism painful tensions, potentialities and complexities. At this point, there is born the will to die, to cancel out the painful tensions of life by returning to the inorganic state. Gradually, however, the tensions and complexities grow too great and too far-reaching to be simply cancelled out. Now they must be (grudgingly, as it were) lived through, or, in the economic metaphor of payment of debt so felicitously adopted by the English translation, 'lived off' (*BPP*, 55).[4]

Freud here produces an ingenious way of expressing the primacy of death instincts over life instincts. Death employs, deploys life, invests in it, putting it to work in its own interests. Unable simply to countermand life, death compromises by orientating the whole of life towards itself. Oddly, Freud can now suggest that self-preservation (which may be identified in some way with the pleasure principle) is itself an expression of the desire for extinction. Self-preservation, self-assertion and mastery are all

> component instincts whose function it is to assure that the organism shall follow its own path to death, and to ward off any possible ways of returning to inorganic existence other than those which are immanent in the organism itself. We have no longer to reckon with the organism's puzzling determination (so hard to fit into any context) to maintain its own existence in the face of every obstacle. What we are left with is the fact that the organism wishes to die only in its own fashion. (*BPP*, 39)

Here, the duality which Freud repeatedly asserts and maintains between life and death is coolly retracted, as life becomes simply a ruse or stratagem, a masochistic diversion on the way to death, a means of ensuring the fact of oblivion. In avoiding the short-cut to death via accident, it is as though the organism had recognized that oblivion will be *all the more complete* a nothingness, or, to adopt an appropriate Beckettian word, a 'lessness', for the fact that life has intervened. The longer the organism can hold out against negativity, the sweeter it will be in the end. Freud here produces a kind of inverted dialectic, which substitutes for the accumulative syntax of Hegel's thesis–antithesis–synthesis triad, in which the positivity of spirit or self-consciousness always gathers into itself the antithetical negations of materiality which it encounters, a rhythm which has life as its antithetical phase, and death in the position of the positive, in the sense of purely material existence which precedes and transcends the conflict of life and death – in the deeper death, the greater nothingness of an oblivion which, once returned to, can never again be broken.

So, where earlier in the essay the death instinct, or the instinct towards conservation or lessening of energy, supplemented the pleasure principle (imperfectly identified, as we have seen, with the life instinct), here the situation is reversed; the formula life (death) = life gives way to death (life) = death. However, it is never entirely clear to Freud or his reader what the final goal of this economy, or of these two economies, might be. The view that the instinct towards conservation and lowering of energy always produces a contradictory gain of pleasure would seem to privilege life, development and 'general positivity'. This reversion to the positive is effected principally through repetition, the very device of death; bombarded with modifications which cannot be avoided, the slug-gish organism responds by storing them up 'for further repetition' (*BPP*, 38). But if repetition is a way of saying no to life, by its nature it also always produces surplus, which tends towards the preservation and prolongation of life rather than its destruction. But this gain of surplus value can then always itself be interpreted as a detour on the organism's self-willed road to death.

It is as though both Smith's principle of general positivity and Freud's preferred primacy of the instinct towards annihilation were shown them-selves to be precipitations from an economic system of exchanges and instrumentalizations, rather than governing principles or end-points. This hyperpenetration of economy then threatens the very dualism by means of which Freud is able to posit the conflict and (economic) relationship of the life instinct and the death instinct. This becomes apparent, for example, in Freud's account of the earliest formation of the death instinct:

> The attributes of life were at some time evoked in inanimate matter by the action of a force of whose nature we can form no conception. It may perhaps have been a process similar in type to that which later caused the development of consciousness in a particular stratum of living matter. The tension which then arose in what had hitherto been an inanimate substance endeavoured to cancel itself out. In this way the first instinct came into being: the instinct to return to the inanimate state. (*BPP*, 38)

Something remarkable happens between the second and third sentences of this quotation. Having said first of all that the formation of life was only *like* the formation of consciousness, Freud then characterizes the tension which arises in the organism in terms which suggest, if not exactly consciousness, then the possibility of purposive effort: 'The tension ... endeavoured to cancel itself out' ('Die ... Spannung ... trachtete darnach sich abzugleichen' (*JL*, 228)). But how can a tension 'endeavour' to do anything, unless it is already part of life? How can death will itself, without already having become a living substance capable of willing? And if so, why should it then will death? Seen in this way, every instance of the will to death, especially in the quaintly individualistic, even egoistic form given to it by Freud when he says that 'the organism wishes to die only in its own fashion' ('der Organismus nur auf seine Weise sterben will') (*BPP*, 39; *JL*, 229), must always belong to, and be the expression of, a kind of life. How, otherwise, can death will itself, can nothing 'noth'?[5]

It is clear that, in their promotion of the opposing principles of general positivity on the one hand and the all-assimilating drive towards death on the other, Smith and Freud are in fact both arresting the play of a complex economy in which positive and negative value (if the word 'value' may continue to be employed for that which puts the positivity of value in question) are exactly at stake. Indeed, the specification of one or other points in this ceaseless transaction as positive loss or gain is always an abstractive arrest of a process which seems to disallow such finality – a process, indeed, which is always renewed precisely by such attempts at arrest. Derrida has pointed, in the course of a discussion of *Beyond the Pleasure Principle* (to which, it will be plain, my own present discussion owes a very great deal), to the structure of detour which governs the relationship of the pleasure principle to the reality principle and the death instinct. He argues that if the reality principle is a vehicle of the pleasure principle, and the pleasure principle itself an indirect vehicle of the death instinct, then this suggests not only that death may be the final destination, reward or (non-)profit, but also that death may be identified with the principle of detour itself, and so may indeed resist the finality of a presence or economic product. 'No *Weg* without *Umweg*', writes Derrida: 'the detour does not overtake the road, but constitutes it, breaks open the path' (TSF, 284). The question of whether life is using death, or death is using life is not susceptible of being phrased in terms of positive benefits or outcomes, since the structure of detour never regains its path long enough for these positive gains – either the positive end of life, or the positive negativity of death – to materialize. Derrida suggests that 'death' might therefore be the name not of the necessary end in the sense of the final result or yielded value of the process of life – though this is an 'actuality' which 'is never present or given' – but of the 'speculative transaction' which ceaselessly barters life for death and death for life:

> From whichever *end* one takes this structure with one–two–three terms, it is death. *At the end*, and this death is not opposable, does not differ, in the sense of opposition, from the two principles and their *différance*. It is inscribed, although non-inscribable, in the process of this structure ... If death is not opposable, it is, already, *life death*. (TSF, 285)

As Derrida has elaborately shown, this produces complex writing effects in *Beyond the Pleasure Principle*. Freud's language and outlook always predisposed him to a blunt positivity – to the view that the objects of his analysis and speculation had a substantial and specifiable existence, as forces, quantities or locations. Throughout his work, Freud struggles with the recalcitrant forms of negativity which resist the positivizing effects of metaphor. This struggle takes a particularly intense form in *Beyond the Pleasure Principle*, since this is the text in which the positive valencies of Freudian science truly encounter their other. Two particular vehicles of this struggle are the metaphorical pairings of binding/dissolution and progress/regression. These form a clear homology in Freud's argument, with binding being equivalent to organic progress, and dissolution being equivalent to regression to the inorganic state. The two are brought together at the point in Freud's argument where he specifies the 'contrary directions' ('entgegengesetzter Richtung') taken by constructive or assimilatory processes on the one hand and destructive or dissimilatory processes on the other (*BPP*, 49; *JL*, 241) There is a close and often disturbing parallelism between the ways in which these metaphors embody the struggle of the life instinct against the death instinct, and the ways in which they serve implicitly or explicitly to embody Freud's own endeavours in this text.

The first pairing becomes most evident in chapter 6 of the essay, in which Freud discusses the power of Eros, whose aim, he has told us, is always 'to combine organic substances into ever larger unities' ('das Organische zu immer größeren Einheiten zusammenfassen') (*BPP*, 42–3; *JL*, 233). This principle of combination, which gradually comes to replace the pleasure principle as the representative form of the life instinct, seems also to govern Freud's own attempts to grasp the complex unity of Eros and the death instinct, as well as his predilection – not, of course, confined to this essay – for intellectual unification of the literary and the scientific, the philosophical and the psychoanalytic, the empirical and the speculative. At one point, Freud justifies his synthetic procedure in *Beyond the Pleasure Principle* by saying that 'it is impossible to *pursue* an idea of this kind except by *repeatedly combining* factual material with what is purely speculative and thus *diverging* widely from empirical observation' ('Die Durchführung dieser Idee ist jedenfalls nicht anders möglich, als daß man mehrmals nacheinander Tatsächliches mit bloß Erdachtem kombiniert und sich dabei weit von der Beobachtung entfernt') (*BPP*, 59 (my emphasis); *JL*, 252), a sentence which articulates into a perplexingly close sequence the ideas of progress and combination on the one hand, and repetition and divergence on the other. The moment when, searching for a scientific account of the origin of the sexual instinct for conjugation, Freud calls upon Aristophanes' myth of the sundering of the sexes by Zeus is, therefore, clearly a crucial one. Building on 'the hint given us by the poet–philosopher', Freud suggests that 'living substance at the time of its coming to life was torn apart into small particles, which have ever since endeavoured to reunite through the sexual instincts' (*BPP*, 58). (This is, of course, in partial contradiction to the claim made earlier in the essay that the coming of life represented the unwelcome intrusion of complexity and differentiation into the undifferentiated simplicity of inorganic life (*BPP*, 38–9).) The long sentence which follows piles speculation upon speculation until it arrives at the idea that 'these splintered fragments of living substance ... attained a multicellular condition and finally transferred the instinct for reuniting, in the most highly concentrated form, to the germ-cells' – at which point Freud suddenly restrains himself with a metaphor that has an uncomfortably close relationship to the metaphors of binding and assimilation – 'But here, I think, the moment has come for *breaking off*' ('Ich glaube, es ist hier die Stelle, abzubrechen') (*BPP*, 58 (my emphasis); *JL*, 251). By breaking off thus abruptly from his account of the process of assimilation, Freud asserts the contrary principle of destruction and dissolution in the service of the death instinct – even though, looked at from another point of view, by breaking off from what is already an extravagant speculative detour in his text, Freud may be bending his essay back to its principal theme, and therefore binding up the gash in his argument which is here beginning to gape.

Not the least of the complexities attending this metaphorology of assimilation and dissolution is its asymmetrical relationship to the concept of binding, which plays such an important part throughout Freud's work. For the value of binding is radically uncertain in *Beyond the Pleasure Principle*. Freud's earlier work had suggested a direct and proportional relationship between, on one side, the production of pleasure and the binding of psychic energies (their organization, connection and unification) and, on the other, the production of unpleasure and the presence of amounts of free or unbound energy. But, as we have seen, Freud suggests in *Beyond the Pleasure Principle* that the task of binding free energies, in the particular instance of battle trauma, where the organism is assailed from outside by stimuli of unassimilable intensity, might actually be prior to the pleasure principle, and might act 'not, indeed, in *opposition* to the pleasure principle, but independently of it and to some extent in disregard of it' (*BPP*, 39). In fact, however, the compulsion to repeat, with which Freud links this 'task of mastering or binding excitations', does precisely act in opposition to the pleasure principle, in that it belongs to the instinct to return to the inanimate condition. So here again, binding seems to suggest at different times, and at the same time, the gathering of energies into the organism, to the ends of Eros, or life, and the mastery of such energies by repetition in the service of death. In an equivalent way, the unbinding of energy suggests both the discharge of unpleasurable tension characteristic of the organism's attempts to cancel out life in itself, and, in certain cases, the means by which forward movement into life, change and development takes place. At one moment in his account, Freud strikingly attributes progression and aspiration in life to the difference between the unfixed demand for the pleasure of satisfaction (in fact, the satisfaction of death) and the limited amounts of pleasure that can be achieved by the binding effects of repression, sublimation and so on. It is this difference 'that provides the driving factor which will permit of no halting at any position attained, but, in the poet's words, "*ungebändigt immer vorwärts dringt*"' (*BPP*, 42). Strachey's translation of Mephistopheles' words in *Faust* ('Presses ever forward unsubdued') does not bring out the force of the idea of 'unbinding' in the word 'ungebändigt'. (In fact, this is a word that Freud uses, as early as the 'Project for a Scientific Psychology', to mean something like unbound, for example when he writes about the unpleasurable effect of memories relating to painful experiences when they are 'ungebändigt'.[6])

The metaphorical pairing of combination and dissolution therefore embodies a risky set of reflections on the value of Freud's own writing in *Beyond the Pleasure Principle*; these are precisely valuable to the extent that they offer a new, more coherent synthesis of ideas about life and death, pleasure and unpleasure, even though the impetus of the essay is to suggest the dominance of the value of unbinding, dissolution and 'breaking off'.

Even more remarkable in this respect are the allotropes offered of the metaphor of progress in *Beyond the Pleasure Principle*. All the way through, the essay represents itself as a stubborn journey, or steady progress towards some as yet unspecifiable goal in the knowledge of the purpose or aim of existence. But this metaphor is compromised precisely to the extent that the goal of existence may not lie ahead in the future but behind in the past, in the state of undifferentiated being to which the organism strives to return. In this sense, the life of the organism can hardly be seen as an orderly progression:

> It is as though the life of the organism moved with a vacillating rhythm. One group of instincts rushes forward so as to reach the final aim of life as swiftly as possible; but when a particular stage in the advance has been reached, the other group jerks back to a certain point to make a fresh start and so prolong the journey. (*BPP*, 40–1)

Here, forward and backward not only alternate, they actually invert. The impulse to rush forward is the death instinct, since to move forward more quickly is to return more quickly to the initial state of non-being, while the conservative instinct to tarry on the journey is in the service of the life instinct. But the inversion can never be complete, and it can never be guaranteed that the desire for forward movement is not in fact the desire for life rather than death, and the desire to hang back not in fact also the expression of the sluggish will not to be.

Freud's language throughout urges conscious intellectual progress ('let us make a bold attempt at another step forward', 'versuche wir kühn, einen Schritt weiter zu gehen' (*BPP*, 50; *JL*, 241)), while also suggesting an uncertainty of goal ('what follows is … an attempt to follow out an idea consistently, out of curiosity to see where it will lead', 'was nun folgt, ist … ein Versuch zur konsequenten Ausbeutung einer Idee, aus Neugierde, wohin dies führen wird' (*BPP*, 24; *JL*, 211); 'it is surely possible to throw oneself into a line of thought and to follow it wherever it leads', 'man kann sich doch in einem Gedankengang hingeben, ihn verfolgen, soweit er führf' (*BPP*, 59; *JL*, 252)). But the direction and outcome of this itinerary are so unpredictable as to produce near-oxymoron at some points, as here: 'for the moment it is tempting to pursue to its logical conclusion the hypothesis that all instincts tend towards the restoration of an earlier state of things' (*BPP*, 37). German syntax here collapses together even more strikingly biological origin and argumentative destination: 'Aber vorher mag es uns verlocken, die Annahme, daß alle Triebe Früheres wiederherstellen wollen, in ihre letzten Konsequenzen zu verfolgen' (*JL*, 227).

Elsewhere, Freud's text betrays a much more fundamental dissatisfaction with the very notion of cultural progress. Freud is forced to confess in *Beyond the Pleasure Principle* to his abandonment of the 'benevolent illusion' that there is 'an instinct towards perfection at work in human beings, which has brought them to their present high level of intellectual achievement and ethical sublimation and which may be expected to watch over their development into supermen' (*BPP*, 42). Such an instinct cannot be primary and autonomous, says Freud, but must be the product of the life/death psychic economy. The desire for progress is in fact nothing other than the baulked and diverted instinct towards death; deprived of the possibility of going backwards to death by a repression stemming from the life instincts, death takes a grudging detour through life, since 'there is no alternative but to advance in the direction in which growth is still free – though with no prospect of bringing the process to a conclusion or of being able to reach the goal' ('bleibt nichts anderes übrig, als in der anderen, noch freien Entwicklungsrichtung fortzuschreiten, allerdings ohne Aussicht, den Prozeß abschließen, und das Ziel erreichen zu können') (*BPP*, 42; *JL*, 233).

In all these negotiations of the metaphor of direction, Freud appears to be unconsciously designating the rhythm of his own enquiry, which displays a similarly uncertain momentum in its dartings forward and lingering divagations, its anticipations and puttings-off, its purposeful drives for home and inconclusive speculations. Its dynamic principle is characterized by Derrida, in the course of a subtle reading of directional metaphors in *Beyond the Pleasure Principle*, as a 'démarche', a (non-) proceeding, or a 'pas de thèse', the organized dance of a non-thesis 'which advances without advancing, without advancing itself, without ever advancing anything which it does not immediately take back, for the time of a detour, without ever positing anything which remains in its position' (*TSF*, 293). As Derrida suggests, the dominating (non-)principle of argumentative movement in *Beyond the Pleasure Principle*, in its alternation of advance and retraction is in fact provided by the fort:da game which, despite its enormous importance in the history of psychoanalysis, plays such an oddly peripheral role in Freud's text (*TSF*, 294–337).

As though to acknowledge the injury inflicted upon the metaphor of progress through his essay, Freud ends *Beyond the Pleasure Principle* with a poetic quotation from Rückert's 'Die beiden Gulden' which answers Mephistopheles' evocation of the unrestrained drive for progress quoted earlier: 'Was man nicht erfliegen kann, muss man erhinken ... / Die Schrift sagt, es ist keine Sünde zu hinken' ('What we cannot reach by flying we must reach by limping ... The Book says that it is no sin to limp' (*BPP*, 64)). A limp is wounded walking, the product of a compromise between advance and recoil, or motion and stasis. The evocation of another famous walking impediment could hardly be more appropriate, for the brave movement of the swollen-footed Oedipus into the future also takes the form of a movement backwards into knowledge of the disastrous past. In apparent contrast to the determination of his earlier work to strike out fearlessly into the future of psychoanalytic enquiry, Freud acknowledges that 'we must be ready, too, to abandon a path that we have followed for a time, if it seems to be leading to no good end' ('man muß bereit bleiben, einen Weg wieder zu verlassen, den man eine Weile verfolgt hat, wenn er nichts Gutem zu Führen scheint') (*BPP*, 64; *JL*, 257). This is to say, if there appears to be no positive value in a particular form of progression, we should not pursue it. But what if the 'end' sought by the organism, and consequently by psychoanalysis itself, were precisely not the good of the individual, or if the 'good' it desired were precisely the end of questions of good or bad? What would it then mean to pursue it as a 'good', or as an 'end'? What, moreover, could it possibly mean to abandon such a pursuit? Would this abandonment be a turning away from the possibility of achieving good, in the sense of positive value for life? Or would it be a productive refusal of that instinct for dissolution which seems to deploy and invest every pursuit of value, and can bring it only to a bad end – and therefore a profitable abandonment?[7]

Bataille and Absolute Expenditure

The investigation of the principle of negative value in the economies of human life and history has been fostered by none so passionately and single-mindedly as Georges Bataille. His subversive refusal of the restrictiveness of economic rationalism and, indeed, of rationalism itself is a source for many of the most distinctive contributions of French thinking of recent years, among them especially the work of Baudrillard, Kristeva, Foucault and Derrida. In noting the legacy of Bataille, we are noting a paradox: for a body of work which promotes loss, waste, excess, refuse and excrement, along with everything that stands against the principles of bourgeois utility, to have become such a rich resource for knowledge is a strange kind of failure. How is it possible to maintain a serious commitment to the values of pure and non-productive expenditure, the values of non-value, when Bataille's own work increases so steadily in positive value?

Bataille's fixation upon the economics of waste dates from his early involvement with Surrealism. His interest in the topic of expenditure derives from the work of Marcel Mauss, who pointed in his *Essai sur le don* (1925) to various practices among primitive peoples which seemed to suggest an economy based on principles radically different from the calculated self-interest characteristic of Western economic systems. The evidence of the *potlatch* in particular, a ceremony practised by the native tribes of the north-west coast of North America, in which prodigious amounts of valuable possessions are ritually and publically destroyed, suggested to Mauss and to many others the existence of a need for expenditure which is in stark contrast to the economic considerations of gain and conservation characteristic of more advanced cultures.[8]

Although Bataille often refers to and depends upon Mauss, he has a much more radical view of the general economic principles revealed by such practices. Concerned to demonstrate the principles of non-materialist reciprocity at work in primitive societies, Mauss does not deny the existence of any form of self-interest or economic exchange in the structures of gift-giving that he analyses. For Bataille, on the other hand, the 'gift' and its intensified sacrificial forms such as the *potlatch* are evidence of a fundamental drive towards non-productive expenditure of energy and goods in human life, a drive which is manifested in forms as various as the love of luxurious but useless items like jewels and precious metals, the practice of ritual sacrifice, sport and competitive spectacles and artistic production of all kinds. In his later work, Bataille explored in greater detail the various challenges to the principles of rational self-interest and an economy based on utility as he saw them enacted through the free expenditure of energy in sexuality, literature, philosophy, mystical and ascetic experience and, finally, political economy itself.[9] Where in his earlier work Bataille had tended to accept the domination of the principles of productive utility in everyday modern life, seeing instances of waste or expenditure as glorious but intermittent episodes within utility, in his most comprehensive account of 'general economics', *La Part maudite* (1949), expenditure is projected as fundamental to the astrobiological economics of the universe. At the centre of our solar system is the sun, which we are accustomed to think of as the source of all life and increase, but which Bataille characterizes as the principle of wasteful luxuriance:

> The origin and essence of our wealth are given in the radiation of the sun, which dispenses energy – wealth – without any return. The sun gives without ever receiving. Men were conscious of this long before astrophysics measured that ceaseless prodigality; they saw it ripen the harvests and they associated its splendor with the act of someone who gives without receiving.[10]

If animal and vegetable life on earth absorb and concentrate the energy of the sun, they do so only in the longer-term interests of further expenditure. Acquisition and conservation are therefore to be seen as auxiliary effects in the service of the expenditure of surplus energy, just as, for Freud, the death instinct uses for its own ends the instinct to conserve life. Humanity is simply the organism in which the transformation of possession into expenditure takes place most energetically:

> Man is a result of surplus energy; the extreme abundance of his noble activities must be defined principally as the brilliant liberation of an excess. Free energy flourishes in him and endlessly exhibits its useless splendour. But this surplus of energy could not have been liberated unless it had first been possessed. Condensation is necessary for expenditure.[11]

The value of culture, in both the widest and the narrowest senses, consists in its capacity to express the 'sovereignty' which Bataille associates with expenditure, as opposed to the 'servility' of production or utility. 'The term poetry,' he writes in 'The Notion of Expenditure', 'applied to the least degraded and least intellectualized forms of the expression of a state of loss, can be considered synonymous with expenditure; it in fact signifies, in the most precise way, creation by means of loss' (*VE*, 120). The essays in *Literature and Evil* examine this principle of sovereignty as it is to be found in the work of Emily Brontë, Blake, Sade and others. The essay on Michelet in that volume explains the superiority of intensity (which belongs to the instant and is not directed towards any ascertainable end or profit in the future) over mere pleasure (which is subordinated to the modest and prudential ends of survival and co-operation in time):

> Intensity can be defined as a value (it is the only positive value), survival as Good (it is the general goal of virtue). The notion of intensity cannot be reduced to that of pleasure because, as we have seen, the quest for intensity leads us into the realm of unease and then to the limits of consciousness ... The value is situated *beyond Good and Evil*, but in two opposed ways, one connected with the principle of Good, the other with that of Evil. The desire for Good limits the instinct which induces us to seek a value, whereas liberty towards Evil gives access to the excessive forms of value. Yet we cannot conclude from this that the authentic value is on the side of Evil. The very principle of Evil wants us to go 'as far as possible'. (*LE*, 74)

Bataille is caught here in some very uncomfortable logical problems. First of all, there is the question of the place occupied by poetry or literature. If it represents the value of absolute excess, the sovereign transgression of an economy based on profit and calculation, then how is it to be related to the 'general economy' elaborated in *La Part maudite*, except as a minor expression of a larger principle? This would be to suggest that literature provides a homeopathic dose of the drive towards immeasurable excess which governs the entire universe. But this is difficult to understand; for what sort of economy could it be that allowed one to distribute degrees of incommensurability and quantities of absolute excess in this fashion? Here we are presented with a general economy which is based on the inherently non-or anti-economic principle of waste, even though that principle cannot be conceived except in economic terms. Derrida has pointed to the parallel here between Bataille's general economics and Freud's economy of death, both of which seem to require us to conceive in economic terms a principle that radically undermines any and every economy:

> How are we to think *simultaneously*, on the one hand, *différance* as the economic detour which, in the element of the same, always aims at coming back to the pleasure or the presence that have been deferred by (conscious or unconscious) calculation, and, on the other hand, *différance* as the relation to an impossible presence, as expenditure without reserve, as the irreparable loss of presence, the irreversible usage of energy, that is, as the death instinct, and as the entirely other relationship that apparently interrupts every economy? It is evident – and this is the evident itself – that the economical and the noneconomical, the same and the entirely other, etc., cannot be thought *together*.[12]

Barbara Herrnstein Smith attends to a different problem in mounting her attack on Bataille's economics of loss, in a reading which widens to include a condemnation of any attempt to project categories of experience or value which lie beyond the reach of the generalized positivity of value. As we have seen, she argues that 'no valorization of anything, even of "loss" itself, can escape the idea of some sort of positivity – that is, gain, benefit or advantage – in relation to some economy' (*CV*, 137). Although she approves to some considerable degree of Bataille's attack on the restricted economy of utilitarianism or pure market capitalism, she nevertheless convicts him of crucial inattention to the ways in which loss always functions, even and especially within his own account, as a value. To the precise degree that the wasting of men and animals in sacrifice, the squandering of money and energy in the purchase of luxuries and competitive games, and the provocation of laughter or horror in literature and the theatre are seen as in any way desirable or preferable to pure monetary gain, then 'there is a gain in the economy of the individual or the community ... a gain or exchange that makes the particular expenditure and riches "rational" in an economic/utilitarian sense: that is, they have some more or less proportional relation to a desired/able outcome' (*CV*, 136). Smith draws upon the work of Bourdieu and others to discredit Bataille's simple faith in the force of 'absolute loss' in the *potlatch* and similar ceremonies. In all such cases, she argues, loss is strategic and temporary, a depletion of material goods in the interests of a gain in social standing. The gift, no matter how extravagantly excessive, always calls for a counter-gift from its recipient; the conspicuous waste of goods always confers power and authority on their destroyer (*CV*, 138–9). Allan Stoekl makes a similar point about Bataille's radical negativity in asking, 'in the very act of writing about various forms of trash, in valuing them by devoting articles to them, does not Bataille simply erect them as new privileged values?' (*VE*, p. xvii).

What these criticisms lack is an awareness of Bataille's own embarrassed awareness of the recursion of value in non-value. Devastating as her account is, Smith concentrates almost entirely on 'The Notion of Expenditure', an essay dating from the early 1930s, which, while it provides a very useful concentration of many of Bataille's principal arguments in a short space of time, does so because it is so much more blunt an account than emerges elsewhere in his work. In *La Part maudite* Bataille in fact considers the arguments about the positive value attached to expenditure in *potlatch* and sacrifice and acknowledges their unavoidable positivity of outcome: 'the squandering of energy is always the opposite of a thing, but it enters into consideration only once it has entered into the order of things, once it has been changed into a *thing*.'[13] A similar anxiety attends his account of the force of literature. Writing of Blake's consecration of the principle of excess, Bataille warns us against giving the power or value of poetry the force of a positive principle. The 'sovereignty' of poetry becomes apparent not in the objectified forms of excess which it gathers together, but in its yearning towards an absolute excess. For poetry to become a domain of value is to betray itself: 'Poetry is right to assert the extent of its empire, but we cannot contemplate this extent without immediately knowing that it is completely elusive: it is not the empire so much as the impotence of poetry' (*LE*, 85). Bataille ends *Literature and Evil* with a surprising condemnation of Genet – surprising because Genet's work would seem to embody perfectly the negative values of transgression and heterogeneity that are so important to Bataille. But it is precisely the fact that Genet's work seems to commit itself to these values as substances that Bataille wishes to condemn. The riotous scandal of Genet's work is seen as a sort of ascesis, an abjection of the self and all its attachments which, as Bataille writes in *Inner Experience*, is always a detour on the way to the procurement of beatific being (*IE*, 21–3) – and Bataille's essay in *Literature and Evil* is written against Sartre's *Saint Genet*, the title of which epitomizes the canonization of the apostate. Although Bataille says he admires *Saint Genet*'s 'passion for nullity', he is also plainly suspicious of its programmatic content, the fact that 'it reaches a form of perfection owing to the continuous expression of abjection' (*LE*, 174). Genet's work fails in its bid for sovereignty, simply because Genet wants to experience and possess pure waste, pure excess, pure transgression, as a mode of being. Genet wants to seize the sovereignty of *dépense* (the term that runs together so usefully for Bataille the dilapidation of the economic and, as *dé-pense*, of thought itself) 'like a positive benefit' (*LE*, 194), but it is precisely this that makes Genet's a 'sovereignty *confiscated*, the dead sovereignty of him whose solitary desire for sovereignty is the betrayal of sovereignty' (*LE*, 204). But this is not a tactical failure on Genet's part, but a structural necessity, since positivity is inescapable – 'a certain utility always alienates the proposed sovereignty' (*LE*, 194). Bataille's recognition of this necessity is in the negative mode of melancholy, in contrast to the more positive mode of Smith's argument:

> Sovereignty ... is the object which eludes us all, which nobody has seized and which nobody can seize for this reason: we cannot possess it, like an object, but we are doomed to seek it ... So we cannot talk of Jean Genet's failed sovereignty as if the accomplished form of a real sovereignty existed ... Never can we *be* sovereign. (*LE*, 193–4)

Oddly, it is only when the principles of waste, loss and sovereignty are, in Smith's words, 'predicated, or otherwise constituted ... as a positivity' (*CV*, 147) that they become open to her critique. Bataille acknowledges his own implication in this recoil of negativity into positivity at the beginning of *La Part maudite*, where he meditates upon the peculiarity of his own investment of time and energy into the production of a work designed to show the pre-eminence of the principle of waste:

> As I considered the object of my study, I could not personally resist the effervescence in which I discovered the unavoidable purpose, the value of the cold and calculated operation. My research aimed at the acquisition of a knowledge; it demanded coldness and calculation, but the knowledge acquired was that of an error, an error implied in the coldness that is inherent in all calculation. In other words, my work tended first of all to

increase the sum of human resources, but its findings showed me that this accumulation was only a delay, a shrinking back from the inevitable term, where the accumulated wealth has value only in the instant. Writing this book in which I was saying that energy finally can only be wasted, I myself was using my energy, my time, working; my research answered in a fundamental way the desire to add to the amount of wealth acquired for mankind.[14]

Or, as Bataille puts it, more succinctly, in *Interior Experience*, 'the word silence is still a sound' (*IE*, 13).

It is astonishing that, given this apprehension, Bataille should have persisted so unswervingly in his attempt to specify and substantiate his view of the purely negative. Undoubtedly, his work remains or repeatedly becomes vulnerable to Smith's charge whenever it claims to have found or named the principle of pure loss in any particular embodied form. However, the force of that critique is less plain when the reversal of negative into positive is made the explicit subject of Bataille's enquiry in this way. We can ('profitably') examine another example of his self-conscious exploration of the paradox of negativity in an essay entitled, oddly, 'The Use-Value of D. A. F. de Sade' (*VE*, 91–102). The essay was produced as an 'open letter to my current comrades' in 1929 or 1930, as part of Bataille's protracted and complex disagreement with André Breton and Surrealism. Here, as elsewhere, Bataille's charge against Surrealism is that, contrary to all its affirmations, its interest in the low, the base, the unconscious and the heterogeneous in human life is not revolutionary but assimilative. In the end, Surrealist aesthetics work to sublimate the eruptive values of the body and of sexuality, rather than to unleash them. Bataille's essay on Surrealism and Marxism, 'The "Old Mole" and the Prefix *Sur* in the Words *Surhomme* and *Surrealism*', which was written at around the same time as the essay on Sade, develops a parallel contrast between the height and 'luminous splendour' of the values associated with Surrealism and the baseness of the 'old mole' of Marx's *Communist Manifesto*, grubbing in the bowels of the proletariat (*VE*, 35). This essay represents one of the earliest forms of Bataille's resistance to the transformations of the Hegelian dialectic and his commitment to articulating everything that lay beyond the reach of *Aufhebung* which, as Derrida puts it, 'reappropriates all negativity for itself, as it works the "putting at stake" into an *investment*, as it *amortizes* absolute expenditure, and as it gives meaning to death'.[15]

In 'The Use-Value of D. A. F. de Sade', Bataille claims that the honour and privilege ritually accorded to Sade among Surrealists depends upon the fact of his work having no real purpose, which is to say, having too *immediate* a purpose, in its aptness to yield a conventional profit of literary value:

> It is no doubt almost useless at the present time to set forth rational propositions, since they could only be taken up for the profit of some convenient and – even in an apocalyptic guise – thoroughly literary enterprise: in other words, on the condition that they be useful for ambitions moderated by the impotence of present day man. (*VE*, 93)

Bataille's sense here that what he has to say is, strictly speaking, 'useless' ('inutile')[16] derives of course from his conviction that the only real utility is futility. But the essay goes further than this. The works of Sade suggest the possibility to Bataille of a 'heterology', a science of the other, of everything that is expelled from consciousness in the interests of maintaining unity or homogeneity, whether of the self, of the state, of history, in psychoanalysis, politics, religion, philosophy or even poetry. The last of these may seem to allow access to the heterogeneous, but, says Bataille, 'has almost always been at the mercy of the great historical systems of appropriation', chief among them being 'a total poetic conception of the world, which can end at any one of a number of aesthetic homogeneities' (*VE*, 97). The logic that governs all these unities is the logic of *appropriation*. If things go as they usually seem to in Bataille's work, then we would expect this to leave the way clear for the promotion of the countervailing principle of pure and unproductive excretion. But in fact Bataille's essay has already made such a move suspect, by its interpretation of expulsion and expenditure as not only vulnerable to dialectical reappropriation, but the very *expression* (this, in all senses, therefore) of the appropriative and homogenizing impulse. As purification, purgation and hygienic partition, excretion is the servant of identity, violently reproducing the hiatus between the full self and the nihilated futility of what is expelled from it. Bataille finds evidence for this equivalence of appropriation and expulsion in the Surrealist reception of Sade:

> The behavior of Sade's admirers resembles that of primitive subjects in relation to their king, whom they adore and loathe, and whom they cover with honors and narrowly confine. In the most favorable cases, the author of *Justine* is in fact thus treated as any given *foreign body*; in other words, he is only an object of transports of exaltation to the extent that these transports facilitate his excretion.
>
> The life and works of D. A. F. de Sade would then have no other use value than the common use value of excrement; in other words,

for the most part, one most often only loves the rapid (and violent) pleasure of voiding this matter and no longer seeing it. (*VE*, 92)

Here Bataille does indeed predictably set forth his alternative, 'positive' view of excremental expulsion, an expulsion not in the service of the self, but one which expends and dissipates it. However, the damage has been done, since it is hard in principle to know how to distinguish between the positive value *for assimilation* of expulsion and its positive value *for dissipation*. Bataille must therefore resist absolute negativity in his account of Sade, since this always risks making excretion 'a middle term between two appropriations' (*VE*, 99).

This is why Bataille speaks, so strangely, of the 'use value' of Sade's work for Surrealism and for the revolutionary cultural politics it seeks to further. Where negativity is captured by positivity, the only response is to resist negativity; so, instead of allowing Sade the position of the negated exterior, Bataille paradoxically himself proposes a utilitarian investment of Sadian values, 'not in the domain of gratuitous impertinence, but rather directly in the very market in which, each day, the credit that individuals and even communities can give to their own lives, is, in a way, registered' (*VE*, 94). This can be seen as an attempt to bluff the system into producing negativity, the logic being: if negativity is always captured and reversed by positivity, then let us begin with a positivity of the negative in the hope that this will then flip into 'pure' negativity. But it may also be seen as an attempt to refuse or rewrite the logic which binarizes and hierarchizes the positive and the negative in the first place. An investment of Sade's values of non-utilitarian *dépense* such as Bataille projects here is from the beginning a complex amalgam of the positive and the negative, which puts their relationship 'en cause'. Derrida's account of Bataille's complex philosophical negotiations with Hegel indicates something similar. Unable to escape being Hegelian even (and especially) in pure and simple denial of the structure of the dialectic, since that structure is designed precisely to incorporate all denials in its ever-widening appropriation of knowledge and meaning, Bataille is forced first of all to inhabit Hegelian logic, to feint to follow it, in order to disrupt (rather than to overturn) its general positivity.[17]

It is in this sense that Bataille's work foreshadows Derrida's own deconstructive project. No less than Derrida, Bataille sees (intermittently, to be sure, and unsystematically) the necessity for avoiding the claims of any discourse to enact or embody the sovereignty of expenditure itself. Poetic (and philosophical) discourse is condemned to the positivity of utterance, the substantiality of words and concepts: but if one avoids claiming to have dissolved all the rules, it may be possible to regulate the sliding of language away from the government of meaning:

> But we must speak. 'The inadequation of all speech ... at least, must be said,' in order to maintain sovereignty, which is to say, after a fashion, in order to lose it, in order still to reserve the possibility not of its meaning, but of its nonmeaning; in order to distinguish it, through this impossible 'commentary,' from all negativity. We must find a speech which maintains silence.[18]

We have encountered one version of this apparent inversion of negative and positive already in Freud's discussion of the ways in which death is forced to inhabit and govern the course of life in the search for a return of non-being, and we will see another version in a moment in Beckett's *Worstward Ho*, in which the only route towards the unrecuperable 'worst' is via the positive imperative to find ways of 'failing better'. In all three cases, what results from this infiltration of negativity into positivity is the strategic and compromised refusal of positive or negative values as such, in the initiation of a principled and probably interminable probation of the value of these values.

Worstward Ho

No writer has evidenced the conceptual problems associated with claims for absolute negativity of value and the absolute value of negativity more than Samuel Beckett. Beckett's aesthetics, and the Beckettian aesthetics which criticism has produced from his writings by prolongation and positive elaboration, follow the recursive trajectory that has been the subject of this chapter. Beckett proclaims a poetics of poverty and an art of impotence, incompetence or failure. His early critical writings stress in a remarkable way the determination to resist not only the values of the commodity and the market-place, but the value of value itself. In his *Three Dialogues with Georges Duthuit* (1949), he speaks famously of the emptiness of means and purpose of the contemporary artist, and the shrinking of the artist's expressive and representational capacities in his 'dream of an art unresentful of its insuperable indigence and too proud for the farce of giving and receiving'.[19] If this exemplifies a modernist aesthetic of the integrity of the artwork against the corruption and emptiness of history — and Beckett's joke about the world and the trousers is an even more concentrated synopsis of that aesthetic[20] — it is less often remarked that Beckett also attempts to refuse the recuperation of value in such an aesthetic, in particular the way in which the artwork's refusal of the occasion of reference can itself form a subject or referential occasion. Beckett affirms that 'the numerous attempts to make painting independent of its occasion have only succeeded in enlarging its repertory', but advises an art of 'ultimate penury' which refuses to participate in any kind of evaluative economy:

> Let us, for once, be foolish enough not to turn tail. All have turned wisely tail, before the ultimate penury, back to the mere misery where destitute virtuous mothers may steal stale bread for their starving brats. There is more than a difference of degree between being short, short of the world, short of self, and being without these esteemed commodities. The one is a predicament, the other not.[21]

Beckett's embrace of the non-positive negation is nicely summarized in 'Gnome', a cleverly self-consuming poem of the 1930s:

> Spend the years of learning squandering
> Courage for the years of wandering
> Through a world politely turning
> From the loutishness of learning.[22]

Learning (and, we may perhaps take it, art) is politely despised by the bourgeois world of gain and utility, but the 'loutishness of learning' can offer no positive principle of resistance to this culture. The years of learning can therefore be no preparation, in the sense of a storing up of a capital resource; they are a 'spending', a 'squandering' of courage, such that the negativity of learning consumes even itself.

This is not say, however, that the transformation of negativity into different varieties of positive value does not declare itself abundantly elsewhere in Beckett's writings and interviews and in critical work on him. The minimalist motto 'less is more' is not only a standard way of interpreting Beckett's texts, but also prescribes the rate of exchange whereby criticism has been able to move the dwindling 'lessness' of his work from the red into the black of cultural profit. Jessica Prinz critically performs the process she describes when she concludes a comparison of Beckett's 'art of inexpression' to that of Duchamp by saying that 'the devaluation of art leads to more art, and the rejection of mastery leads to masterpieces'.[23] Interestingly, Bataille himself was one of the first to capitalize upon Beckett's work, in a review of *Molloy* in 1951, the last paragraph of which simultaneously recruits Beckett to a literature of absolute loss and banks on the positive value of that literature:

Literature necessarily gnaws away at existence and the world, reducing to *nothing* (but this *nothing* is horror) these steps by which we go along confidently from one result to another, from one success to another. This does not exhaust the possibilities available in literature. And it is certain that the use of words for other than utilitarian ends leads in the opposite direction into the domain of rapture, defiance and gratuitous audacity.[24]

The economy of assimilation is nowhere better illustrated than in those revealing texts which mark the meeting of the aesthetic and the economic, the jacket blurbs of Beckett's books. Here is what we are told on the back of the British edition of *Worstward Ho*:

> This extraordinary text is not just a presentation of the pain of the human condition clothed in a new language of audacious originality and startling beauty. It is also rich in anecdote, contains unforgettable imagery and a poetry that is as visual and musical as it is literary. As so often before, Mr. Beckett has created magic, transforming the emptiest of voids and insubstantiality of material into a whole unforgettable world that will live with the reader and become part of his experience.[25]

There is a certain economic necessity that this blurb responds to directly; the punter who is being asked to spend £7 or more for a book 47 pages long, printed in type large enough to be read at twenty paces, clearly needs a bit of reassurance that less is, despite all appearances, more. You might not get much for your money, the blurb is saying, but what you do get has 'audacious originality', is 'rich in anecdote' ('have you heard the one about the two shades and the staring skull?'), and apparently even consists of more than just words, since its poetry 'is as visual and musical as it is literary'. The final sentence of the blurb then characteristically effects the transformation it speaks of, substituting expansion, wholeness and permanence for limitation, emptiness and insubstantiality. This kind of blurb is an easy target, of course, and these points would not be worth labouring were it not for the fact that the table of conversion instanced here governs much if not most criticism of Beckett, which has learnt to give every extremity of dilapidation in his work a positive reflex of value.[26]

There is no way to guarantee absolutely against such harvests of value from negativity (and perhaps no reason why one should seek such an absolute guarantee). However, what makes such assimilations seem like underdescriptions of *Worstward Ho* is precisely the awareness within and through the text of this very problem of recuperation. For, in *Worstward*

Ho, Beckett is clearly conscious of the necessity of living through, or, in Freud's terms, 'living off', the reversibility of value.

The text begins with the bleakest and tiniest 'pas de thèse', in Derrida's phrase, setting out the oscillation of assertion and retraction, advance and retreat which will characterize it throughout. Here, every item of narrative is invoked and revoked almost immediately, every attempt to 'say' automatically translated and cancelled as 'be missaid':

> Say a body. Where none. No mind. Where none. That at least. A place. Where none. For the body. To be in. Move in. Out of. Back into. No. No out. No back. Only in. Stay in. On in. Still. (*WH*, 7)

The very rhythm of these stunted, grudging phrases seems to enact the desire to make as little trace as possible on the immaculacy of silence, to leave no unnecessary stone turned in its itinerary to non-being. The text mimics and urges closure, its repetitions corresponding with great exactness to Freud's account of the elementary organisms in which minimal levels of animation are no sooner brought about than shrugged off, 'constantly created afresh and easily dying' (*BPP*, 38). The cancellation of the alternatives for movement 'out of' and 'back into' the narrative space designated and opened up by the text attempts to preclude the accretion and involuntary storage of any surplus, so the sentences mirror each other, a mirroring that is itself mirrored in the closeness of fit between 'on' and 'in' and in the grim little palindrome of 'on' and 'no'. Like Freud's elementary organism again, the text seems to resist the agglutination of elements into larger unities, carefully maintaining the separability of its semantic particles – though we should observe here that the principle of reversibility and auto-cancellation itself always seems to require a minimal but nevertheless crucial degree of binding.

We should note too one small but important detail in the paragraph just quoted. Beckett kindles the first of the many jokes in the text from the slight asymmetry of two cancellations: 'Say a body. Where none. No mind. Where none.' The rhythm of alternation here requires a positive to be countermanded by a negative, a negative that gives the positive statement the status only of a posited hypothesis: 'Say a body. Where none' – 'There is no body but (let us say) there is a body.' But the second coupling confounds (and yet also, because of the fact that it is a reversal, confirms) this rhythm, since what is posited and denied is itself a negation: 'No mind. Where none' – 'There is no mind and/but (let us say) there is no mind.' Here, the very redundancy of the negation creates a tiny surplus, the first smear of what will build into an Augean deposit of negative affirmations.

The next paragraph begins the long debate about failure and success which is to run through *Worstward Ho*. Everything is as it has always been, that is to say, destined to end in failure; but the text vows to itself that this will be a different kind of failure: 'All of old. Nothing else ever. Ever tried. Ever failed. No matter. Try again. Fail again. Fail better' (*WH*, 7). The next paragraph suggests what it might mean to fail better. 'Try again. Fail again. Better again. Or better worse. Fail worse again' (*WH*, 8). It is unclear whether to 'fail better' means to fail more comprehensively, in a way that approximates more closely to total failure, or whether it means to fail less comprehensively, to fail in such a way as to reserve some measure of success. The two alternatives might in one sense coalesce (though only, as it were, momentarily, and not in a way that analysis can hold together), since to fail absolutely, 'for good and all' (*WH*, 8), insofar as it is a desired end, must always constitute some kind of success.

So the worst failure has to be brought about 'with care', with an agonizing vigilance to the dangerous possibilities of gain (here the acoustic as well as the economic sense seems appropriate) in every utterance. An important sequence in the middle of the text demonstrates the urgent desire to effect an absolute deterioration without allowing loss to constitute a positivity:

> First one. First try fail better one. Something there badly not wrong. Not that as it is it is not bad. The no face bad. The no hands bad. The no –. Enough. A pox on bad. Mere bad. Way for worse. Pending worse still. First worse. Mere worse. Pending worse still. Add a –. Add? Never. Bow it down. Be it bowed down. (*WH*, 21)

Here the text is suspicious even of its own positive resolve to avoid positivity as it is implied in the imperative to avoid increase, 'Bow it down', and substitutes the subjunctive 'Be it bowed down'. Here, as elsewhere, the attempt to automatize the workings of the text is a desirable removal of the worrying heterogeneity of authorial agency, but increases the possibilities that, without strict and continuous supervision, the text will spontaneously begin to pile up reserves of meaning. In fact, later on, in a move that resembles Bataille's attempt to exert limited control over the process of slippage of meaning, Beckett acknowledges the inescapability of increase, hoping however to be able to use it in the interests of diminishment:

Back unsay better worse by no stretch more. If more dim less light then better worse more dim. Unsaid then better worse by no stretch more. Better worse may no less than less be more. (*WH*, 37)

Affirmation is better (worse) than negation, because affirmation leaves room for further denial: 'Ask not. No. Ask in vain. Better worse so' (*WH*, 19).

Therefore, rather than unilaterally eschewing the language of gain, the text actively seeks it out, multiplying instances of economic clichés in order to 'unutter' them. This can take the form of simple inversion, as when we are told, with regard to the images of an old man and child that the text has succeeded (or failed) in conjuring up, that 'any other would do as ill' (*WH*, 12). The simplicity of this inversion is deceptive. To do 'well' as an example of impoverished or defective imagination is obviously always to do 'ill' – but to do 'ill' as defectiveness always suggests the possibility that the images are not defective enough, that they are somehow short of deficiency. Like everything else that can be uttered or reflected on in language, 'ill-ness' is not an absolute negative, but a relative quantity, which is susceptible to comparisons and degree, as becomes apparent a moment later: 'Any others would do as ill. Almost any. Almost as ill' (*WH*, 13). Here it is the word 'almost' which discloses the positivity of ill-ness, in its suggestion of an ill-ness which falls short of the ideal maximality of ill. The word 'almost' is used here as elsewhere in the text at once to predicate and to disclaim the coincidence of zero and totality, suggesting the plenitude, the 'all' and the 'most' of nothing, even as it enacts the necessary falling-short from absolute nothingness (later on Beckett refers to the 'leastmost all', (*WH*, 33)). It is for this reason that the text retreats from the suggestion that its aim is to achieve nothingness:

> Naught best. Best worse. No. Not best worse. Naught not best worse. Less best worse. No. Least best worse. Least never to be naught. Never to naught be brought. Never by naught be nulled. (*WH*, 31–2)

The 'most' that can be attained is the asymptotic approach to zero, a worst that is always maintained short of the zero degree.

This play on the economies of nothing is also enacted through variations on the phrase 'better than nothing', as in 'a little better worse than nothing so' (*WH*, 23), 'better than nothing so worsened for the worse' (*WH*, 27) and 'better than nothing worse say stare from now' (*WH*, 44). For something to be 'better than nothing' in ordinary language is for it to comprise a desirable quantity of something, but such quantity is always undesirable in the inverted economy of *Worstward Ho*, which is why better than nothing is always worse than nothing. A similar play is enacted with the ideas of cost and lack. Early on, the text attempts to protect itself from the consequences of gathering too much knowledge about its subjects: 'Why up unknown. At all costs unknown' (*WH*, 17). There is a miniature hilarity in the idea of a text being willing to risk the sacrifice as cost of all its resources in order to maintain the value of a non-knowledge (a *dépense*) which is itself a willed squandering of intellectual resources. There is a similar play with the idea of scarcity and resource through *Worstward Ho*. When the text returns to its image of the 'plodding twain', it is with the words 'Back to them now for want of better on and better fail' (*WH*, 30–1). Here the 'want' of better is clearly a scarcity not of good narrative subjects, but of bad or lacking subjects; the 'plodding twain' are most in need of degeneration, as being the 'least worse failed of all the worse failed shades' (*WH*, 31). What is wanting is in fact want itself; the text is scarce in scarcity. Elsewhere, in a moment of retraction late in the text, Beckett undermines the rhetoric of abundance and scarcity embodied in the expression 'much less': 'Back unsay shades can go. Go and come again. Shades cannot go. Much less come again' (*WH*, 40). The casual intensifier 'much less' here inserts an expectation of argumentative quantity into an argument that wishes to deplete. The expression 'much less' usually has the function and connotation of building or accretion, the function of the *a fortiori*, but here, with the oxymoronic coalescence of 'much' and 'less', it is made to *mean* much less (and the oxymoronic collocation of 'much' and 'less' is typical of *Worstward Ho*).

As Freud and Bataille point out, the play of scarcity and abundance, loss and gain, is necessarily played out not only in time, but also with time. *Worstward Ho* describes the double movement analysed by Freud in *Beyond the Pleasure Principle* in which movement forward in time is both the painful compulsion of life and the means used to escape it. If the first words of *Worstward Ho* suggest a resistance to the painful entry into duration and sequence, the text finds itself unable to avoid amassing itself in time, and must also, as it were, amass deposits *of* time, in order subsequently to expend and annul them. As with Freud then, the drive towards death consists both in resisting forward movement and in surrendering to it, retarding and propelling it. If the best (worst) of all would be not to enter upon duration, the next best (worst) is to acknowledge that duration is necessary to the process of worsening: 'No once. No once in pastless now. No not none. When before worse the shades? The dim before more? When if not once?' (*WH*, 38). Correspondingly, the text needs its syntax of 'first', 'next', 'again', 'on' and 'back', and can lament, 'No future in this. Alas yes' (*WH*, 10).

In *Worstward Ho*, Beckett seeks to economize on time, to resist the waste of time by a procedure of remote control, which is announced as early as the first page: 'Say for be said. Missaid. From now say for be missaid' (*WH*, 7). This technique of automated substitution attempts to keep a regulating hold over the text's future, controlling time at a distance and collapsing the lapse of time between affirmation and negation. Duration itself is problematic in *Worstward Ho*, since many of the advances in response to the imperative 'on' in fact consist of retrospections, the unsaying or worsening of what has already been said, which yields the recurrent hybrid 'on back' or 'back on'. When Beckett attempts late in the text to shrink the interval in which 'on' is reversed to 'back', this constitutes a shrinkage of time itself: 'Back is on. Somehow on. From now back alone. No more from now now back and now back on. From now back alone. Back for back on. Back for somehow on' (*WH*, 37). But to resist the pull forwards into time is deeply paradoxical where the only route to the end of time 'for good' is through duration. This has already been recognized at the end of a sequence in which the text proposes a numerical shorthand to distinguish between the three images it has conjured up:

> From now one for the kneeling one. As from now two for the twain. The
> as one plodding twain. As from now three for the head. The head first said
> missaid. So from now. For to gain time. Time to lose. Gain time to lose.
> As the soul once. The world once. (*WH*, 20)

The Christian economy of value suggests the unprofitability of gaining the whole world if one loses one's soul, but now there is no prospect of profit or saving from this transaction, since both 'world' and 'soul' are saved only in order to be lost. Here is another version of Freud's organism which stores up time and the modifications it imparts in order the more effectively to expend them on its path to death, or Bataille's vision of condensation as a stage of dissolution. The general economy which Beckett seems to be elaborating here cannot but occur in time (it is only time which allows for the difference between profit and less to come into being), even though time is also a product of that same economy, and is subject to the same incessant reversibility of gain and loss. 'Faintly vainly longing for the least of longing' the mind imagined by the text may be (*WH*, 36), but the longing for cessation itself prolongs and prolongs itself. In the same way, the 'preying' or 'gnawing' to be gone (*WH*, 41) is precisely what prevents the shades, the dim and the void from ever being fully consumed by negativity. The hunger for absence keeps creating the cake it wants not to eat, and the attempt to 'throw up and go' and 'throw up for good' (*WH*, 8) always leaves a surplus of value which must itself be consumed by or expelled from consciousness. The play between corporal expulsion and accumulation is enacted in the word 'secretes', which comes to be the preferred term for the words uttered by the imagined skull in *Worstward Ho*; to secrete is both to hide and hoard, to contain expenditure, and to produce a wasteful superfluity (the sluggishness of secretion perhaps itself an impossible compromise between the principles of containment and expenditure, as Freud's limp is the compromise between advance and retreat).

As the narrative inevitably but reluctantly advances, so it finds itself accumulating a kind of reef of time, the time that it has both secreted as waste product and involuntarily hoarded. The urge to maintain the disaggregation of particles, to prevent the binding of energies, and to keep the levels of cathexis as low as possible itself results in more and more complex forms of binding. It is the will to return to elementary segregation which itself lengthens out the complex strings of molecular aggregation in the text: 'For poor best worst of all' (*WH*, 24), 'How all but uninane. To last unlessenable least how loath to leasten. For then in utmost dim to unutter leastmost all', 'Unmoreable unlessable unworseable evermost almost void' (*WH*, 24, 33, 43).

The last words of the text proclaim as if by desperate or defeated fiat that there is 'Enough. Sudden enough' (*WH*, 46). (But of what? Of lack? Of surplus? Both?) The hunger of the text is suddenly satisfied by the attainment of a condition of stasis and disaccumulation, a sufficiency of deficiency.

> Enough. Sudden enough. Sudden all far. No move and sudden all far. All least. Three pins. One pinhole. In dimmost dim. Vasts apart. At bounds of boundless void. Whence no farther. Best worse no farther. Nohow less. Nohow worse. Nohow naught. Nohow on.
>
> Said nohow on. (*WH*, 46–7)

Here the text attempts to unbind all its economic chains, in a final expiring act of will to command dissolution, dying, as Freud says, 'only in its own fashion' (*BPP*, 39). But even in this cooled down, disaggregated universe the possibility for accumulation remains, in the tiny flutter of self-reflexion with which the text ends: 'Said nohow on' (*WH*, 47). This is the merest trace of positive awareness, the smallest possible yield or gain from expenditure, but it cannot be wiped out.

Plainly, there is nothing to guarantee that this attempt to push negation to its limit will not itself be reconfigured as a form of critical or cultural value; indeed, it will be apparent that my own reading here evidently and inescapably predicates value in the play of value and non-value in *Worstward Ho*. But this is a value that cannot without violent abbreviation merely be cited, mentioned or transmitted by a critical discourse, since it consists in a perturbed transaction of thought that has always to be renewed, lived through or off, in order to be known. If Beckett's work suggests the metaphor of limit in the way it presses towards or transgresses accepted boundaries of possibility, this metaphor of the limit is itself a vehicle of the dialectical logic that alternates positivity and negativity as positive quantities, allowing one to constitute the denial or surpassing of limits as a heroic negation of a negation. We might do better to borrow Foucault's account of what he calls Bataille's 'nonpositive affirmation', which suggests that we can characterize Beckett's investigation of value and non-value as an internal dissolution of the evaluative vehicle of the limit metaphor itself:

> Transgression contains nothing negative, but affirms limited being – affirms the limitlessness into which it leaps as it opens this zone to existence for the first time. But correspondingly, this affirmation contains nothing positive: no content can bind it, since, by definition, no limit can possibly restrict it. Perhaps it is simply an affirmation of division; but only insofar as division is not understood to mean a cutting gesture, or the establishment of a separation or the measuring of a distance, only retaining that in it which may designate the existence of difference.[27]

Warping the topography of extremity and limit inwards on itself, Beckett's work suggests ways in which the resistance of cultural negativity may resist its own incorporation *as* resistance, its own capitalization as non-value.[28]

Wasting Time

What, under these circumstances, becomes of the principle of generalized positivity which forms the basis of Barbara Herrnstein Smith's critique? In one sense, its force and threat are undiminished. Here, once again, is her formulation: '*anything* that is indicated, predicated, or otherwise constituted either as a positivity within some economy or as the object of a need, desire, or interest (individual or collective) is measured, in the very moment that it is put forward as such, as so much "good" ' (*CV*, 147).

But does this argument not appear in one respect tautologous? For it depends, surely, on temporality, the temporality of the 'very moment' at which negativity is 'put forward' as positivity. The very moment a negativity is set out in positive terms, it becomes positive. The question then is, can there *be* any other 'moment'? Can a negative exist as a negative before or otherwise than in its formulation in language? The answer here would seem to be no, if we continue (as we surely must) to accept the axiom that negatives can exist nowhere else *but* in language. So we have a paradoxical situation. Negative value can exist only in language, since only language allows for the possibility of negativity. But the very fact that language is economic in its nature (based on exchange, equivalence and distribution) means that any element of it can and, in the end, must become a positive. Language both insists on and disallows the possibility of negative value.

Perhaps the problem lies in the language which makes us think that all escapes must be absolute and positive. One way to begin an argument against Smith's generalized positivity is to suggest that, in always projecting negation in a positive form, it creates its own self-confirming object. All negativities are positivities for the principle of generalized positivity for the reason that nothing else shows up on its instruments. Bataille's absolute loss can be taken to be contradictory only because it has been artificially condensed into the positive coherence of a concept or value. This principle is also apparent in Smith's own dismissal of Derrida's reading of Bataille, which she says represents a mere recruiting of Bataille to Derrida's own nihilism:

> The evocation of a totally disassembled or nihilistic perspective on human activity has its purposes in certain theoretical discourses, and it is evidently thus that Derrida would restate and thereby conserve the value and productivity of Bataille, translating his paradoxes and absolute inversions into a neutral nihilism. (*CV*, 214)

The suggestion here is that Derrida's work produces a usable philosophical commodity out of Bataille's work and that he has to misread Bataille in order to do this. But to say that Derrida produces or conserves from Bataille's work anything as helpful and useful as a 'neutral nihilism' is brutally to simplify his argument; here the positivity of rhetorical gain is dependent on a reading which has already decided in advance what the outcome of Derrida's engagement with Bataille will have been, has calculated the theoretical profit and discarded as 'noise' all its waste products. Smith needs to be inattentive to all the forms of attention paid by Bataille and Derrida to the inversive and problematic status of negativity, in order to make out its case for Bataille and Derrida themselves being insufficiently attentive to that problematic status.[29]

We may suggest in opposition to this that language and economies of representation generally do tolerate negativity, but not 'absolute' negativity. Paradoxically, for a negation to be 'truly' negative, it cannot be true, since this will always make it a kind of positive. Positivity is resisted, therefore, not by negativity, but by indeterminacy (which, therefore, naturally cannot 'resist' it). Smith's mistake is to collapse all economic activity into its outcomes, speaking of processes of evaluation in terms of precipitated values. If it is always the case that a negative can be cashed in as a positive, there is always the uncertainty as to what that value will be, which may amount to an uncertainty about whether or not it is a positive value. If uncertainty or risk were not a part of the economic field, then economy would be a matter of prices rather than transactions.

To understand this, we may turn usefully to the work of Pierre Bourdieu. In his *Outline for a Theory of Practice*, Bourdieu specifies two different kinds of mistake that it is possible to make about the symbolic practices of primitive or archaic societies. One is to see them as entirely non-economic, which is to impose the (anyway artificial and unsustainable) Western distinction between base and superstructure, economic and non-economic activity, on to these societies and to fail to recognize the economic nature of all symbolic, social and cultural exchange. The other mistake, however, is to objectivize such activities as *totally and exclusively* economic, which is to miss the element of risk and uncertainty which are always at work within them. Every transaction (symbolic or otherwise) *can* go wrong, not only as a matter of accident, but as a structural principle. (Is this to say that it can ever actually fail to be economic? Bourdieu does not say so, and Smith would probably demur.) As his later work, especially *Distinction*, makes plain, Bourdieu does not deny that the labour of dissimulation whereby economic relations are concealed in socio-symbolic practices is itself economic, or suggest that, in the end, there could be anything that did not belong to the general economics of social life and history. But he does protest against the flattening out of the risk and irresolution which inhabit all economic systems by the objectivist account of symbolic economy. This is for

Bourdieu fundamentally an issue of temporality. Economic activity takes place hazardously over time, while economic analysis (itself always part of economic activity, of course) spatializes this activity:

> If it is true that the lapse of time interposed is what enables the gift or counter-gift to be seen and experienced as an inaugural act of generosity, without any past or future, i.e. without *calculation*, then it is clear that in reducing the polythetic to the monothetic, objectivism destroys the specificity of all practices which, like gift exchange, tend or pretend to put the law of self-interest into abeyance. A rational contract would telescope into an instant a transaction which gift exchange disguises by stretching it out in time; and because of this, gift exchange is, if not the only mode of commodity circulation practised, at least the only mode to be fully recognized, in societies which, because they deny 'the true soil of their life', as Lukács puts it, have an economy in itself and not for itself.[30]

Bourdieu here counsels against the 'self-mystifying demystification' which collapses the specificity of socio-symbolic transaction into the positivity of economic outcome *in the end*, though Bourdieu's own language in fact always suggests that he regards the 'real' activity of the societies he discusses as economic. But, even if this is to push Bourdieu further than he would wish to go, the negativity of value must be considered not as any form of exterior to value or economy (there is no such simple exterior), but as an interior principle of their workings. This is to say, that it exists in *time*, or in the fact of temporal duration (which cannot be specified or exemplified without making it non-temporal). An economics of generalized positivity is a plenum of outcomes, a diagram which achieves its flattened positivity by squeezing out duration and risk.

The principle of temporality, though rarely approached directly in Bataille's general economics, proves to be crucial to it. Anticipating contemporary critiques of Hegelian Marxism, he criticized the productivist economic theory of state communism on the grounds that, in subordinating the present to a projected future, it annulled the possibility of time as instantaneity and passage:

> In Communism the goal, the altered world, situated in time, in the future, takes precedence over existence, or present activity, which is only significant in as far as it leads towards the goal: *the world must change.* Communism, therefore, raises no problem of principle. The whole of humanity is prepared to subordinate the present moment to the imperative power of a goal. Nobody doubts the value or questions the ultimate authority of action. (*LE*, 152–3)

Usually, Bataille's response is to promote the intensity of life lived in the insubordinate instant, without orientation to any projected gain in the future. However, the development of his general economy, which is itself orientated towards a future of entropic waste or dissolution – a kind of universal death instinct – requires him to reintroduce the concept of extended time and indeed of a temporal destination which governs time in passage. If, as is argued in *La Part maudite*, accumulation is only a stage in the process of universal *dépense*, then in the 'long run', dissolution must be the final goal of the universe; but, seen in this way, the open time of the instant or of undirected *durée* is not free expenditure at all but, precisely, the subordination of the present moment 'to the imperative power of a goal' – here, the goal of dissolution.

Attention has recently been paid to the intersection of time and economics by Jean-François Lyotard. Although Lyotard is himself sceptical about the 'value' of Bataille's cult of waste, arguing that the privileging of sacrifice, of *la part maudite*, over all other forms of activity is 'useless pathos', he seems to reinstate a Bataillean privileging of expenditure over utility in his discussions of time (*D*, 142). Lyotard argues that the dominion of the discourse of economics in the world today expresses itself in terms of an instrumentalization which not only requires the medium of time in which to operate, but actually makes time a commodity. According to this analysis, profits are not only realized over time, but involve the gain of the abstract or 'stocked-up time' which is money or goods (*D*, 176). The labour and production costs of any good are seen by Lyotard as so much lost time which must be redeemed in the form of this profit, which can then be exchanged for real time. In the economic structure of thought which dominates the world, any activity, event or 'cession' in the present is considered as a form of loan or investment which must be paid back or include within itself the fact of its economic return. The aim of this system is therefore always to narrow the gap between the 'cession' and the 'counter-cession' of return or profit, to produce a gain of abstract time over real time. Value therefore comes to consist, especially in advanced multinational capitalism, not in specific yields or products but in the very speed of the economic process itself – literally the 'rate' of exchange rather than the objects of exchange. This is as true of ideas and of philosophical texts as of anything else:

> Reflection requires that you watch out for occurrences, that you don't already know what is happening. It leaves open the question: *Is it happening?* [*Arrive-t-il?*] It tries to keep up with the now [*maintenir le maintenant*] (to use a belabored word). In the economic genre, the rule is

that what happens can happen only if it has already been paid back, and therefore has already happened. Exchange presupposes that the cession is canceled in advance by a counter-cession, the circulation of the book being canceled by its sales. And the sooner this is done, the better the book is. (*D*, pp. xv–xvi)

In a world in which value is speed, such uses of language as the philosophical or the poetic seem to Lyotard to promise the wasteful integrity which offers a resistance to what he has recently called the 'neg-entropic' urge to store up and control time. If the principle of reason is to rush to its goal with the minimum delay, the principle of philosophy and art may still be 'not at all to determine the reply as soon as possible, to seize and exhibit some object which will count as the cause of the phenomenon in question. But to be and remain questioned by it, to stay through meditation responsive to it, without neutralizing by explanation its powers of disquiet.' In such forms of language, as in contemporary theoretical discourse like deconstruction and Deleuzian nomadism, 'time remains uncontrolled, does not give rise to work, or at least not in the customary sense of the verb "to work"'.[31] In contrast to a generalized positivity in which value has always already arrived, such discourse would attempt to delay the arrival or eventuality of value in the interests of keeping alive the transacting of the 'arrive-t-il?', of the always-virtual 'event'.

Obviously, this wasteful or non-productive time of speculation can be assimilated with no strain to all the various non-utilitarian claims for the specificity of the cultural since the last century, and, to the degree that Lyotard is arguing for the loss of time as any kind of absolute negation of the economic, then it is amply recuperable, if not within utility, then certainly within the law of generalized positivity. In fact, however, Lyotard's proposal for the value of lost time is more provisional, less metaphysical than may appear. He asks for a time in which conclusions and economic returns are suspended and put into question, rather than denied. Delay here is inserted into the interval between non-time and the resolution of economic return, giving or maintaining a kind of extension to the moment of uncertainty at which value is in the process of being decided, what Derrida calls 'the swoon from which it is awakened by a throw of the dice'.[32]

We might pause here to note a congruity with Freud's account of the death instinct. On a couple of occasions, Freud turns to time in an attempt to resolve his perplexity over the nature of the economy of pleasure, which, he recognizes, does not permit us to identify pleasure and unpleasure simply with the diminution or increase of quantities of excitation. Freud suggests that 'the factor that determines the feeling is probably the amount of increase or diminution in the quantity of excitation *in a given period of time*' (BPP, 8). The suggestion is repeated later in *Beyond the Pleasure Principle* without being developed (BPP, 63), and in 'The Economic Problem of Masochism' (1924), where Freud modifies the idea of time to suggest that pleasure and unpleasure might be the result not simply of rates of increase or decrease over time, but of 'the rhythm, the temporal sequence of changes, rises and falls in the quantity of stimulus'.[33] But there is also a moment in *Beyond the Pleasure Principle* where Freud suddenly affirms not only that unconscious processes are in themselves timeless, but also that 'our idea of time seems to be wholly derived from the method of working of the system *Pcpt.-Cs.* and to correspond to a perception on its own part of that method of working' (BPP, 28). This is to say that the economic movement which produces pleasure not only takes place in time, but is also a rhythm which binds and unbinds, accumulates and expends, concentrates and diffuses *time itself*, in short, which economizes with and on time. Time is produced economically even as time is the necessary medium in which all economy takes place. But, as we have seen, the work of Freud, Bataille and Beckett suggests the transaction of value in an economy which is so general that it never takes place, never arrives at its last instance.

Cultural Value

Of the three writers with whom we have been concerned, only Bataille offers an explicit and developed account of the value of culture, an account which, in simply identifying the value of literature and art with the sovereign principle of *dépense*, falls victim to Bataille's own critique of productivist economy. But there are in all three writers, and perhaps particularly in *Beyond the Pleasure Principle* and *Worstward Ho*, different calculations of the complex reckonings between culture, economy and negativity.

In *Beyond the Pleasure Principle*, as so often in his work, Freud simultaneously promotes and restricts the value of the literary-aesthetic. At a couple of crucial points in his essay, he turns to literary examples to further his argument, most notably in the use of the story of Tancred's unwitting double murder of his beloved Clorinda from Tasso's *Gerusalemme Liberata* to illustrate the repetition compulsion, and Aristophanes' story of the splitting of the sexes, which illustrates mythically the origin of the organic need to return to an earlier state of things (*BPP*, 22, 57–8). In both these cases, as also in the references to Mehpistopheles' words in Goethe's *Faust*, to Schiller and to Rückert, there is very little self-consciousness on Freud's part. Their justification is provided at the end of the second chapter where, having just concluded his discussion of the fort:da game, Freud briefly considers the analogous instance of tragedy, which shows that 'there are ways and means enough of making what is in itself unpleasurable into a subject to be recollected and worked over in the mind' (*BPP*, 17). Freud then turns away from the subject of aesthetics, but not before he has suggested that 'the consideration of these cases and situations, which have a yield of pleasure as their final outcome, should be undertaken by some system of aesthetics with an economic approach to its subject-matter' (*BPP*, 17).

So Freud has put the question of the aesthetic to one side, as being inadequate to his present purpose of demonstrating that which lies beyond, rather than in the grasp of the pleasure principle; but this putting aside forms part of that recurrent pattern of fort:da in which, as Derrida shows, Freud abandons ideas in order to be able to retrieve them at some later stage (TSF, 302–37). In fact, Freud repeatedly uses literary examples in precisely the way he has said they have no use for him in his search for something other than the pleasure principle. In their very exemplarity, the examples from Tasso and Plato allow themselves to be expropriated and put to work by Freud's text, to be 'recollected and worked over'. There is a contradiction here, for Freud is aiming to use the literary examples to 'show' the operations of a repetition compulsion or death drive which remain otherwise obscure and inaccessible. In using these examples to show the beyond of the pleasure principle, Freud undermines his demonstration; to the very degree that the examples are successful, they demonstrate the continued dominion of the pleasure principle.

But the contradiction goes further than this. As Derrida 'shows', there is a residual force of the uncanny in the use of the reference to Tasso which is not so easily to be disposed (of) in a final outcome of exemplarity. What is uncanny is the status and functioning of the example, the fact that it anticipates or repeats in advance the theory of the death drive, making of Freud's text a mere repetition, in a displacement that can never quite be subdued by putting the example to work in the service of Freud's argument (TSF, 342–3). Freud's text cannot grasp this uncanny anticipation in the form of a theme, evidence or instance, since repetition is here the form of his text, its ungraspable but imperative 'scene of writing'.

This is, if anything, even more apparent in the later literary appropriation of Aristophanes' account of the sundering of the sexes as it is itself recounted in Plato's *Symposium*. Again, there is the contradiction between what Freud wishes the story to illustrate, the origin of the need to return to an earlier state of things, which lies beyond or before the pleasure principle, and the subordination of the example in its exemplary function to the pleasure principle (Freud says plainly that, although it is a myth, he will reproduce it, simply because 'it fulfils precisely the one condition whose fulfilment we desire' (*BPP*, 57)). Freud uses this example in the mode of combination or synthesis; as he reminds us a page or so later, 'it is impossible to pursue an idea of this kind without repeatedly combining material with what is purely speculation, (*BPP*, 59). Of course, the story is also about the need to bind or recombine, though in a way that makes the meaning or value of binding very uncertain (the desire for bound or unified existence in Aristophanes' fable involving reversion and not progress). And the binding of the Aristophanic fragment into the body of Freud's argument depends upon the fact that it has itself been torn from its original context, a context which, as Derrida reminds us, is not itself whole or complete, since Aristophanes' story, the story of 'a lacuna and of supplementation at the origin of love' (TSF, 373), is told in response to a request that he fill in any gaps that might arise in the discussion through ignorance or forgetfulness.

So if, in one sense, Freud draws on the literary as a resource of value, his use of the literary amounting to the realization of certain calculable measures of profit or return, in another sense, it suggests a transaction in which the economic outcome is far from reckonable. This is not to suggest, as some have, that it is exactly or ascertainably Freud's 'literariness', as opposed to his scientificity, which produces the open-endedness of his concepts and explorations, since this would be to give the literary the substantive 'value' of interminability, in much the same way as Smith tells us that Bataille unwittingly gives a positive value to absolute loss. Rather, it is to propose that the encounter or exchange between the literary and the non-literary, the scientific, the biological, the philosophical, etc. allows or provokes the transaction of value between them, a transaction that at any and every moment *can* be cashed in for the positivity of gain (or of loss), but that does not consist in and is not strictly identifiable with this regularity of return.

Beckett's *Worstward Ho* has no explicit consideration of its cultural-aesthetic status, even though, as we have seen, it comes complete with an instruction kit for its ideological reassembly into cultural capital. A predictable move would be to read Beckett via Bataille, as the refusal of this structure of gain, as an attempt to effect a pure spending or squandering of meaning. A politicized version of this position is even conceivable, one that aligns Beckett's negativity with the refusal of institutional and economic structures of art characteristic of Dada. Both of these accounts, however, are in the grip of the economic logic which they would wish to oppose or to circumvent, since both of them still consist in converting negativity, or the transaction of negativity, into forms of cultural or political advantage. There can be little doubt that Beckett's own cultivation of silence, and his strategic (and inconsistent) refusals to co-operate with the culture and criticism industry, are themselves caught up with this structure of exchange: the less Beckett gave to criticism the greater the potential yield of value from his work. There is a huge distance between the specificity of Beckett's writing practice and the economic function served by his work (either as cultural or directly as economic commodity), but this distance is precisely what energizes the process of positivization. (The widening ratio of less to more is instanced with amazing exactitude by Beckett's *Stirrings Still*, a piece of about 1,000 words which was first issued in a limited edition costing £1,000. That the text was also available for 25 pence in a national British newspaper does not contradict, but rather intensifies, the cultural-economic harvest from the gap between less and more.[34])

But, read through with the transaction of the negative in Freud and Bataille, Beckett's work may allow at least for a widening of the circuit which rounds negativity home to the positive eventualities of value. This need not be to argue the positive value of literature or of culture as a resource of self-reflexion, non-utility or negativity (though there is also nothing to guarantee that this transformation will not take place). The 'value' negotiated by the cultural in and between the negative aesthetics of Freud, Bataille and Beckett might lie not in any absolute positivity (absolute, essential value, value *an sich*), nor in its absolute negativity, nor again in the pragmatic possibility of yield or return within economies which telescope the time of transaction of value to nothing; rather, it may be produced in the rhythm of delay, the delay of rhythm, in the space of which the transaction of value may always be about to be occurring.

If this seems quietistic, a simple return to aestheticist or liberal claims for the autonomy and non-utility of art, then this is only from a perspective which insists on a general positivity of outcomes, insisting on cashing in the kind of transacted delay I have in mind here for a negotiable and exchangeable value (here the value of non-utility). Of course, an outlook such as the one I am suggesting here will always be calculable to the person who requires positive outcomes of various kinds as quickly as possible, and with the least expenditure of time or noise, as pure vacuity, or as a temporizing in the interests of the *status quo*. But this could be to make a serious mistake about the *status quo* and about the free-market economics which, as I write, look set to move into the stage of total saturation, with the jettisoning of centralized economies in most of Eastern Europe. In such a market, the requirement to produce substantial value is paramount; nothing that does not produce or cannot be registered on a scale of value can be recognized. What is more, nothing is left out of such a general economy; when everything can be produced, sold and exchanged, even (especially) knowledge and the experience of culture, then it is precisely the insistence on the production of value (whether it be a metaphysical *real* value, use-value, fundamental value or the value yielded for the pragmatist from the general economy of human needs and interests) which cannot avoid serving the interests of the *status quo* of the global market.

NOTES

1 This general economy is adumbrated in Pierre Bourdieu, *Outline of a Theory of Practice*, trans. Richard Nice (Cambridge: Cambridge University Press, 1977), pp. 171–97; Bourdieu, *Distinction*; and Jean Baudrillard, *For a Critique of the Political Economy of the Sign* (1972), trans. Charles Levin (St Louis, Mo.: Telos Press, 1981).

2 See Jean-François Lyotard, *Economie libidinale* (Paris: Editions de Minuit, 1974).

3 J. Laplanche and J.-B. Pontalis, *The Language of Psycho-Analysis* (London: Hogarth Press, 1983), pp. 322–5.

4 The German reads 'abgelebt werden müssen' (*JL*, 248).

5 This piece of imaginary Heideggerianism is instanced scornfully by Peter Gench, in his *Mental Acts: Their Content and their Objects* (London: Routledge & Kegan Paul, 1957), p. 10. I encountered it via Peter Middleton's 'Linguistic Turns', *Oxford Literary Review*, 11 (1989), p. 142.

6 Sigmund Freud, 'Entwurf einer Psychologie', in *Aus der Anfängen der Psychoanalyse* (London: Imago, 1950), p. 459. See too the discussion of binding in Laplanche and Pontalis, *Language of Psycho-Analysis*, pp. 50–2.

7 In the course of his highly suggestive articulation of Freud's *Beyond the Pleasure Principle* with Nietzsche's and Heidegger's writings on death, difference and repetition, in *The Question of Value: Thinking through Nietzsche, Heidegger, and Freud* (Carbondale and Edwardsville: Southern Illinois University Press, 1989), James S. Hans is equally attentive to the interweavings of the values of life and death brought to light by Freud's work. But, in arguing for a form of resistance to the 'discursive' revulsion against time,

finitude and change which characterizes the death instinct, a resistance which would consist precisely in the 'recursive' acceptance of temporality – which is to say, acceptance of the dialectic of life and death – Hans appears to argue for a definitive, but gratuitous choice of life over death which, however fervently it seems to be desired in Freud's *Beyond the Pleasure Principle*, is also, I believe, disallowed by it. I concur with what I take to be one of the principal points of Derrida's reading of *Beyond the Pleasure Principle*, namely that the simple and affirmative embrace of the value of life, or its analogues such as the Eternal Return or Heideggerean Being, cannot be secured against or in permanent contradistinction to the economy of death. Although I first read Hans's book after having completed the writing of this chapter, I find myself having proleptically contracted a large debt to it.

8 Marcel Mauss, *The Gift: Forms and Functions of Exchange in Archaic Societies*, trans. I. Cunnison (New York: Norton, 1967).

9 See Georges Bataille, *L'Expérience intérieure* (1943), trans. Lesley Anne Boldt as *Inner Experience* (Albany: State University of New York Press, 1988); *Sur Nietzsche* (Paris: Gallimard, 1945); 'Hegel, la mort et le sacrifice', *Deucalion*, 5 (1955), pp. 21–43; *L'Erotisme* (1957), trans. Mary Dalwood as *Eroticism* (London: John Calder, 1962); *La Littérature et le mal* (1957), trans. Alistair Hamilton as *Literature and Evil* (London: Marion Boyars, 1985).

10 Bataille, *La Part maudite* (1949), trans. Robert Hurley as *The Accursed Share* (New York: Zone Books, 1988), pp. 28–9.

11 Bataille, 'L'Economie à la mesure de l'univers', in *Oeuvres Complètes* (Paris: Gallimard, 1976), vol. 7, p. 14 (my translation).

12 Jacques Derrida, *Margins of Philosophy*, trans. Alan Bass (Brighton: Harvester Press, 1982), p. 19.

13 Bataille, *The Accursed Share*, pp. 68–71, 193.

14 Ibid., pp. 10–11.

15 Derrida, 'From Restricted to General Economy: A Hegelianism without Reserve', in *Writing and Difference*, trans. Alan Bass (London: Routledge & Kegan Paul, 1978), p. 257.

16 Bataille, 'La valeur d'usage de D. A. F. de Sade (lettre ouverte à mes camarades actuels)', *Oeuvres Complètes*, vol. 2 (Paris: Gallimard, 1970), p. 57.

17 Derrida, 'From Restricted to General Economy', pp. 257–8.

18 Ibid., p. 262.

19 Samuel Beckett, *Disjecta: Miscellaneous Writings and a Dramatic Fragment*, ed. Ruby Cohn (London: John Calder, 1983), p. 141.

20 'LE CLIENT: Dieu a fait le monde en six jours, et vous, vous n'êtes pas foutu de me faire un pantalon en six mois. LE TAILLEUR: Mais Monsieur, regardez le monde, et regardez votre pantalon' ('La Peinture des Van Velde ou le Monde et le Pantalon', ibid., p. 118).

21 Ibid., pp. 142, 143.

22 Samuel Beckett, *Collected Poems in English and French* (London: John Calder, 1977), p. 7.

23 Jessica Prinz, 'The Fine Art of Inexpression: Beckett and Duchamp', in

Beckett Translating/Translating Beckett, ed. Alan Warren Friedman, Charles Rossman and Dina Sherzer (University Park and London: Pennsylvania State University Press, 1987), p. 105.

24 Bataille, Review of *Molloy*, first published in *Critique* (15 May 1951), trans. Jean M. Sommermeyer, in *Samuel Beckett: the Critical Heritage*, ed. Raymond Federman and Lawrence Graver (London: Routledge & Kegan Paul, 1979), p. 63.

25 Samuel Beckett, *Worstward Ho* (London: John Calder, 1983).

26 I attempt to examine this process of critical assimilation in the chapter entitled 'Repetition and Power' in my *Samuel Beckett: Repetition, Theory and Text* (Oxford: Basil Blackwell, 1988), pp. 170–201. This discussion begins to seem to me now too much the vehicle of the logic it criticizes, whereby negation is simply turned into positivity, whether to be approved or denounced.

27 Michel Foucault, 'Preface to Transgression', in *Language, Counter-Memory, Practice: Selected Essays and Interviews*, ed. Donald F. Bouchard, trans. Donald F. Bouchard and Sherry Simon (Oxford: Basil Blackwell, 1977), pp. 35–6.

28 I am helped here by Andrew Benjamin's characterization of the 'resistance' of value, which, he says, cannot be reduced to 'a simple refusal or negation of tradition' and is better thought of as 'that moment of tension opened up by an incorporation of tradition (or elements of tradition) but where that incorporation no longer provides the dominant logic of the object of interpretation. Resistance is diverse and resists a synthetic thematization' ('The Redemption of Value: Laporte, Writing as Abkürzung', *Paragraph*, 12 (1989), p. 25).

29 This false positivization is, of course, difficult to avoid and it would have to be acknowledged that the account offered of Hegel's dialectic by Bataille and Derrida and, following them, by me similarly freezes into narrow utility or concrete positivity a structure of thought which may be said to anticipate all the conceptual mobility of Bataille and Derrida. For a reading which attempts to triangulate Bataille and Derrida with Hegel in this way, see Tony Corn, 'La Negativité sans emploi (Derrida, Bataille, Hegel)', *Romanic Review*, 76 (1976), pp. 65–75.

30 Bourdieu, *Outline of a Theory of Practice*, p. 171.

31 Jean-François Lyotard, 'Time Today', trans. Geoff Bennington and Rachel Bowlby, *Oxford Literary Review*, 11 (1989), pp. 17–18.

32 Derrida, 'From Restricted to General Economy', in *Writing and Difference*, p. 261.

33 Freud, 'The Economic Problem of Masochism', in *Standard Edition*, vol. 19, p. 160.

34 Samuel Beckett, *Stirrings Still* (London and New York: John Calder and New Moon, 1989).

5

The Ethics of Discourse:
Habermas, Lyotard and Rorty

After so long a time in which even to utter the word 'ethics' in mixed critical company was to commit the worst of social gaffes (a worse blunder, even, than blurting out the word 'aesthetic'), the 'ethical turn' which seems currently to be taking place in the various provinces of critical theory, in feminism, Marxism, deconstruction, discourse theory, psychoanalysis and so on, is surprising and also gratifying.[1] If it is possible to welcome such a development as a sign of the long-overdue politicization of some aspects of literary theory, it is also possible to see the ethical as the latest alibi for, or displacement of, the political. And there are, as usual, as many varieties of the ethical as there are critics to recommend them; when Wayne C. Booth heralds the return of the ethical, it is plain that though we may indeed be witnessing a toughened, wirily self-aware kind of humanism, this still need not be the same thing at all as the ethico-political criticism which has for so long been the demand of critics such as Terry Eagleton.

This chapter considers one version of the ethical turn, though it perhaps has a representative status: that is, the concern with the ethics of discourse. This smooth phrase, the 'ethics of discourse', is in fact a remarkable, near oxymoronic splicing of two subjects which have traditionally been seen as radically antipathetic. For many philosophers since Plato, ethics has required as a condition of its possibility the notion of absolute or invariant standards of conduct and judgement, and for such philosophers, language, and that particularly hallucinogenic form of language we call literature, has sharply imperilled such absolute standards. For Plato, the virtues of honesty and truth to self which are essential to ethical life are always threatened by the dishonest and dissimulatory powers of literary and poetic language. Skipping a thousand years or so, we find Nietzsche, at the alleged end of the Western metaphysical tradition, inverting the Platonic hierarchy of ethical truth and the powers of language but, as Tobin Siebers has pointed out, relying on exactly the same structure of binary opposition between them: for

Nietzsche, truth and the morality founded upon truth is just the mirage of metaphor, but, rather than seeking to rescue ethical truth from language, he prefers to affirm the destructive–creative power of language itself.[2]

The inverted Platonism of the assertion of language against ethics may be said to characterize much of the textual politics of critical theory over the last two decades or so. Julia Kristeva's 'The Ethics of Linguistics' is a usefully explicit statement of the doctrine of language *contra* ethics or, to be more accurate, linguistic against non-linguistic ethics. Here, non-linguistic ethics means the 'coercive, customary manner of ensuring the cohesiveness of a particular group through the repetition of a code'. Against this, there stands language, or that trickster version of language that is all 'free play of negativity, need, desire, pleasure, and jouissance', along with the criticism that ethically champions its polyphiloprogenitive *élan* against duty, responsibility, commitment and other such dreary ethical compulsions.[3] The ethics of language are similarly affirmed all the way from *Tel Quel* through Colin MacCabe's revolution of the word, French feminism's 'écriture féminine' and Toril Moi's 'sexual/textual politics' to Jean-François Lyotard's promotion of the heterogeneity of language games and incitement of the differend.

Somewhere along the line, however, this ethic of language against ethics has hardened into something less wish-fulfilling than I may so far have made it sound. The transformative factor here has been the development in various quarters of powerful theories of *discourse*. Even if we admit the vast and unconscionable inflation which the word 'discourse' has undergone, making it compulsory to use it wherever and whenever one might previously have used its homely cousin 'language', the word does still signal a useful distinction. If we may restrict the term 'language' to the formal structures of grammar, phonology, syntax, lexis, etc., what characterizes theories of discourse in Mikhail Bakhtin to John Austin and John Searle to Michel Foucault and Michel Pêcheux is their emphasis on of the social uses and practices of language. Discourse theory requires us to grasp the fact that we don't merely use language as a neutral medium of exchange in which to conduct or reflect on our social life, for our social life *is* the language in which we conduct it. Language not only represents the world, it orders, makes and remakes it. Hence the central insight and insistence of speech-act theory that, in John Austin's famous motto, we not only say things in words, we *do* things *with* words.

Theories of discourse make language and the social uses of language the vehicle of power; for Foucault, discourse and power are strictly inseparable, for every instance of language-use resides within or congregates about it a disposition of differential power-relations, and every such disposition needs to be made manifest in discursive form. As a result of this concern with discourse, the questions asked by a critic of a literary text, for example, may shift markedly. We can stop worrying about the question of how accurately an industrial novel portrays mid-nineteenth-century social conditions, and ask instead what kind of world it *makes*, and what kind of relations of power the literary text enters into, starting perhaps with the litany of questions asked by Edward Said: 'Who writes? For whom is the writing being done? In what circumstances?'[4] Such questions can obviously be asked at different levels, and of different objects; so one might equally well enquire into the discursive relationships of literature as such, or of literary criticism.

Given that one of the things we most compulsively and habitually do in language is inflict violence, enforce exclusion and maintain relations of injustice, this new orientation in critical theory and linguistics (literary and otherwise) can hardly fail to raise with regard to discourse all of those questions, about goodness, justice, agency and responsibility, which have traditionally exercised political and ethical theorists concerned with human action more generally. At this point, the ethics of discourse is born. What distinguishes contemporary debates about the ethics of discourse, from, say, Renaissance or Victorian codes of conduct with regard to speech, is their sense of the centrality and standing of discourse. The otherwise disparate ethical theories of discourse developed by such writers as Jürgen Habermas, Jean-François Lyotard, Michel Foucault and Richard Rorty share the assumption that discourse is not one area of ethical concern among others, but a crucial and exemplary area of ethical concern.

This is most manifestly the case with Habermas, whose work since the publication of his massive *Theory of Communicative Action* in 1981 has been intended to demonstrate the immoderate (not to say outrageous) claim that the ethical universals which had progressively shrivelled away during the last two centuries could be retrieved from the structures of discourse itself.[5] Habermas argues that discursive exchange has as its ideal outcome the achievement of rationally based consensus, or 'the intersubjective communality of mutual comprehension, shared knowledge, reciprocal trust and accord with one another' (UP, 3). Agreement depends on the degree of validity claimed and accomplished in four different ways: the comprehensibility of what is being said, the truth of what is being said, the sincerity of the speaker and the appropriateness of fit between what is said and the social context in which it is said (UP, 2).

To be rational and legitimate, such consensus must be unforced, which is to say, free of every kind of duress, distortion or constraint, and must be governed by no strategic or purposive intention other than that of establishing truth. It is hard to imagine what kind of discursive encounter, short of a conversation between angels, could possibly meet all these austere conditions, since every discursive encounter embodies and enacts inequalities and irregularities of some kind. For Barbara Herrnstein Smith, this vision of consensus beyond conflict is a fatuous pipedream:

> [I]t is clear that, in defining genuine communication as something altogether uncontaminated by strategic or instrumental action, Habermas has secured a category that is quite sublime ... but also quite empty: for, having thus disqualified and bracketed out what is, in effect, the entire motivational structure of verbal transactions, he is left with an altogether bootstrap operation or magic reciprocality, in which the only thing that generates, sustains, and controls the actions of speakers and listeners is the gratuitous mutuality of their presuppositions. (*CV*, 110)

This kind of objection is commonly made about Habermas's notion of the 'ideal speech situation', and perhaps embodies a sophisticated version of the belief that goodness is undesirable because it is so dull compared with wickedness. We should notice, however, that what Smith objects to here is the suggestion that one might work towards the installation in the present (by some sort of sinister 'social engineering' (*CV*, 111), Smith suggests) of such an ideal speech situation. But, arguably, the force of Habermas's account lies precisely in its evocation of a utopian orientation within the structure of discourse; although this may indeed imply the desire to close the gap between actuality and ideal, it does not stake everything on the possibility of accomplishing that convergence. Just as the improbable prospect of universal peace and goodwill on earth does not and should not prevent one trying to minimize actual conflicts in the here and now, so one might think, in a similar way, that the ideal speech situation may be described and recommended as a motivating and operative orientation within discourse without needing to be or necessarily to become actual.

For Smith, ethico-discursive ideals such as the one proposed by Habermas are also implausible because of the irreducible heterogeneity of human interests and the inevitability of conflict which this entails. But this mistakes ethical for ontological universalism, the claim that ethical imperatives should operate indifferently for the claim that there is no essential difference between people. In fact, it could be said that the heterogeneity of human interests is precisely what makes the orientation towards consensus most necessary and desirable, not in order to annul this heterogeneity, but to preserve it. If the conflicts of interests which imperil the structure of responsible intersubjectivity are precisely what seem to require the continuing supposition of such intersubjectivity in moral argument, then, far from it being the case that an ideal speech situation is impossible or undesirable in our corrupt sublunary world, this is the only world in which there would be any point in maintaining an orientation towards the ideal speech situation. It has to be acknowledged however, that this reading of Habermas goes somewhat against the grain of much of his writing on the topic of communicative ethics, in which there is indeed an explicit and sustained desire to give the notion of the ideal speech situation a scientific foundation, by showing that language is primarily intended for or grounded on the goal of achieving consensus. In other words, Habermas seems to want to establish the visible *actuality* of the orientation towards ideal consensus in the structure of discourse, as well as the potential for or desirability of such consensus. Whether or not we agree to submit to its force, language is structured by the expectation of the ideal speech situation.

One of the recurring problems with Habermas's account is that it has so little to say about why or how anyone should be brought to submit to this ethico-discursive force, other than to avoid contradicting in their discursive performance the performative conditions of the language they are using; and, even here, Habermas would have little to say to the person who did not recognize the danger of self-contradiction as any kind of disincentive. As Seyla Benhabib points out, there is a circularity at work in the argument that the norms of symmetry and reciprocity presupposed by the structure of speech situations also necessarily embody democratic and egalitarian norms. To interpret the structure of speech situations in this way is to assume what is supposed to be demonstrated:

> Universal pragmatics proceeds at a level of abstraction from the standpoint of which each and every individual is considered as a being capable of consensus. This is a highly counterfactual assumption, which already assumes a moral standpoint that disregards all existing natural and social differences as irrelevant in defining the moral core of one's humanity ... What is said to be binding about the ideal speech situation are certain normative conditions which first need to be argued for. One extracts from the ideal speech situation what one has already put into it.[6]

One of the forms in which Habermas attempts to show the actuality of this normative force is in the establishing of a strict separation between uses of language which authentically embody 'communicative action', or the orientation towards understanding, and those which embody 'purposive-rational action', or the use of language to achieve certain strategic ends. One can readily see why Habermas should want to maintain this as an actual distinction between different kinds of language-use, rather than as two different ways of looking at any given language-use, since it is the vehicle of his political project to rescue the lifeworld from its Weberian colonization by instrumental reason, with the absolute split this implies and maintains between a knowing rational subject and the world it brutally objectifies, and restore to that lifeworld the possibility of authentic communication, founded not on the subject/object split, but on structures of mutually responsible intersubjectivity. However, it is very difficult to demonstrate the absolute distinction Habermas proposes here, since, no matter how scrupulously a speaker in a discursive situation tries to maintain the orientation towards 'achieving understanding *with*' rather than 'exerting an influence *upon* others',[7] there are always likely to be ways in which it will be possible to exert power through or gain some kind of reward or advantage from the discursive encounter; communication is always liable to slip into strategy, ideal speech into rhetoric.

This is partly because of the famous difficulty at the heart of the speech-act theory upon which Habermas stakes so much, that it is impossible to be sure where any particular communicative encounter or, within such an encounter, any particular speech act, begins or ends. For any communicative encounter, no matter how authentic it may seem at its alleged moment of occurrence, can always become inauthentic at some later stage, as a result of some recontextualization. If I were to spend an afternoon authentically communicating with Jürgen Habermas and were then subsequently to decide to publish my account of this exchange, in the hope of turning a profit in various ways, by making money, plumping out my c.v., gathering institutional prestige and so on, what would have happened to the ideal speech situation which once magically obtained? One answer is that it would simply have been corrupted, that communicative action would have given way to strategic action. But how could one ever be sure that I did not secretly, unknown even to myself perhaps, have the intention, or leave open to myself the possibility, of making use of the exchange in strategic ways? How could one be sure that the situation itself did not leave open this possibility, in ways that were not evident at the time? If this were the case, then it would be possible and necessary to reanalyse the exchange in the light of my later actions, and reveal its inauthenticity. But now the theory of the absolute separability of communication from rhetoric is in severe difficulties, for it seems that communication can always be made to serve some strategic end, in ways which would require this kind of reanalysis. In the face of this, Habermas is forced to some pretty extreme defensive manoeuvres, as, for example, in defending his consensus theory that truth is whatever emerges from dialogue, by which he must mean authentically communicative rather than strategic discourse:

> In order to distinguish true from false statements, I make reference to the judgement of others – in fact to the judgement of all others with whom I could ever hold a dialogue (among whom I counterfactually include all the dialogue partners I could find if my life history were coextensive with the history of mankind).[8]

The silliness of this is staggering; the history of *mankind*? If this kind of defence is necessary to protect the distinction between truth and strategy, it is also the sign of the fragility of that distinction. On the other hand, one can see that, once committed to the project of showing the actual existence and the actual priority of communication not merely as an aspect, but as a distinct kind of discourse, Habermas is also committed to making this kind of strong universalist claim. One wonders, however, just why it is necessary to maintain such an absolute distinction between truth and strategy in the first place. This aspect of Habermas's recent work has given the greatest difficulty to his supporters and detractors alike.[9]

One of the most striking features of the discourse ethic proposed by Habermas is that it is simultaneously dense with political implication and rarefied to an extreme pitch of abstraction. Habermas is in no doubt that just as discursive violence and oppression are not mere accessories to but the principal agencies of injustice in the contemporary world, so the orientation towards consensus which is buried as deeply as a DNA code within every discursive exchange embodies a utopian political promise. Habermas's claim about the relationship of discourse and utopia has the same chutzpah as Matthew Arnold's claim that poetry can save us: 'the truth of statements is linked in the last analysis to the intention of the good and true life.'[10] On the other hand, Habermas's account of the ethics of discourse may also be said to be purely formalistic, in that what matters most are the procedures of rational and unconstrained discourse, rather than the content of that discourse. This point is sometimes made by those concerned to defend Habermas against the accusation that his ideal discursive forms are absolutist and restrict plurality. For Richard

Wolin, for example, it is precisely the formalist nature of Habermas's discursive ethics which guarantees its tolerance of diversity:

> [I]t seems unarguably clear that the discourse ethic, instead of being a dogmatic rationalism, presents an impassioned and principled justification of political pluralism. This is true precisely by virtue of its 'formalism,' or 'proceduralism,' which in principle remains compatible with an infinite variety of practical norms or 'forms of life.' Moreover, only a 'formalistic' approach to ethics such as Habermas's can be truly pluralistic, since it in no way attempts to prejudge the *content* of the decisions that are ultimately reached.[11]

There is a certain absurdity built into this account, which would suggest, for example, that it would be possible to view as legitimate a consensus about the desirability of exterminating all persons with red hair over the age of 50, providing it had been reached according to established discursive procedures. In practice, of course, such an example might seem self-contradictory, since it is unlikely that such a consensus could have arisen without riding roughshod over the views of 51-year-old redheads on the matter of their extermination, such that the consensus would have to have depended on an illegitimate constraining of the discursive situation. Like other liberal-democratic theories, Habermas's ethic of communication tolerates any discursive norm except those that contradict its own principle of tolerance, that is to say, systematically disable or constrain certain parties in the discursive exchange.

One problem with this account is that, by insisting on the identification of moral agency with discursive capacity, it systematically rules out the possibility that those without discourse – children, animals, trees and rocks – could ever have rights or legitimate interests which would count in human discourse in their own terms, which is to say, separate from the interests or prudential judgements of adult human beings. There would be no way in which one might argue in Habermas's terms against a universal human consensus about the disposability of the natural world (foolish though such an idea may seem in terms of human self-interest), since there would be no medium of access to any speech situation, ideal or otherwise, for the natural world to argue its interests. For those who are convinced by Habermas's model, and therefore accept that legitimate rights may be possessed only by those creatures who can articulate them discursively, this is not a problem of course, since where there are no legitimate rights there can be no injustice. But, if a discursive agent wished to press the cause of animal rights against a human consensus, arguing that human discursive norms were unjust *because* they excluded animals and the natural world, the problem would already have arisen of how to have the argument, since the way in which the argument was allowed to take place would always have decided in advance the question of what kind of argument ought to be allowed.

This is an instance of a more general problem with Habermas's account, namely the fact that it is exceedingly hard in practice to maintain the strict separation that he requires between the ethical form of discursive exchanges and their arbitrary content. How do you decide whether or not certain forms of discursive behaviour do or do not provide the ideal conditions required by Habermas? More importantly, according to what rules do you negotiate a disagreement of this kind, when what are in question are precisely the rules for negotiating such disagreements? Such problems may seem abstruse, but they in fact occur whenever there is debate or disagreement about any aspect of constitutional or political procedures, which is to say, nearly all the time. Habermas suggests that in situations such as this, it is indeed possible to shift adaptably and reflexively from level to level, from discursive paradigm to discursive paradigm, but the fact that these shifts are always to be governed by the orientation towards consensus, as described by Habermas, only moves the problem back a stage; this is because in any real situation it may be necessary or desirable to question the authenticity of the very discursive frame which governs the shift of level (and, of course, so on, almost infinitely). For in practice it is very hard to be sure whether ideal speech or the orientation towards ideal speech are in fact in evidence in any given situation. Is it more accurate to say that the hostile exchanges between George Bush and Saddam Hussein and their representatives in the run-up to the Gulf War were governed in their interior logic by a shared orientation towards understanding, or that they reflected a fundamental disagreement about what should even count as just or rational discursive exchange?

Jean-François Lyotard, as is well known, is not convinced by a single particle of Habermas's argument. In his addiction to Enlightenment ideals like reason and truth, Habermas is, for Lyotard, the last victim of the habit of metanarrative which postmodernity ought so categorically to have kicked. Where Habermas argues for the hierarchy of certain forms of language game over others – notably, of course, rational communication over purposive or instrumental language – Lyotard urges and assumes the decentring and multiplication of language games, and denounces as oppressive any attempt to subordinate one kind of language game to another. Where Habermas aims to establish a systematic and total account of the operations and orientations of language, Lyotard proclaims the endless openness of the linguistic field. And where

Habermas assumes and promotes the ideal of consensus, Lyotard calls upon theory and criticism to tolerate, even to provoke and proliferate, difference and dissensus. For Habermas, Lyotard's rejection of the ideal of rational consensus is dangerous irrationalism, while for Lyotard, Habermas's espousal of this ideal can lead only to new versions of Auschwitz and the Gulag.

It may seem unpromising, given the bitter and unyielding antagonism between Lyotard and Habermas, to look for points of convergence between them. Surprisingly, perhaps, such points of convergence are evident. For one thing, Lyotard and Habermas have in common a conviction of the centrality of discursive ethics to moral and political reasoning in general, and share a remarkable tendency to translate political into linguistic questions; this is evident most notably in Lyotard's rewriting of the Holocaust in discursive terms ('the linkage between the SS phrase and the deportee's phrase is undiscoverable because these phrases do not arise from a single genre of discourse' (*D*, 106)), which seems almost to suggest that the worst thing the Nazis were guilty of was a failure of rhetorical protocol. (Of course, whether or not you view this translation of political action into discourse as a fatuous diminution will depend to a very large extent on whether you have already decided to view language as subordinate to 'real' actions.) In Lyotard's case, there is a striking inconsistency here. For Lyotard, the principle of justice lies in the heterogeneity of language games, the irreducibility of any one language game to another. Lyotard has a rather fluid conception of what a language game is, gathering under this term different rhetorical ends and uses of language, such as exhortation, prescription, denotation and so on, as well as what one might call different public or institutional idioms (which might more familiarly be called discourses), such as the philosophical use of language, the economic, the legal and so forth. It is true that in his more recent work, such as *The Differend* (1984), Lyotard has preferred to rely less heavily on the undifferentiated notion of the language game and has introduced some distinctions between the smaller and larger dimensions of language pragmatics, dividing them into 'phrase-regimens' and 'genres of discourse'. But this does not seem to immunize his argument from the objection that it can only establish its principle of the necessary heterogeneity of forms of language-use by means of a preliminary homogenization of what one essay quaintly calls 'the flood of human events' in terms of *language* itself. Lyotard assumes that everything, from the Holocaust to the history of ethical and metaphysical thought, can be thought of as a kind of speech act and, what is more, a speech act that may be analysed according to a pretty invariant grid of terms and agent-positions, which may seem oddly to resemble the 'universal pragmatics' of speech acts posited by Habermas. Lyotard's argument about the incommensurability of different forms of language-use depends crucially on the fact that language provides this kind of common denominator between what have been taken as discrete areas of experience, most markedly by the Kant whose distinction between the different areas of judgement, practical morality and pure reason Lyotard otherwise seems to have so much respect for. In short, Lyotard is in a position to reject the principle of translatability between particular languages and language games only as a result of having first translated everything *into* language.

This paradox is one that in fact afflicts the notion of incommensurability itself, since to say that two different areas of activity cannot be measured according to the same scale always requires the positing of just such a common scale; you must in some way measure the two incommensurable things together in order to decide that they cannot be measured together. In fact, we might say that the very notion of the 'incommensurable' itself provides a kind of scale of comparison or correlation. This need not cause problems in ordinary uses of the term, but it certainly does in attempts like Lyotard's to affirm the *absolute* incommensurability of language games. What applies to the notion of incommensurability applies by extension to the idea of translation. If a language were absolutely resistant to translation (that is, to measurement in the terms of another language), we would actually have no way of being sure that it was a language, rather than just a complicated way of breathing.

How would Lyotard respond to this criticism that, in reducing everything to language, he was inflicting the very discursive injustice he decries? Presumably he would be forced, like Habermas and others interested by the idea of an ethics of discourse, to argue the legitimacy rather than merely the heuristic advantage of the linguistic model, to argue that this correlation between action and language corresponded in some sense to the way things *are*. If this were not the case, it would scarcely be possible to derive the principle that Lyotard does in fact derive, of 'just play', or desirable heterogeneity. But this leads to another internal contradiction in Lyotard's argument. For any defence of the accuracy of his account of the field of human language would actually offend against his principle of the incommensurability of prescriptive and denotative language (in more familiar terms, the fact/value problem or the dichotomy of 'is' and 'ought'). If you cannot derive values from facts, as Lyotard claims you cannot, then his painstaking descriptions of the narrative pragmatics of the Cashinahua or the Gestapo are supremely beside the point, and rest on the illegitimate promotion of the language game of denotation over that of prescription. Of course, there is a last-ditch defence of this apparent arbitrariness, since Lyotard could say that if facts and values are indeed utterly distinct, then it is quite self-consistent of him to derive values arbitrarily from facts. According to this option, the weaker his argument, the less founded on verifiable or plausible descriptions, the stronger it is. There is not much one could do logically against such a defence, but, since it would involve Lyotard cutting off his nose, ears and eyebrows to spite his face, there is not very much one would be required to do either.

The work of Habermas and Lyotard is also united by another feature, namely the assumption of moral universalism. Again, this might seem like a tricky line to pursue, given Lyotard's explicit and sustained campaign against all universals and universalisms, and his junking of the metanarratives that underwrite them. Universal truths and norms are to be explained, like so much for Lyotard, as the operation of a particularly sinister linguistic violence, in which the force of a particular 'we' subsumes and assimilates the force of the 'you' and the 'they'. But if we pause a moment to consider the grounds for Lyotard's critique of metanarrative, we realize that what is being criticized is not so much universalism as *false* universalism, the illegitimate claim of a particular group or society to speak for and represent the whole of humanity. But how could such a claim be regarded as illegitimate, except by being insufficiently universal? In this sense, the 'suspicion of metanarratives' is a profoundly and traditionally ethical suspicion, which is grounded in a sense of norms and responsibilities that should apply indifferently across all like cases. Put briefly, if the suspicion of metanarratives were total, then there would be no grounds for continuing to suspect them.

Lyotard's covert universalism has two dimensions, which are, respectively, protective and imperative. To assimilate others forcibly to one's own project of emancipation or cultural style more generally is an unjust violation for Lyotard, precisely because he assumes, as he must assume, the universal right of all peoples, groups and even individuals, not to have their autonomy violated in this way. Such an assumption would be disclosed by asking the question, who could Lyotard possibly wish to exempt from the protection of this ethical norm? How could he make such an exemption without practising the same violence as he is condemning? Here, of course, the self-contradiction criterion would apply to Lyotard's ethics of discourse in precisely the same way as it does to Habermas's, for Lyotard would presumably extend such ethical protection to any and every culture, of any and every period in history, except those whose discursive and other actions systematically violated the discursive rights of others. The imperative dimension of Lyotard's ethics of discourse would be disclosed correspondingly by asking the question, who would he wish to exempt from the responsibility of not unjustly violating the discourse of others?

In both of these senses, Lyotard seems to be offering a universal discursive norm which is very similar to that offered by Habermas, namely, that all subjects and groups of subjects shall be permitted access to discourse, and no subject or group of subjects shall be hindered by compulsion, whether internal or external to discourse, which will constrain or prevent such access.[12] The difficulty here is that, unlike Habermas, who repeatedly states his adherence to such a norm, Lyotard only rarely does so, even though, for most of the time, this norm howls for recognition in the very form taken by his critique. Of course, even this could be taken to illustrate the Habermasian principle that the ethical orientation towards the norm of ideal speech is inherent within rational discourse itself. On this view, Lyotard most thoroughly exemplifies the Habermasian orientation towards ideal speech precisely where he criticizes the universalizing claims of such a notion, since his criticism of Habermas must rest on the Habermasian presuppositions specified just now.

This is not to say that there is no difference between an ethical norm that is explicit and specified and one that is implicit and unspoken. In the sense that it is the issue which divides and distinguishes Lyotard and Habermas, this is a difference which makes all the difference in the world. For Lyotard, there would be no possibility of embodying a universal norm in practice, since such a thing is, or is always likely to be, unjust, whereas, for Habermas, as we have seen, everything is staked on this possibility. So there is a crucial difference in the form of ethical orientation imagined by each philosopher; for Lyotard, ethical orientation must be without arrival at embodied forms of value, whereas for Habermas, orientation means nothing without the possibility of such arrival. This is because Lyotard rejects the notion of communicative action which is so central to Habermas's argument, insisting that, since all language is strategic, a matter of gaming and winning rather than a matter of communication leading towards understanding, communication in Habermas's sense would only ever be seen as a particular form of strategic ruse. Lyotard therefore struggles with the problem of the statement of norms or imperatives. His ethics of discourse are governed by the imperative to avoid arbitrary imperatives, and so cannot state their own imperative without the performative self-contradiction described by Habermas. It is not possible for Lyotard to accept Habermas's distinction between the normative forms of ethical discourse and the variable and unspecified contents of that discourse, and so he cannot believe in the possibility of setting out rules for just discursive practice which would not actually be a kind of strategy, unjustly serving the interests of some particular group.

This impossibility of stating the universal ethical imperative to avoid ethical imperatives is consequently a source of considerable and instructive unease in Lyotard's work, and nowhere more so than in the relatively relaxed situation of the discussions recorded in *Just Gaming*. This book ends with a burst of what seems like embarrassed laughter at the problem of formulating the 'justice of multiplicity', that 'prescriptive of universal value ... [which] prescribes the observance of the singular justice of each game', a laughter described drily by Samuel Weber in his afterword to the book as that which arises 'when a forbidden representation succeeds ... in imposing itself despite the inhibition affecting it'.[13] And in *The Differend* too, Lyotard is driven to try to imagine new ways of describing the activity of prescribing in which he is engaged. According to one account offered in *The Differend*, political discourse avoids being a form of discursive subordination by not being a genre of discourse at all: 'Were politics a genre and that genre to pretend to that supreme status, its vanity would be quickly revealed. Politics, however, is the threat of the differend. It is not a genre, it is the multiplicity of genres, the diversity of ends, and par excellence the question of linkage' (*D*, 138).

But all this actually points to another interesting parallel between Habermas and Lyotard. For both of them, the principle of discursive justice is entirely formal. For Habermas, as we have seen, the ideal speech situation regulates only the rational procedures of discourse and has no influence at all upon its content. For Lyotard, the norm of discursive justice is also simply a matter of form, or, as he describes it in *Just Gaming*, an 'empty transcendence'.[14] Discursive justice (which, as we have seen, can subsume every other question of justice for Lyotard) is not tied to any particular values or principles, but aimed purely at the possibility of its own continuance. For Lyotard, 'absolute injustice would occur if the pragmatics of obligation, that is, the possibility of wanting to play the game of the just, were excluded. That is what is unjust. Not the opposite of the just, but that which prohibits that [*sic*] the question of the just and the unjust be, and remain, raised.'[15] Interestingly, Lyotard and Habermas share a preference for Kant, and his attempt to derive universal rules out of the structures of rationality itself, over Hegel, who urged the historicity of all rules and norms. And Lyotard and Habermas are also both somewhat paralysed by the problem of the interference between form and levels, the fact that the empty transcendence keeps getting drawn back into the arena of the actual, and becoming itself the subject of linguistic and ethical determination.

Habermas attempts to cope with this problem by progressively sharpening the distinction between the universal ethics of discursive forms and the culturally and historically specific actions and beliefs which are articulated through discourse. Lyotard attempts to maintain this distinction even more emphatically, by insisting, as we have seen, that the politics which attempts to regulate and account for the multiplicity of genres is not itself a genre, or, equivalently, that the philosophy which tries to legislate the field of linguistic legislations which is discourse in general is not itself legitimate in the strong sense: 'The stakes of philosophical discourse', he writes, 'are in a rule (or rules) which remains to be sought, and to which the discourse cannot be made to conform before the rule has been found' (*D*, 97). Where political value and purpose lie for Habermas in extending the force and dominion of rational, egalitarian discourse, value and purpose lie equally for Lyotard in the determination to resist, with a sort of vigorous melancholy, the impersonation of the utopian future by the present. Drawing on Kant's account of the ennobling effect of the French Revolution, Lyotard suggests that the most important ethical principle is that of the gap between idea and actuality, between the ideals of freedom and justice aimed at by the French Revolution and the violent reality of the Terror. This is much more like an aesthetic than an ethical response, and an aesthetic response that belongs particularly to the Romantic theory of the sublime, which stresses the gap between the vastness of the mind's apprehension of natural forms, and its capacity for representing that vastness.

> As for a politics of the sublime, there is none. That would only be Terror. But in politics there is an aesthetic of the sublime. The actors, the heroes of the political drama are always suspect and must always be suspected of acting out of particular and interested motives. But the sublime response manifested by the public for the drama is not suspect.[16]

It is at this point that Lyotard makes that move towards what might be called the 'ethics of the aesthetic' which has seemed to open up the largest breach between his work and that of Habermas. For a regulating principle of non-regulation, a universal rule of absolute singularity, to have force, its force must be directed against itself. The guiding principle of ethical action for Lyotard must therefore be an absolute suspicion of all such guiding principles. This means that, rather than seeking to confirm and substantiate the rule of law, ethical consciousness must represent an endless putting of the law into question. If, as Terry Eagleton has suggested, the aesthetic has functioned historically as a model for the spontaneous self-legitimation of ethical and political law, Lyotard suggests that ethical and political discourse ought to be thought according to the self-delegitimations of the avant-garde work of art.

> When Cézanne picks up his paint-brush, what is at stake in painting is put into question; when Schoenberg sits down at his piano, what is at stake in music; when Joyce grabs hold of his pen, what is at stake in literature. Not only are new strategies for 'gaining' tried out, but the nature of the 'success' is questioned ... Aren't the stakes analogous ... to those that orient the 'philosophical' genre? A painting will be good (will have realized its ends, will have come near them) if it obliges the addressee to ask about what it consists in. Everything is political if politics is the possibility of the differend on the occasion of the slightest linkage. (*D*, 139)

So, although we have seen that in one sense Lyotard follows Habermas in maintaining a distinction between the 'empty transcendence' of discursive ethics and the actual playing out of language games – in Habermas's terms, this would be the distinction between the realms of the norm and the law, discursive procedure and discursive content, communicative and strategic action – here that distinction is collapsed. In the ethics of the aesthetic which Lyotard proposes, the norm (the rule of the work of art) is put into question in the very process of being applied. Reversing Habermas's derivation of strategic from communicative action, Lyotard makes norms the posterior residue of discursive action.

Lyotard's ethics are therefore radically and acknowledgedly self-contradictory; indeed, insofar as they revolve around the principle of maintaining rather than resolving contradiction, self-contradiction is of their essence. Driven on the one hand by a positively Habermasian commitment to universal norms which would guarantee preservation of discursive diversity and freedom (though, as we have seen, this commitment rarely comes to discursive consciousness), Lyotard's bitter antagonism to what he sees as the dominative form of ethical universalism espoused by Habermas's philosophy is an antagonism against himself. Given this, it is not entirely clear how one should describe the 'debate' between Habermas and Lyotard – a curious kind of debate, this, in which not only have the two alleged opponents never got into the rhetorical ring with each other, but each seems hardly to be able to bear the

mention of the other's name; nevertheless, the division between
Habermas and Lyotard has increasingly been made to exemplify the rival
claims of modernity and postmodernity.[17] Is Lyotard's rejection of
universals to be described (in Habermasian terms), as a different form of
universalism, in which case Lyotard's argument is made to demonstrate,
in its very form, the 'speech-act immanent obligation' towards rational
consensus (UP, 64) which Habermas is concerned to show as primary
and irreducible in language? Or, on the contrary, is Habermas's attempt
to maintain an ideal of pure, non-strategic communication to be read (in
Lyotard's terms) as the unjust promotion of one particular language
game, or form of discursive strategy, over all others? But, if this latter is
the case, Lyotard seems to be accepting Habermas's claims in order to
refute him, using the Habermasian orientation towards universalism
to criticize Habermas's false universalism. The problem here seems
undecidable; since if we decide in favour of Lyotard, we seem also to be
confirming Habermas; but if we decide in favour of Habermas, we may
also therefore be granting Lyotard the force of his universalist critique of
Habermas's universalism.

This paradox is made even denser by the fact that the disagreement
between Lyotard and Habermas essentially concerns the question of what
kind of disagreement might actually be taking place between them. If we
accept Lyotard's characterization of the conflict, then we must call it a
differend, or a situation in which two discursive worlds are in opposition
without the possibility of a higher principle of discursive justice with
which to mediate that opposition. But, if we adopt Habermas's account
of the opposition, then we must call it a disagreement (though Lyotard's
word would be a 'litigation'), since, for Habermas, the very structure
of intersubjective speech, which one needs to enter into even to have a
disagreement, presupposes a universe of shared rational norms. But
then this might look quite like the assimilative tyranny objected to
by Lyotard, since it would then never be possible to disagree with
Habermas without actually accepting his terms and hence showing that
he is right. This impossibility of deciding whether the relationship
between the two is one of Lyotardian differend or of Habermasian orientation towards consensus represents the undecidability of the question
of whether the question is itself decidable or undecidable. To press no
further than this. It is as much as to illustrate the point that there are no
ways of negotiating problems regarding the ethics of discourse without
exemplifying the very problems one is trying to solve in one's own
discourse. But it is perhaps only from the Habermasian side of the argument that this might seem to obviate the possibility of rational debate

continuing about ethical possibility. The gnarled form of this unsub-latable stand-off recalls that of the confrontation between the objectivist and the relativist evoked at the end of chapter 2.[18] And this is no acci-dent, for such a condition is always reached by any theory of value which seeks to abstract and autonomize one side of the paradox which coils together absoluteness and relativity. Just as any attempt to affirm forms of absolute and unconditional value always returns one to the field of relativity and exchange, so any attempt to validate relativity as a principle recoils into the very forms of fixity and transcendence which are denied by the principle of relativity. Each side needs the other to affirm its own unconditionality.

However we choose to describe it, the fundamental disagreement between Lyotard and Habermas has been triangulated by the pragmatic philosophy of Richard Rorty, who rejects what he sees as the extremity of both positions; rejects, that is to say, the hands-on ethic of discourse exemplified in Habermas's absolute imperative to ideal speech grounded in rational norms, and the hands-off ethic of discourse exemplified in Lyotard's absolute imperative to multiply differences. What matters most for liberal-democratic politics according to Rorty – and here there is a certain consonance between him and Habermas – is not foundational or universal values, but simply the existence of forms of free and uncon-strained discussion. Accepting, as Habermas does, the Peircean notion of truth as consensus, Rorty believes that 'if we take care of political free-dom, truth and goodness will take care of themselves' (*CIS*, 84). So, to some degree, Rorty shares with Habermas the idea of the importance of free discussion and undistorted communication, but is much more sanguine than Habermas about the possibility of achieving this. In contrast to those, like Barbara Herrnstein Smith, who believe that the ideal speech situation is impossible and chimerical, Rorty sees this ideal as lying within the grasp of any more or less developed democratic polity such as presently exists. If Habermas's speech ideal is angelically austere, then Rorty's is affably laid back: unconstrained discourse 'is simply the sort which goes on when the press, the judiciary, the elections, and the universities are free, social mobility is frequent and rapid, literacy is universal, higher education is common, and peace and wealth have made possible the leisure necessary to listen to lots of different people and think about what they say' (*CIS*, 84).

Of course, the rub for both Habermas and Lyotard is how to be sure that freedom actually exists in any of these areas. Rorty objects to the view that any kind of strenuous or systematic enquiry would be needed to establish exactly what was free or constrained about any form of discursive activity, and therefore sees no value in the notion of the critique of ideology. Since ideology means nothing more dramatic or sinister for Rorty than bad ideas, there is no need to rid ourselves of ideology *first* before we can go about subjecting such bad ideas to the ameliorative influences of unconstrained discussion. This might seem to lead Rorty into the same kind of self-reflexive paradox that we pointed out a little earlier in the work of Habermas, namely that it is hard to be sure that one is discussing a problem under conditions of discursive freedom when what may be at issue in that discussion is the nature of discursive freedom itself. But Rorty has a Zen-like knack for turning aside such paradoxes, arguing that since they are merely the product of an unhelpful way of thinking, all that is needed is to give up the way of thinking for the paradox to vanish, leaving only a whiff of sulphur behind it. There is no problem about trying to lift ourselves out of ideology by our own bootstraps for Rorty, because if we had been meant to fly we wouldn't have been given boots in the first place. Or, as he put it in a debate with Lyotard, the pragmatist can dispense with the project of emancipation, because '[h]e believes that there has never been anything to emancipate and that human nature has never been in chains'.[19]

Rorty aims to mediate between the alternatives represented by Lyotard and Habermas with the idea of the 'ironic liberal'. This ideal would appropriately, which is to say, moderately, pragmatically, allow some of the claims of ironists such as Lyotard, Foucault and Derrida, for example, the claim that there is no such thing as absolute truth, universal human nature and so on. But it would also allow the idea of the desirability of improvement achieved by democratic discussion and freely achieved consensus. This means navigating between the extremes represented by irony without liberalism (Foucault, Lyotard, Derrida) and liberalism without irony (Habermas).[20] If the difference between Lyotard and Habermas is the difference in the status of the 'we' in their work, Lyotard rejecting the possibility of universal community, Habermas subordinating everything to this ideal, then Rorty proposes a more moderate kind of orientation towards community, in which the 'we' does not need to abandon or suspect its own nature in order to acknowledge the interest or claims of others: the liberal-democratic 'we' can afford to be ethnocentric if this is 'the ethnocentrism of a "we" ("we liberals") which is dedicated to enlarging itself, to creating an ever larger and more variegated *ethnos* ... the "we" of the people who have been brought up to distrust ethnocentrism' (*CIS*, 198).

One of the most important ways in which Rorty agrees with Lyotard against Habermas is in the standing that he gives to the literary and the aesthetic. For Rorty, it is the literary or poetic sense which allows the kind of self-correcting irony of which he approves, and he therefore welcomes the interest in literary-aesthetic questions among many contemporary Continental philosophers precisely to the degree that this reflects a notion that philosophy is not involved in the search for truth, or the discovery of foundations, but rather in the creation of more or less rich and accommodating metaphors and narratives. The history of philosophy is therefore for Rorty not the history of a slow development of knowledge with respect to something outside itself, but a history of self-weaving and unweaving. When it comes to questions of politics, Rorty proposes a similar kind of aesthetic ideal, in the notion of a poeticized rather than a rationalized or scientized culture. Crucial to this apprehension is the sense that truth is made rather than found: 'A poeticized culture would be one which did not insist we find the real wall behind the painted ones, the real touchstones of truth as opposed to touchstones which are merely cultural artifacts. It would be a culture which, precisely by appreciating that *all* touchstones are such artifacts, would take as its goal the creation of ever more various and multicolored artifacts' (*CIS*, 53–4). If this appears to reduce the business of negotiating cultural values to a form of handicraft, it nevertheless connects with an important strain of critique within recent debates about the ethics of discourse. For many writers, the ethics of discourse require a refusal of the narrow definition of discourse offered by Habermas, and an attempt to include within the sphere of the ethical all those forms of discourse apparently undervalued in Habermas's account of the priority of communicative action, and especially aesthetic discourse.

Habermas is curiously inattentive to the question of the literary-aesthetic throughout his work, and has been disappointing in his attempts to defend and compensate for this inattention in his recent responses to criticisms. For Habermas, the aesthetic and the literary in particular are simply not as significant as 'serious' rational discourse. The literary is taken to be a second-order form of discourse, derived from and falling short of communicative action. It is principally 'non-serious' language, for Habermas, language which neither submits to nor could survive the various validity tests undergone in rational discourse, and so cannot have a legitimate role either in intellectual critique or in the generation of forms of social life and value. This is because communicative action of a serious kind must engage with and be tested and modified by the world, whereas, says Habermas, literary language has no such responsibility, or procedure for being tested and modified (*PDM*, 205).

In his recent work, Habermas has been more prepared to allow some limited value to the claims made for the literary and the aesthetic more generally. He goes as far as agreeing with some of his critics that modernist literature and art in particular, insofar as they are or may be experimental, critical and innovatory, can indeed open the rigorously self-knowing rational ego to otherness, can create new worlds or disclose to us the experience of this world in new and valuably defamiliarized ways. Modernist aesthetic consciousness also imparts

> increased sensitivity to what remains unassimilated in the interpretive achievements of the pragmatic, epistemic, and moral mastery of the demands and challenges of everyday situations; it effects an openness to the expurgated elements of the unconscious, the fantastic, and the mad, the material and the bodily, thus to everything in our speechless contact with reality which is fleeting, so contingent, so immediate, so individual-ized, simultaneously so far and so near that it escapes our usual categorial grasp.[21]

Stephen K. White, who is sympathetic to Habermas's account of the function of the aesthetic, summarizes it thus: 'The radical decoupling of the aesthetic sense from the imperatives of society and tradition has the potential for informing consciousness about how we normally interpret our desires and feelings in ways which unreflectively mirror the prevail-ing value standards of the culture around us.'[22]

However, it is plain that this complimentary view of the aesthetic still marginalizes it as discursive action; for example, Habermas sees the ironic reversals and dissolutions of rational categories practised by litera-ture as always in the end presupposing and finally reinforcing the categories which are reversed or dissolved.[23] The aesthetic remains an enhancement of, or nutritional supplement to, rational discourse, which helps to keep that discourse in trim without ever posing any threat to its healthy self-identity. Habermas remains unconvinced by the claims that poeticity (Rorty), metaphor (Derrida) or narrative (Lyotard) can or should have any serious part to play in the legitimate determination of social action, or in 'linguistically mediated processes such as the acqui-sition of knowledge, the transmission of culture, the formation of personal identity, and socialization and social integration [which] involve mastering problems posed by the world' (*PDM*, 205).

But this is an argument which merely demonstrates its presupposi-tions: in fact one could think of lots of examples of the ways in which literature, or the literary conceived in a wider sense than as mere world-innovation or 'world-disclosure', could have concrete effects in the areas said by Habermas to be the particular preserve of legitimated rational discourse. Indeed there would seem to be serious grounds for suspecting that the formation of identity and the creation of forms of social integration in fact take place emphatically through literary or rhetorical processes such as narrative, metaphor, myth and so on, and that the reproduction of social life is not and has never been regulated by the kinds of serious communicative action supposed by Habermas. Of course, it would be possible to agree with this judgement from Habermas's perspective and yet see it as a cause for regret, urging that the claims of the ideal speech situation implied within all rational discourse have yet to be redeemed partly because of the distorting influences of the literary on rationality. This would maintain the normative distinction between communicative action and derivative and degraded discursive forms such as literature. But it is just this distinction that, without these presuppositions, would be in question. Everything depends here on Habermas's claim that the orientation towards the ideal speech situation can actually be shown to be a constitutive part of all discourse. But the subordination and marginalization of the literary that seems to be the effect of this claim is in fact its enabling condition. As Jonathan Culler has argued: 'the ideal speech situation, the model for an ideal society said to be inescapably presupposed in communicative action itself, emerges as the result of a series of exclusions of those communicative actions which do not seem to presuppose these norms.'[24]

Those who have opposed themselves to Habermas on the question of the aesthetic, Rorty, Foucault and Lyotard, would presumably share Culler's suspicion of the claim that the communicative norms of rational discourse are foundational and resist the demotion of the literary-aesthetic (and, indeed, other forms of language-use as well) which is the consequence of this claim. It may seem as though we have arrived back at the starting point for this chapter, which was the opposition between an ethics based upon universal and absolute norms and a linguistics attentive to all the slippage and aberrancy of language in its general character as 'literature'. As Culler remarks, literature has long fulfilled the function for foundational philosophy of 'a margin close at hand, into which problematical aspects of language could be shunted so as not to complicate normative accounts, as the name for everything non-serious or abnormal which permits accounts of language to focus on so-called normal, serious communicative action'.[25]

However, there are various ways in which Habermas's account of literary-aesthetic discourse can be contested from this perspective. Perhaps one of the least promising is Rorty's strategy of inversion, his suggestion that we simply replace the foundationalist description of how language (and philosophical language in particular) works with a poetic account, which stresses aesthetic-rhetorical qualities of persuasiveness, coherence and capacity to interest and delight over the Habermasian claims for validity, truth and rationality. Like most such inversive strategies, the simple replacement of truth with poetry may give credence to the structure of ideas which produced the subordination of poetry as the derivative supplement of truth in the first place. (The persistence of the original/derivative structure in Rorty's writing may be detected in a sentence such as this one: 'It took Hegel a lot of hard work to manage the dialectical inversions he then pretended to have observed rather than produced' (*CIS*, 134).) Rorty's resistance to the rational linguistic ideals of Habermas in fact resembles closely I. A. Richards's promotion of poetic language over scientific language, on the grounds that it presented provisional 'as-if' worlds which were in principle untestable by criteria of truth or falsity. In a similar way, Habermas sees literary-poetic speech acts as being dependent upon a suspension of binding illocutionary forces which 'removes them from the sphere of usual discourse, and thereby empowers them for the playful creation of new worlds – or, rather, for the pure demonstration of the world-disclosing force of innovative linguistic expressions' (*PDM*, 201). In contesting Derrida's account of the relations between philosophy and literature, Habermas actually produces a negative version of Rorty's position, in order to try to persuade his readers of the weakness of Derrida's criticism of philosophical language. Habermas represents Derrida and his followers as simply substituting literature for philosophy, dismissing as rhetoric the claims of truth. Habermas believes that, in contrast to Adorno, who attempts to maintain a critique of the identity-thinking of philosophical discourse from within that discourse, Derrida chooses to step outside philosophy altogether. This has the advantage of protecting him from the lacerations of performative self-contradiction to be found in Adorno's work, but the disadvantage of depriving his critique of any substantive truth-claim, since 'whoever transposes the radical critique of reason into the domain of rhetoric to blunt the paradox of self-referentiality, also dulls the sword of the critique of reason itself' (*PDM*, 210). But this criticism presupposes what is precisely in question in Derrida's work, which is to say, the necessary authority of reason over rhetoric, the glinting sharpness of critique over the cloudy dullness of poetry. Such an authority can hardly be demonstrated without self-contradiction; it must simply be asserted, but the force of such assertions can be precisely the cutting edge of violence, the sword's argument that it is mightier than the pen.

More damaging than this is Habermas's misconstruing of Derrida's account of the relations between philosophy and literature. For Derrida does not simply argue the claims of the literary over the philosophical, or simply reduce philosophy to literature, in the way that Habermas (disapprovingly) and Rorty (approvingly) suppose. Habermas here exorcizes a spectre of his own making, since there is no deconstruction which simply dissolves truth into trope. Derrida has explicitly repudiated the 'rhetoricism' that has been attributed to deconstruction, claiming, for example, that the result of his enquiry into the insistent effect of metaphor in philosophical language is not simply to assimilate thought to metaphor, but to propose a new way of understanding the relationship between concept and metaphor.[26] This produces a relationship of paradoxical undecidability, in which the hierarchy of truth and rhetoric is neither dissolved or inverted, but subject to a ceaseless contortion of exchange.

This tendency to polarize claims for the aesthetic over and against the rational may bear the imprint of the institutional struggles between disciplines such as literature and art history on the one hand and the social sciences on the other, with the rival claims of rationality and the aesthetic standing in for the claims made by such rival disciplines for the commanding priority of their subject and approach. (In some highly mediated fashion, this disciplinary rivalry of ideas and values gets re-enacted in the cultural splits between art and science, 'life' and technology, and so on.) The argument about the ethics of discourse and the competing claims of pure rational norms and literary embodiments is in this sense clearly to be seen not as an example of communicative action, but as a strategic 'contest of faculties' for intellectual pre-eminence. This is plainly visible in the work of many of the literary critics who follow Rorty in seeing Derrida's work as a simple legitimation of poetic truth over rational truth, but it is also apparent in Habermas's critique of the disturbances in the intellectual order of things wrought by Derrida's influence. Although Habermas's recent work sometimes seems to be generously attentive to the complementary differences between the spheres of philosophy and the aesthetic, with an almost Lyotardian insistence that the distinct forms of discourse represented by philosophy and the aesthetic should not contaminate each other, this always turns out in the end to be protecting the priority of the philosophical discourse of truth over all others. Habermas therefore reproves literary scholars for uppishly affecting to engage in the critique of metaphysics, while wagging his finger at philosophy for slumming it among rhetoric and tropes.

However, these struggles can take place within as well as between disciplines, and this may suggest a more complex and positive way of thinking about the place of ethico-discursive questions in literature and more generally. For literature is not merely the other of communicative action, or, as Habermas would want to see it, a simply 'non-serious' use of language in which validity claims are entirely suspended. For if literary discourse is not serious 'communicative action', it seems clear that it is also not exactly or exclusively 'strategic action', not entirely orientated towards the achievement of rhetorical effects, or towards the coercive and ideological replication of structures of power. For literary texts commonly make large cognitive claims, not all of them separate from the kinds of rational claim made in philosophy; claims to be presenting a certain kind of warrantable truth about the social or natural world, and appeals to a presupposed ideal community of readers. Nowadays, such claims tend to be dismissed as much by opponents of the notion of truth as by its supporters. And yet, isn't there a sense in which *Middlemarch* or *Ulysses* are as serious an attempt to consider the nature of right actions as any ethical or political discourse? And, in doing so, do they not also constitute a kind of self-reflexive investigation of the differing claims to ethical and political authority of different forms of discourse, including the 'literary'? Obviously enough, literary texts cannot abide by all the four criteria of validity announced by Habermas; if a literary text can claim in some sense to be 'true', it is not clear in what sense it could be seen as 'truthful' or sincere (or, for that matter, insincere). And if literary texts have more or less warrantable claims to comprehensibility, then how are we to measure the appropriateness to context of a form of language that, by definition, has no obvious or immediate context? But in fact the ethico-discursive claims of literary discourse rely precisely upon this variability or uncertainty of context, on the structural fact of the literary text's distance from actual strategic or speech-act situations. In summoning up, alluding to or seeming to install itself in such contexts, the literary text also always breaks with them, allowing the reader and interpreter to see the text as a citation of and commentary upon the context as well as being determined by it.

A characterization of literary writing in these terms may seem simply to imply that literature cannot be measured according to the validity criteria specified by Habermas, which might, depending on one's point of view, be taken as either bearing out or contradicting the idea of the superiority of communicative action. But it is possible to argue in stronger terms for the validity-claims of the literary. This would involve the suggestion that *literary discourse permits and promotes the analytic appraisal of the very distinction between valid and invalid discourse which traditionally has constituted it.* A novel such as *Ulysses* might seem at first glance to be constituted entirely of the kind of language-use which Habermas sees as derivative and secondary, which is to say strategic or rhetorical language, language expressing and enacting relations of power and struggle between competing linguistic forms. Among the many styles and languages which throng and mingle in the book, the languages of advertising, of popular fiction, of journalism, of philosophy and aesthetics, of political bigotry, of sexuality, there seem conspicuously to be no examples of ideal speech, or rational language undistorted by desire, compulsion or ideology. And yet it is still possible to recognize the particular ways in which *Ulysses* as a text co-ordinates and combines these languages. This is to say that *Ulysses* consists simultaneously of a demonstration of the incommensurability of languages and a claim to have made them commensurate. The more *Ulysses* seems to refute the idea of a common horizon uniting the agonistic differences of discourse, the more it actually proposes and constitutes such a horizon. This suggests a distinction between the speech acts represented in *Ulysses* and the speech act constituted by *Ulysses*. The more the claims of ideal speech are disintegrated at one level, the more those claims reassert themselves at the other (and must, in the name of ideal speech, themselves come under suspicion). This is to say that a text such as *Ulysses* presents a simultaneous extremity of strategic language and of communicative action, an extremity at which each is allowed ethically to interrogate the other. My discussion of *Ulysses* in chapter 8 will extend this analysis considerably.

This would be to suggest that the suspension of validity-claims in literary writing is not of the simple kind proposed by Habermas and those convinced by his account. Literary discourse is not merely non-serious – the other or mirror of seriousness – but that kind of language which permits and provokes the question of what constitutes the distinction between serious and non-serious language. The non-seriousness of literary discourse is therefore not what establishes it as a category but, on the contrary, what defines it as a suspension and interference of categories. Literary discourse can suspend validity-claims in such a way as to suspend (in the sense of putting into question rather than dissolving or doing away with) the claim of validity itself, to constitute a principled and ethical assault on the notion of rational validity in language, while all the time continuing to presuppose an orientation towards consensus similar to that supposed of rational discourse. Any effort to disentangle completely these two dimensions, for example by suggesting (as I did a moment ago) that there is a permanent distinction to be made between the speech acts represented in it and the speech act represented by *Ulysses*, or that the discursive disruptiveness of such a text proves the horizon of ideal speech by presupposing it (as we saw a little earlier that Habermas does), must fail to do justice to the ways in which these two levels tirelessly recompose and decompose, in that renewed conflict between the strategic and the communicative, between rhetoric and truth, between language as power and language as critique of power. This is not to claim that literature has a special status, exempting it from all the normal sorts of discursive responsibility, rather that, in literature, the question of responsibility is posed in a particularly intense way. In literary language, or in valuable forms of it (though, of course, value is precisely what such valuable forms distinguish themselves by subjecting to open question), the corrupt and the utopian are impacted together.[27]

However much it may look like it, this is not an attempt to characterize all literary texts on the modernist model of *Ulysses*; this would be as dubious as all the other theories of the essence of literariness which have been brought forward by theorists from Jakobson to de Man. In fact, my characterization of the 'nature' of literature sits most happily with the sort of claim made by Terry Eagleton and others, that 'literature', if it is taken to mean a particular category of linguistic objects having certain identifiable properties in common, simply cannot be said to exist.[28] Rather, 'literary' texts are simply texts that we have agreed to treat as or call literary, that is to say, to accord certain (variable) values to. This categorial uncertainty may be as much as we can say, and indeed as much as we need to say, in the way of defining literature. Hence, the celebrated uncertainty or vacuity of the category would be part of its dynamic definition; not that certain texts were and would remain for all time privileged examples of categorial indeterminacy, but that where such indeterminacy existed as a structural condition of the work and its reception, naturally by particular readers in particular histories, one could recognize the presence and effect of the literary. In this sense, literary discourse is not easily to be gathered together as a disciplinary field or resource, since literary discourse would be at work in social representations, narratives, games and figures of speech of all kinds. A literary department of the utopian kind I would like to imagine would be very poor indeed if it were not able to engage with the complex ethicity of jokes, for example; for jokes present just that friction of alternative worlds, that clashing of the dimensions of the communicative and the strategic which I have claimed for a work such as *Ulysses*.

Without crudely attempting to split the difference between Lyotard and Habermas, this account of the literary might remain true to the sense that both philosophers share of the prevalence of violence and exclusion in discursive relations themselves and the responsibility of philosophy and critical theory to analyse and resist such violence and exclusion. Surprisingly, perhaps, I have suggested that Habermas and Lyotard also share a sense of the immanent universalist horizon of discourse. At its best, and despite its rebarbative systematicity, Habermas's elucidation of the theory of ideal speech locates the aspiration towards community and the responsibility for extending it within the textures of discursive exchange. Although Lyotard refuses what he sees as the cramped singularity of this model of discourse, his very refusal is driven by an encompassing, urgent sense of the general responsibility to refuse the distortions, subordinations and violences done by discourse on discourse, or in other words by an orientation towards universal rules for the resisting of false and violent universalisms. As we saw above, it is impossible to decide whether Lyotard's critique of Habermas's ideal speech situation takes place on its inside or on its outside, whether it represents the rejection of the ideal speech situation or a turning of this norm upon itself.

The discursive ideal that I wish to derive from this grotesque synthesis of Lyotard and Habermas is one that is itself grotesque or catastrophic rather than elegantly self-consistent. For it would be an ideal of inter-subjective community in discourse that would recognize the continuing need to tolerate interior structural crisis, as the norms that governed and constituted discursive community were themselves in the name of that community perpetually subject to critique. If, with Lyotard and against Rorty, this would provoke a continuing suspicion of stabilities and hierarchies of every kind, then, with Habermas against Lyotard and Rorty this might also involve a principled attachment to the formation of those institutions which would enable this ironic structure of critique to take place and continue.

It seems to me, for example, that the cultural institution of the university and, within that, the study of cultural practices such as literature provides an interesting starting point for such a paradoxical ideal of discourse. This is particularly so because the 'speech situation' of the university, so to speak, is already paradoxical. The university triangulates an encounter between the languages of those who arrive inside it as its clients, the languages that they encounter there (the languages, for example, of literary texts) and the languages of those who manage and direct this encounter. In what ensues, interesting and fundamental negotiations can and should take place about the nature and authority of language as such and, at its best, the university ought to allow and infinitely to extend this participation in the formulation of crisis. This notion of the role of the university is counter-factual, to put it mildly, since the university is characterized much less by its promotion of discursive crisis than by its careful legislation of discourse, governed by a notion of ideal speech that is itself a form of violence. (Thus, if this appears as a defence of an elitist institution it is so only to the extent that it requires the demolition and reworking of everything that maintains exclusion and fixation in that institution.) It seems to me that where this strategy can encounter the most productive difficulties is in those areas of the university where the subject under negotiation is also the means and arena of the negotiation itself, which is to say in literary and linguistic study, or those subjects which allow themselves to be affected by it. Of course, this would require a considerably enlarged conception of what literature was, in which the literariness (in the sense specified earlier) of signifying practice as a whole would be the subject of enquiry, and in which one would seek productively to maintain the non-categoriality of the category of literature. The point of such an exercise would be to make what takes place accidentally and occasionally in departments of literature, namely the acknowledgement of the crisis of discourses, something systematically and collectively available. The ethics of discourse are founded upon the notion that language does not merely represent the world, it makes it; and the point of thinking of our practice in departments of literature in the way I am recommending is in order to begin (re)making the world.

NOTES

1   For evidence of the 'ethical turn' in deconstruction, see Miller, *The Ethics of Reading*; in psychoanalysis, see John Rajchman, 'Lacan and the Ethics of Modernity', *Representations*, 15 (1986), pp. 42–56; in Foucauldian discourse theory, Michel Foucault, 'On the Genealogy of Ethics: An Overview of Work in Progress', in *Michel Foucault: Beyond Structuralism and Hermeneutics*, ed. H. Dreyfus and Paul Rabinow (Chicago and London: University of Chicago Press, 1983), pp. 229–52 and John Rajchman, 'Ethics after Foucault', *Social Text*, 13/14 (1986), pp. 165–83. See too Martha Nussbaum, 'Perceptive Equilibrium: Literary Theory and Ethical Theory', in *The Future of Literary Theory*, ed. Ralph Cohen (New York and London: Routledge, 1989), pp. 58–85 and Andrei Plesu, 'Elements for a Restoration of Ethics', *Cahiers Roumains d'Etudes Littéraires: Revue Trimestrielle de Critique, d'Esthétique et d'Histoire Littéraires*, 1 (1987), pp. 110–17. For an excellent

overview of the question of ethics and criticism, see Tobin Siebers, *The Ethics of Criticism* (Ithaca, NY and London: Cornell University Press, 1990).

2 Ibid., pp. 30–1.

3 Julia Kristeva, 'The Ethics of Linguistics', in *Desire in Language*, trans. Thomas Gora, Alice Jardine and Leon S. Roudiez (Oxford: Basil Blackwell, 1980), p. 23.

4 Edward Said, 'Opponents, Audiences, Constituencies, and Community', in *The Politics of Interpretation*, ed. W. J. T. Mitchell (Chicago and London: University of Chicago Press, 1983), p. 7.

5 Jürgen Habermas, *The Theory of Communicative Action*, vol. 1: *Reason and the Rationalization of Society*; vol. 2: *Lifeworld and System: A Critique of Functionalist Reason* (Boston: Beacon Books; Cambridge: Polity Press, 1984, 1987). A useful condensation of Habermas's argument for the utopian orientation of social discourse is to be found in his essay 'What is Universal Pragmatics?' (1976), in *Communication and the Evolution of Society*, trans. Thomas McCarthy (London: Heinemann, 1979), pp. 1–68.

6 Seyla Benhabib, *Critique, Norm, and Utopia: Study of the Foundations of Critical Theory* (New York: Columbia University Press, 1986), pp. 291–3.

7 Habermas, *Theory of Communicative Action*, vol. 1, p. 286.

8 Habermas, 'Wahrheitstheorien', in *Wirklichkeit und Reflexion: Festschrift für Walter Schulz*, ed. H. Fahrenbach (Pfüllingen: Neske, 1973), p. 219, quoted in Thomas McCarthy, *The Critical Theory of Jürgen Habermas* (Cambridge: Polity Press, 1984), p. 299 (McCarthy's translation).

9 The most lucid account of the difficulty of maintaining the communicative/strategic distinction is Jonathan Culler's 'Communicative Competence and Normative Force', *New German Critique*, 35 (1985), pp. 133–44.

10 Quoted without source in McCarthy, *Critical Theory of Jürgen Habermas*, p. 307.

11 Richard Wolin, 'On Misunderstanding Habermas: A Response to John Rajchman', *New German Critique*, 49 (1990), p. 144.

12 This formulation derives from the synthesis of Habermas's position offered by Robert Alexy in 'Eine Theorie des praktischen Diskurses', in *Normenbegrundung und Normendurchsetzung*, ed. Willi Oelmüller (Paderborn: Schöningh, 1978), pp. 40–1, quoted in Stephen K. White, *The Recent Work of Jürgen Habermas: Reason, Justice and Modernity* (Cambridge: Cambridge University Press, 1988), p. 56.

13 Lyotard and Thébaud, *Just Gaming*, pp. 100, 103.

14 Ibid., p. 69.

15 Ibid, pp. 66–7.

16 Jean-François Lyotard, 'Post-Script on the Terror and the sublime', in *Le Postmoderne expliqué aux enfants: Correspondance 1982–1985* (Paris: Galilée, 1986), pp. 111–13 (my translation).

17 See, for example, Richard Rorty's 'Habermas and Lyotard on Postmodernity', in *Habermas and Modernity*, ed. Richard Bernstein (Cambridge, Mass.: MIT Press, 1986), pp. 161–76.

18 See discussion above, pp. 30–1.

19 Richard Rorty, 'Le Cosmopolitisme sans émancipation: en réponse de Jean-François Lyotard', *Critique*, 41 (1985), p. 570 (my translation).

20 This formula is derived from Rorty's comparison of Foucault and Habermas (*CIS*, 61–9).

21 Jürgen Habermas, 'Questions and Counter-Questions', *Praxis International*, 4 (1984), p. 236.

22 White, *Recent Work of Jürgen Habermas*, p. 149. White's helpful discussions of Habermas's recent attitudes towards the question of the aesthetic are to be found on pp. 31–6 and 134–53.

23 Jürgen Habermas, 'Reply to my Critics', in *Habermas: Critical Debates*, ed. J. Thompson and D. Held (Cambridge, Mass.: MIT Press, 1982), p. 271.

24 Culler, 'Communicative Competence and Normative Force', p. 141.

25 Ibid., p. 142.

26 Jacques Derrida, *Limited Inc*, 2nd edn, ed, Gerald Graff, trans. Jeffrey Mehlman and Samuel Weber (Evanston, Ill.: Northwestern University Press, 1988), pp. 156–7.

27 My argument here may recall Fredric Jameson's notion of the concealed utopian aspiration to be found as the political unconscious of literary texts, in *The Political Unconscious*. The difference between my argument and his is that mine is posed at the level of discourse itself. As will become clear in my discussion of the treatment of value in Jameson's *Political Unconscious*, I would also prefer a realizable utopia of maximally free transaction that could be positively anticipated from the crisis and contingency of value within (for example) literary texts to a utopia which required the translation of those conditions of crisis into an imagined and thoroughly imaginary plenitude of 'real' value; see discussion below, pp. 148–53.

28 Terry Eagleton, *Literary Theory: An Introduction* (Oxford: Basil Blackwell, 1983), pp. 1–16.

6

Exchanging Utopia: *Marxism, Aesthetics and Value*

The arguments of this book have so far been based upon an apprehension of the complex silence surrounding the question of evaluation
in contemporary critical discourse – complex because it is a silence
pressurized by the unspoken force of evaluative imperative. There are
two areas of contemporary theory, however, in which this judgement
about the silencing of value may seem inappropriate. If Marxism and
feminism offer abundant evidence of the turning away from evaluation
and towards interpretation, then it has also been the case that neither of
these approaches has been able to ignore for long, or with any easy
conscience, the nagging problems of value. Arguably, Marxism arises
from and depends upon a theory of the question of economic value, a
theory which is itself based upon a powerful evaluation of the economic
conditions which it describes. This makes it very hard for Marxist
cultural theory to elide the question of value. As we shall see in chapter
7, feminist theories of culture, though less unified than Marxist theories,
are based in a similar way upon a recalcitrant refusal of dominant values,
in a way which repeatedly provokes self-consciousness about the question of value. And yet it is also striking that the question of value as
such, and in particular the question of the ways in which aesthetic value
is articulated within and against cultural and economic value more
broadly, has, until recently, been left unexplored in Marxist cultural
theory.

An exemplary instance here might be the work of Raymond Williams.
Clearly, anyone setting out to convict Williams of inattention to the
question of cultural value is going to cause some raised eyebrows, for
in one sense it is obviously the single question which nags and throbs
throughout Williams's huge, magisterial corpus. Everywhere, it seems,
from the early, passionately affirmative studies of dissentient cultural
traditions, to the foundational works on cultural studies, and the last
work on the complex sociological history and structure of the notion of
culture itself, the question of value is paramount. Indeed, Williams must

be said to have provided a kind of genealogy of cultural value, which is both rich in historical specification and theoretically supple. But his work does all of this with hardly a mention of the question of value as such. Is it not remarkable that the subtle and unceasing responsiveness to the concrete dynamics of value should have yielded no single explicit, extended discussion of the concept of value in the whole of Williams's work?

It may be replied that the immanence of value in Williams's work, as embodied, for example, in the complex, ironical reserve of his style, in which the values of community and solidarity are to be deduced from the sinuous and responsive balancing of perspectives rather than in any easy or explicit affirmation, is precisely the strength of his contribution to Marxist aesthetics. It is clearly important for Williams to resist such emphatic declarations of value in order precisely to maintain the precarious balance between the historical imagination, which refuses to take the aesthetic or the products of high culture at their own account, and the aesthetic imagination, which refuses to collapse cultural and especially artistic objects and processes into mere historical data, refuses, in short, to collapse value into fact. But the opposite effect of this immanence is that value is made ungraspable, in a certain sense unavailable for analytic discourse. For Williams, the civilizing value of the work of historical and cultural enquiry just *is*; there would be no profit in subjecting it to evaluative enquiry and, indeed, there would be no reliable language in which to perform such an act of meta-evaluation.

If Williams's work represents one, highly influential mode of Marxist cultural analysis, then the work of Terry Eagleton and Fredric Jameson may embody a rather different mode. If the profit of Williams's work is a fully fledged model for a sociology of culture, then its cost is a certain donnish insulation from the most crucial theoretical debates of the 1970s and 1980s. Eagleton and Jameson have attempted to respond much more directly than Williams to the many assaults upon the values of meaning, totality and determinable truth which have been so much in evidence during this period. In particular, these two latter theorists have responded to the grotesque bifurcation of attitudes towards the aesthetic in postmodern theory, in which the specificity of the aesthetic is either entirely liquidated in favour of some general notion of cultural representation, or grossly inflated in the Nietzschean extremity of a Deleuze or early Lyotard. Eagleton's and Jameson's responses have involved the attempt to grasp the category of the aesthetic in a fully dialectical manner, which is to say, allowing and developing the critique of what Eagleton has called the ideology of the aesthetic – the concealments, fixations and false totalizations embodied in the ideal of the aesthetic in the last couple of centuries – while simultaneously refusing to abandon the possibility of discussing artistic works and practices in terms of their value. Both Eagleton and Jameson attempt to stand at once inside and outside the question of the aesthetic, which is to say, inside and outside the question of value. This means refusing the hallucinatory authority implied by the notion of the 'cultural analyst', whose knowledge of the historical contingency of cultural values depends upon inhibiting the vulgar urge to make evaluative judgements, or discuss evaluative criteria. But at the same time, it makes the business of evaluation, whether of ideologies of the aesthetic or of specific examples of it, a tenaciously, perturbedly self-conscious act.

Eagleton and the Marxist Sublime

Eagleton's work displays a particularly stubborn determination to continue speaking of the question of value, recognizing that for a socialist critic to turn high-mindedly away from the contaminated discourse of value is actually to surrender that discourse to the right. The first emphatic stage of Eagleton's attempt to wrest the topic of value back from the brutal intuitionism of the liberal-humanist consensus in literary studies is to be found in the concluding chapter of *Criticism and Ideology* (1976), on the topic of 'Marxism and Aesthetic Value'. After limning a Machereyan 'science' of the literary text in the preceding chapters, Eagleton aims in the final chapter to provide a correspondingly scientific account of the nature of literary value. His first move is to re-enact the inaugurating moment of Marxist political economy by considering the question of value as principally a question of literary production. Eagleton carefully warns himself against the danger of ignoring the relativities of circulation and consumption, which, in the case of literary texts, must be said in some sense to dissolve the production/consumption division at the outset: 'there is no immanent value – no value which is not *transitive*. Literary value is a phenomenon which is *produced* in that ideological appropriation of the text, that "consumptional production" of the work, which is the act of reading' (*CI*, 166–7). The value of a literary text, Eagleton continues, is therefore never more (or less) than '*relational* value: "exchange value"' (*CI*, 167) rather than value in itself. This acknowledgement of the relativity of judgements is no mere subjectivism, since, for Eagleton, the contingencies of evaluation are primarily ideological, and 'the literary text is always the text-for-ideology, selected, deemed readable and deciphered by certain ideologically governed conventions of critical receptivity to which the text itself contributes' (*CI*, 167).

However, Eagleton may have given away here more than is good for his subsequent argument, which is indeed, as he has promised, an account of the production end of literary value, and correspondingly vulnerable to the criticism that it objectifies the value of particular literary texts, which are kept too far away from the vicissitudes of taste and value-construction. For Eagleton, value is produced in a literary text as a result of a characteristic effect of the aesthetic, involving 'a certain bracketing, whereby the work dissolves and distantiates the real to produce it as signification. The aesthetic is that which speaks of its historical conditions by remaining silent – inheres in them by distance and denial' (*CI*, 177). It is this suspension of direct referentiality, this interior *lapsus* in the literary work, that enables the reader to gain access into the complex ideological conjuncture from which it speaks but of which it may not speak fully. Eagleton here gives the example of Dante, whose work is valuable, he says, 'not ... because it "speaks of" an important historical era, or "expresses the consciousness" of that epoch. Its value is an effect of the process whereby the complex ideological conjuncture in which it inheres so produces (internally distantiates) itself in a play of textual significations as to render its depths and intricacies vividly perceptible' (*CI*, 177–8).

It is hard to know precisely what is being said in the second sentence here. Is it that literary texts allow a certain analytical reading of a complex ideological conjuncture, or is it rather that they permit access to a certain process of 'internal distantiation' in the literary text itself? What follows indicates that it is both at once. In the work of a writer such as Yeats, who has a tangential, adversary relation to the hegemonic bourgeois ideology of his period, 'the hegemonic formation is produced from a particular dissentient conflictual position within it, and ... the resulting problematic throws the "fault-lines" of that formation into partial relief' (*CI*, 181). Here, the value of Yeats's work clearly seems to be as some kind of symptomatic history, permitting an X-ray view of ideological conflict. At the same time, it is possible to say that, for writers such as Eliot, Hardy, Joyce and Lawrence, it is the question of textual production that predominates, since 'the ideological question is implicit in the aesthetic *problem* of how to write; the "aesthetic" – textual production – becomes a crucial, overdetermined instance of the question of those real and imaginary relations of men to their social conditions which we name ideology' (*CI*, 181).

It is not entirely clear that these two elements, the laying bare of ideological conflict, and the heightened self-consciousness of the textual
production of ideology, have the same kind of value. The first kind of
effect seems to embody the strategic value of knowing your enemy;
writing, for instance, of the ideology of conservative classical humanism
in Ben Jonson, Eagleton suggests that it 'becomes the productive instrument by which a resourceful ideological world is so "internally dis-
tantiated" as to yield up the wealth of its prejudices and perceptions' (*CI*,
186). Clearly the trove of value opened up here has nothing to do with
the productive or progressive nature of the ideologies involved; rather,
its value lies in its diagnostic usefulness for the socialist cultural
historian. However, when Eagleton goes on to compare Walter Savage
Landor with William Wordsworth, a different criterion of value seems to
emerge, one that belongs with more familiar accounts of the aesthetic.
Both Landor and Wordsworth may be said to be in full flight from
history, Eagleton says, and yet 'the contradiction and complexity of that
movement in Wordsworth's case are a condition of superior value. It is
a contradiction inscribed in the very form of Wordsworth's text: *The
Prelude* is a poem about the poet's preparation to write an epic which
turns out to be *The Prelude*' (*CI*, 187). This formal hesitation conjoins
in a significant manner with the text's insecure ideological self-
possession:

> *The Prelude* is creased and haunted by the aesthetic and ideological
> ambiguities of its moment. It is haunted by certain spiritual and historical
> possibilities, by the ghost of certain powers and values which its formal
> ideology is forced to censor; and it is in the rifts created by this radical
> lack of unity with itself that its play of meanings becomes most fertile. (*CI*,
> 187)

Eagleton's account of value has persistently activated a kind of
geomorphology, which figures the emergence of value in the seismic
contention of the earth with itself, with 'the impaction of value upon
value' (*CI*, 180), in the 'fault-lines' of ideology thrown into relief by literary texts (*CI*, 181), or their 'flexing and compacting of senses' (*CI*, 185).
Here, this seismology throws up one last, climactic instance, in the 'rifts'
opened up by *The Prelude*'s lack of unity with itself. The cumulative effect
of this train of metaphors is to suggest the obduracy of natural matter,
and its strife with some elemental force which 'bursts triumphantly
through the fault-lines' (*CI*, 180) to manifest itself in a fertile, eruptive
flow.

The primary index of this particular figure may, I think, be found earlier in the essay, in the argument that Eagleton mounts for the moral force of Marx's analysis of the contradiction between productive forces and the social relations of production. Since it derives from a claim about the nature of human beings, that they are 'capacity-producing and repro-ducing creatures' (*CI*, 175), the concept of a productive force may be seen as the unity of fact and value, says Eagleton (*CI*, 176). If this is so, then it would be impossible to take the diagnosis of the contradiction between forces and relations of production merely in a factual sense, and not to accept the moral imperative that it implies, namely the need to liberate these forces from the unjust constraints of capitalist relations of production. Elsewhere in his discussion, Eagleton characterizes the liber-ation of Marx's productive forces in terms which cohere suggestively with the metaphorical pattern of geomorphic disturbance that we have just noted. Eagleton refers to Marx's famous discussion of the aesthetics of revolutionary form in *The Eighteenth Brumaire of Louis Bonaparte* and suggests that, to forge a true revolution that would not merely repeat the forms of the past, it is necessary to rethink the very form/content oppo-sition, a rethinking which is at once a matter of politics and of aesthetics:

> For *The Eighteenth Brumaire*, it is not simply a matter of discovering the expressive or representational forms 'adequate to' the content of the social-ist revolution. It is a question of rethinking that opposition – of grasping form no longer as the symbolic mould into which content is poured, but as the 'form of the content': which is to say, grasping form as the structure of a ceaseless self-production, and so not as 'structure' but as 'structura-tion'. It is this process of continual self-excess – 'of the content go(ing) beyond the phrase' – which is for Marx the poetry of the future and the sign of communism, as it is for us the secret of the materialist analysis of the literary text. (*CI*, 184)

Seen in this way, the value of the aesthetic lies not so much in the stra-tegic insight it offers into the complex conjunctures of ideology, but in a certain proleptic enactment of Marx's 'poetry of the future', that bursting of productive forces beyond measure into utopian measurelessness. The ending of *Criticism and Ideology* reminds us emphatically that the Marxist solution to the reifications of the aesthetic is not to abolish the category, but to extend it indefinitely: 'Men do not live by culture alone: far from it. But the claim of historical materialism is that, in effect, they will. Once emancipated from material scarcity, liberated from labour, they will live in the play of their mutual significations, move in the ceaseless "excess" of freedom' (*CI*, 187). It is precisely the element of play, of instability, the suspension or problematizing of ideological value, which is the warrant of the aesthetic work's value. The metaphors of geological tension, conflict and flow enact in Eagleton's argument the aesthetic freeing of productive forces, which would represent a surpassing not only of the form/content division, but of the very structures of exchange that allow value to be thought.

The aesthetic, in this sense, seems both to constitute real, or intrinsic value, and yet also to predict the suspension, or liberation into limitless productivity, of value. Where Kant, and the tradition that he inaugurated, saw the aesthetic as representing value in itself, standing for the disinterested value of value, Eagleton proposes that the value of the aesthetic lies in its interruption or problematizing of structures of value, in a productive disablement that opens up some new, strictly inconceivable mode of constituting value: 'It is a matter of a certain curvature in the ideological space in which the texts play – a curvature produced by the impaction of value upon value, signification upon signification, form upon form' (*CI*, 180).

These arguments, fragmentary as they are in *Criticism and Ideology*, are taken up in the more richly diversified account of aesthetic value in Eagleton's *The Ideology of the Aesthetic*, and especially in the chapter on Marx. Where most discussions of the aesthetics of Marxism in the past have attempted to derive an aesthetics from Marx's political theory, Eagleton's audacious claim in *The Ideology of the Aesthetic* is that Marx's theory of value is in fact best understood in terms of the categories of nineteenth-century idealist aesthetics, and that therefore his political theory is already a kind of aesthetics. The risk with this sort of argument is that it ends up merely aestheticizing the political; but the effect of Eagleton's analysis is a reimagining of the very notion of the aesthetic in its relations with the political in a way that makes the simple homological contrast between fiction (aesthetics) and reality (politics) – on which the superstitious dread of the aesthetic among left political theorists is based – untenable.

The Ideology of the Aesthetic takes up the suggestion made at the end of *Criticism and Ideology* that Marx's politics of human liberation are essentially aesthetic, in that they are orientated towards the free and unrestricted exercise of human capacities as ends in themselves, but now gives that judgement a more specific force, in identifying in particular the liberation of the body as the source of Marx's utopian politics: 'Only when the bodily drives have been released from the despotism of abstract need, and the object has been restored from functional abstraction to sensuously particular use value, will it be possible to live aesthetically'

(*IA*, 202). The irony is that the rejoining in aesthetic theory of spirit and sense, intellect and body, form and content, is simultaneously an authentic attempt to restore the immediacy of the human body from its brutal abstraction into exchange-value and an abstract idealization which is the very sign of the sundering that it attempts to heal; the aesthetic is here both wound and cure. It is for this reason that Marx's implied association between the wholeness of the aesthetic and the immediacy of use-value is so vulnerable to the objection that it sustains the very idealism which it denounces.

Eagleton attempts to outflank this particular objection by arguing that Marx's aesthetics are in fact of two radically different kinds. In the first of these, the ideal society is indeed imagined in terms of a Romantic aesthetic of the beautiful, as an interfusion of abstract law and sensuous experience, of form and content. Eagleton again turns to *The Eighteenth Brumaire* to identify the second aesthetic form governing Marx's thought. In the reflection on the semiotics of revolutionary form to be found in that work, Eagleton finds an aesthetic not of the beautiful, but of the sublime, which is to say, an aesthetic not of the measured adaptation of form to content, but of the measureless outstripping of form by content. If previous revolutions have been governed by the aesthetics of the beautiful, attempting to contain their revolutionary content within the forms inherited from the past, Marx's vision, writes Eagleton, is of a revolution that is 'excessive of all form, out in advance of its own rhetoric. It is unrepresentable by anything but itself, signified only in its "absolute movement of becoming", and thus a kind of sublimity' (*IA*, 214).

Eagleton argues that in Marx's own work, there is a struggle between, and perhaps also a precarious synthesis of, the political aesthetics of the beautiful and the sublime; this is necessary because the Kantian notion of the beautiful 'is too static, too harmoniously organic for Marx's political purposes', while, on the other hand, the Kantian sublime is too formless, too unregulated by law. 'The condition of communism could be envisaged only by some blending of the two – by a process which has all of the sublime's potentially infinite expansiveness, but which nevertheless carries its formal law within itself' (*IA*, 217). This presents a problem. For what are the aesthetics of the blending which Eagleton proposes in this attempt to move beyond the limitations of nineteenth-century formal aesthetics, but an aesthetics of harmonious synthesis, of the reconciliation of law and impulse; in other words, the return of the reifying aesthetics of the beautiful?

What Eagleton says here of the aesthetics of the political might be extended to the question of the politics of the aesthetic. Though it is true that *The Ideology of the Aesthetic* is concerned more with investigating the force and nature of aesthetic thought, rather than with making judgements about the value of aesthetic and cultural practices in themselves, the suggestions made here and elsewhere cohere with the judgements reached in *Criticism and Ideology* fifteen years earlier. It would seem that the value of the aesthetic lies in its premonition or promise of an utterly unprecedented blending of form and content, which is nevertheless also a surpassing of the idealized and reified ways in which their resolution has been imagined hitherto in the formal aesthetics of the beautiful. What this means is that the aesthetic is both a utopian foretaste of a realm of achieved value, and a constant reminder that, for a world brutally alienated from itself by the abstractions of exchange-value, such a realm must remain unthinkable. '[I]f Marxism has maintained a certain silence about aesthetic value, it may well be because the material conditions which would make such discourse fully possible do not as yet exist', Eagleton had already declared at the end of his earlier discussion of aesthetic value (*CI*, 187). If the aesthetic of the beautiful promises a closing together of form and content, abstraction and particularity, in some all-too-imaginable synthesis, then the political aesthetics of the sublime maintain a prohibition on attempting to imagine the achievement of such a synthesis. For such aesthetic projections of perfect futures consist in a wish-fulfilling spring out of the degraded conditions of the present, which provides consolation precisely to the degree that it atrophies the will to discover the ways in which the present might realistically be led into such a future. Paradoxically, therefore, the most valuable form of political thought is that which refuses to proclaim the achievement of value, embodying its orientation towards value precisely in that work of negation or counter-valuation which is 'able to trace within the present that secret lack of identity with itself which is the spot where a feasible future might germinate – the place where the future over-shadows and hollows out the present's spurious repleteness' (*IA*, 229–30).

Eagleton's account here moves surprisingly close to that of Jean-François Lyotard, who has similarly proposed a 'politics of the sublime', a politics, this is to say, which systematically resists the premature identi-fication of reality with political utopia, the actual with the ideal. As we have already seen in chapter 5, Lyotard draws on Kant's reading of the French Revolution, which proclaimed the value of the idea of liberty for those who looked on from other countries, even in the face of the excesses of the Terror which followed the institution of the French Republic. 'As for a politics of the sublime,' declares Lyotard, 'there is none. That would only be Terror. But in politics there is an aesthetic of the sublime. The actors, the heroes of the political drama are always suspect and must always be suspected of acting out of particular and interested motives. But the sublime response manifested by the public for the drama is not suspect.'[1] Eagleton acknowledges his debt in *The Ideology of the Aesthetic* to Lyotard's characterization of the Marxist sublime; and there is indeed a certain affinity between that 'vigorously melancholic' political temperament which Lyotard at one point suggests might be the attitude of the sublime and Eagleton's own suspicion of ersatz utopias (*D*, 179).

And yet it hardly needs to be said that there is also a crucial difference between Eagleton and Lyotard. For Eagleton embraces a teleology of the sublime which Lyotard obstinately resists, which is to say, Eagleton insists that the route towards the achievement of the aesthetic condition of the sublime is through history, arguing that the great originality of Marx is to propose that an aesthetic society be produced not by bypassing the vulgar instrumentality of material life but by passing through and transforming it (*IA*, 206). The problem with poststructural-ist thinkers, according to Eagleton, is that in urging us to abandon truth and instrumental reason for the Nietzschean delights of delirium and dance, they offer a premature aestheticization which may actually forestall the achievement of an aesthetic existence for all (*IA*, 227). Of course, this account of poststructuralism does more justice to the Lyotard of *Economie libidinale* than to the less jaunty Lyotard of *The Differend*, for the latter seems to regard it as a matter of political honour to disallow utopian political thought of any kind except the rigorously impossible, and to restrict political action to a fitful fevering of resistance on the interior of an all-encompassing system of economic performativity. But Lyotard's movement from excess to asceticism may itself be a confirmation of the secret identity of premature utopianism and defeatism.

The question of the sublime has in Eagleton's argument a crucial bear-ing on that most central and yet in many ways most mysterious of Marxist concepts, use-value. For Marx, as is well known, the exploitation and alienating effects of exchange-value act to dissolve the immediacy of use-value, in which human labour produces objects which meet certain needs and are entirely consumed in meeting those needs. Use-value here seems to mean the immediate and entire equivalence between need and satisfaction. The problem is that though it is possible, even theoretically necessary, to posit forms of social existence and organization in which use-value is predominant, the concept of use-value must in some sense be unavailable to those who enjoy it. Paradoxically, it is only with the development of a single form of equivalence, capable of measuring the relative value of everything else in its terms, namely the money-form, and the consequent development of the possibility of variable exchange-value, that use-value becomes visible. Use-value becomes therefore both a vanished ideal and a utopian dream, available to consciousness only by deduction or extrapolation. Indeed, one might go even further and say that, like the sublime, use-value seems to represent a certain kind of unthinkability. For use-value embodies the paradoxical notion of a value that lies beneath or goes beyond the notion of exchange, that is, of relative estimation of all kinds. But what sort of value could this be, since the possibility of relative estimation, based as it must be on some scale of commensurability, seems to be an essential and irreplaceable part of any value?

The Marxist problem of use-value is a version of the problem of value as such, which dominates philosophy, and especially philosophy of the aesthetic, from the beginning of the nineteenth century onwards; namely, the problem of how to define or legitimate forms of absolute or transcendent value, in ways that do not depend upon structures of relativity which immediately and precisely contradict any claim to transcendence. It is for this reason that the doctrine of use-value has come under such sharp attack by those wishing to demonstrate and decry the metaphysical bases of classical Marxist theory. No attack has been more thorough-going than that mounted by Jean Baudrillard in a series of works from the early 1970s, most especially *For a Critique of the Political Economy of the Sign* (1972), *The Mirror of Production* (1973) and *L'échange symbolique et la mort* (1976).[2] Baudrillard's method is to transform the paradoxical insight that the nature of use-value becomes apparent only after the advent of exchange-value into a causal sequence. For Baudrillard, spontaneous and unmediated utility does not come before the possibility of exchange, but after it. If Marx correctly analysed the fetishism of the commodity, the manner in which the commodity effaces from itself the marks of labour and production, seeming to offer itself to the consumer in immediate autonomy, he failed to extend this analysis to the notion of use-value, which is, Baudrillard suggests, an instance of just the same fetishism. For use-value, or immediate, concrete utility, is precisely the metaphysical form in which exchange-value cloaks itself. It is a secondary effect of exchange-value, its intensification rather than its opposite. For all their natural or innate appearance, our individual and species needs are in fact always produced and sustained by what is already a semiotic system of needs. In the language of later Baudrillard, we could say that use-value is a grotesque simulacrum produced out of exchange-value. Naturally, this has serious consequences for a revolutionary socialism founded upon the idea of transcending the dominion of exchange-value:

> If the system of use value is produced by the system of exchange value as its own ideology – if use value has no autonomy, if it is only the *satellite* and *alibi* of exchange value, though systematically combining with it in the framework of political economy – then it is no longer possible to posit use value as an alternative to exchange value. Nor, therefore, is it possible to posit the 'restitution' of use value, at the end of political economy, under the sign of the 'liberation of needs' and the 'administration of things' as a revolutionary perspective. ('Beyond Use Value', *CPES*, 139)

It is all too easy to imagine a political position which would accept the critique mounted here by Baudrillard while dispensing with all its apocalyptic colouring. For is not the ideology of the free market precisely this belief that the structures of exchange will not only supply human needs in the most efficient way, but can also authentically generate those needs? But in Baudrillard's work of this period, one senses an extreme hostility to the degradations of exchange-value, a hostility which is nevertheless unable to root itself in any countervailing economic ideal. Indeed, so total is the dominion of the law of exchange over the workings of value that Baudrillard's only resistance is a resistance to the concept of value itself. This is named variously in *For a Critique of the Political Economy of the Sign* as 'ambivalence' and 'symbolic exchange', but it is the latter term that concretizes in the title of Baudrillard's most developed account of the resistance to value. Drawing heavily on Bataille's critique of positive utility and his general economy of expenditure, Baudrillard suggests that the totalitarianism of positive value is haunted everywhere by the possibility of its failure, in certain kinds of gratuity, gift-giving or glorious wastefulness:

> What we need is what is bought and sold, evaluated and chosen. What is neither sold nor taken, but only given and returned, no one 'needs.' The exchange of looks, the present which comes and goes, are like the air people breathe in and out. This is the metabolism of exchange, prodigality, festival – and also of destruction (which returns to non-value what production has erected, valorized). In this domain, value isn't even recognized. ('Desire in Exchange Value', *CPES*, 207)

The account of 'symbolic value' which is given cryptically in *For a Critique of the Political Economy of the Sign* and developed in *L'échange symbolique et la mort* is open to an objection which we have already encountered in Barbara Herrnstein Smith's critique of Bataille's economics of expenditure, that there is in fact nothing which anyone could affirm as beyond or outside the law of value which would not in that very affirmation be presented as a value relative to other things, and so fall once again under the sway of that law; nothing which could be affirmed as excessive or immeasurable which would not in that very moment constitute a kind of measure, if only the measure of excess itself.[3]

But a different kind of objection is also conceivable, which would focus on Baudrillard's point of critical departure from Marxism, the notion of use-value. For it is by no means plain that all Marxists, or even Marx himself, have adhered to the rampantly metaphysical notion of use-value assumed by Baudrillard, in which given and innate human needs are satisfied simply, immediately and in perfect reciprocity. As Douglas Kellner valuably observes, needs and their corresponding use-values are not merely natural or given for Marx, but may themselves be socially mediated and produced.[4] There are two ways of taking this. One might be that Marx's acknowledgement of the production of needs, for example in his analysis of advertizing in the *Economic and Philosophical Manuscripts of 1844*, is a hazardous anticipation within his work of precisely Baudrillard's point, that human needs and use-values are produced by the forms of exchange-value (and I think that Kellner is not sensitive enough to this particular danger in his argument). But a stronger reply to Baudrillard's critique is to be found in that entirely alternative conception of use-value articulated by Eagleton. For Eagleton, the dissolution of the dominion of exchange-value will not bring about a mere return of humanity to its pregiven, essential nature, a circling back to the primitive beginnings of history which would effectively cancel history out. Rather, the entry into use-value signifies 'the all-round liberation of a multiplicity of particular use values, where the only absolute would seem development itself ... [a] self-delighting plurality of human powers'. At this point, Eagleton insists, history might effectively *begin* (*IA*, 215). Eagleton's recognition in the discussion of Marx in *The Ideology of the Aesthetic* that the emancipation of human productive forces includes an emancipation of the capacity to create oneself anew represents a significant advance on the arguments of *Criticism and Ideology*, which had asserted in a straightforward manner the primary and irreducible value of the liberation of human productive powers. A conception of use-value as dynamically self-productive adds to the Romantic model of revolution as the simple liberation of pre-existing capacities a Habermasian sense of the need to enter in unconstrained

ways into the evaluation of those capacities, by no means all of which
may be said to be positive. In other words, the actualization of use-values
would mean the coming into being of the possibility of (r)evaluating value
itself, the possibility of forming rather than merely realizing identity.

This view of use-value undoubtedly conforms to the political aesthet
ics of the sublime rather than of the beautiful (though we need to note
that, strictly speaking, nothing could exactly *con*form to that category
which Kant defines as the *Unform*), in that it adumbrates that which is
currently unthinkable and unrepresentable. In fact, there are some striking parallels between the way in which the realm of use-value is spoken
of here, and Baudrillard's account of symbolic value. In both cases, for
example, it is necessary to define that which goes beyond exchange-value
in negative or proleptic terms, since to do otherwise would be to fall into
the trap of thinking the future in the degraded terms of the present, or
thinking the dissolution of value in terms of the positivity of currently
existing forms and criteria. For both Eagleton and Baudrillard, an acute
sense of the elastic capacity of capitalism to turn every oppositional value
to its service leads to a logic of intensification rather than of dialectical
opposition: the liberation of use-value is a matter, for Eagleton, of turning history against itself, transforming it from within; the realization of
symbolic value for Baudrillard is a matter of pushing the system of simu-
lation to the point of catastrophic collapse, of making the irreversible
law of value encounter the death or absence of value that is its only exteriority.[5] Naturally, there are also some very striking differences between
the two, notably in the fact that where, for Eagleton, the escape from
exchange-value brings about for the first time the historical possibility of
producing value under conditions of freedom, the only escape which the
Baudrillard of *L'échange symbolique et la mort* can imagine is a morbidly
exultant dissolution of all value. We might align this contrast with the
one which Eagleton himself draws between the otherwise strikingly
similar views of Marx and Nietzsche on the aim of liberating human
capacities from the historical constraints of structures of value, namely
that what Marx (Eagleton) represents as a self-transcendence which is
to be achieved by collective effort in the material world, Nietzsche
(Baudrillard) can imagine only as a purely ideal and aristocratically indi-
vidualist act of will (*IA*, 245–6).

This is especially the case since, for the later Baudrillard, the total
dominion of exchange-value includes those aesthetic and cultural realms
which, for Eagleton and others, constitute a partial, contradictory resistance to the law of the commodity. For Baudrillard, the traditionally
antagonistic spheres of the aesthetic and the industrial have collapsed

into each other; just as 'art has entered the phase of its own indefinite *reproduction*', circulating according to the sweetly delirious logic of the commodity, so conversely the sphere of production has itself become aestheticized, in its investment in the production of signs and self-reflexive images: 'Art and industry can thus exchange signs: art, in order to become a reproductive machine (Andy Warhol) without ceasing to be art, since this machine is only a sign; and production, in order to lose all social purpose and thus to verify and exalt itself at last in the hyperbolic and aesthetic signs of prestige that are the great industrial combines, the 400-meter-high business blocks and the statistical mysteries of the GNP.'[6] Where it was still possible for Baudrillard to hint, in the aftermath of May 1968, at the capacity of culture to generate resistant forms of symbolic value from within, that hope has evaporated by the time of *L'échange symbolique et la mort*. Eagleton, as we have seen, cleaves to a dialectical sense of the possibility that the aesthetic might offer, in the very midst of its subordination to the law of exchange, a point of leverage, or resistance, an underground tunnel to a desirable future. Interestingly, *The Ideology of the Aesthetic* is no longer concerned to offer such an account as a criterion for judging particular works of art, but rather as a way of grasping the positive possibilities of the aesthetic as such. What this then leaves unexplored is the whole question of how one is to judge or evaluate which particular works or cultural activities might qualify as 'aesthetic' in this embattled, yet still aspirational sense. This is really to say that many of the problems of value remain in all their old tenacity.

Eagleton's view of the ambivalence of art draws extensively from the work of the Frankfurt School, and perhaps especially from the work of Marcuse, probably the last representative of the Schillerian tradition of aesthetic Marxism, Benjamin and Adorno. And of these, it is Adorno who most emphatically and systematically elaborates the paradoxical situation of the aesthetic in contemporary developed capitalism. For Adorno, the strength of the aesthetic is precisely its incapacity; it is only the utter discrediting of art, its categorical expulsion from authority by a thoroughly instrumentalized and rationalized world, which can guarantee its continuing authenticity. If Adorno does allow us to think of the work of art, in its austere autonomy of form, as an enactment of pure use-value, then this utopian promise is systematically denied by the very enabling condition of that insight, which is precisely the powerlessness of art to intervene in the brutally reified world. If art allows a vision of non-dominative synthesis, a form of ordering which does not subordinate the sensuous particularity of the non-identical to the conceptual demands of what Adorno names 'identity-thinking', then it can do this only in a virtual and unrealizable way. Art can pose a challenge to identity-thinking only and exactly to the degree that its challenge is unreal, without practical consequence. As Jay M. Bernstein has put it, 'Art is the remainder, the result of the exclusions that allowed an autonomous economy to centre itself without the encumbrances of the claims to sensuousness or teleology (the submersion of use value by exchange value), and it is equally the periphery forever threatening and threatened by the centre.'[7] Adorno insists on the recalcitrance of this paradox, and is much more unwilling to extrapolate selectively from either its hopeful or pessimistic side than some of his commentators.

The importance of Adorno for a Marxist cultural theory concerned to reply to the challenges posed by Derridean deconstructive thought is that he anticipates many of the qualities of that thought, in his unsparing rigour of negativity, his desire to think contradiction without reducing it to identity and his enactment of the aporias of meaning in the very style and substance of theoretical writing itself, in which, as Eagleton puts it, 'each phrase must become a little masterpiece or miracle of dialectics' (*IA*, 342). But where Derrida seems to many on the left (and they are mistaken, in my view) to offer only critique without the horizon of eman-cipation, Adorno, for all his suspicion of affirmation, nevertheless still seems to embody the hope 'that we might go through the aesthetic and come out in some unnameable place on the other side' (*IA*, 360). Bernstein finds a different and more specific sort of affirmation in Adorno's aesthetic theory, drawing attention to the call to ideal solidarity or collectivity which that theory promises, the subjunctive instancing of 'a "we," a substantial community for whom the question of history can be raised again'.[8]

Jameson and Utopia

No writer has argued more emphatically for an attention to the utopian orientation of the aesthetic than Fredric Jameson. If some of the appar-atus of interpretation in *The Political Unconscious* (1981) now seems rather creaky and laborious – the notion of the four interpretative levels, the Greimasian semiotic rectangle, retrieved here from Jameson's *The Prison-House of Language*, dusted down and set dutifully whirring – and if the ambition which this apparatus subserves of bringing to visibility the ideological unconscious of literary works seems to express a more opulent confidence in the powers of unifying interpretation than is now current even among Marxist theorists, then the principal stake of this work, that the political unconscious of literary texts consists not merely of guiltily repressed political knowledge, but also of a scarcely articulable aspiration towards the emancipation of value, retains its considerable and uncircumventable force. Acknowledging, as so many others have done, the power of Walter Benjamin's dictum in *Theses on the Philosophy of History* that 'there is no document of civilization which is not at one and the same time a document of barbarism', Jameson nevertheless believes that it is possible to read this dialectical formula dialectically, and to argue that 'the effectively ideological is also, at the same time, necessarily Utopian' (*PU*, 286). Jameson is therefore prepared to deploy a 'positive hermeneutic' with regard to even the most degraded and dominative of cultural forms – say, the art and mythology of Fascism – in order to make visible in them the 'symbolic enactment of collective unity' (*PU*, 296), the utopian aspiration towards the transcending of the very divisions which are officially enforced in those cultural forms.

So, like Adorno, Jameson reads the autonomizing features of modernist art as both an alienation and a utopian hunger. He detects in the work of Conrad, for example, a strategy of aestheticization, in the intense, hallucinatory highlighting of the individual senses, especially that of sight. This strategy of aestheticization arises historically as the hypertrophic effect of an actual partition of the senses from instrumental reason. Driven out by a money economy based upon strict criteria of calculable return, sense perception 'can only reorganize itself into a new and semi-autonomous activity, one which produces its own specific objects, new objects that are themselves the result of a process of abstraction and reification' (*PU*, 229). The resulting artistic forms, such as impressionism, or the pure abstraction of colour, or, in this case, the intense and mysterious sensuality of Conrad's descriptive style, are simultaneously the embodiment of the pitiful dissociation of the senses from social life as a whole, and the enactment of 'a Utopian vocation' (*PU*, 230), a counter-value which aims to transcend the regime of commodities and profit.

The compacting of the negative with the positive hermeneutic in the manner of reading proposed by Jameson, the interweaving of ideology-critique and the discernment of utopia, represents a specifically Marxist version of the familiar problem of fact and value in interpretation. For such a dual focus requires not only a functional analysis of the ways in which texts cohere with ideology, but also what Jameson calls a '*collective-associational* or *communal*' mode of interpretation (*PU*,

296), in other words, one which measures the value of the work as well as its manner of functioning. Yet here there is a problem. For Jameson, as for Eagleton, it is not possible to speak unequivocally of value when one is dealing with cultural objects so enmeshed in social and economic structures in which relations of value are systematically distorted and estranged. Jameson sets himself this riddle – 'how is it possible for a cultural text which fulfills a demonstrably ideological function ... to embody a properly Utopian impulse, or to resonate a universal value inconsistent with the narrower limits of class privilege which inform its more immediately ideological vocation?' (*PU*, 288).

One answer to this riddle would seem to be that any affirmation of value must be accompanied by and indeed conduce to a Marxist version of Nietzsche's 'transvaluation of all values', in which the simple ethics of yes and no, good and evil, give way to an account of the historical determinations of all such ethical structures. But the larger answer is that it is in fact impossible to go beyond the ideological logic of class-based good and evil until the arrival of some wholly new mode of collective thought and being. 'In this sense,' writes Jameson, 'to project an imperative to thought in which the ideological would be grasped as somehow at one with the Utopian, and the Utopian at one with the ideological, is to formulate a question to which a collective dialectic is the only conceivable answer' (*PU*, 286–7). In other words, it will be possible to affirm value as such only once the dominion of exchange-value has been gone beyond. Until that time, all values are provisional and ambivalent, all ethical categories are partial and dishonest.

We can see, therefore, that Jameson is here working with a notion of value which partakes of the structure of the sublime specified by Eagleton. To represent value is always to misrepresent it, since, it seems, the very structures of value which dominate our thought are what prevent us from apprehending the nature of value in itself. The only way to conceive the liberation of use-value is as an absolute surpassing of exchange-value. This conceptual structure seems to compel simultaneously the orientation towards value in *The Political Unconscious* and a certain inhibition of the topic. Although the long final chapter of the book is concerned almost exclusively with the question of value in Conrad's work, and especially in *Lord Jim*, it is notable that this question is displaced into the thematic content of the work. Jameson's starting point is that Conrad's work comes into being at a moment when the problem of the value of human activity presents itself with a particular intractability. In this situation, the social divisions between activity and value, or, as one might equally say, between labour and profit, wrought by the logic of exchange, produce something like a systematic aporia in the text of *Lord Jim*, as it struggles to produce that 'unimaginable and impossible resolution and *Aufhebung*; the union of activity and value, of the energies of Western capitalism and the organic immanence of the religion of precapitalist societies' (*PU*, 255). Jameson maps *Lord Jim*'s baffled but obstinately renewed enquiry into the condition of value on to the semiotic rectangle of A. J. Greimas mentioned above, using it to generate a quadrilateral *combinatoire* of possibilities, in which the textual instances of value, activity, non-value and non-activity, as well as their mediating terms, are discovered in *Lord Jim* and seated in their places around the rectangle: hence, the 'deck-chair sailors' mentioned scornfully by Jim mediate between non-value and non-activity, the passive pilgrims on the *Patna* mediate between value and non-activity, Gentleman Brown embodies the fusion of activity and non-value, while Lord Jim himself stands for the (idealized) mediation of the primary terms, activity and value.

However, if this procedure allows Jameson to read the text's aspiration to overcome the antinomy of activity and value, its net result is also to show how impossible such an overcoming must be. Afflicted by the division of value from life, the text can only crave elaborately for their rejoining, while the hermeneutic that brings this process to visibility in turn has no choice but to shadow it, in all the intricacy of its thwarting. The value of this work, even on its good or utopian side, can be read only as negative prolepsis, as value-towards-value. As such, there is a strange reduplication in Jameson's own inability to generate a here-and-now hermeneutic reconciliation of the analytic and the evaluative, the ideological and the utopian, of the problematic gulf between activity and value which he analyses in Conrad.

The reason for this disablement may be found in the short but telling section in which Jameson situates *Lord Jim*'s enquiry into value with regard to other contemporary instances of this enquiry. The most important and representative names for Jameson are those of Nietzsche and Weber, both of whom, he says, mount an unprecedented enquiry into the nature of values and value as such, attempting to project a standpoint of absolute exteriority to the turbulent, 'inner-worldly' realm of values in order to allow, respectively, the 'transvaluation of all values' and the development of 'value-free science'. Jameson wishes to specify the historical determinants which make such a problem manifest and articulable in the first place. In order to do this, he adopts what is of course a Weberian kind of analysis, which centres on the secularization of life under capitalism, and especially the breaking up of traditionally organized societies with the extension of market capitalism. The result of this is that 'for the first time in any general or irreversible way, the realm of values becomes problematical, with the result that it can, for the first time, be isolated as a realm in itself and contemplated as a separate area of study' (*PU*, 249). Jameson goes on to describe in more detail this superseded realm of traditional society, beginning the description as a formally distanced paraphrase of the Weberian attitude towards such societies, but moving imperceptibly into agreement with it. In a traditional or precapitalist society, the problem of value in the modern sense cannot arise, since in such societies 'each activity is symbolically unique, so that the level of abstraction upon which they could be compared with one another is never attained: there is no least-common-denominator available to compare iron-welding or the preparation of curare with basket-weaving or the making of bread or pots' (*PU*, 249–50).

The problem of value arises precisely when it becomes possible to compare and evaluate these activities relative to each other, with the development of such a common denominator; for Marx, of course, this common denominator is equivalent labour-power and its representative, the money-form. Jameson wishes to stress here the paradoxical nature of the notion of value, which, he says, 'becomes visible as abstraction and as a strange afterimage on the retina, only at the moment in which it has ceased to exist as such ... [T]he study of value, the very idea of value, comes into being at the moment of its own disappearance and of the virtual obliteration of all value by a universal process of instrumentalization' (*PU*, 250, 251). What is striking about this analysis – and by this point Jameson's own position has clearly begun to articulate itself through the paraphrase of Weber and the Frankfurt School – is a certain sleight of hand in it. The notion of a movement from precapitalist structures of value to capitalist instrumentalization of value becomes the myth of a Fall; instead of a mutation in the structure of value, we now have the loss of value 'as such'. As with most such myths, the Fall here promises a redemption, namely the freeing of use-value, as a realm of pure and uncontaminated singularity and incommensurable immediacy, from the ghastly effects of exchange-value, in which, because everything can be exchanged for everything else, nothing may really be said to be worth anything in itself. It is just this impossibility of authentically conducting the question of value under the conditions of exchange-value which entails for Jameson that deferral or displacement of the question of value until a future in which value will have returned to the world. The provisional value of this gesture (which is compromised precisely because it works by substitution and deferral) is its own recognition of the impossibility of value.

There is, however, reason to suspect that, in defining value so utterly and absolutely in terms which go beyond exchange-value, Jameson is in fact evacuating it of all force or human relevance. Far from embodying the possibility of value *as such*, the universe of absolute incomparability which Jameson sees as coming before and, presumably, after the era of exchange-value, would in fact allow for no possibility of value *at all*, since a universe in which nothing could be compared with anything else by any shared scale of measurement would be a universe of absolute inertness, or valuelessness. The idealist notion of use-value which Jameson here inherits has an odd similarity to that postmodern condition so famously described by Lyotard. As has been argued already, Lyotard's insistence on the value and necessity in postmodernity of absolute incommensurability is radically self-contradictory, since the very recognition of incommensurability, let alone its positive estimation, in itself constitutes a kind of measurement according to a shared scale.

Jameson's mistake here would seem to lie in mistaking the particular and historically limited forms of exchange-value for exchangeability as such. For exchange-value has two quite contrasting aspects, the one being the multiplicity and indeterminacy of all values, the other being the fixity and singularity of the scale of value; indeed, it is the latter which enables the former. Jameson takes one side of the dialectic of exchange-value and inflates it at the expense of the other, emphasizing the problem of indeterminacy, and the corresponding desire for the fixity of value, at the expense of the restriction on evaluative forms and activity represented by the narrowing force of economic exchange-value. In the course of her desperately dense but still highly suggestive discussion of the question of value in Marxism, Gayatri Spivak articulates a theory of the textual nature of Marx's theory of value which, I think, coheres with this critique of Jameson. Believing that, for Marx, use-value is not a foundation or historical destination, since 'it is use-value that puts the entire textual chain of Value into question', Spivak suggests that a Marxist 'horizon of full realization [of value] must be indefinitely postponed'.[9] She offers instead 'the pluralized apocalypse of the practical moment, in our particular case the set of ideology-critical, aesthetic-troping, economically-aware performative or operational value-judgement'. In conscious contrast to Jameson's positive notion of fulfilled or liberated value, Spivak suggests that 'the practical moment is not a "fulfillment." In the pluralized apocalypse, the body does not rise.'[10]

Jameson is followed by a number of contemporary Marxist cultural analysts, who have responded to the embrace of indeterminacy on the part of poststructuralist thought with an overcompensation on the side of fixed or determinate value. An example here might be David Harvey, whose recent critique of postmodern theory relies too heavily on the analogy it draws between the hyper-relativity of value in advanced global capitalism and the postmodern aesthetics of slippage and drift, surface and instantaneity.[11] The 'unitary principle' of late modernism and postmodernism, which in this respect are continuous for Harvey, is Marx's notion of 'value in motion'. It is, of course, the irresistible reduction of all forms of value to serial exchangeability by means of the money-form which enables this extraordinary mobility of values in modernity. Harvey's distinctive contribution has been to point out the ways in which the revolutionary compression of space by advanced capitalism (which Harvey defines as the reduction of space to time), combines with capitalism's attempt to cope with the chronic problems of over-accumulation by compressing time, especially increasing the rate of turnover, to produce a crucial involution in the sphere of value. For the use of the credit and banking system to create profit, by means of betting on or discounting the future (as, for example, in currency dealings, bond markets and futures markets), puts money itself, the universal medium of exchange, into doubt, drawing it into what Marx referred to as the 'general corruption' of exchange and speculation. As Harvey points out, this drawing into exchange of the very medium of exchange creates 'a breakdown of money as a secure means of representing value', which is to say, radical uncertainty as to the 'value of value' itself (*CP*, 298, 106–7). Aesthetic-cultural practice has an interesting relation to this. Harvey suggests that the rapid expansion of capital into the cultural sphere is one of the most striking ways in which capitalism can harness the future, by shortening the time-scale of consumption and accelerating the cycles of need and desire in fashion (*CP*, 285), in a process of scarcely regulated volatility. Harvey sees a pretty faithful relation between this accelerated indeterminacy of value, in which 'the central value system, to which capitalism has always appealed to validate and gauge its actions, is dematerialized and shifting, time horizons are collapsing, and it is hard to tell what space we are in when it comes to assessing causes and effects, meanings or values' (*CP*, 298) and the forms of postmodernist culture, with their emphasis on surface, instantaneity and schizoid drift. But if postmodernist art and culture are primarily a reflection or enactment of the dissolution of the value of value, then, at the same time, certain parts of the aesthetic-cultural realm, especially the art market, can function in precisely the opposite way. For Harvey, the art market can be seen as a guarantee of long-term security amid the general flux of an inflationary era, such that the commercialization of cultural production may be seen not only as an attempt to accelerate profits, but also as an attempt 'to store value under conditions where the usual money forms were deficient' (*CP*, 298).

The contradiction here, which is undoubtedly a contradiction in the situation Harvey describes as well as in his argument, means that the commercialization of culture is both a means of discounting the future into the present, of accelerating time, and a means of sustaining the present into the future, of decelerating time. This relates closely to a complex dichotomy within twentieth-century cultural forms to which Harvey devotes considerable space. On the one side, Harvey suggests, the modernist response to the increasing relativity of value is the search for forms of mythological permanence, of fixed and timeless value; such reactionary modernism, of which Heidegger's philosophy of Being (though in a carefully whittled-down form) is taken to be a representative instance, resists temporal transience by fetishized spatialism, by an appeal to the earth and the destiny of place (*CP*, 35, 207–9). Against this form of spatialized aestheticism must be set the modernist (and subsequently postmodernist) embrace of flux, ephemerality and speed, as expressed all the way from Charles Baudelaire to Paul Virilio. Of course, these two aspects of modernism are held together in a systematic unity, which ultimately derives from the theory of exchange-value itself, and is thus enacted in the very form of the commodity, which, at least for Terry Eagleton, is 'a kind of grisly caricature of the authentic artefact, at once reified to a grossly particular object and virulently anti-material in form, densely corporeal and elusively spectral at the same time' (*IA*, 208). In Harvey's terms, this produces an uncomfortable and inauthentic choice between earth and air: culture as 'fictitious capital', in Marx's interesting phrase, as speeded-up time, is part of the art of the ether, of an airborne aesthetics as opposed to a grounded ethics; but culture as grounding is a fetishism, a denial of time which can become an equivalent aestheticization.

Running through Harvey's account is a desire to affirm the possibility of value in itself, the use-value posited by Marx, though it seems this can never articulate itself in forms which are not instantly alienated into one or other of these aestheticisms. For the analysis of the systematic interinvolvement of earth and air in postmodernity is so strong in Harvey's work that it actually compromises his own attempted solutions. The protest against what Harvey calls 'the shift from ethics to aesthetics as [a] dominant value system', against the aestheticizing of ethical issues,

for example in the deployment of images of urban poverty and home-
lessness as mere 'atmosphere' or cultural style in certain postmodern
films, represents a rejection of only one side of the aesthetic dichotomy
of modernism, the aesthetics of air and space. But it relies repeatedly on
the language and concepts of rooted, foundational value which Harvey's
own account has discredited as belonging to a different, reifying
aesthetic.[12] It is a language which obsessionally and apparently unselfconsciously sets grounding, depth, radicality and foundation against the
airy insubstantiality or miasmatic opacity of the cultural, speaking of 'the
invariant elements and relations that Marx defined as fundamental to any
capitalist mode of production', which are 'omni-present beneath all the
surface froth and evanescence, the fragmentations and disruptions, so
characteristic of present political economy' (*CP*, 187, 179). In insisting, as
he does, that 'cultural forms are firmly rooted in the daily circulation
process of capital' (*CP*, 299), Harvey is not choosing the ethical over the
aesthetic, but submitting the ethical to that aesthetic of rooting which his
own analysis has identified as the hallucinatory epiphenomenon of the
'circulation process of capital'.

    The result is a condemnation of relativity as such, rather than the
particularly commodified, regularized forms of relativity that result from
the narrow domination of economic interests in the marketing of global
culture. As we have seen, Jameson too is drawn towards a utopian
account of value that, by attempting to go beyond exchange as such
rather than effecting a transvaluation or catastrophic unconstraining of
exchange from subordination to one code or form, wishes value away
into a strictly unattainable future. Eagleton too, though he falls victim
less often to the ruses of use-value, nevertheless adopts something of the
aestheticizing idealism against which his work is otherwise aimed, in
his recurrent attraction to the Schillerian rather than, shall we say, the
Nietzschean side of Marxist aesthetics. This leads him too often to
conceive a revolutionary aesthetic utopia in terms of achieved ideals of
wholeness, in the healing of body and spirit, the union of subject and
object, the blending of the beautiful and the sublime, the reconciliation
of universal and particular, the conjoining of fact and value. If Eagleton
is right in his demand that we abandon bad or imaginary utopias in
favour of the projects of emancipation that will make possible and actual
the good utopia which will enable history to begin, then he is surely
mistaken in seeking to orientate the discursive-productive powers that
socialism strives to liberate towards such forms of wholeness, for this
risks falling back into the aesthetic ideology which has so stiflingly reified
Marxist theory of value. Rather than setting the false wholeness of

aesthetic ideology against the authentic wholeness of that which lies beyond exchange-value, socialism needs to begin the long work of abandoning the ideal of wholeness altogether – although in full and dialectical awareness that to abandon wholeness altogether would be a paradoxical impossibility, since total abandonment is a kind of wholeness too. But, if both Jameson and Eagleton fail to recognize that they are wishing themselves beyond the problem of value, rather than critically and transformatively inhabiting that problem, it is nevertheless possible and necessary to read in the conceptual contortions induced in their work by the problem of value, the first move beyond reification and fixation into the productive possibilities of the unconstrained evaluation of value, not in any paradise of whole meanings or achieved values, but rather in the intensification of that very 'impaction of value upon value, signification upon signification' (*CI*, 180) which their different forms of critique attempt to resolve.

NOTES

1   Lyotard, 'Post-Script on the Terror and the Sublime', in *Le Postmoderne expliqué aux enfants*, p. 113 (my translation).
2   Jean Baudrillard, *For a Critique of the Political Economy of the Sign; The Mirror of Production*, trans. Mark Poster (St Louis: Telos Press, 1975); *L'échange symbolique et la mort* (Paris: Gallimard, 1976).
3   See Smith's objection to Baudrillard's symbolic exchange in precisely these terms (*CV*, 215).
4   Douglas Kellner, *Jean Baudrillard: From Marxism to Postmodernism and Beyond* (Cambridge: Polity Press, 1989), pp. 35–6.
5   Jean Baudrillard, 'Symbolic Exchange and Death', trans. Charles Levin, in *Selected Writings*, ed. Mark Poster (Cambridge: Polity Press, 1988), pp. 123–4.
6   Ibid., p. 146.
7   Jay M. Bernstein, 'Aesthetic Alienation: Heidegger, Adorno, and Truth at the End of Art', in *Life after Postmodernism*, ed. Fekete, p. 111.
8   Ibid., p. 116.
9   Gayatri Chakravorty Spivak, 'Scattered Speculations on the Question of Value', in *In Other Worlds: Essays in Cultural Politics* (New York and London: Methuen, 1987), pp. 162, 175.
10 Ibid., p. 175.
11 David Harvey, *The Condition of Postmodernity*.
12 For more extended commentary on David Harvey's work, see my article 'Between Earth and Air: Value, Culture and Futurity', *Block* (forthcoming, 1992).

7

Feminism and Value:
Ethics, Difference, Discourse

Feminism is unthinkable apart from the question of value. As an activity of critique, feminism involves the tireless work of revaluation, concerned as it is with the identification, inversion or diversification of patriarchal values, and, in general, with resisting that devaluation of the female so angrily defined by Ursula le Guin when she says that 'we are told by their deafness, by their stone ears, that our experience, the life experience of women is not valuable to men – therefore not valuable to society, to humanity'.[1] As deeply interested critique, feminism must also always involve the formation or affirmation of counter-values; as Kate Full-brook has recently written, 'no variety of feminism defines its purpose, or makes its demands for access to justice or power, without an appeal to values' (*FW*, 2). So only a fool, it seems, could accuse feminism of contributing to that evaporation of the question of value which is so typical of contemporary theory, since, like Marxist critique, feminism is permeated by the question of value.

And yet there is a sense in which the very urgency of the tasks of re-evaluation with which feminism has concerned itself, in the academic disciplines and beyond, has made for a curious inattention to the question of value as such and reluctance to theorize it. (This may have something to do with the fact that the lines of force in feminism have hitherto pointed from the political world inwards to the academy rather than outwards from it, thus perhaps discouraging the excesses of self-reflexion characteristic of other forms of critical theory.) Where, in Marxist critique, the question of value remains a central theoretical issue, feminist critique has concerned itself more locally and pragmatically with the analysis of values as such, avoiding, as it were, the move from the imma-nent to the transcendent. A recent example of this might be Carey Kaplan and Ellen Cronan Rose's *The Canon and the Common Reader* (1990), a meticulous and empirically dense account of the processes of canon-formation and change in the US literary academy, which curiously never extends its criticisms of the gender exclusions of the literary canon into a theoretical account of the processes and value of canonicity. It is not that the book lacks an evaluative dimension; for its concluding words make the position of its authors plain:

> Endorsing, then, openendedness and questioning, oscillation rather than dialectic, reluctantly eschewing the myth of progress, we conclude with the hope that our moment is one of the more expansive and humane episodes in the process, complex and dynamic, by which humans make culture.[2]

It is hard to imagine anyone who would not share the general approval of expansiveness, tolerance and dynamism voiced here. But in the absence of an argument which considers the nature of such values and their relationship to feminism, their affirmation remains a kind of formality.

Another, very different example of the priority of affirming value over theoretically exploring it is Mary Daly's *Gyn/Ecology* (1979), despite the fact that its subtitle promises an investigation into 'the metaethics of radical feminism'. Daly suggests at the beginning of her book that feminist 'metaethics' must subject the ethical and evaluative structures of patriarchal civilization and history to remorseless critique, in order to reveal the 'background of the background' of Western and Eastern ethical systems in male domination, exploitation and murderous cruelty (*G/E*, 12). But the definition of metaethics provided by Daly is a curious one. If the prefix 'meta-' suggests some movement of a discourse into a higher logical level, enabling it to stand apart from and above its own operations, it also signifies a residual, usually problematic doubling. A metacritique differs from a critique in that it must share a certain substance with what, in itself, it subjects to critique. Just as a metanarrative is a narrative about other narratives, and a metacommentary is a commentary upon commentary, so, whatever the mutation it wrought in the sphere of ethics, a metaethics would have still to be considered as a kind of ethics. But it is just this reduplication which Daly's approach seems phobically to refuse, for she wishes to distinguish absolutely a radical feminist metaethics from the 'boundless boringness' and onanistic self-absorption of male theory about ethical theory: 'Gyn/Ecology is hardly "metaethical" in the sense of masturbatory meditations by ethicists on their own emissions. Rather, we recognize that the essential omission of these emissions is of our own life/freedom. In the name of our life/freedom, feminist metaethics O-mits seminal omissions' (*G/E*, 13). Despite the fact that at one point Daly even suggests that, in relation to male metaethics, 'gynography is meta-metaethical' (ibid.), her desire for absolute decontamination from the values which are subjected to critique seems to imply a 'spring into free space ... [in which] the phallocratic categorizations of "good" and "evil" no longer apply' (*G/E*, 12). But, in affirming that there is no possibility of congress between, or even a common ethical scale to relate, corrupt male values and the values of radical feminism, Daly simultaneously exalts and undermines the value of what she proposes, since to deny any relationship of exchange between male and female values is to deprive oneself of any way of measuring the superiority, or even the relative desirability, of the latter. In fact, what Daly calls metaethics are really powerfully and passionately argued *alternative values*, counterposed to, but not in any sense incommensurable with, patriarchal values. Again: the commensurability of feminist or female values with patriarchal or male values does not imply reducibility of one to the other, but only the possibility of evaluating them relative to each other. In this and in other respects, Daly's metaethics resembles the 'transvaluation of all values' deceitfully promised by Nietzsche, in whose work the alleged movement 'beyond' good and evil comes down in the end to the installation of an alternative set of goods or ethical invari-ables – power, ecstasy and virile self-creation over truth, reason and the collective good. For Daly, 'Gyn/Ecological metaethics ... functions to affirm the deep dynamics of female be-ing ... Refusing their assimilation, we experience our Autonomy and Strength. Avoiding their elimination we find our original Be-ing. Mending their imposed fragmentation we spin our Original Integrity' (*G/E*, 13, 423). Indeed, the danger that, by refusing to engage critically with one's precursors, one may end up unconsciously repeating their errors, is demonstrated in the fact that Daly not only reproduces Nietzsche's strategies of transvaluation, but also the flagrantly misogynistic values of power and self-making on which Nietzsche relies; there is an authentically Nietzschean smack, for example, about Daly's suspicion of what she calls the 'tyranny of toler-ance [which] is often the source of the silencing/erasure of strong-minded Hags' (*G/E*, 381) – the mythical figure of the Hag here playing the part of the *Überweib*.

Some of the problems with Daly's attempt to generate a purely or distinctively female system of ethical values recur in the debate about the nature and possibility of a female or feminist aesthetic. The problem here seems to be one of how to imagine a way of transcending patriarchal norms and systems of aesthetic value without denying to oneself all evaluative terms whatsoever – or, to put it the other way round, how to affirm the value of female art and cultural practice without drawing on systems of aesthetic evaluation that must be regarded as patriarchal. A recent example of the necessity of rethinking norms of value even as one employs them, and the difficulties attendant upon not doing so, is furnished by Christine Battersby's *Gender and Genius* (1989). The book offers an impressive and convincing history of the concept of genius in Western thought from Aristotle onwards, showing how the concept effects a double exclusion of women; first of all by a logic of denial in which woman is systematically defined as the frame, context or (alternatively inhibiting and fecundating) ground against which the self-creating artist–genius is figured, and secondly, since the late eighteenth century, by a logic of appropriation that curiously stresses the capacity of the individual male genius to *include* the feminine in itself. Battersby offers ample evidence of the need for a revaluing of the evaluative category of the genius that has operated as a principal cultural force of patriarchy. At the same time, her book is curiously tentative in the approach it makes, as her subtitle puts it, 'towards a feminist aesthetics'. Though she criticizes two other feminist revisionists of aesthetic value, Roszika Parker and Griselda Pollock, because in their *Old Mistresses* (1981) 'there is ... no distinctively female perspective on art: a feminist aesthetics has to accept the values of a patriarchal society, and merely deconstruct these standards from within',[3] Battersby's own version of feminist aesthetics is surely vulnerable to precisely the same charge; the fact that it 'uses cultural history to validate a feminist aesthetics that renders visible, interprets and also evaluates the achievements of great, individual women artists' means that it cleaves to the very category of genius which it so thoroughly discredits.[4]

Feminist discomfort over the question of value has sometimes taken the form of a simple refusal of the concept. One extreme example here is Christine Delphy's bitter, hilarious attack on Annie Leclerc's *Parole de Femme* (1974), a book which had argued that the principal task for feminism was to revalue all those forms of female and especially domestic labour which patriarchy held in such contempt. The ease with which Leclerc is able to reverse the social valencies of cooking, sweeping and nappy-changing, proclaiming them to be 'a rare delight, a form of work akin to ecstasy, of supreme value, as valuable as life itself',[5] seems to reduce politics to rhetoric and positive thinking – as though, for example, the worst thing about being thrown into gaol as a political prisoner were being forced to succumb to society's oppressively negative evaluations of the experiences of confinement, malnourishment and torture. 'Taking the effect (the devaluation) for the cause (exploitation) ... the analysis implies that we must change *not the reality of* women's lives but the subjective evaluation of this reality', writes Delphy (PA, 83). In arguing purely about the perceived worth of women's work, Leclerc never touches on the question of why it is that women's work should have been identified with unpaid domestic labour in the first place. Thus, in ignoring the material conditions of women's exploitation, writes Delphy, Leclerc reproduces rather than dismantles ideology, since 'the reversal of causality – the belief that the ideological superstructure (the devaluation of women) is the cause and not the effect of the social structure – is not one idealist interpretation among others: it is the dominant ideology itself' (PA, 86). Indeed, Leclerc not only fails to get to the root of women's exploitation, her lauding of the life-giving essence of woman also reproduces the very male evaluative structures she deplores: 'While Leclerc's book strives to revalue women's procreative functions, it also strives to imprison us in them: to reduce our being, our pleasures, our value (and even our whole value, "The undeniable, original value of woman", the quality of life-possessing, etc.) to them' (PA, 91).

Delphy's attack on Leclerc's line of argument (though it must be said that the latter is scarcely typical of contemporary feminist theory) may perhaps serve as a useful warning against the dangers of turning politics into rhetoric, by abstracting the question of value from material conditions. However, Delphy is not above a bit of rhetorical artifice herself. For where at one moment she claims an absolute distinction between value (as ideological superstructure) and fact (in the economic infrastructure), she can claim at another that value is intrinsically or objectively part of the latter, arguing that 'it is the relations of production within which a task is done which explain, simultaneously, its subjective interest and its objective (i.e. its social) value' (PA, 95). But such a view encounters all the problems attaching notoriously to the notion of an 'objective value' (including, for example, the puzzling possibility that a value could exist without ever being acknowledged by any individual human or collective being whatsoever). If the relations of production which determine the lowly status of domestic work are absolutely determining, then it is hard to know where the critical-evaluative impulse comes from which rejects those relations of production as unjust. Clearly, the question of value exerts a residual, and here untheorized, force in any critique such as Delphy's.

However, there are signs that in recent work in feminist studies the question of value and the nature of a feminist transvaluation of value is taking on a new prominence and urgency. Some of these theoretical debates concern and are stimulated by a desire to clarify the position of feminism in relation to the various mutations in the valuing of value characteristic of what is called postmodernism (though feminism is itself surely one of the most important of these mutations). Others connect with the renovated debate in feminism (and beyond) about the nature of ethical bonds and prescriptions. As with Marxist theory, these debates in feminist theory have also brought the question of the ethical and the political into close and complex conjuncture with the question of cultural and aesthetic value.

Feminism, Postmodernism, Enlightenment

Is feminism properly to be thought of as an extension of the activity of enlightened critique associated with modernism and embodied in movements such as Marxism? Is it, this is to say, an elaboration of the claims of foundational reason characteristic of most forms of critique of this kind, an extension of the belief that reason enables us to distinguish the true from the false, fact from illusion, and real from false or degraded values? Or is feminism to be associated rather with an entirely other evaluation of value, one suggesting not the inherence but the inherent indeterminacy of value? In which case, is feminism then not more authentically on the side of a ceaseless reinvention of values without any attempt at grounding or ultimate legitimation, without any attempt to distinguish an ethical or evaluative bottom line? A particular way which this last question has been posed in feminist thought is with regard to the insistent problem of identity. If foundational values derive their legitimacy from the idea of the ontological identity of all human beings (all human beings are equal because all partake universally in human nature), and if the value of identity can be shown to be in collusion with certain insistent forms of cultural degradation of women, then surely feminism cannot stand on the ground of identity to protest against its effects? Hence the argument within and around feminism about the ethics and politics of difference. Is a feminist system of values or critique of values possible that does not ground itself in assumptions about the nature or identity of women and men? Is it possible (or desirable) to imagine a transvaluation of patriarchal values founded not on allegedly higher or more inclusive values, but on pure transvaluation itself, on the mobile and recursive differentiality of difference, rather than on systems of differentiation which may be shown in the end to be distributed by and in the service of a patriarchal notion of the same? Should (or can) feminism partake of a form of Enlightenment critique which itself seems to be part of the problem of oppression; and if not, what form of critique would it be that abandoned or surpassed the forms of critique themselves? One might pose this as a problem of transcendence; if transcendence as an ethico-political creed is invalidated, then how are feminists to transcend transcendence, except by a reversion to an immanence which seems to be complicit with everything that provoked the critique of transcendence in the first place?

Some of these alternatives have been exemplified and tested in recent feminist work. Jane Flax, for example, has influentially argued for the centrality of feminism within the critical discourses currently gathered together under the rubric of postmodernism. If the Enlightenment values of modernity are the stability of the self, the objectivity and universality of reason, the attainability of absolute Truth and the transparency of language, then, argues Flax, 'feminist notions of the self, knowledge, and truth are too contradictory to those of the Enlightenment to be contained within its categories'.[6] Instead of trying to transcend the partiality and relativity of values in the contemporary world, feminism should attempt 'to further decenter the world ... Feminist theories, like other forms of postmodernism, should encourage us to tolerate and interpret ambivalence, ambiguity, and multiplicity.'[7] Flax proposes, in other words, a form of the transcendent immanence offered proleptically in the work of Lyotard and other theorists of postmodern value; a transvaluation of the values of reason, truth and equality not in the name of higher or more authentic versions of those values, but for the purposes of transvaluation itself. The result of such a transvaluation (though it is hard to know how one could possibly tell when such a process was ever complete enough to judge of its result) would be not a more orderly and rational world, but a reality which appeared 'even more unstable, complex, and disorderly than it does now'.[8]

Flax concentrates usefully the claims of a number of different feminist theorists, including Kristeva, Cixous and Irigaray (to name those most influential in Britain and the US) who argue what seems to be the paradoxical value of the fluid indeterminacy of value, rooted precisely upon depthlessness, identified with the instability of all identity, and involving the total rejection of all totalities. If this form of feminist utopian critique would indeed seem immune from contamination by the discredited, violently exclusive structures and systems of value characteristic of male universalism, then, like other examples of such postmodern ultraleftism, it falters precisely because of insufficient attention to its own evaluative impulses, which is to say, it is inattentive to the structure of intense ethical paradox which characterizes it. Such a critique, as evidenced, perhaps, in Kristeva's 'The Ethics of Linguistics', proposes an ethics of the dissemination of all ethics based upon customary solidities and solidarities, but without offering at the same time any account of how one might recognize, develop, institutionalize, sustain and protect such an ethics, and without offering an other than implicit claim for the value of such transvaluation. It is true that in later work, and in an unsystematic and rather left-handed fashion, Kristeva has suggested that a female ethics of dispersion ought not to fall into the unbridled and, to that degree, collusive negativity which, as Drucilla Cornell and Adam Thurschwell have noted, 'finds itself reinscribed in the monological value system that it opposes, effacing the otherness of the other in whose name the ethic was promulgated' ('Feminism, Negativity, Intersubjectivity', *FC*, 153). Far from being naturally or constitutively on the side of negativity, or being, as Jane Flax (following Freud) suggests, the 'enemies of civilization',[9] Kristeva writes that a woman's role in reproduction means that she 'takes social constraints even more seriously, has fewer tendencies toward anarchism, and is more mindful of ethics', such that her negativity is never likely to take the disdainful forms of Nietzschean critique of social values.[10] Elsewhere, Kristeva seems to suggest a model for a feminist thinking of ethical value in the practice of the psychoanalyst, who must steer a tricky course between the totalitarian imposition of meaning and the delirious outpourings of difference, in order to build 'a strong ethics, not normative but directed'.[11] Suggestive though her association of psychoanalytic and political practice is, Kristeva offers little sense of how a mediation between the two regions might be effected. This uncertainty accompanies and is perhaps the effect of a certain lack of confidence that it would ever be possible to institute a politics of difference, which is to say, to constitute the legitimacy and the substantial social embodiment of the value of the endless dispersion and exchange of values. The absence of such a specified account, paradoxical though it would have to be, is all the more remarkable since the ethical force of the critique of patriarchal ethics is so palpable in Kristeva's work and the work of other feminist theorists arguing in similar ways for the value of otherness, difference and dissemination of value.

If this may be seen as the strong version of a postmodern ethics of difference in feminist theory, then there is a correspondingly moderate version in feminist work which draws on the communitarian postmodernism associated with Alisdair Macintyre and Richard Rorty. This version of postmodern ethics, which is often mistakenly confused with the position associated with Foucault and Lyotard, does indeed share with the latter a mistrust of Enlightenment values and ambitions; but where Lyotard and Foucault both attempt to evade the allegedly totalitarian ambitions of the Enlightenment by somehow surpassing them, working in a language that urges transcendence even of transcendence, Macintyre and Rorty are content with a much more modest form of moral and evaluative pluralism, which loiters cautiously beneath the threshold of universalism and transcendence. Macintyre bases his postmodern ethics (not his phrase) on a notion of the embeddedness of all social life and individual identity in shared and inherited narratives. 'I can only answer the question "What am I to do?"', declares Macintyre, 'if I can answer the prior question "Of what story or stories do I find myself a part?"'[12] He argues that there is no universal dimension into which we can justifiably hoist ourselves to allow rational arbitration between the plurality of overlapping and competing social and cultural stories. Like Rorty, Macintyre counsels local, pragmatic adjustment rather than the attempt at universal adjudication, and assumes the need for confidence in one's inherited stories rather than systematic suspicion of them. In striking contrast to Lyotard's vision of the incommensurability of language games, Macintyre concedes the possibility, even the desirability, of overlap between and mutual accommodation of different cultural and political stories. But, animated as it is by the desire for gentle progress and not by that stern desire for transcendence which still mutely haunts Lyotard's work, the communitarian perspective of Macintyre and Rorty maintains the necessity of remaining affirmatively oneself, and refusing to put traditions and inherited forms of life into radical question.

Kate Fullbrook has recently suggested that the Macintyre model of ethical negotiation is appropriate for a feminist reworking of notions of value. This is because, in her view, it resists both the danger of an absolute relativism, which would deny to feminists any grounds for objecting to the exclusion and subordination of women in patriarchal systems of value, and the opposite but related danger of value absolutism, which is evidenced not only in inherited official moralities, but also in the 'feminist leaps into mystic, or, at times, even totalitarian thinking' brought about by 'the desire to secure the foundations of ethical thought' for women (*FW*, 2). Fullbrook advances the considerable argument against theorists such as Daly, Chodorow, Cixous and Irigaray that, precisely by attempting to establish and legitimate the absolute *otherness* of woman and female values, such theorists and theories continue to incarcerate women 'in a psychological, if purportedly privileged ghetto that locks them outside the making of meaning, culture and history' (*FW*, 3). Associating Macintyre's and Rorty's notion of the progressive evolution of stories with the ethical thought of women such as Simone Weil and

Iris Murdoch, and in particular their arguments for 'an ethics based not on adherence to tradition and law, but one based on attention to experience, memory and intense apprehension of the other', Fullbrook finds in the work of a number of twentieth-century women novelists the model for a feminist reworking of cultural values:

> This ethical dimension of women's writing does not try to establish a set of timeless rules or universal moral laws. Rather, it works to create conditions for alternative ethical judgements within particular historical situations – usually viewed in new ways from new points of view – and thus create new futures through consciousness of the possibility of revision of values. (*FW*, 7–8)

The modest pluralism resulting from this outlook is a long way indeed from the ethics against ethics proposed by Kristeva. Fullbrook is resistant to the hypostatizations that suggest it would be possible all at once to step outside systems of cultural value and into some entirely new ethical beginning. And if she favours a turn to female values, such as the 'profound egalitarian generosity' evidenced in Gertrude Stein's work (*FW*, 67), or the political attention to the affectively particular in Woolf's (*FW*, 112), or the fluidity and flexibility evidenced in twentieth-century women's fiction more generally, it is not in order to reproduce their embodiment in women alone, but insofar as such values promise a scheme of the good which admits 'the entirety of the human race to participation in its performance and design' (*FW*, 213).

The pragmatic version of feminist postmodernism instanced in Fullbrook's work is very different from Kristeva's, then, and especially insofar as, by declining to assert any form of absolute value, it seems to avoid the paralysing condition of paradox or performative self-contradiction which I have detected in Kristeva. But there is a curious sense in which the pragmatist position also reproduces paradox. For where Kristeva implicitly affirms but cannot explicitly assert the absolute value of negativity, Fullbrook cannot help but affirm forms of value which it seems she has already discredited in advance. In particular, it seems strange to spend so long resisting the notion of universal norms, and arguing the irreducible variousness of human freedom, and then, in a closing sentence, to affirm the value 'for the entirety of the human race' of the ethical fluidity recommended. It is not so much that universalism and universal variousness cannot be thought together (I am trying here and elsewhere to argue that they must be), as that the form of Fullbrook's pragmatism seems to hold them artificially apart, which makes for a certain irresolution in her position, or – more accurately perhaps, since it may not be a matter principally of resolution or non-resolution – a certain failure to occupy the specific nature of the ethical difficulties of any attempt to think in collective and general terms about the ways in which generalism may be resisted and the authority of the particular re-established.

Some of these difficulties are diagnosed usefully in a recent feminist critique of Macintyre's ethical postmodernism. Sabina Lovibond's 'Feminism and Postmodernism' (1989) resists what she sees as the apathetic parochialism consequent upon Macintyre's recommendation that we abandon universalizing ethical theory, indeed, insofar as it involves the attempt to gain access to forms of rigorously legitimated, non-contingent truth, that we abandon theory as such, devoting our-selves instead to 'the construction of local forms of community within which civility and the intellectual and moral life can be sustained'.[13] As we have seen, this seems to mean working within inherited norms, conventions and mythologies rather than putting them in any radical sense in question. Lovibond tries to show simultaneously that such a moral scheme must lead to quietism and that, insofar as it allows any possibility of critical revision of ethical norms, it cannot without self-contradiction rule out the possibility of universalist critique. If Macintyre allows the possibility of revision, contention and corrective debate within his ethical scheme, Lovibond wonders by what process of spontaneous tact this interior criticism would rein itself back from asking larger or more inclusive questions about matters such as the justice of gender stereotyping, and the nature of human freedom:

> If discursive communities are capable of self-criticism in principle, we might ask, then who is to dictate how far they shall take it? Won't there always be room for more, so long as *any* intelligible criticism can be addressed to the moral or cognitive order under which we live? And what is this limitless commitment to the dialectical revision of theory and prac-tice, if not precisely the Enlightenment commitment to haul up everything in life before the tribunal of reason?[14]

Much the same objection might be mounted against Fullbrook's repre-sentation of the process whereby values are submitted to critique and revision: 'Values are humanly devised, and it is only changing con-sciousness of the fractures within accepted thought which makes the process of transformation of values possible ... [Twentieth-century women's novels] build conceptual frameworks with which the fractures in received moral ideas may be identified and alternative values established' (*FW*, 7, 8). For on what rule, other than some strange universal rule of non-universalizability, would it be possible in principle to prevent this process of critique from spilling out of local or parochial contexts, to encompass questions of human justice and freedom from a totalizing perspective?

On the other hand, the identification of this kind of contradiction within postmodern ethical pragmatics need not necessarily lead where Lovibond subsequently makes it lead, which is to say, to the relegitimation of Enlightenment values as such. There is a sense in which postmodern pragmatism, like its more uncompromising cousin, the postmodern theoreticism of the kind embodied in Kristeva's work, still wants to grasp or account for the question of value all at once, rather than recognizing the irreducible, paradoxical temporality of a process which moves productively within and between ethical alternatives without ever reducing them to the instantaneity of total comprehension. If postmodern feminist ethics elevates heterogeneity prematurely to the status of a principle, then the simple reversion to the other pole of the paradox of value that is found in Lovibond's defence of Enlightenment values of universalizability also remains in the grip of Adorno's 'identity-thinking'. The argument between modernity and postmodernity as it has been conducted in recent feminist work on the question of value remains too much in the grip of the logic of non-cooperative opposition, in which either modernity or postmodernity win the day, with the only available third option being forms of synthesis or reconciliation which in fact end up reproducing the subordination of heterogeneity to identity or vice versa.

Nevertheless, there are areas of feminist theory in which another way of thinking these alternative evaluations of value, namely in *non-synthetic interimplication*, is being developed. The alternation between the values of Enlightenment modernity – privileging identity, universalizability and rational truth – and the values of the postmodern critique of Enlightenment – privileging heterogeneity, particularity and poetic invention – typically encodes a disciplinary (but also cultural) division between two distinct areas of social life, between the sphere of the moral/cognitive and the cultural-aesthetic: to put it crudely, the Enlightenment value of truth tends to confirm the priority of scientific-rational discourse over poetic and artistic discourse, while the postmodern critique of Enlightenment truth tends to invert this hierarchy. It will become apparent that the feminist rethinkings of the value of value cannot easily be confined within the sphere of the political, the ethical or the aesthetic as traditionally constituted, since they can scarcely avoid effecting seismic disturbances in the structure of differentiation which connects and distinguishes these realms.

Irigaray and the Ethics of Difference

Unlike the other French feminist theorists of difference who have exerted such a strong individual and combined influence in Britain and the US, Luce Irigaray has maintained a theoretical as well as a strategic grip upon the question of value. From its beginnings in the critique of the Western logocentric tradition through to her more recent work on the ethics of sexual and cultural difference, Irigaray has been concerned not merely to contest particular patriarchal structures of value which work to exclude or silence women, but also to examine the field of value as such and in its totality.

However, the point of this for Irigaray is precisely to show how the field of value is not a totality, by grasping and articulating the fact of its radical exclusion of women. Irigaray follows Claude Lévi-Strauss's analysis of elementary kinship structures in certain primitive peoples, in which women function as the objects rather than the agents of exchange, but generalizes his conclusions and, naturally, subjects them to angrily negative evaluation. In two essays from the 1970s, 'Women on the Market' and 'Commodities among Themselves', later gathered together in her collection *Ce sexe qui n'en est pas un* (1977), Irigaray argues that women function universally as the objects of every kind of exchange, economic, familial, sexual, psychic, aesthetic, religious, linguistic. Far from being just one form of social organization among others, she suggests, this asymmetry is the founding condition for all society and all systems of social and cultural value, for 'the passage into the social order, into the symbolic order, into order as such, is assured by the fact that men, or groups of men, circulate women among themselves' (*TS*, 170).

'Women on the Market' explicates this situation in terms of an expanded Marxist anthropology, in which the economic exchange of women seems to be given a foundational status. The essay begins by stressing the asymmetry of men's and women's relations to exchange, whereby women are the objects of transaction and exchange exclusively among men; if women are exempt from owning and exchanging commodities, men are exempt from being used and circulated like commodities. The consequence of this asymmetry is, despite all appearances to the contrary, to forbid commerce between men and women; for there can be commerce only between owners and buyers, not between them and the commodities which they buy and sell. Social orders founded upon the exchange of women (which is to say, social order as such) simultaneously forbid male homosexuality, since this would open up the possibility of men being exchanged rather than doing the exchanging, and depend upon them, since 'the possibility of our social life, of our culture, depends upon a ho(m)mo-sexual monopoly ... The law that orders our society is the exclusive valorization of men's needs/desires, of exchanges among men' (*TS*, 171). In the essay 'Commodities among Themselves', this point is repeated and extended with the claim that 'Woman exists only as an occasion for mediation, transaction, transition, transference, between man and his fellow man, between man and himself' (*TS*, 193).

The rest of 'Women on the Market' is taken up with an attempt to read the conditions of women's commodification in terms of Marx's analysis at the beginning of *Capital* of the structure of the commodity. First of all, Irigaray points to a paradox arising from the commodification of women. Women are not valuable to men in themselves, for the usefulness of their bodies or natures, but in terms of their value relative to other woman-commodities, or, rather, relative to the abstract scale of equivalence which enables them to be so exchanged. Like the commodity which she resembles (is?), woman is simultaneously reduced to the status of a dumbly material thing and evicted from her physical being and identity for the purposes of exchange:

> When women are exchanged, woman's body must be treated as an *abstraction*. The exchange operation cannot take place in terms of some intrinsic, immanent value of the commodity. It can only come about when two objects – two women – are in a relation of equality with a third term that is neither the one nor the other. (*TS*, 175)

Woman is thus doubly alienated: first alienated from her own physical nature into the condition of a commodity, and then alienated by the abstract structure of exchangeability from her own value in herself. Her value as commodity can never be known in itself, nor indeed even by means of the mirror image of another woman-commodity; but only by some 'ek-static reference' to 'a preeminent mirror, transcending the world of merchandise [which] guarantees the possibility of exchange among commodities' (*TS*, 181). It is not quite plain how the analogy with Marx's theory of the operations of exchange-value works here; where, for Marx, it is the money-form as the abstract system for measuring labour-power which makes for exchangeability among commodities, Irigaray proposes that women are exchanged 'as women reduced to some common feature – their current price in gold, or phalluses – and of which they would represent a plus or minus quality' (ibid.). Irigaray goes on to gloss the puzzling notion of a 'price in phalluses' by saying that women as commodities represent varying amounts of male social and symbolic labour. But this seems to make women themselves the medium of exchange, a kind of abstract labour-power; in terms of Marx's analysis, they would then have to be identified not as commodities, but as the money-form itself. Throughout the rest of the essay, Irigaray does not really attempt to resolve the issue of whether women are to be seen as alienated commodities or as the *general equivalent* which enables exchange among commodities to take place, whether they are elements in the syntax of economic language or the syntax itself. One of the particular problems with this account of women's absorption into the market as commodities which represent male labour is that it seems to make it impossible to speak of the alienation of female labour by the symbolic-economic market. It may be true, of course, that the most important thing to be understood about female labour that it is indeed invisible in economic terms, alienated, as it were, from the alienation of the market, but by absolutely refusing to women the status of economic agents or any other relationship to the market than of actually constituting it, Irigaray's analysis tends to reproduce this occlusion by economic structures of the economy of women's labour.

However, though it might upset a purist looking for a point-for-point analogy between Marxist economics and feminist critique, this uncertainty is useful rather than damaging to Irigaray's argument, for it enables her to theorize a number of different ways in which woman is split by being primarily the object rather than agent of exchange; split, first of all, between her natural 'being' and her being as commodity, and then, within her condition as commodity, between her function as 'the materialization of an abstract human labor ... objectivization or crystallization as visible object, of man's activity' (*TS*, 179) and her dissolution into a ghostly, ungraspable slippage of value by which the commodity, like the sign, can be measured only in terms of other, absent commodities.

Irigaray goes on to generalize this economic model to other dimensions of cultural life, though in 'Women on the Market' it appears that the economic code remains the dominant and determining one. She finds in the notion of the proper name or the name of the father the point where economic and linguistic structures meet. Named with the father's name, exchanged in terms of the husband's name, the 'trans-formation of women's bodies into use values and exchange values inaugurates the symbolic order' (*TS*, 189). Irigaray then goes on to make manifest the parallel between the commodity and the sign which has been latent throughout her essay:

> Women, animals endowed with speech like men, assure the possibility of the use and circulation of the symbolic without being recipients of it. Their nonaccess to the symbolic is what has established the symbolic order. Putting men in touch with each other, in relations among themselves, women only fulfill this role by relinquishing their right to speech and even to animality. (*TS*, 189–90)

The structure of economic exclusion also extends into the psychosexual domain. Masculine sexuality and sexual pleasure, writes Irigaray, are to be understood in economic terms, of laborious productivity, abstraction and rivalrous relations between the (Oedipal) economic competitors of father and son. 'Does pleasure, for masculine sexuality,' she asks, 'consist in anything other than the reappropriation of nature, in the desire to make it (re)produce, and in exchanges of its/these products with other members of society?' (*TS*, 184). Irigaray prefers not to specify whether this is 'an essentially *economic* pleasure' because economic structures bear the imprint of masculine sexuality, or whether masculine needs and desires are '*the effect of a social mechanism*, in part autonomous, that produces them as such' (ibid.). Women's desire, on the other hand, seems compelled to be the economic relay or mediation of men's desire, without ever having any value for itself: 'if woman is asked to sustain, to revive, men's desire, the request neglects to spell out what it implies as to the value of her own desire. A desire of which she is not aware' (*TS*, 27).

Elsewhere, Irigaray specifies other areas of symbolic or imaginary life (the realm of what she calls 'semblance' (*TS*, 171)) that seem to be readable in terms of the economic structure of exclusion analysed in 'Women on the Market'. One of the most important agencies of women's psychological exclusion from exchange, for example, is the Freudian doctrine of penis envy:

> Her lot is that of 'lack,' 'atrophy,' (of the sexual organ), and 'penis envy,' the penis being the only sexual organ of recognized value. Thus she attempts by every means available to appropriate that organ for herself: through her somewhat servile love of the father–husband, capable of giving her one, through her desire for a child–penis, preferably a boy,

through access to the cultural values still reserved by right to males alone and therefore always masculine. (*TS*, 23–4)

Irigaray is also critically attentive throughout her work to the exclusion of women from intellectual agency in Western philosophy and, in recent work, has drawn attention to the religious exclusion of women from the acts of sacrifice (for example in Christianity) which have typically inaugurated and sustained the social order. Women, she writes, are both excluded from these founding rites of sacrifice and also partake of them precisely by being their hidden sacrificial objects: 'doesn't the founding sacrifice precisely correspond to this *extradition* from the celebration of religion, this exile from the places where the ultimate social decisions are taken?'[15]

Against all these kinds of exclusion, Irigaray argues the vital necessity for women to generate 'a religion, a language, and either a currency of their own or a non-market economy'.[16] In contrast, therefore, to those feminist theorists who argue for the installation of alternative values which are less prejudicial to the interests of women, she argues for nothing less than a catastrophic mutation in the very structure of value itself. Different answers are offered in Irigaray's work to the question of how this is to be achieved. In 'Commodities among Themselves', she examines the position of female homosexuality within psychoanalysis and society. Given the exclusion of women from relationships of exchange, and the fact that it is 'out of the question for them to go to "market" on their own, enjoy their own worth among themselves, speak to each other, desire each other, free from the control of seller–buyer–consumer subjects' (*TS*, 196), female homosexuality is in some sense also impossible, except as an imposture of masculinity by women (*TS*, 193–4). But there is also a radical potential in this impossibility, or at least unrepresentability. For if female homosexuality exists, as it palpably does, then may it not be that it represents a wholly other form of economy or structure of value? At the end of her essay, Irigaray launches into a rhapsodic evocation of this paradoxical other economy, this exchange-beyond-exchange:

> Exchanges without identifiable terms, without accounts, without end ... Without additions and accumulations, one plus one, woman after woman ... Without sequence or number. Without standard or yardstick. *Red blood* and *sham* would no longer be differentiated by deceptive envelopes concealing their worth. Use and exchange would be indistinguishable. The greatest value would be at the same time the least kept in reserve. Nature's resources would be expended without depletion, exchanged

without labor, freely given, exempt from masculine transactions: enjoyment without a fee, well-being without pain, pleasure without possession. As for all the strategies and savings, the appropriations tantamount to theft and rape, the laborious accumulation of capital, how ironic all that would be. (*TS*, 197)

This utopian vision has parallels with a certain version of a Marxist utopia, in which the serializing and homogenizing effects of exchange-value are utterly annulled, to release the transformative abundance and energies of pure use-values, as well as with Bataille's vision of an economy of sovereign excess, which can burst asunder the structures of profit and accumulation. Like Bataille, Irigaray sees this economy of excess both as the impossible transcendence of an economy of exchange and accumulation, and as its secret interior principle, suggesting that 'this mode of exchange has undermined the order of commerce from the beginning – while the *necessity of keeping incest in the realm of pure pretense* has stood in the way of a certain economy of abundance' (ibid.). There are analogies for this form of utopianism to be found elsewhere in feminist theory. Jane Gallop, for example, in the course of a complex dialogue with Jacques Lacan and Stephen Heath, draws out, with at least partial approval, Lacan's characterization of woman as excessive to all structures of knowledge and authority:

Tout, the contained, the universalized, leads to exchange value, not use value. Lacan refers to woman as the *pas-tout* (not-everything), which term is a displacement not an assumption of Freud's notion of the woman as castrated, here, in Marxian terms, that which exceeds exchange value ... On the side of the *pas-tout*, an alternative practice, outside exchange value: let us think here of Lévi-Strauss's exchange of women. The system of the name-of-the-Father implies authorized possession of the woman, who since possessed can be exchanged. Infidelity is a use value, the use of the woman one does not possess, one is not authorized to exchange.[17]

Margaret Whitford has recently drawn attention very usefully to the utopian dimension of Irigaray's thought, arguing that the evocation of exchange beyond current economies of value is one such utopian moment, to which, therefore, we need to ascribe a subjunctive rather than an indicative force: 'we should see [such utopian moments] in terms of the imaginary, rather than as literal accounts of a possible future, or engagement with current (economic or anthropological) theories of exchange.'[18] But there are different forms of utopia and utopianism within Irigaray's work, which it is useful to try to distinguish. Here, in this vision of value beyond or surpassing exchange or the possibility of exchange, we have indeed a purely imaginary utopia, a utopia that is not only not currently actual, but is strictly inconceivable under any circumstances whatsoever, insofar as it asserts the value of transcending what cannot ever be transcended without negating the possibility of value altogether, namely exchange *itself*. If it were possible to move beyond exchange, with its necessary features of 'identifiable terms ... accounts ... additions and accumulations ... sequence[s] or number[s] ... standard[s] or yardstick[s]' (*TS*, 197), which is to say, beyond relativity itself, it would no longer be possible to perceive or affirm the value of such a surpassing, because it would no longer be possible to perceive or affirm the value of anything at all. In this, Irigaray's vision is like (and is probably best seen as a version of) the Bataillean vision of a transcendence of the economy of accumulation, discussed in chapter 4, which can be affirmed only in terms of a positivity that shows its continuing dependence upon the system it allegedly transcends.[19] The problem here is exactly congruent with the problem of any Marxist utopia which aims to move beyond exchange-values into the realm of purely incommensurable use-values. As we saw in chapter 6, such a dream could never be actualized, since use-value conceived in this way would mean the annihilation of value as such.

This purely imaginary utopianism may be produced in Irigaray's work as a necessary reflex to what is already an overtotalized view of structures of exchange. If Marx insists that exchange-value comes into being in specific ways and at specific points in history, Irigaray seems in some of her work to believe that the reduction of women to exchange-value is primal and universal. But if it were really primally and universally true that all societies of any kind have been founded and sustained upon the sacrifice and silencing of women, and that the exclusion of women from exchange and their reduction to objects of exchange has characterized every conceivable area of public and private life within these societies, then it is very hard to understand not only how this situation might ever be changed, but also how or why it might ever have come critically to light. (Irigaray might argue that it has indeed effectively taken centuries to come to light, but the point is that somehow, in the end, and perhaps also at various points along the way, it *has* done so.) Visions of total domination tend to produce utopias which are correspondingly impossible of realization, and I think that this is the case with Irigaray's. But it is surely dangerous to assume that women are entirely and inescapably silenced and objectified within economy, language and representation; such a vision assumes the homogeneity and self-identity of a system of exclusion that is and has been dominant, but perhaps nowhere has ever been total.[20] Has it always and everywhere been impossible for women to determine and represent values to and for each other, with and against men, in any other fashion than as '*a mirror of value of and for man*' (*TS*, 177)? In assuming a sort of ontological barrier to the participation of women in the formation of value and values, Irigaray sometimes risks perpetuating the very condition from which she is aiming to escape, as well, of course, as denying the possibility of the revaluation which her work itself so powerfully requires and enacts.

But there is another form of utopianism, which we might call *virtual* rather than *imaginary*. Since the late 1970s, this has been running alongside and may perhaps gradually have displaced its more sublime sister in Irigaray's work. This form of utopia asserts the value not of moving beyond exchange as such, but of moving beyond the limited and unjust structures of exchange which currently exist, structures which measure exchange-value in terms of a single abstract standard alone. It asserts the necessary value of opening exchange rather than transcending it. It is measured against the ideal form of something more than an other-worldly pseudotopia, namely, a utopia that is conceivable within the terms of and releasable from within current conditions. But, ironically, this shift from an imaginary to a virtual utopian mode has taken place precisely as a result of a perplexing move in Irigaray's work away (some might feel, even further away) from the sphere of political and economic actualities. Where her early work had centred on a notion of exchange which is at root economic, her work during the 1980s has centred on the question of the ethics of sexual difference. If the economic exclusion of women from exchange was what underlay and negated the possibility of sexual reciprocity between the sexes in that early work, in her more recent work it is precisely the image and possibility of sexual love which seems to promise a revaluation in the economics of gender relations. Hence the modulation in that work from economics, anthropology and psychoanalysis to ethics, theology and poetics.

In this later work, and especially in *Ethique de la différence sexuelle* (1984), Irigaray continues to argue, as she had in *This Sex which is Not One*, for woman's status as interval, indeterminacy or multiplicity, in opposition to the authoritative singularity of male phallogocentrism. As in earlier work, this condition is one of both systematic disadvantage and epistemological privilege, in that the extradition of woman from self-possession allows her to resist or open up the oppressive self-identity of the phallus. The difference seems to be that female difference is no longer the sign and promise of a female economy of meaning and value which would be wholly other to and transcendent of patriarchal systems of value. Or no longer this *alone*, for woman's status as interval now also embodies the promise of an alliance or interconnection between the sexes. Where the lips of the female genitalia earlier served as an image of the interior 'speaking together' of the female, in a self-communing that went beyond male structures of exchange, they are now read as 'this *threshold* which has never been examined in its own terms … threshold which is always *half-open* … threshold and reception of exchange' (*EDS*, 24).[21] This exchange is not read as the commensurability of equals, for Irigaray maintains her distrust of an abstract notion of universal equality that has always acted in the service of the male, but an exchange or reciprocity that could never be the 'accomplishment of consummation … [since] one sex cannot be entirely consumed by the other' (*EDS*, 20). The ethics of sexual difference depend upon a notion, which Irigaray borrows from Descartes, of *admiration*; the non-possessive, non-appetitive acknowledgement of that which can never be brought under the dominion of the concept, the other who can never be assimilated to the self without residue. This Irigaray calls the 'inaugurating passion of love, of art, and of thought, the place of man's and woman's second birth, the birth into the other's transcendence' (*EDS*, 84).

The fact of women's exclusion from exchange, economic and symbolic, nevertheless still requires that, as a first stage, women must enter into exchange rather than being its medium. This requires a certain female narcissism, or love between women; but this is now not the opposite of relationships with men, as it had arguably been represented in Irigaray's earlier work, but the very enabling condition of male–female intersubjectivity; 'The enveloping between mother and daughter, daughter and mother, between women, will not be a closure, or enclosure, protecting itself against a "for the other" in seduction, or a servitude which abolishes all subjective possibility. Love of the same, in the same, is the care for an interiority which can open itself to the other without loss of the self or the other in the bottomless abyss' (*EDS*, 70–1). And the development of female identity or interiority does not mean simply giving women access to male values and systems of value, but rather 'women putting in place new values corresponding to *their* creative capacities. Society, culture and discourse would then be seen to be *gendered*, rather than the monopoly, as universal values, of one sex which misrecognizes the effects of the body and its morphologies on imaginary and symbolic creation' (*EDS*, 70).

Nor is this a matter simply of redeeming women's value, or women for value. Although, perhaps understandably, Irigaray does not devote much space to the ways in which men as well as women are alienated by patriarchy, there are moments, even in her earlier work, in which she reminds her readers that the asymmetry of the field of value means that men are locked into a sterile economy of the same, and denied the possibility of intersubjective encounter with women, and among each other; if they are 'exempt from being used and circulated like commodities' (*TS*, 172), another way of saying this is that they 'have to *give up* the possibility of serving as commodities themselves' (*TS*, 193 (my emphasis)). The evaluative shift from privilege (being 'exempt from' commodification) to disadvantage (having to 'give up' the possibility of commodification) here signals an interesting ambivalence about the idea of the commodity, which in turn marks Irigaray's qualification of orthodox Marxist theory. If reduction to the status of a commodity is in one sense a grim denial of the possibilities of one's humanity, then it is also true that, in order to have and represent value for others in intersubjective relationship, it is also necessary to accept in some positive sense the shared participation – even as a commodity – in symbolic and economic economies. The ethics of sexual difference in Irigaray's later work are therefore principally, but by no means exclusively, in the interests of women. A similar point has recently been made by Michèle le Doeuff, though in a very different philosophical idiom. In an interesting defence of the discursive ideal of non-dominative intersubjectivity, le Doeuff points out that under conditions of constrained or unequal dialogue it is not only the suppressed or objectified interlocutor who is denied their freedom, but also the one apparently benefiting from the suppression or objectification. Since it is only when subjected to the corrective and transformative force of trans-personal communication that it is possible to become free of obsession, illusion, ideology and all the other automatizing and infantilizing forces which make freedom impossible, men too are the victims of a situation in which meaning, power and value reside only on their side of an unequal exchange.[22]

Irigaray faces the difficulty in *Ethique de la différence sexuelle* of writing about the ethics and politics of love in a culture which has traditionally expelled love from the public sphere of ethics and politics into the private realms of the aesthetic and the affective. Nevertheless, it is plain that, for her, the relation of love between the sexes is a pattern and example of the possibility of what she repeatedly calls 'fecundity'; this means that her love is the very transcendence of the traditionally limited value of love in the Western tradition, in a 'perpetual transvaluation, permanent becoming' (*EDS*, 33). In a similar way, the fecundity of sexual difference would also involve the 'production of a new era of thought, art, poetry and language; the creation of a new *poetics'* (*EDS*, 13). This must partly encompass a new inversion of values, in that art and poetry will be valued alongside technological power. But if Irigaray's utopian ethics-as-poetics of sexual difference is really to be seen as encompassing transvaluation, then it is not enough simply to read the poetic here as embodying 'fictions of a different mode of social organization', as Whitford calls them, since to identify the poetic merely with the fictional is surely to fall into the traditional evaluative dichotomy of the ethico-political and the aesthetic-imaginative which Irigaray's work would require to be dislodged.[23] Love, for Irigaray, stands at the point of juncture between the aesthetic and the political, unsettling and recombining the values of both.

Irigaray's work, like that of Kristeva and Cixous, has of course long been recognized as stressing the political force of all those forms and experiences which have traditionally been relegated to the status of the personal, the psychic or the aesthetic, and her work joins with theirs in agitating this structure of relegation, and arguing the impossibility of abstracting questions of language, feeling and identity from the political. Recently, however, there have been signs of feminist dissatisfaction with the aestheticization of the political (and vice versa) as it is found in Irigaray and others. These are expressed most emphatically in Rita Felski's *Beyond Feminist Aesthetics* (1989), a book which cautions against the danger of assuming that language, art and representation alone can be trusted to yield significant emancipatory change in the social and personal lives of women. Felski argues powerfully that feminism and aesthetics must exist in a dialectical relationship rather than one of simple identity in which such aesthetic features as formal self-reflexivity, structural paradox, semantic indeterminacy and the defamiliarization of the real are taken as necessary guarantees of progressive effect. For Felski, the suggestion that aesthetics and politics are always in exact alignment ignores the historical relativity of the significance of the aesthetic; at one moment, it may seem necessary to subordinate questions of artistic form to the urgency of political struggles, while at another there may be good political reasons for resisting the instrumentalization of the aesthetic.[24] Seen in this light, the exclusive emphasis on aesthetic rather than political subversion seems like what Terry Eagleton has characterized as premature utopianism, the imagination of a perfect liberation which is permitted under the conditions of relative autonomy of the aesthetic precisely to the degree that the bourgeois separation of the aesthetic from social and political power nullifies its force.[25] Felski concludes therefore that:

The value of a text as art, if one means by this a self-reflexive symbolic structure which generates multiple meanings and is not directly reducible to ideological interests, does not therefore constitute a sufficient basis for the specific needs and interests of a feminist politics of culture, which also needs to situate itself more concretely in relation to the ideological dimensions of the text and the praxis-oriented interests of an oppositional feminist public sphere.[26]

Such a critique would seem to compromise the ethics-as-poetics proposed by Irigaray in *Ethique de la différence sexuelle*, and exemplified especially in the extraordinary final chapter of that work, 'The Fecundity of the Caress', a rhapsodic 'reading' of a short section from Emmanuel Levinas's *Totality and Infinity*.[27] The chapter conducts an exploration into such themes as the erotics of touch, the capacity of lovers to transcend the self, the relationship between love and divinity, the various lures and dangers of voluptuousness that makes one partner the object to be consumed by the other, and the paradoxical binding and unbinding of self and other that is the ethical promise of love. The resistance of the text to sequential paraphrase, the necessity for Irigaray of evoking the shifting, intangible effect of what is in Levinas much more of an evocation than anything that might be called a description or analysis, would seem to indicate that here we have an attempt to enact rather than merely to describe the poetics of the ethical.

'The Fecundity of the Caress' might therefore seem vulnerable to Felski's critique, in its apparent displacement of the political into the aesthetic. But, from Irigaray's point of view, it might be said that such a critique merely continues to assume what it is precisely the intention of an ethics-as-poetics to disrupt, namely the necessary separation of the aesthetic and the political, the private and the public, and the subordination in each case of the former to the latter, a subordination moreover which is not an accidental accompaniment to the oppression of women but its very form. Irigaray's demand for some entirely new and expanded economy of cultural value would entail suspicion of the attempt to form a feminist counter-public sphere such as that recommended by Felski insofar as this precisely accepted that very organization of the field of 'public' as opposed to 'private' value which is built upon the sacrifice and silencing of women. However, a further rejoinder is possible at this point, which is that it is actually Irigaray who reproduces the privative opposition of private and public, precisely by drawing back from attempting to join her mystical vision of erotic community-in-difference with its playing out of 'the most terrible demand of the ethical ... [the] confrontation, here and now, with the mystery of the other' (*EDS*, 190) to an account of collective as well as private life. The irony of Irigaray's claim for an erotic ethics which dissolves the fixity of every ethical siting, dwelling in the threshold between fixed places, is that it keeps itself under house arrest, confined to the fine but obscurely private place of love between two commingling singularities; nowhere does the ethical relation seem to encompass a properly intersubjective opening of the self on to the collective other.

Feminism and Discourse Ethics

Nevertheless, this dimension has the force of a determinate absence in Irigaray's ethics, insofar as it depends upon the desire to create the conditions for a 'culture of difference' rather than a culture which systematically refuses or regulates difference. Indeed, her most recent work shows signs of moving away from the privatized sphere of erotic divinity and back towards a consideration of collective life.[28] As such, her work comes to have an interesting congruity with a body of feminist critique which might seem at first sight to have a very different attitude towards the question of value for the female, that Habermasian feminism exemplified over recent years in the work of such writers as Rita Felski, Nancy Fraser, Seyla Benhabib and Drucilla Cornell.[29] These writers have by no means attempted simply to annex Habermas for feminism, or indeed vice versa, but, rather, by asking feminist questions of Habermas's programme of discursive ethics, to enlarge that programme, adapting and transforming it for the purposes of a feminist theory of ethics and politics of cultural value. For all these writers, the central question for feminism is not just how to reverse or modify those values which embody or contribute to the domination and exploitation of women, revaluing that which has been systematically disvalued under patriarchy, or setting 'female' values alongside or against 'male' values. Like Irigaray, Habermasian feminists are concerned with intervening in and transforming the field of value as such, by theorizing the ways in which women's exclusion from the collective determination of value can be overcome. It is in this respect that feminist critique can draw profitably on Habermas's shift of Marxist theory towards a concern with the operations of discourse, his defence of the utopian orientation towards non-coercive communication and consensus within all discourse, and his identification of freedom with the universal emancipation from discursive constraints of all kinds.

However, as we have seen, there is a danger inherent in Habermas's

enterprise, namely that in defining its discursive ideal it needs to perpetu-
ate divisions and evaluative hierarchies – for example between the
rational and the aesthetic – which ought in principle to be available for
re-evaluation. Nancy Fraser has argued that one of the most notable
continuing fixations of value in Habermas's theory is a model of the
social determination of value that seems systematically blind to gender,
and therefore excludes women. Fraser shows how, by staking too much
on what appears to be an absolute opposition between the public world
of 'system' and the private 'lifeworld', and encouraging too precipitate an
identification of these analytic categories with the actual realms of the
workplace and the home, Habermas is insufficiently attentive to that
feminist critique of the public/private opposition, which shows how
thoroughly power and strategic reason operate, mostly in the interests of
men, in the home as well as in the public workplace. Habermas's defence
of the value of the lifeworld, and desire to decolonize it of the invasive
forces of strategic rationality (for example, in the form of the bureau-
cratic welfare state), therefore depends upon a dangerously sentimen-
talized view of the sphere of the lifeworld traditionally associated with
the female. 'In short,' writes Fraser, 'the struggles and wishes of contemporary women are not adequately clarified by a theory that draws the
basic battle line between system and lifeworld institutions. From a feminist perspective, there is a more basic battle line to be drawn between the
forms of male dominance linking "system" to "lifeworld" *and us*'
('What's Critical about Critical Theory?', *FC*, 55).

Nevertheless, despite her criticisms of some of Habermas's conceptual
apparatus and evaluative assumptions, Fraser continues, in this essay and
elsewhere, to acknowledge the value of Habermas's ideal of unconstrained discourse and 'the replacement of normatively secured contexts
of interaction by communicatively achieved ones' (*FC*, 53).[30] Fraser's
critique shows how feminism can turn Habermas's theory reflexively
against itself; indeed, it illuminates the central problem of reflexivity
within that theory itself which I have discussed in chapter 5, namely the
problem of establishing intellectual procedures and social institutions
which allow for the unconstrained determination of value, without
assuming in the very form of those procedures and institutions evaluative
structures which themselves work to limit or constrain intersubjective
dialogue.

A similar problem of reflexivity is identified by Seyla Benhabib in her
discussion of the question of 'female ethics' and its relation to the work
of Habermas. Benhabib centres on the notorious controversy between
psychologists Lawrence Kohlberg and Carol Gilligan about the nature of

moral awareness in men and women. She begins by offering a distinction between the different kinds of moral awareness valorized by Kohlberg and Gilligan in terms of their respective constitutions of the self–other relationship. The 'postconventional' ethics valorized by Kohlberg, and allegedly found to be more dominant in men, depends on a formal and legalistic notion of the other, as possessed of precisely the same rights and duties as those we would wish to prescribe for ourselves. The 'generalized other' assumed and required by this form of ethical theory, must be abstracted from the contingencies and particularities which constitute the other's actual personal identity. One of the problems to be coped with by a Habermasian feminism is that Habermas not only has common roots with Kohlberg in Kantian morality, but also at times depends heavily upon Kohlberg's scheme of growth into postconventional moral awareness, seeming to share Kohlberg's view of the centrality of an ethical relation to a generalized other based on abstract substitutionality. By contrast, an ethical orientation towards the 'concrete other', found by Gilligan to be dominant in women, depends upon a responsiveness not to what is generalizable about the humanity of the other, but what is most particular about them. In the first ('male') form of relationship, the self is bound to the other by 'norms of *formal equality* and *reciprocity*: each is entitled to expect and assume from us what we can expect and assume from him or her'; in the second ('female') form of relationship, the self is bound by 'norms of *equity* and *complementary reciprocity*: each is entitled to expect and to assume from the other forms of behavior through which the other feels recognized and confirmed as a concrete, individual being with specific needs, talents and capacities' ('The Generalized and the Concrete Other', *FC*, 87).[31]

There are obvious problems with a scheme of morality that refuses any form of generalization, or refuses to prescribe any norms that would govern individuals abstractly and in advance of their actions. How far, after all, should we feel constrained to embrace the 'concrete individuality' of the anti-Semite? What sort of interactive 'bonding and sharing' is envisaged with the rapist? With what 'sympathy and solidarity' do we measure the 'specific needs, talents and capacities' of the camp-commandant? In saying that the 'interactive' rather than 'substitutionalist' ethic of Gilligan confirms 'not only your *humanity* but your *human individuality*' (*FC*, 87), Benhabib risks neglecting that collective dimension intrinsic to ethical thought. On the other hand, by no means every ethical question has this kind of clarity, and indeed the desire for such clarity, and the willingness to distort ethical encounters into it may be precisely one of the effects of the dominance of the Kohlberg model. For, where the Gilligan model of the 'concrete other' may overindividualize, the Kohlberg model of the 'generalized other' surely overabstracts ethical questions. Benhabib shows that the assumption of the ethical inter-changeability of co-operating or conflicting moral agents tends to makes that other purely abstract, by assuming in Kantian fashion that all knowledge about his or her particular identity must be suspended. Thus, in assuming what Benhabib calls 'the disembedded and disembodied generalized other' (*FC*, 88), this ethical perspective effectively abolishes the other by making it an exact mirror of the same, making reciprocity between different viewpoints impossible.

In fact, unlike some other feminist theorists of ethics, Benhabib does not propose simply to install a female ethic of the kind described by Gilligan in the place of the Kohlbergian ethic of the disembodied subject, since she recognizes the irreducible importance for ethics and politics of the capacity to read the general in the particular. On the other hand, she is also aware of the feebleness of merely adding the qualities of flexible, situational understanding on to universalist morality.[32] Instead, she proposes a strategically expanded version of Habermas's communicative ethic. In this, it is necessary not just to measure conduct by fixed moral norms, but to make moral norms available for scrutiny and collective determination.

> From a metaethical and normative standpoint, I would argue, therefore, for the validity of a moral theory that allows us to recognize the dignity of the generalized other through an acknowledgement of the moral identity of the concrete other. The point is not to juxtapose the generalized to the concrete other or to see normative validity in one or another standpoint. The point is to think through the ideological limitations and biases that arise in the discourse of universalist morality through this unexamined opposition. I doubt that an easy integration of both points of view, of justice and of care, is possible, without first clarifying the moral frame-work that would allow us to question both standpoints and their implicit gender presuppositions. (*FC*, 92)

This blending and self-questioning of values is intended to have more than a merely corrective force. In contrast to the 'closed reflexivity' (*FC*, 94) of the ethical models proposed by Kohlberg, Rawls and, one might add, Habermas, who assume that the situation of collective moral reasoning is governed by certain fixed values, value is open-ended and developing in the 'communicative ethic of need interpretations' proposed by Benhabib. For it would be aimed at not only the prescription, actualization or protection of value, but also the generation of new forms of value. In it, 'the object domain of moral theory is so enlarged that not only rights but needs, not only justice, but possible modes of the good life, are moved into an anticipatory-utopian perspective. What such discourses can generate are not only universally prescribable norms, but also intimations of otherness in the present that can lead to the future' (*FC*, 93).

Is this the point at which the question of the aesthetic dimension of the cultural, traditionally so absent within moral and political theory, is obliquely signalled? For if the rational determination of value is to be enlarged to allow both unconstrained reflexivity and the intimations of otherness, then is there not some curious restraint or failure to transvalue in the continuing exclusion of the aesthetic from these negotiations? If the universal and the particular, the public and the private, along, we might add, with the actual and the anticipatory, the serious and the non-serious, are to be in some sense thought with and through rather than against each other, then it would be hard to know on what grounds the aesthetic was to be kept out of the rational imagination of freedom. The sphere traditionally constituted as the aesthetic is perhaps the same kind of determinate absence in the account offered by Benhabib as the sphere of collective political action is in the work of Irigaray.

There seems therefore to be an intimation here of a way in which the utopian ethics–poetics of transvaluation of Irigaray, Kristeva, Cixous and others might be read alongside a productive politics of diversity of the kind recommended by Fraser and Benhabib. Such a *rapprochement* is indeed suggested by Drucilla Cornell and Adam Thurschwell, who argue the necessity of going beyond what sometimes seems in Kristeva's work and in other forms of gynocentric theory to be an ethics of pure negativity, based on a wish to speak woman but able to articulate itself only in a total refusal of an allegedly 'universalist' system of value that itself has thoroughly and systematically excluded women. Cornell and Thurschwell propose a reading of Kristeva via Adorno's negative dialectic which enables the positive and negative aspects of Kristeva's ethic to be brought, and thought, together. Negativity, for Adorno, is neither to be restored to the positive and self-perpetuating authority of the self nor to be fetishized as absolutely negative other. Rather, negative dialectics allows the paradoxical opening of some alternative between or beyond the greedy imperialism that assimilates the other into itself and the lonely imperialism that expels it for ever beyond its reach. The implications of this for feminism are that the conventional distinctions between universalism and gynocentrism, a politics of the same and a politics of difference, are actualized in dynamic interplay rather than involving stark, once-and-for-all choices. 'The deconstruction of gender categorization', they write, 'affirms multiplicity and the "concrete singular," and at the same time opens up the possibility of communicative freedom in which the Other is not there as limit but as supportive relation, the "ground" of my own being' ('Feminism, Negativity, Intersubjectivity', *FC*, 161).

On both sides of the feminist question of value, then, the French side encompassing difference, deconstruction and the poetic, and the Habermasian side encompassing universalism, reconstruction and the political, there seems to be a growing imperative not only to open up a space for women in the production of value, but to open up the field of value itself to new forms of exchange and production in general. Though both are orientated towards utopia, neither nourishes a purely imaginary utopia which would depend upon some epochal reversal or transcendence of systems of value: rather, it is the inauguration in positive and present form of new ways of thinking the question of value which can bring about this expansion of the field of value as such.

NOTES

1 Ursula le Guin, 'Bryn Mawr Commencement Address', in *Dancing at the Edge of the World: Thoughts on Words, Women, Places* (New York: Grove Press, 1989), p. 155.
2 Carey Kaplan and Ellen Cronan Rose, *The Canon and the Common Reader* (Knoxville: Tennessee University Press, 1990), p. 165.
3 Christine Battersby, *Gender and Genius: Towards a Feminist Aesthetics* (London: Women's Press, 1989), p. 10. Battersby is here discussing Roszika Parker and Griselda Pollock, *Old Mistresses: Women, Art and Ideology* (London: Routledge, 1981).
4 Battersby, *Gender and Genius*, p. 11.
5 Annie Leclerc, 'Parole de Femme' (1974), extract reprinted in *French Feminist Thought: A Reader*, ed. Toril Moi (Oxford: Basil Blackwell, 1989), p. 76.
6 Jane Flax, 'Postmodernism and Gender Relations in Feminist Theory', *Signs: Journal of Women in Culture and Society*, 12 (1987), p. 625.
7 Ibid., pp. 642, 643.
8 Ibid., p. 643. For a range of different perspectives on the relationship between feminism and postmodernism, see *Feminism/Postmodernism*, ed. Linda J. Nicholson (London: Routledge, 1990).
9 Sigmund Freud, *Civilization and its Discontents* (New York: W. W. Norton, 1961), pp. 50–1, quoted in Flax, 'Postmodernism and Gender Relations', p. 643.

10 Julia Kristeva, 'Woman Can Never Be Defined', *New French Feminisms*, ed. Elaine Marks and Isabelle de Courtivron (New York: Schocken, 1981), p. 138.

11 Kristeva, 'Psychoanalysis and the Polis', trans. Margaret Waller, in *The Politics of Interpretation*, ed. W. J. T. Mitchell (Chicago and London: University of Chicago Press, 1983), p. 98.

12 Alisdair Macintyre, *After Virtue: A Study in Moral Theory* (London: Duckworth, 1981), p. 201.

13 Ibid., p. 245.

14 Lovibond, 'Feminism and Postmodernism', pp. 20–1.

15 Luce Irigaray, 'Women, the Sacred and Money', trans. Diana Knight and Margaret Whitford, *Paragraph*, 8 (1986), pp. 8–9.

16 Ibid., p. 9.

17 Jane Gallop, *Feminism and Psychoanalysis: The Daughter's Seduction* (London: Macmillan, 1982), p. 49. Gallop is referring in this discussion to Stephen Heath's characterization of Lacan's characterization of the feminine in language in, respectively, 'Difference', *Screen*, 19 (1978–9), p. 108 and *Le séminaire livre xx: Encore* (Paris: Seuil, 1975), p. 89.

18 Margaret Whitford, *Luce Irigaray: Philosophy in the Feminine* (London and New York: Routledge, 1991), p. 186. A similar defence of Irigaray is offered by Carolyn Burke, who, in 'Irigaray through the Looking Glass', *Feminist Studies*, 7 (1981), pp. 288–306, suggests that the poetics of the body in Irigaray's work do not depend upon any kind of belief in women's essential biological nature, but rather upon an evocation of forms of possible resistance to patriarchal appropriations of the female body.

19 See above, pp. 71–7.

20 The total exclusion of women from language and representation alleged by such thorists as Irigaray is criticized by Deborah Cameron in *Feminism and Linguistic Practice* (London: Macmillan, 1985).

21 Translations from *EDS* are my own.

22 Michèle le Doeuff, *Hipparchia's Choice: An Essay concerning Women, Philosophy, Etc.*, trans, Trista Selous (Oxford: Basil Blackwell, 1991), pp. 278–9.

23 Whitford, *Luce Irigaray*, p. 188.

24 Rita Felski, *Beyond Feminist Aesthetics: Feminist Literature and Social Change* (London: Hutchinson Radius, 1989), p. 178.

25 See discussion above, pp. 141–2.

26 Felski, *Beyond Feminist Aesthetics*, p. 179.

27 This chapter has appeared in an English translation by Carolyn Burke in *Face to Face with Levinas*, ed. Richard A. Cohen (Albany: SUNY Press, 1985), pp. 231–56.

28 See Irigaray, *Je, tu, nous: pour une culture de la différence* (Paris: Grasset, 1990).

29 The most representative texts here are Rita Felski, *Beyond Feminist Aesthetics*, Nancy Fraser, *Unruly Practices: Power, Discourse and Gender in Contemporary Social Theory* (Cambridge: Polity Press, 1989) and *Feminism as Critique*, ed. Benbabib and Cornell.

30 A more positive view of the usefulness of Habermas for feminism is articulated in Fraser's 'Toward a Discourse Ethic of Solidarity', *Praxis International*, 5 (1986), pp. 425–9.

31 See Lawrence Kohlberg, *The Psychology of Moral Development: The Nature and Validity of Moral Stages* (San Francisco and London: Harper & Row, 1984). Carol Gilligan's critique of Kohlberg's views is to be found in her *In a Different Voice: Psychological Theory and Women's Development* (Cambridge, Mass.: Harvard University Press, 1982).

32 The question of ethics has become increasingly important for feminism in recent years. Among the most significant and representative considerations of the relationship between feminism and ethical theory are Lesley Davies, *Caring: A Feminine Approach to Ethics* (Canterbury: University of Kent, 1990); *Science, Morality, and Feminist Theory*, ed. Marsha Hanen and Kai Nelson (Calgary: University of Calgary Press, 1987); Jean Grimshaw, *Philosophy and Feminist Thinking* (Minneapolis: University of Minnesota Press, 1986); *Women's Consciousness, Women's Conscience: A Reader in Feminist Ethics*, ed. Barbara Hilkert Andolsen, Christine E. Gudorf and Mary D. Pellauer (San Francisco and London: Harper & Row, 1987); and *Feminist Ethics*, ed. Claudia Card (Kansas City: University of Kansas Press, 1991).

8

Ethics without Ethos:
Levinas, Derrida, Joyce

To put the question of ethical value to, and together with, the theory of deconstruction is to bring about a strange and difficult conjuncture; for, at first sight, the concerns and debates traditionally associated with ethics may seem to have little enough to do with the incendiary glamour of deconstruction. If deconstruction aims to move in a Nietzschean trajectory beyond good and evil, promising liberation, release, rebirth, subversion, energy, then ethics has often been associated with everything that deconstruction is held to range itself against, legislation, restriction, codification, responsibility. Nevertheless, recent years have seen among deconstructive writers a number of attempts to think these two mutually resistant dimensions of thought together. For if it is true that deconstruction is characterized by its close and sometimes antagonistic scrutiny of the assumptions, metaphysical and otherwise, which lie behind systems of ethics, as well as of systematic thought in general, then it is also the case that there is a certain irreducible ethical force within deconstructive thought itself – even if this force has not always made itself easily available for self-conscious analysis. We might note straight away that this ethical stimulus may not necessarily lead straight to the kind of issue usually designated by the ethical. For to discuss the ethics of deconstruction is to be concerned not with specific values comported or promised by deconstruction, or the principles of right conduct held to be implicit within it, but rather with the ethical force or responsibility which is already in being whenever one begins to perform the work of a deconstructive analysis. Enquiry into the ethics of deconstruction therefore concerns itself with the kind of primary questions asked by Simon Critchley: 'Why bother with deconstruction? ... What or who calls for deconstruction? What necessity governs Derrida's work?'[1] There is an ethical force involved in attempting to answer such questions, as there is in investigating what is at stake within them. So it is a matter, as Arkady Plotnitsky has said, not only of a deconstruction of all 'permanent, universal, absolute, objective (or, conversely, subjective) values', but also of 'the development of a theory accounting for "metaphysical" values; that is, precisely, for their *value* or necessity'; and, we might add, the value or necessity of such a deconstructive theory of value or necessity (and so on).[2] In fact the ethics of deconstruction will turn out to involve a characteristic self-reflexion, in the examination of the ethics of ethics, and the principled and sustained analysis of the ethical question itself, which Derrida, in his early essay on Emmanuel Levinas, calls 'a community of the question about the possibility of the question' (VM, 80). In more recent work, Derrida has become more emphatic in his statements regarding the irreducibility of value and ethics, and has willingly accepted that the deconstructive scrutiny of values and ethical commitments by no means implies a simple or definitive denial of the possibility of value and ethics as such. Arguing, for example, against the ethico-political force of the subordination of various kinds of 'non-serious' speech conditions in speech-act theory, he insists that 'such conditions, which may be anethical with respect to any given ethics, are not therefore anti-ethical in general. They can even open or recall the opening of another ethics.'[3] And, as opposed to those, like Plotnitsky, who counsel the Nietzschean replacement of 'truth value' by 'value without truth', Derrida has declared that 'the value of truth (and all those values associated with it) is never contested or destroyed in my writing, but only reinscribed in more powerful, larger, more stratified contexts'.[4]

For a long time, the demand has been made of deconstruction that it demonstrate a programme of attainable goals and imperatives and desirable political outcomes. These demands have become particularly pressing because of the progressive breakdown of the temporary, always uneasy alliance between political criticism of the left and the techniques of deconstruction. Where political critics such as Terry Eagleton began by embracing the critical possibilities presented by deconstruction (if only in the rather end-stopped fashion once regretted by Christopher Norris[5]), his later work is much more sceptical about the radical claims of deconstruction. At the same time, there has been a political challenge from another direction, the revived liberalism of neo-pragmatism, with its claim to have jettisoned metaphysical or universalist thinking in favour not of a discourse of emancipation, but of practices of prudential self-interest. Deconstruction therefore has to face the twin challenges of a political criticism that will tolerate no theory that does not earn its keep in what Derrida has called 'that thing obscurely and tranquilly named "real life"',[6] and the growing prestige of a postmodern pragmatism which claims that real life requires and admits of no kind of theory.

What has happened in the mean time of course is the widespread and, to some, unexpected institutional success of deconstruction in the US and elsewhere. If it is really true, as Derrida and others have always claimed, that deconstruction is inimical to institutions, then what are we to make of this institutional success? There is obviously a certain pungency in the suggestion that some of the discourses ranged under the name of deconstruction may have served merely to manufacture and maintain the energizing effects of crisis without at any point risking the dissolution of its own authority. It is perhaps in response to these criticisms and in uncomfortable awareness of the fact of the triumph of theory in general and deconstruction in particular that many deconstructive writers have begun to try to supply the ethico-political dimension that is regularly claimed to be absent in their work. One might instance the work of Barbara Johnson here, whose most recent book *A World of Difference* openly attempts, as she puts it, 'to transfer the analysis of difference ... out of the realm of linguistic universality or deconstructive allegory and into contexts in which difference is very much at issue in the "real world"'.[7] Derrida's own work has instanced a similarly worldly turn in the last few years, with his work on nuclear arms and on the politics of race. And, most notably, there has been the Paul de Man affair, which, more than anything else, has highlighted such important questions about the politics of deconstruction.[8]

The problem for deconstructive criticism of this worldly kind, however, has been how to harness or redeem in ethico-political terms a form of critique which has habitually been characterized (though not always by its practitioners) as resistant to any form of the sedimentation of value and whose energies have primarily been expended in a kind of negative capability, in the hermeneutics of suspicion, resistance and negation rather than in acceptance and positive affirmation. A representative account of the way in which the question of value is deployed in deconstruction is provided by Plotnitsky, whose study of the question of value in Derrida makes a fundamental and, at first sight, rather surprising distinction between interpretation and evaluation. Evaluation, says Plotnitsky, is what brings interpretation to a halt. If interpretation is an open and transactive process, an interminable and unoriginated following through of traces, and traces of traces, then the arrival at an evaluation always represents a more or less artificial fixing or arrest of that process. 'The limits of our interpretations are evaluations,' writes Plotnitsky, 'or rather evaluation inscribes itself in relation to such limits. We begin or stop at some point and/or select one or other alternate trajectory of traces to follow because, under the constraints of the moment, it is "the best" we can do.'[9] Alan Kennedy adopts the distinction made by Plotnitsky for his own purposes, proposing in the light of it a distinction between 'ethics' and 'Value'. Kennedy claims that ethics, because it involves beliefs held in a community, is always likely to be the realm of ideology, in which thinking is really conducted via precomprehension. However, we are in this realm of ethics whenever we make any kind of decision or choice. The thinking of Value, on the other hand, represents the attempt to subject our own values and ethical investments to scrutiny – to measure the value of value itself:

> When we make a determination of value ... we leave the realm of Value and enter that of the ethical, or the realm of value. In the instant prior to making a statement of value, we operate in Value – precisely so long as we consider, or are suspended between, a conflict of values are we genuinely operating in Value. The category of Value is an uncertain one, one in which responsible thinking of alternatives takes place.[10]

Kennedy then gives an example of what this might mean:

> A discourse that says 'No Abortion' is ethical in that it operates according to values or sentiments, or 'felt value'. So is one that says 'Abortion'. Neither is a discourse of Value. The discourse of Value is the one that asks whether or not there is an answer to the question, an ultimate answer, about killing foetuses. To occupy both ethical positions is perhaps liberal in some sense, but it is the position of Value.[11]

This kind of example is obviously a gift for the radical or political critic anxious to convict deconstruction of liberal fence-sitting. But it is not its irresolution which troubles me so much as the fact that Kennedy here sits so unselfconsciously (and, as we might say, 'undeconstructively') on one side of a familiar dichotomy between 'interested' criticism and 'disinterested' examination of first principles. Somewhere behind it lies the Kantian notion that the only really ethical reflections are those which are utterly disinterested and non-utilitarian. But such denials of utility always seem to turn out in fact to have been merely delayings or gearings-up of utility, in which, characteristically, a limited form of gain is sacrificed or invested in the interests of a wider, more encompassing gain that is thought likely to arise further down the line. In this example, the suspension of judgement about the question of abortion is clearly intended to precipitate the investigation or production of 'higher' values or principles, which will have more, or more extensive, utility and application.

The kind of claim presented by Kennedy has become characteristic of deconstructive approaches to the question of value. For Andrew

Benjamin, for example, the most urgent question for critical theory is not to determine the value of writing in general, or of particular pieces of writing, since 'any redemption of value must be predicated upon the actuality of a revaluation of value itself'.[12] For Benjamin, this involves a deconstructive *Nachträglichkeit* of tradition, a working-through-with-difference, which seems to require a certain suspension of, or resistance to, the need to affirm value. Gregory S. Jay shows a similar attitude towards the question of value in his essay 'Values and Deconstructions' (1987), in which he suggests that Derrida's response to the demand that deconstruction set out its ethical and political principles is to begin a genealogy of the nature of such principles, in an 'active withdrawal of allegiance to previous values and an attempt to think not this or that value, but the essence of valuation'.[13] But, as with the similar evaluative ideal proposed by Alan Kennedy, it is not clear whether this constitutes a permanent withdrawal from questions of value, or a promise of their eventual resumption. Jay concludes that 'the "intermediate stage" of our postmodernism, in criticism and politics, may never end, and this may turn out to be its crucial value, for this will signal the interruption of logocentrism by a resilient historicity that will generate, rather than fore-close, the production of new values'.[14] So this is surely another instance of delayed utility, the temporary sending away of questions of value in order to prepare for the production of new and better values at some future stage. In deconstruction as elsewhere, it seems, a theory that requires the permanent suspension of value cannot help but predicate the value of such a suspension in such a way as to suspend the suspension.

All these deconstructive discussions of the nature of value and choice seem to me to be caught in the jaws of this particular dichotomy – the dichotomy between an absolute and uncompromising suspension or dissemination of value, and an absolute betrayal or compromising of that suspension in one or another form of fixation or return (though, as we have seen, for Derrida at least, such an impacting of the dissemination and affirmation of value is far from being merely catastrophic). The viability of the question of value for deconstruction, I believe, depends upon enlarging the repertoire of options to allow for something other than the predictable alternation between these two absolute forms.

Ethics against Ethics

Recently, it has become clear how important an influence the work of Emmanuel Levinas has been in formulating questions of ethics and value for deconstruction. It is a work which poses in an intense form the evaluative questions just identified. Such questions exist not merely as the theme or content of Levinas's work, but arise equally in the very form of the appropriation of that work by writers like Derrida, for such appropriation throws into visibility the problem of deriving positive and actual value from an ethical system that seemingly resists such positivization as its very principle. Levinas's project begins with the Heideggerean grasping of existence as *Dasein*, or being-in-the-world, and with the indictment of metaphysical thinking that this entails. We do not exist, could not ever exist, apart from those conditions of our experience which metaphysical thought would separate off as contingent, for example spatiality and temporality. These are not accessory but necessary to our being, and constitutive of it. But Levinas believes that, for all its alleged break with metaphysics, Heidegger's thought remains metaphysical, because of its stress on the objectivizing consciousness, whose task is to grasp the conditions of its being-in-the-world. In his early work, Levinas tries to understand and articulate the condition of the *il y a*, the *there is*, by which he means pure existence, prior to its being fixed and distributed in the forms of subjectivity and objectivity, or sedimented into particular existents:

> To be conscious is to be torn away from the *there is*, since the existence of a consciousness constitutes a subjectivity, a subject of existence, that is, to some extent a master of being, already a name in the anonymity of the night. Horror is somehow a movement which will strip consciousness of its very 'subjectivity'. Not in lulling it into unconsciousness, but in throwing it into an *impersonal vigilance*, a *participation*.[15]

In his later work, Levinas will develop this position into a full-blown critique of the Western philosophical tradition, which struggles against the force of the *il y a* and against the authentic 'participation' which Levinas says it provokes. Philosophy consists of the gradually increasing dominance of an ontology of the same, in which a knowing self struggles to subordinate the alien objects of its thought to its dominion. Being thus becomes the object, that target and the subordinated other of knowing. Levinas believes that philosophy has always attempted to breach the gap between knowing and being by forms of violent appropriation: 'the known is understood and so *appropriated* by knowledge and as it were *freed* of its otherness. In the realm of truth, being, as the *other* of thought becomes the characteristic *property* of thought as knowledge.'[16] Modernity, for Levinas, means the attempt to move beyond the mere appropriation of being by knowledge to a condition in which they become absolutely interchangeable, in which 'identical and non-identical are identified', and 'the labour of thought wins out over the otherness of things and men'.[17] The evidence of this is to be found as much within the philosophy of Husserl and Heidegger as in the dominance of technological consciousness in the twentieth century.

Levinas suggests that this violent subjugation of the other (by which he means not only other beings in particular, but also Being itself in general) will always be brought about by a philosophy that subordinates ethics to ontology – that insists on first knowing what man *is* before attempting to formulate what he *should do*. For Levinas, the primary fact of being is not anything that could be formulated in terms of knowledge, theory or even 'experience', but is rather an anxious openness to the immediacy of the *il y a*. As soon as this can be known or conceptualized, it has already been subjugated to the sovereignty of the ego and the subject/object dichotomy it enforces. Another way of putting this, however, is that the ego itself is formed as a response to this crisis; it is a kind of scar tissue, which is to say, both a violent self-defence and a continuing ethical wound. 'The ego', Levinas writes, 'is the very crisis of the being of a being in the human domain. A crisis of being ... because I begin to ask myself if my being is justified, if the *Da* of my *Dasein* is not already the usurpation of somebody else's place.'[18]

Levinas wants to argue that the ethical relation, and not the ontological condition, is primary, that 'ethics is first philosophy'. Oddly, this depends on what seems to be an ontological claim about the primacy of the unaccommodated encounter with the other. Before the ego, before consciousness, before knowledge, says Levinas, comes exposure to the naked 'face' of the other, and the proximity and threat that it embodies. It is a threat not only in its unbearable closeness and nakedness, but in its terrifying vulnerability. It stands for the fact of death, the death of the observing ego and the death of the face that it observes. It is by throwing the ego's defences into crisis that this becomes an ethical relationship and, indeed, for Levinas, ethics centres not on the self-constituting and freely choosing ego, but on its dilapidation in the encounter with the other:

> In its expression, in its mortality, the face before me summons me, calls for me, begs for me, as if the invisible death that must be faced by the Other, pure otherness, separated, in some way, from any whole, were my business ... The Other becomes my neighbour precisely through the way the face summons me, calls for me, begs for me, and in so doing recalls my responsibility, and calls me into question.[19]

It has come to seem to many that if deconstruction has an ethics, then it must be of the kind that Levinas proposes, which is to say an ethics of otherness, based not on the principle of identity and the considerations of utility, rational self-interest or the common good which might spring from it, but on the very crisis of identity. For Simon Critchley, for example, what Levinas and Derrida have in common is an attempt 'to displace and think anew ethics by locating its condition of possibility and impossibility in the *Autrui*, the singular other'. Both of them aim for 'a certain point of exteriority with respect to traditional philosophical conceptuality, and they both seek this point by giving a privilege to an "infrastructural" matrix of alterity (*Autre* or *Autrui*), which, while still depending upon the resources of philosophical discourse, tries to displace that discourse and change its ground'.[20] This might seem to presuppose and make predictable a number of specifiable and desirable ethical outcomes from deconstruction: for example, the relaxation of the grip of dominant (Western, logocentric) forms of thought and language, the opening on to marginal and silenced areas of discourse and the dissolution of rigid hierarchical distinctions – in short, the diminishment of the discursive and conceptual violence involved in every form of centring. Alan Kennedy is perfectly happy to make this kind of ethical claim for deconstruction: 'Deconstruction decentres the world of English literature – not, note, so that non-literature takes over, but so that other literature can be seen. Deconstruction is a literary-critical (and of course also philosophical, etc.) decentring that has contributed to a major change resulting, for instance, in the recent awarding of the Nobel Prize to a Third World writer.'[21]

But it would seem that the Levinasian ethics inherited by certain forms of deconstruction would also be forced to resist the suggestion that the value of the ethical relation could ever be authentically measured in such beneficial outcomes in the real world. In fact, as we have seen, the ethics that deconstruction is concerned with resists formalization into codes of conduct and specifiable social values. As Derrida observes, 'Ethics, in Levinas' sense, is an ethics without law and without concept, which maintains its non-violent purity only before being determined as concepts and laws' (VM, 111). For Jean-François Lyotard, who also acknowledges a great debt to the work of Levinas, ethics consists not in the assimilation of one kind of language game to another – the subordination of description or denotation to ethical prescription, for example, or the measuring of the value of an activity by its practical outcome in the world – but in the refusal to allow such assimilation. So far is the ethical encounter from achieving any kind of gain in any kind of language game, economic or artistic, that it cannot even be represented without falsifying it. The only authentic writing of the ethical relation would therefore be one that did not attempt to 'weave a mastery, an experience, a text together with what has no text, no experience, and no mastery', but was rather 'the testimony of the fracture, of the opening onto that other who in the reader sends a request to Levinas, of a responsibility before that messenger who is the reader' (*D*, 113). Levinas therefore provides for Lyotard a kind of empty ethics, that refuses the orientation towards success or practical application that characterizes every other form of discourse: Lyotard speculates that the ethical genre may be 'the one whose rule is to admit no rule but that of obligation without conditions' (*D*, 117).

In his resistance to the objectification of ethics into law and precept, Levinas comes oddly close to the Heidegger against whose allegedly violent abstractive ontology his own philosophy is developed. Pressed to provide an articulation of the ethical system which seems implicit in the concept of *Mitsein*, or Being-for-others in *Being and Time*, Heidegger's response was his 'Letter on Humanism' (1947), in which he claims that ontology, the study of Being, must always be prior to ethics, the theory of right actions. But what is striking about what Heidegger says about the question of values in the 'Letter on Humanism' is how it anticipates the Levinasian theme of resistance to the objectification of concepts and values:

> To think against 'values' is not to maintain that everything interpreted as a 'value' – 'culture,' 'art,' 'science,' 'human dignity,' 'world,' and 'God' – is valueless. Rather it is important finally to realize that precisely through the characterization of something as a 'value' what is so valued is robbed of its worth. That is to say, by the assessment of something as a value, what is valued is admitted only as an object for man's estimation. But what a thing is in its Being is not exhausted by its being an object, particularly when objectivity takes the form of value. Every valuing, even where it values positively, is a subjectivizing. It does not let beings: be. Rather, valuing lets beings: be valid – solely as the objects of its doing. When one proclaims 'God' the altogether 'highest value,' this is a degradation of God's essence. Here as elsewhere thinking in values is the greatest blasphemy imaginable against Being. To think against values therefore does not mean to beat the drum for the valuelessness and nullity of beings. It means rather to bring the lighting of the truth of Being before thinking, as against subjectivizing beings into mere objects.[22]

Levinas, like Heidegger, wishes to found an ethics not in the possibility of rational or prudential choice, which is to say, choice in the service of the self-regulating ego, and the return of advantage to the same, but in the breaching or primal crisis of the ego. For Levinas, as for Heidegger, therefore, the pursuit of non-violence means something like the 'letting be' of the other, and the surrender of the mastery of identity. This letting be involves the refusal to objectify the other by giving it a value, or to conceptualize the non-conceptualizable relation to the other in terms of ethical schemes. Values and ethics, in the traditional sense, therefore, seem to be ruses of the same, ways of violently subordinating the other to the same. Heidegger, though apparently more concerned with how to avoid inflicting violence on Being than on people, is as appalled as Levinas by the reduction and objectification involved in values and valuing as conventionally thought. Indeed, the closeness between Levinas and Heidegger here becomes even more apparent when, a little later in his argument, Heidegger writes that 'that thinking which thinks the truth of Being as the primordial element of man, as one who eksists, is in itself an original ethics'; even though he quickly cancels this out by saying that 'this thinking is not ethics in the first place, because it is ontology'.[23] However, the problem of the recursion of positive value affects Heidegger quite as much as we will see that it does Levinas. Heidegger defends himself against the charge that the thinking of Being, as opposed to the assignation of objective values, is merely theoretical, and without any practical application in our own lives, by arguing that 'such thinking is neither theoretical nor practical. It comes to pass before this distinction ... Such thinking has no result. It has no effect. It satisfies its essence in what it is.'[24] But the notion of a satisfaction, even the 'satisfaction of an essence', with its implication of the possibility of some painful or relatively undesirable non-satisfaction, necessarily predicates a form of positive value. Inasmuch as you might ever recommend anyone to devote time to the thinking of Being, in preference to hopscotch or hoovering, it would always already have registered on some scale of practical utility or desirability, and this not as a mere adjunct or idiom of some hypothetically 'true' nature or value, but as its very actualization.

Ethics is the traditional name for the philosophy of morals in general, which is to say, the philosophy that deals with questions of right and wrong, duty, responsibility and choice. The word 'ethics' derives, of course, from the Greek *ethos*, which means, in the singular, 'character' and, in the plural, 'manners' or 'customs'. Embodied within the word therefore is a conception of the continuity between the singular and the plural, between character and custom, and, indeed, ethics has traditionally been considered the theory which attempts to bring these two realms together. Occurring at the point at which singularity and the generality of the social converge, ethical systems have often depended upon or led to assumptions about the nature of the bond between self and society, as well as general claims about the nature of both. Now, it is just such claims that are habitually undermined by the relay which runs from Heidegger to Levinas to Derrida, for all of whom, as we have seen, the *ethos* is an unjust and limiting reification of value, which systematically prevents the thinking of value beyond the mastery of the ego, constraining the ethical gift of the self to the other.

But is this damaging for a deconstructive ethics? The suspicion that it may be impossible to maintain the pure separation of the thinking of value from actual values as such may lead one to wonder whether there can ever be such pure value, or an ethics without *ethos*. For Tobin Siebers, such a thing is indeed impossible. Siebers's discussion of deconstruction in *The Ethics of Criticism* (1988) allows the ethical impulse of deconstruction, but argues that it is profoundly disabled by its unwillingness to acknowledge the idea of ethical 'character'. The ethical force of deconstruction is apparent in its minute and conscientious attention to the modes of violence in discourse, indeed, in its sense that all writing, insofar as it involves opposition, difference and structure, constitutes a kind of violence. So, in his essays on Lévi-Strauss in *Of Grammatology*, Derrida joins to Lévi-Strauss's Rousseauesque condemnation of the intrusive effects of writing on non-Western cultures a condemnation of Lévi-Strauss himself for the ethnocentric violence of his own sentimental assumptions about the unfallen nature of the Nambikwara Indians before the arrival of writing. For Derrida, the violence of writing is originary and universal; there could not conceivably ever have been a time of pure non-violence before the arrival of writing.[25] The question that Siebers rightly wants to ask about this is: what does the universal violence of writing violate, if there is nothing before or outside it? Siebers argues that, if Derrida is a radical follower of Rousseau in his attention to the modes of violence in writing and representation, in social and linguistic structures themselves, nevertheless, he deprives himself of the possibility of an ethics which would resist violence by refusing to follow Rousseau in positing some possibility of a natural condition of man that once was non-violent, or could conceivably be restored to the condition of non-violence.

Siebers argues in a parallel way about the work of Paul de Man. De Man's criticism is so hypersensitive to the violence involved in every will-to-system that the only theory he is willing to contemplate is a theory that absolutely resists system. The problem is that this theory is itself so powerful and all-encompassing ('nothing can overcome the resistance to theory because theory *is* this resistance', thunders de Man[27]) that it risks itself subsiding into the violent condition of system and ideology. In ethical self-preservation, de Man retreats into what Siebers calls the condition of critical 'martyrdom': by which he means the willed self-annihilation of a criticism that believes every form of encounter with the other is likely to become a form of violence. But the apparent purity of this absolute non-violence is a violence in itself, precisely because of its refusal to engage with the other.

> The only possible value to be given to martyrdom consists in its refusal on ethical grounds to stand for the aggressive and exclusionary impulses of some forms of systematic thought. Once martyrdom becomes a theory, however, it fails to direct its aggression neither toward its enemies nor toward itself. It becomes a system bent on its own destruction as the first step in destroying the violence that it associates with others. Its motivations are ethical, but ethically misguided because it trades a less sure form of violence for one that strives to encompass everything. Nihilism in the modern world may be defined as the preference for nothingness over the risk of committing an act of violence. Since nihilists cannot escape the equation within the philosophical tradition between violence and negativity, however, they must accuse themselves of violence as well.[28]

What connects this critique of de Man with Siebers's critique of Derrida is the belief that the negation of the self, and of the possibility of a human nature partially or variably instanced in that self, deprives deconstruction of the possibility of an ethics. There may be an ethical impulse in the negative capability of deconstruction, but it is just this negativity that vitiates its ethics: 'A moral philosophy that does not include the self may seem faultless, but its perfection rests in reality on the enormous void left by its rejection of the human. Removing the human from ethics leaves it without a basis for existence, since ethics is by definition profoundly anthropocentric.'[29] Deconstruction, on this account, resembles a Sartrean dissolution of the bad faith and inauthenticity characteristic of the *en-soi* which has been carried through to the choosing agency of the *pour-soi*. Here, the ethical self can only ever be an intermittent flicker of negativity, refusing to risk the visibility which might bring with it culpability.

Undoubtedly, Siebers here has isolated one of the most important problems regarding deconstructive ethics and, one might add, the ethics of any form of theory which is entirely mistrustful of the category of the self or of human nature. However, his error is to assume too precipitately that this complete suspension of the self and liquidation of the value embodied in it in fact takes place in deconstruction, or indeed is necessarily implied in it. The paradox suggested in Siebers's analysis of de Man, for example, which suggested that a purely non-violent theory could become a form of ethical violence, is anticipated by Derrida in an important comment on the ethics of Levinas:

> Implied by the discourse of *Totality and Infinity*, alone permitting to *let* be others in their truth, freeing dialogue and the face to face, the thought of Being is thus as close as possible to nonviolence.
> *We do not say pure nonviolence.* Like pure violence, pure nonviolence is a contradictory concept ... Pure violence, a relationship between beings without face, is not yet violence, is pure nonviolence. And inversely: pure nonviolence, the nonrelation of the same to the other (in the sense understood by Levinas) is pure violence. Only a face can arrest violence, but can do so, in the first place, only because a face can provoke it. (VM, 146–7)

I take it that what Derrida is saying here is that the dream of pure non-violence, the absolute avoidance of the risk of violence by avoidance of contact with the other, is in itself a kind of violent denial of that other. To put it for a moment in the terms offered by Lyotard: the justice embedded in the principle of the absolute incommensurability of cultures, 'name-worlds', and 'phrase-regimens', is unjust precisely because, insofar as it proclaims the contradictory principle of *absolute* incommensurability, it deprives itself of the possibility of measuring and maintaining the incommensurability of cultures. The principle of incommensurability is contradictory because it is this principle which precisely provides the common scale of comparison that indicates the impossibility of any common scale of comparison. This common scale is necessary to establish the principle of justice embodied within incommensurability, even as it contradicts it. The principle of justice is therefore itself unjust; the principle of the inviolability of language games is itself a kind of violence.

If this is an aporia, it is not, I think, a lethal aporia, which would simply and definitively kill off the ethical project of deconstruction. Indeed, insofar as the ethics of deconstruction involves a continuing willingness to interrogate the principles of ethics themselves, it may be that there is nothing that would always and reliably fit the description of a deconstructive ethics; since any ethics that attends scrupulously (ethically) to its own principles is likely to encounter these sorts of problem. If deconstruction became the name of the subdiscipline that would predict these problems in advance, then it would be the very contrary of an ethics.

If the question still remains, 'why do it?' 'why be ethical?', it may be that the very posing of the question already presupposes an ethical answer. That is to say, the putting into question of ideas of value, profit, advantage, the 'good', has always already entered the sphere of value. For how could one possibly give a negative answer to this question that would not instance the contradiction of constative and performative, in other words that would deny value in what it said but affirm value in the very affirmation of its denial? If one replies negatively to the question 'why be ethical?' – if one says, one should not be or need not be ethical, because ethics is just a sham (Nietzsche), or because the desire to accumulate value is secondary to the death instinct or desire for waste (Freud, Bataille), then one will always be establishing an ethics of negation in the very negation of ethics. For one will have entered into discourse, which, insofar as it always implies and embodies relationships at once of power, violence and justice, is always already ethical. There can be no entirely non-violent discourse, but there can equally be no discourse which is not to some degree the just deferral of violence.

It is because the ethical relation is principally a discursive relation, and vice versa, that it may be possible to advance a little beyond, or move a little deeper back into, the impasse represented variously by deconstructive attempts to rethink the question of value as such, by the reading of a text which articulates the ethical and discursive relations together, and curiously triangulates the encounter between Levinas and Derrida. Such a divagation into the textual and ethical thematics of wandering and return in Joyce's *Ulysses* may prove in the end to be the shortest way home. In reading Derrida reading Levinas through reading a text such as this one, in which the relations of reading, speaking and responsibility are intimate and intricate, we may arrive at a more complex and responsive account of the ethical relations between the self and the other, as well as of the ways in which the aesthetic and the ethical cross and convene in these relations.

Ulysses Jewgreek

At the meeting point of two forms of extremity, the extremity of artifice and the extremity of realism, *Ulysses* also insists on the importance of questions of right and responsibility, value and prescription; that is, on questions of ethics. Such questions are inescapable because every attempt to refuse them at the level of character and action, of what is represented in the novel, can only displace them into questions of representation itself. Why write this novel? Why read it? What kinds of ethical force and value are embodied in its address to its readers and those readers' response to it?

For those critics who set out to assimilate *Ulysses* to the norms and functions of the realist novel, the ethical question gathers around the question of the self and its social relations and responsibilities. For this kind of critic – whom we may designate 'ethico-realist' – the central problem dealt with in *Ulysses*, that of the relationship of the artist Stephen and the citizen Bloom, is also the central problem dealt with *by Ulysses*. The extreme, almost, at times, inhuman complexity of the work, which provides a challenge to the authority of form, is what eventually allows a humanizing of form, an ethical mediation between abstraction and actuality, theory and experience. For Charles Peake, the moral vision of *Ulysses* depends on 'the scrupulous refusal to lift questions of moral discrimination out of the bewildering context of ordinary life'. This vision is 'penetrating, extensive and coherent. Its complexity may be difficult to grasp on a first reading, but, because it is a complexity founded on every reader's own experience, it is ultimately not merely comprehensible, but clarifying and illuminating.' For Patrick Parrinder, the 'moral justification' of Joyce's particularity, his parody, his mockery of system, lies in its 'challenge to the claims of orthodox religion and morality to pre-empt human value', and his rejection of the impersonal structures of history and value in favour of the unifying force of 'private consciousness and the informal and unofficial creation of meanings'.[30]

For a more recent generation of critics, the novel has often been taken to provide an instance of a *linguistic* ethics, which is no longer rooted in the idea of ethical character, but takes its force from its refusal of the closure of traditional constructions of the self. This form of criticism – which we might as well call 'ethico-linguistic' – wishes to assert the primacy of language and representation, in all their shifting indeterminacy, over the narrow, citizenly ethics of the bourgeois; to assert, as it were, the ethical ascendancy of the linguistic over the ethical.

For writers impelled by versions of linguistic ethics such as Julia Kristeva's, the ethical distaste for narrow definitions of ethics based on the singular, responsible self or the coercively cohering community is often so great as to require the prohibition of the language of ethics altogether, although this is never enough to complete the concealment of the ethical force impelling such arguments.[31] Both for the ethico-realist critic and for the ethico-linguistic critic, the question of language is paramount; for the former, it represents a bewildering contingency that must be brought into ethical cohesiveness, for the latter, it is the very contingency of language which guarantees its ethical force.

The ethico-realist reading of *Ulysses* may be said to be governed by a reversionary thematics of the same: this involves an ethical rhythm in which the self is drawn away from its enclosure into an embrace of otherness, only to be returned to itself, enlarged, pluralized but reinforced. Such an account might concentrate in particular upon Stephen's halting characterization, against the sardonic interventions of Lynch's Cap, of the artist's self-estrangement in 'Circe':

STEPHEN: Here's another for you. (*he frowns*) The reason is because the fundamental and the dominant are separated by the greatest possible interval which ...

THE CAP: Which? Finish. You can't.

STEPHEN: (*with an effort*) Interval which. Is the greatest possible ellipse. Consistent with. The ultimate return. The octave. Which.

THE CAP: Which?

(*U*, 411)

Stephen here struggles to complete a sentence which, in its own gaps and hesitations, imitates the series of 'empty fifths' which he has just been picking out on the brothel piano (*U*, 410). Suddenly, the sentence is drawn together, ellipsis completed in ellipse, as Stephen sets out the incarnational processes of self-othering in religious, artistic and commercial terms:

STEPHEN: (*abruptly*) What went forth to the ends of the world to traverse not itself, God, the sun, Shakespeare, a commercial traveller, having itself traversed in reality itself becomes that self. Wait a moment. Damn that fellow's noise in the street. Self which it itself was ineluctably preconditioned to become. *Ecco*!

(*U*, 412)

Commenting on the 'Circe' chapter in which this passage appears, Charles Peake writes that 'for each of the two men, the brothel chapter represents the dominant of their fundamentals, the aphelion of their orbits ... In their extremities, when their paths meet, they may through their encounter complete the realization of their potential selves.'[32] But the rhythm or shape that Stephen sketches out here may describe not only the ethical structure of the book, but also its aesthetic structure; *Ulysses* is a book which hedges its immense expenditure of time and energy on multitudinous particularities with the promise that these particularities will all come to have meaning and value, will have been returned with profit to their point of origin. The book can be seen as the wager on a return, on the return of its wager. If this generalized economic metaphor can be seen at work in all narratives, since all narratives extend and expend themselves in time, with the promise of a return of aesthetic profit at the end of the process, then what surely characterizes *Ulysses* is the extreme *risk* of the undertaking, the huge distance and lapse of time between the initial outlay and the final return. And of course it is precisely this ratio, along with the close relationship between the idea of ethical character and the question of form in the novel, which makes the question of value so inescapable for it.

The dichotomy between outlay and return may be seen as an economic allotrope of the more familiar Lukácsian split between existence and essence, the sensuous phenomenality of being and the underlying laws which govern it. Terry Eagleton has recently suggested another kind of economic analogy for this split in *Ulysses* in the 'curious time of the commodity' in early twentieth-century capitalism, the commodity which is simultaneously entirely present as sensuous being and entirely constituted by abstract economic processes. In this system, 'human subjects are on the one hand held fast in the mire of immediacy, atomised and decimated by the commodity and its operations, and on the other hand dimly aware of themselves as subjected to the dominion of global iron laws with all the naturalised fatality of the world of myth'.[33] In fact, the striking thing about *Ulysses* is how little need there is to resort to the mode of analogy to measure the functioning of the economic in its ethico-narrative structure, precisely because the book itself so conspicuously takes this analogy as its subject, measuring the distance and dialectical equivalence not only between experiential phenomenon and organizing principle in the realm of the aesthetic, but also between the realms of the aesthetic and the economic themselves. The book gives us an allegory of this, of course, in the very relationship of Stephen, the artist, and Bloom, the citizen. The ethical lengthening of the aesthetic consists in the artist's encounter with the world of the economic, the world of the 'commercial traveller'. And, if the commercial is the stage of ethico-economic self-estrangement for the aesthetic, then, from Bloom's point of view, the aesthetic represents the possibility of a profitable economic detour for the commercial, as in his plans for remunerative concert tours, or for making money by writing short stories in the manner of Philip Beaufoy. If Stephen sinks artistic capital into the world of commerce, then Bloom invests resources in the world of art. In both cases, the investment is simultaneously economic and ethical.

Or we might also say that the ethical seems here in its very syntax and functioning to be economic. Ethical odyssey is a supplement to aesthetic closure, aesthetic closure is the profit derived from an expenditure of the self that turns out all along to have been a wise investment. If in one sense the economic is merely a stage through which the aesthetic must pass, a commercial travelling of the aesthetic principle to the ends of itself, in another sense the very structure of the aesthetic encounter with and transfiguration of the world is itself an economic one from start to finish.

The most important principle of this ethical self-distancing is the fact that it is an odyssey with a homecoming, an ethics that depends on an eventual return to the *ethos*. The essential feature of the metaphor of incarnation for Stephen as an artist is not the outward journey, but the return of the fallen substance of the world to its divine nature, via the intermediary function of art. In the passage from 'Circe' quoted above, Stephen may be meditating on the process by which the divine is drawn into the vicissitudes of history, but his emphasis falls on the trajectory of the self's return to the 'self which it itself was ineluctably preconditioned to become', and is dependent upon the silencing of the distractions of that 'noise in the street' (*U*, 412). And if the Odyssey of the day represents for Bloom a number of opportunities for loss of self in the other, these are all in fact avoided or turned to account; Bloom is tempted by the brutality of hunger in 'Lestrygonians' only to compromise with the urgent demands of the body with his modest cheese sandwich and glass of burgundy. In the same way, he is tempted into political argument with the Citizen in 'Cyclops', lured by lachrymosity and sentiment in 'Sirens' and 'Nausicaa' and, most notably, by the dreams of glory and grandiose self-enlargement in 'Circe'. In each case, Bloom is shown being able to return to himself, preserved and enlarged by the encounter with the other. We may take as paradigmatic Bloom's mistrust of the pseudo-Odysseus in the cabman's shelter, with his dubious globe-trotting tales, and substitution of a more modest idea of a trip to London via the South Coast, and the notion of 'a concert tour of summer music embracing the most prominent pleasure resorts', which he thinks 'might prove highly remunerative' (*U*, 512). Perhaps the most extreme of Bloom's ethical expeditions into the other is his masochistic adoption of female identity in 'Circe'. But this is clearly presented as a male fantasy of femaleness, the voluptuous surrender of the self to humiliation, restraint and punishment in order to reinstate the authority of the self in terms of its pleasure principle. Wayne Booth reads a passage from *Ulysses* in terms of such profitable recursion to the same, although he displaces the ethical enlargement of character in the book to its ethical effect on the reader. Booth uses *Ulysses* to instance the ways in which fiction necessarily calls forth, in forms of identification and reader-projection, the kind of projection of the self into the other that Stephen seems to evoke in 'Circe'. Booth insists that the ethical effect of reading is to transform the self, perhaps even fatally to compromise its essential reality: 'regardless of what I may want to be or to become – I, the true I, the sincere person of integrity, the "self" that was already compromised by my reading such stuff instead of doing my work as a Mormon missionary among the lost souls of Chicago – I am now become *somewhat* Joycean.'[34] But, for all his apparent rejection of the notion of the essential self, and embrace of the ethics of otherness, Booth's account remains tied to an ethics of accumulation which is at bottom economic, in the sense that it is orientated towards productivity and return. The process of reading, he says, is a process of establishing larger and larger syntheses and amalgamations of competing narratives, since 'to be bound to any one story would be to surrender most of what we care for'. The self, in this account, may not be an 'essential' self, but it is a self whose boundaries can never be burst by its 'ever-expanding collection of metaphoric worlds'.[35]

But if *Ulysses* yields richly to such readings, this is precisely because it also offers such conspicuous resistance to them. The novel seems regularly to refuse the consolations of totality, either in terms of the self or in terms of artistic form. The most arresting example of this occurs in 'Ithaca', the very episode which claims to enact the *nostos*, or homecoming, in a passage which seems to contradict Stephen's vision in 'Circe' of the ethical and aesthetic homecoming of the self. Bloom feels that the various ideas for continuing his relationship with Stephen beyond their evening encounter are 'rendered problematic' by the following considerations:

> The irreparability of the past: once at a performance of Albert Hengler's circus in the Rotunda, Rutland square, Dublin, an intuitive particoloured clown in quest of paternity had penetrated from the ring to a place in the auditorium where Bloom, solitary, was seated and had publicly declared to an exhilarated audience that he (Bloom) was his (the clown's) papa. The imprevidibility of the future: once in the summer of 1898 he (Bloom) had marked a florin (2/–) with three notches on the milled edge and tendered it in payment of an account due to and received by J. and T. Davy, family grocers, 1 Charlemont Mall, Grand Canal, for circulation on the waters of civic finance, for possible, circuitous or direct, return.
>
> Was the clown Bloom's son?
> No.

Had Bloom's coin returned?
Never.

(U, 571)

This passage represents the failure and mockery of the entire aesthetic wager on speculation and return that *Ulysses* advances; the father is an impostor, the coin never returns, either directly or circuitously. Indeed, the passage may suggest a different economy of the ethical altogether, an ethics based not on recursion but on improvident expenditure, not on the closure of totality but on the openness of infinity. Such a writing could not be thought of as an investment, but rather as a pure giving, without the hope of return which is present even in the structure of gratitude. Such improvidence is precisely the force of the ethical relation as defined by Levinas, that relation which Derrida finds so fascinating and problematic in his responses to Levinas's work. Interestingly, it is in evoking this improvidence in 'Violence and Metaphysics' that *Ulysses* seems to make its first, subliminal appearance in Derrida's text:

> Truthfully one does not have to wonder *what* this encounter is. It is *the* encounter, the only way out, the only adventuring outside oneself toward the unforeseeably other. *Without hope of return* ... In describing liturgy, desire, and the work of art as ruptures of the Economy and the Odyssey, as the impossibility of return to the same, Levinas speaks of an 'eschatology without hope for the self or without liberation in my time'. (VM, 95)

The metaphors of 'economy' and 'odyssey' employed here have wide reference, of course, but will prove at the end of Derrida's essay to have a particular appropriateness to *Ulysses*, the novel in which these two features are so structurally important. Derrida here does seem to suggest that it might be possible to mount a reading of the ethics of such a text as *Ulysses* by means of this Levinasian principle of primordial openness and obligation to the other, an openness which is constitutive and non-profitable. Such a reading would need to look again at the large symbolic structures in the novel, and especially the structures of Economy, Odyssey and Paternity, and try to open a difference from the conventional reading of these symbols, as leading to profit, homecoming and familial unity.[36] The novel would then be seen as elaborating as a continuing principle, rather than as an occasional aberration, wasteful expenditure, wandering without return and absolute alienation of the father's ethical relation to the son. The passage about the clown and the non-returning coin would, on this account, be the internal allegory of another *Ulysses*, a text in which the profitable return to the same is denied, and in which there is a pure opening on to the other.

There are a number of ways in which such an ethics might seem to be thematized in the text of *Ulysses*. There is, most notably, the attempt throughout the book to refrain from or to displace the force of violence, mostly, of course, through the mild civic heroism of Bloom. Bloom resists the violence of the Citizen, protesting against 'persecution ... perpetuating national hatred among nations' (*U*, 271), and asserting the superiority of love over violently fixated national identity. Violence is often associated for Bloom with cannibalism, the self-consumption of the same. As he watches Holy Communion, the letters 'I.N.R.I' interpret themselves for him as 'Iron nails ran in', while the swallowing of the Host causes him to reflect, 'Rum idea: eating bits of a corpse. Why the cannibals cotton on to it' (*U*, 66). The 'Lestrygonians' episode furnishes other examples of this association, especially among the rapacious carnivores in the Burton restaurant, who make him think, 'Eat or be eaten. Kill! Kill!' (*U*, 139). The oral rage which Bloom witnesses here even seems to stifle the expressive capacities of discourse, which is reduced to a retentive gagging and cramming: 'Other chap telling him something with his mouth full ... I munched hum un thu Unchster Bunk un Munchday' (ibid.). It is no wonder that Bloom leaves, thinking, 'Every fellow for his own, tooth and nail. Gulp. Grub. Gulp. Gobstuff' (ibid.). The theme of self-consumption is continued in the episode with Nosey Flynn snuffling up his dangling dewdrop, and the terrier which 'choked up a sick knuckly cud on the cobblestones and lapped it with new zest' (*U*, 147); but it is also opposed with Bloom's memory of the passage of food between mouths, in the seedcake shared with Molly on Howth Head (*U*, 144). Here, as elsewhere, the ethical openness to the other in love seems to be signified in the opening of the body to the outside.

The most often-remarked example of the displacement of violence in the book is, of course, Joyce's refusal to parallel the slaying of the suitors in the *Odyssey*, as enacted in Bloom's mood of 'abnegation' and 'equanimity' on arriving home, and his sense of the futility of violent retribution in the light of 'the lethargy of nescient matter: the apathy of the stars' (*U*, 604). His entry into the matrimonial bed has been 'circumspect', 'prudent' and 'reverent'; encountering there 'the imprint of a human form, male, not his', he reflects calmly on his own displacement, thinking that 'each one who enters imagines himself to be the first one to enter whereas he is always the last term of a preceding series even if the first term of a succeeding one, each imagining himself to be the first, last, only and alone whereas he is neither first nor last nor only nor alone in a series originating in and repeated to infinity' (*U*, 601).

Arguably, Bloom slays Molly's actual and imaginary suitors by gradually repossessing her thoughts and fantasies during her long nightspeech, progressively insinuating himself in place of his rivals. But this is not an absolute or violent displacement of the other, or colonization of Molly's thoughts. The final section of Molly's monologue seems to run together the seedcake-chewing episode on Howth Head and an earlier memory of Molly's concerning Lieutenant Mulvey in Gibraltar. Bloom's imaginative repossession of Molly therefore takes place, if at all, within a transferential reminiscence in which neither the Howth Head episode nor the Gibraltar episode has priority. A non-violent slaying of this kind gains its victory in a surrender to the other.

One might argue that this opening to the other is also what is attempted by the move towards the discourse of the feminine in the final section of the book, and perhaps throughout Joyce's work as a whole, as suggested, for instance, by Bonnie Kime Scott in writing that '*Ulysses* and *Finnegans Wake* raise questions about the "moral nature" that has held the ascendancy in culture ... Largely through representations of female consciousness, Joyce demonstrates the vulnerability of rational absolutes, the truth of contradictions, the power of desire, the multiplicity of language and style.'[37] Christine van Boheemen-Saaf puts matters even more strongly. Even though she wants to resist what she calls the 'hypostasis of "the Other"' in critical readings of Joyce, she can still declare that ' "Penelope" is the *mise en abyme* of the otherness of *Ulysses* ... even if "Penelope" stands outside and apart ... by repeating, clarifying, and intensifying the style of writing in the body of the text [it] affirms and signs the alterity of *Ulysses*'.[38] Those readings which claim that feminine language in 'Penelope' and in *Ulysses* more generally represents a kind of pure prodigality, an excess that cannot be contained by conceptual structures or logocentric thinking, may be seen as congruous with Levinas's arguments for the ethical force of language in general; he suggests that 'absolute difference, inconceivable in terms of formal logic, is established only by language. Language accomplishes a relation between terms that breaks up the unity of a genus ... Language is perhaps to be defined as the very power to break the continuity of being or of history.'[39]

If Levinas offers a way of reading the ethical force of female language in *Ulysses*, then his work also accords a central place to that other preoccupation of Joyce's text, paternity. Struggling in *Time and the Other* (1947) with the problem of how to conceive a relation to the other which is not in fact one version or another of the egological violence practised by the self in its attempts to master the other, Levinas focuses, a little surprisingly perhaps, on the paternal relationship between father and son:

> Paternity is the relationship with a stranger who, entirely while being Other, is myself, the relationship of the ego with a myself who is none the less a stranger to me. The son, in effect, is not simply my work, like a poem or an artifact, neither is he my property. Neither the categories of power nor those of having can indicate the relationship with the child. Neither the notion of cause nor the notion of ownership permit one to grasp the fact of fecundity. I do not *have* my child; I *am* in some way my child ... Then again, the son is not any event whatsoever that happens to me – for example, my sadness, my ordeal, or my suffering. The son is an ego, a person. Lastly, the alterity of the son is not that of an alter ego. Paternity is not a sympathy through which I can put myself in the son's place. It is through my being, not through sympathy, that I am my son. The return of the ego to itself that begins with hypostasis is thus not without remission, thanks to the perspective of the future opened by eros. Instead of obtaining this remission through the impossible dissolution of hypostasis, one accomplishes it through the son.[40]

Here, paternity, as the remission of the ego's return to itself, is close to the experience of eros, which, for Levinas, is a paradigm of the ethical relationship not because it transcends the singularity of the ego in fusion, but precisely because it consists in 'an insurmountable duality of beings'. In eros, 'the other as other is not here an object that becomes ours or becomes us; to the contrary it withdraws into its mystery'.[41]

The preoccupation with fatherhood in *Ulysses* has been much discussed, of course, and the subject evidences in miniature the critical split between a recursive ethics and an excursive ethics. For Sheldon Brivic, fatherhood and filiality in Joyce's writing represent a struggle of life and death, which is finally overcome by a kind of merging of father with son, converting loss into victory, death into life:

> In the long run, the role of the son is to win, while that of the father is to lose. In the early 'Hero' phase, Joyce's work is driven by a need to be right at the expense of the world. But the later phase accepts the possibility of being overwhelmed by experience. The inevitable victory of the son tends to be destructive to others, while the defeat of the father is creative. The son takes life while the father gives. Yet the victories of sonship are ultimately justified as preparation for fatherhood, and Joyce became his own cause only by accepting the secret, fateful identity of his enemy.[42]

Read from a Lacanian perspective, the interchange of father and son in Joyce may seem less likely to come to rest in any gathered or reconciled identity as is projected here. For Jean-Michel Rabaté, *Ulysses* is driven by the desire for filial/paternal 'atonement' which it nevertheless always resists, for 'the entire conception of paternity as founded upon the void and incertitude rules out any such reunion and stresses difference'. Ellen Carol Jones argues in a similar way that the law of the father, as *logos*, as *lex eterna*, gives way in *Ulysses* to 'the law of dissemination, a sowing of infinite repetition, proliferation, and supplementation'.[43] We may say that readings of paternity in *Ulysses* via Lacan stress the undermining of the law of the father from the point of view of the insubordinate son, where Levinas's reading of paternity takes up the position of the father in order to imagine and project the ethical undermining and enlargement of the paternal self. But of whatever kind it may be, such a preoccupation with male paternity is, of course, always vulnerable to the charge which Luce Irigaray seems to level against it, that it may be a means for the male ego of restoring itself to itself, by means of the intermediary figure of woman, here reduced to a mere interval in the male circuit of egoity: 'The aspect of fecundity that is only witnessed in the son obliterates the secret of difference. As the lover's means of return to himself outside himself, the son closes the circle. The path of a solitary ethics that will have encountered, for its own need, without nuptial fulfillment, the irresponsible woman, the loved one.'[44] Derrida seems to anticipate such a critique in a footnote to 'Violence and Metaphysics', in which he remarks, with extraordinary offhandedness, that Levinas's *Totality and Infinity* 'pushes the respect for dissymmetry so far that it seems to us impossible, essentially impossible, that it could have been written by a woman. Its philosophical subject is man' (VM, 320–1). The fact that the remark is prompted by a reference to the phrase 'woman's reason' in *Ulysses* seems to suggest that the association of the two texts may be more than merely adventitious, and that Derrida sees *Ulysses* too as a male text precisely to the degree that it desires the decentring of the male. We shall see a little later on how Derrida returns in his later essay on Levinas to this footnote which both opens up and precipitately closes off the question of the ethics of sexual difference.

This returns us to a version of the problem which has recurred throughout this discussion. For as soon as the ethical relation has been set forth visibly in language, it has been betrayed; the ethical relation, as 'the extreme exposure and sensitivity of one subjectivity to another', can only be frozen into rigidity and distance by removal into the realm of utility and actual moral event.[45] Just as the ethical relation as set out so exhaustively by Levinas can never really be projected in conceptual form or persuasively instanced without subjecting it to violent reduction, so, for *Ulysses* to embody within it an ethics of alterity, an opening on to the infinity of the other, would therefore always be to retain the possibility of its own profit or aesthetic advantage. The possibility of an ethical anti-economy based on pure expenditure and contingency which seems to be embodied in the episode of the paternal impostor clown and the non-returning coin is therefore undermined at the moment that it is set forth. For *Ulysses*, the contingency of value exemplified in this passage comes to have that strategic value of contingency for the book itself, the book whose very structure depends upon this kind of speculation with contingency. As such, this passage and the heterogeneity it embodies would not constitute any pure or autonomous disruption of the economy of return in the book so much as its riskiest but most profitable speculation.

The game that Bloom plays here is a version of the fort:da game described by Freud in *Beyond the Pleasure Principle*, for it involves a sending away of himself, in the hope of a return that will guarantee mastery over absence and loss. But at the same time, this moment in the narrative of *Ulysses* represents a sending away of *itself*, in the interests of narrative authority, pleasure and profit which are all the more intense for their sojourn in death and absence. In this, we may say of *Ulysses* what Derrida so aptly says of Freud's account of the fort:da, which is that the structure of the game described by Freud enacts or folds over exactly on to the relationship between the game and its narration in *Beyond the Pleasure Principle*. Freud tells the story in order to dismiss it from his argument, to show that it is not a good example of anything beyond the pleasure principle, but, like the cotton-reel which is despatched by his grandson in order that it may be retrieved, the game comes back insistently through Freud's argument about the interrelationship of life and death, just as it is reeled back insistently into psychoanalytic discourse (TSF, 355). If the force of the non-returning coin and the false son for Bloom is disruptive, an ethical (in the Levinasian sense) estranging of the self into what 'Ithaca' calls 'aliorelative' rather than 'ipsorelative' identity (U, 581), then the way in which *Ulysses* so scrupulously asks and answers its own question about this alterity pulls it back within its own orbit, returning this alterity to itself, and mastering the fact of absence by giving it the meaning of absence.

What this seems to imply is that *Ulysses* will not tolerate a reading that simply replaces the ethics of the same with a Levinasian ethics orientated to the other. Indeed, as we have seen, Derrida argues in 'Violence and Metaphysics', there is a kind of abstractive violence implied in the very exactitude of this division between the violence of the same and the non-violence of alterity which is allegedly prior to it. In this sense, there could never be a pure, or purely non-violent, ethics of alterity. It would seem that

> the expression 'infinitely other' or 'absolutely other' cannot be stated and thought simultaneously; that the other cannot be absolutely exterior to the same without ceasing to be other; and that, consequently, the same is not a totality closed in upon itself, an identity playing with itself, having only the appearance of alterity, in what Levinas calls economy, work, and history. How could there be a 'play of the Same' if alterity itself was not already *in* the Same? (VM, 126)

Sameness can therefore no longer be opposed to alterity, since the difference between them is really only a difference within each. The consequence of this is that it is also impossible to found an ethics upon the notion of a purely non-violent opening of the ego to the other. This is because the other cannot be regarded as *purely* other, cannot be completely innocent of being reappropriated as an *alter ego* (though Levinas sees this as the egological violence of the same), since its absolute alterity could be registered only insofar as it were acknowledged to be an ego like my ego – 'The other as alter ego signifies the other as other, irreducible to *my* ego, precisely because it is an ego, because it has the form of an ego' (VM, 125). This is to say that the absolute alterity of the other, on which the ideal of ethical non-violence is based, is not an absolute at all. Pure non-violence always requires a certain violence in the very act of acknowledging the other to be an other. The denial of all violence would be the denial of all relationship, which is itself violent. (There may be an allegory of this in Mr Deasy's sinister joke about Ireland being 'the only country which never persecuted the Jews ... Because she never let them in' (*U*, 30).)

If pure non-violence always contradictorily entails violence, then, on the other side, pure or absolute violence, which is to say, a relationship 'between beings without face', a relationship in which the ego denies the status of otherness to the other, could never actually be a violence, since violence also requires acknowledgement of the other. As Derrida puts it, 'Only a face can arrest violence, but can do so, in the first place, only because a face can provoke it' (VM, 147).

This contradictoriness at the heart of Levinas's thought also relates crucially to the question of language. Levinas argues that the ethical relation of obligation to the other is primordially a discursive relation: 'The relation between the same and the other, metaphysics, is primordially enacted as a conversation (*discours*), where the same, gathered up in its ipseity as an "I," as a particular existent unique and autochthonous, leaves itself.[46] The principal ethical feature of language for Levinas is its *vocativity*; even though language always has the capacity violently to objectify the other, it is the force of its address which is ethical for Levinas:

> The word that bears on the Other as a theme seems to contain the Other. But already it is said to the Other who, as interlocutor, has quit the theme that encompassed him, and upsurges inevitably behind the said ... In discourse the divergence that inevitably opens between the Other as my theme and the Other as my interlocutor, emancipated from the theme that seemed a moment to hold him, forthwith contests the meaning I ascribe to my interlocutor. The formal structure of language thereby announces the ethical inviolability of the Other.[47]

But, again, what Levinas proposes as a fundamental split between the objectifying content of language and the ethical form of its vocativity Derrida reads as paradoxical. For, if it is true for Levinas, as Derrida writes, that 'the dative or vocative dimension which opens the original direction of language, cannot lend itself to inclusion in and modification by the accusative or attributive dimension of the object without violence' (VM, 95), then the whole of Levinas's exposition of his ethical philosophy must be exactly this kind of violence. The very notion of *exteriority*, for example, which is so important as a metaphor for Levinas, signifying as it does the ethical opening of the ego beyond the closure of its ipseity, itself belongs to and recapitulates the violent spatializing of existential relations in language which it aims to transcend. For Levinas, the struggle to articulate the ethical relation is a struggle against the Greek *logos*, a conceptual language which equates truth with absolute intelligibility or presence; Greek language, he says, construes truth always as 'what can be represented in some eternal here and now, exposed and disclosed in pure light'.[48] This represents a freezing of temporality and history into totality, a totalization which is always violent. The task of the ethical thinker is therefore to try to recover a non-Greek or Judaic lexicon of alterity from within this dominant language of concepts.

But this is as impossible as trying in practice to separate out the vocative from the referential functions of language, for it is always necessary to speak of alterity according to the Greek lexicon of intelligibility, which is to say closure or totality. Derrida criticizes Levinas for trying to effect such a pure separation of the two intermingled tongues, even as he praises Levinas for initiating a 'rupture of the logos', for attempting to hear another voice within the Greek voice. In fact, what Levinas's work really promises is an insight into the insoluble interweaving of Greek and Judaic, presence and alterity, violence and peace, within the *logos* itself:

> By definition, if the other is the other, and if all speech is for the other, no logos as absolute knowledge can *comprehend* dialogue and the trajectory toward the other. This incomprehensibility, this rupture of logos is not the beginning of irrationalism but the wound or inspiration which opens speech and makes possible every logos or every rationalism. A total logos still, in order to be logos, would have to let itself be proffered towards the other beyond its own totality. (VM, 98)

One main strand of Derrida's first essay on Levinas is a defence of Heidegger against Levinas's charge that his ontology is a philosophy of violence. This defence rests on the grounds that Heidegger's work actually already opens up within Greek ontotheology the intimate rupture of the *logos* that Levinas wants to initiate. It is for this reason that Derrida concludes 'Violence and Metaphysics' not with the simple expulsion of the Judaic (as 'the dream of a purely *heterological* thought. A *pure* thought of *pure* difference' (VM, 151)) from the house of Greek philosophy, in what would be a reassertion of ontology against ethics, Heidegger against Levinas, but with an image of a vexed, uncertain but hospitable entertaining of the Jew within the house of the Greek. It is an image which alludes to the final encounter of Stephen and Bloom, Christian and Jew, who must always meet on the grounds of the *logos*: 'still less may the Greek absent himself, having loaned his house and his language, while the Jew and the Christian meet in his home' (VM, 152).

The final paragraph of the essay uncoils a series of questions concerning the meeting of Jewish and Greek philosophical traditions. The questions enact, but are also generated from, the particular difficulty of framing the question of philosophical identity from an ethical point of view at all. If we ask 'Are we Jews? Are we Greeks?', we may always be assuming a Greek or Jewish answer. If we answer, as Derrida does, quoting Lynch's Cap in the 'Circe' episode of *Ulysses*, 'Jewgreek is greekjew. Extremes meet' (U, 411), then we must go on to ask whether the mutuality of Jew and Greek is a Jewish or Greek mutuality:

> Does the strange dialogue between the Jew and the Greek, peace itself, have the force of the absolute, speculative logic of Hegel, the living logic which *reconciles* formal tautology and empirical heterology ...? Or, on the contrary, does this peace have the form of infinite separation and of the unthinkable, unsayable transcendence of the other? (VM, 153)

If we are asking this question of *Ulysses* alone, rather than using *Ulysses* to ask it of philosophy as a whole (though we must still be using philosophy to ask the question, via *Ulysses, of* philosophy), then we might be asking, does the reconciliation or meeting of opposites in Stephen and Bloom belong to a violent metaphysics? Does the drawing together of divergences into accord, the gathering of the heterogeneous particulars of this text into totality, represent what Derrida colourfully calls 'the asphyxiation of the same', the 'autistic syntax' of the Greek dream of merged opposites? (VM, 149, 152)? Is the much-celebrated ethical hospitality to the contingent and the indeterminate in *Ulysses* just an extreme form of modernity's rapacious appetite for the unthought? Or is this reconciliation of contingency and structure to be read against itself, as a Judaic opening on to the history, contingency and otherness it seems to annul?[49] Does the coming together of Stephen and Bloom represent that violent/peaceful acknowledgement of the other as ego which is the only means to an ultimately peaceful/violent acknowledgement of the freedom of the other as other?

A reading of the second kind would need to pay heed to all the comic resistances to reconciliation included in the final encounter of Stephen and Bloom in Eccles Street, and perhaps especially to the passage in which they exchange views about Irish and Hebrew and the similarities of Catholicism and Judaism in 'their dispersal, persecution, survival and revival', and the possibilities of a return to a homeland (*U*, 564). In fact, here as elsewhere, Joyce stresses the incompleteness and unsatisfactoriness of the shared experience of diaspora and aspiration to homecoming, for example in the anthem which Bloom chants (this is later to become the national anthem of the state of Israel) 'partially in anticipation of that multiple, ethnically irreducible consummation', and which is broken off 'in consequence of defective mnemotechnic' (ibid.). Stephen's reply is to sing the ballad of 'Little Harry Hughes', describing the murder of a little child by a Jew's daughter. His commentary on the ballad and Bloom's reaction may seem to measure egotistic self-identification against the refusal of identity. Stephen reads the ballad in terms of his own grandiose sense of mission and betrayal, and the vocative dimension of his discourse clearly embodies some kind of threat to his host:

> One of all, the least of all, is the victim predestined. Once by inadvertence, twice by design, he challenges his destiny. It comes when he is abandoned and challenges him reluctant and, as an apparition of hope and youth, holds him unresisting. It leads him to a strange habitation, to a secret infidel apartment, and there, implacable, immolates him, consenting. (*U*, 567)

Stephen's violence here is of two kinds: firstly, in the appropriation of the experience of the ballad as his own and, secondly, in his assimilation of Bloom to the role of other, as the 'secret infidel'. Bloom offers no commentary of his own, but, in a manner that is typical of him, internally resists and deflects the ethical violence of the tale and its commentary: 'He wished that a tale of a deed should be told of a deed not by him should by him not be told' (*U*, 567). The easiest way to make sense of this puzzling sentence might be to split it between its eleventh and twelfth words, with the second clause, beginning 'of a deed', being grammatically consequent on the opening words 'he wished that a tale'. The sentence would then mean: 'He wished that a tale be told (by Stephen) but also wished that he (Stephen) had not told a tale of a deed not his (Bloom's)', i.e. had not violently attributed to Bloom the violence that he had. But the sentence could also mean that he (Bloom) wished that he (Stephen) had not told a tale of a deed which was not his (Stephen's), i.e. he wished that Stephen had not identified himself in his commentary. But these by no means exhaust the possible meanings of this odd sentence, which seems at once so grammatically deficient and excessive. Indeed, the very point of the sentence seems to be its anxious indeterminacy about who is speaking to whom about whose deed, as it inverts and complicates the structures of referentiality and vocativity. As a wounding, an ethical reproof and a gentle recompense at once, the sentence enacts a tremor in the principle of identity which governs Stephen's view of the artist and the ethics of reconciliation promoted throughout *Ulysses*. Bloom's language seems to testify both to the pained unwillingness either to inhabit his identity, or to allow the simple merger of identities. We might suggest that what is occurring here is a species of ethical transference, in which identities shift without ever being (in either sense) entirely *given*.

As we have seen already, even if it were possible to multiply such instances from the text of *Ulysses*, this could never amount to a demonstration of a Levinasian ethics within it. It is rather in some mode of the text's vocativity, in its resistance to the ethics of the same that such a relation may be, if at all, intuited. Such a resistance may be enacted in the interior of every reading, as part of its movement against totality, but could never be the demonstrable outcome of such a reading. Rather than using *Ulysses* to help him choose the Greek against the Jew, the same against the other, Derrida uses the novel to read what is at stake within that choice. So that, by the time Joyce is identified, in the final words of 'Violence and Metaphysics', as 'perhaps the most Hegelian of modern novelists', we can no longer be sure what that means – whether the meeting of Greek and Jew is here a Greek or a Jewish meeting, a 'jew-greek' or a 'greekjew' assimilation. The impossibility of simply deciding in favour of one or other of the two ethical responses we began by distinguishing suggests that the ethical compulsion of *Ulysses* in fact involves the very question of how to read the question of ethics, how, non-violently, within a discursive economy of violence, to read the question of alterity within the same. It is the quiver of categories induced by the call to ask the ethical question, while simultaneously questioning what that question is and how it must be asked, and while being, indeed, called by the need to question that question, which constitutes the ethics of *Ulysses*.

In Performance: War and Peace

Derrida's critique of the notion of an absolutely achieved alterity is resumed and extended in his second essay on Levinas, 'At This Very Moment in This Work Here I Am'. The essay seems to respond un-knowingly and, as it were, in advance to the essay 'Wholly Otherwise', which Levinas contributed to the volume of essays in which the English version of Derrida's text first appeared, for Levinas ends that essay by respectfully defending the pure alterity of his ethical philosophy against deconstruction. He does so by insinuating that, for all his precautions, Derrida falls back into the form of what he is attempting to escape – the thematics of Being set forth in a positive language of concepts. It is true, he concedes, that Derrida subjects every such concept and every such ambition to self-present Being to rigorous suspicion, but he asks never-theless, 'is not the attempt at a positive utterance of the failure of pres-ence to itself still a way of returning to the presence with which this positivity merges?'[50] As such, Levinas maintains, Derrida remains within the order of ontology, rather than breaking into the order of ethics; or, another way of saying the same thing, Derrida remains in the domain of the constative Said, and is inattentive to the ethical relation presupposed in every instance of vocative or performative Saying.

But this last issue is precisely that which is taken up by 'At This Very Moment'. The essay, and its title, are put together out of a number of quotations from Levinas's work, in all of which Levinas appears to be trying to affirm a kind of pure Saying, the immediate and uncom-promised opening to the other which would tear or interrupt the thread of conceptual discourse. Derrida's critique of Levinas's performativity parallels his critique, in *Limited Inc*, of the notion of performative self-presence in the speech-act theory of John Searle (and, in effect, in the discourse ethics of Habermas). This is to say, it depends upon demonstrating the structural necessity of iterability in every performative, which means, among other things, that no performative utterance, no matter how sufficiently it appears to be determined by its context – in the presence of a speaking and intending 'I', a comprehending other, the existence of shared conditions to interpret or validate the utterance – can avoid the possibility of being deported from its own context and resettled in new ones. If it is impossible to be sure of the intrinsic self-presence of Searle's performatives, it is equally impossible to be sure of the uncontaminated alterity of Levinas's ethical performatives. The capacity to be repeated of any statement in and of the now, any attempt to embody or instance pure Saying in the language of the Said, means that a performative of Levinas's kind is no more immune to reversal, displacement and betrayal than one of Searle's kind. To show this, Derrida quotes a passage from Levinas's *Otherwise than Being, or Beyond Essence* (1974) in which the phrase 'at this moment' occurs twice, in nearly identical form, but with absolutely different imports. Here is the passage:

> It will of course be objected that if any other relation than thematisation may exist between the Soul and the Absolute, then would not the act of talking and thinking about it *at this very moment* [Derrida's italics], the fact of enveloping it in our dialectic, mean that language and dialectic are superior with respect to that Relation?
> But the language of thematisation, which *at this moment* [Derrida's italics] we are using, has perhaps only been made possible itself by means of that Relation, and is only ancillary. (quoted in ATVM, 23, no page reference given)

The first 'at this very moment' announces the betrayal of the ethical relation by the false positivity of language: in Derrida's words, it 'thematizes the thematization that envelops, covers up, or dissimulates the Relation' (ATVM, 24). The second 'at this moment' does the opposite: it 'thematizes the unthematizable of a Relation that does not allow further envelopment under the tissue of the same' (ibid.). This enables Derrida to demonstrate the way in which the very performance of the performative brings about a doubling in Levinas's text, folding together the Saying and the Said, the vocative and the thematic, the ethical and the ontological:

> Although, between the two 'moments,' there is a chronological, logical, rhetorical, and even an ontological interval – to the extent that the first

belongs to ontology while the second escapes it in making it possible –
it is nevertheless the *same moment*, written and read in its difference, in
its double difference, one belonging to dialectic and the other different
from and deferring from (*différant*) the first, infinitely and in advance
overflowing it. (ΛTVM, 24)

This is to say that it is necessary to be aware of the irreducible
interconnectedness of the two dimensions distinguished and associated
by Levinas's repeated phrase, which is in turn to argue what had been
argued in 'Violence and Metaphysics', the inalienable possibility of passage between the ethical and the unethical, non-violence and violence.
Derrida's critique of Searle and, behind him, the discourse ethic of
Habermas, is that it assumes that intersubjective relations can be captured
and formalized within conceptual thought and put without risk to the
service of a (narrowly conceived) rationality. Although it has sometimes
(but still too often) been said that Derrida's work abandons rationality
and therefore also abandons sociality and intersubjectivity, Derrida's
critique of speech-act theory depends to a large extent on a Levinasian
sense of the intersubjective vocation of all discourse, along with a sense
of its uncapturable excessiveness to all conceptual and consensual
thought. But here, in responding to Levinas, Derrida is also forced to
show the limits of Levinas's doctrine of the uncapturable excess of
intersubjectivity, by indicating that it can never be entirely immune from
recapture by the 'thematization' which he appears to object to in Searle,
Habermas and others.

In order to mount this critique of Levinas, Derrida has to adopt in an
even more intense way than usual the technique of immanent critique,
shadowing Levinas's work on the inside in order to show its limits,
rather than claiming to occupy a position of exteriority with regard to
it. Derrida's own performance or enactment of his critique therefore
performs and enacts the point that he wishes to demonstrate, that pure
self-identity and pure difference can never be thought separately and in
strict opposition. This is why 'At This Very Moment' is so impelled and
imperilled by the problems of giving, obligation and gratitude, the problem of how to render homage to Levinas in a way which would authentically resume the irreversible openness to the other which is claimed by
that work, and therefore avoid in any sense reinstituting an economy of
the same in merely restoring that work to him. Levinas's radical altruism
seems, in short, to forbid gratitude. The problem that Derrida here sets
himself seems to be anticipated in some earlier remarks made about
Joyce's writing, though not in *Ulysses* so much as in *Finnegans Wake*.

Such writing might be seen, he conjectures, as a gesture towards a purely unreturnable and non-profitable gift:

> There is first of all the greatness of s/he who writes in order to give, in giving, and therefore in order to give to forget the gift and the given, what is given and the act of giving, which is the only way of giving, the only possible – and impossible – way. Even before any restitution, symbolic or real, before any gratitude, the simple memory, in truth merely the awareness of the gift, on the part of giver or receiver, annuls the very essence of the gift. The gift must be without return, without a sketch, even a symbolic one, of gratitude. (TWJ, 146)

The answer to the problem of how to write gratefully about the philosophical gift of Levinas (and perhaps also of Joyce) seems to be that, in order to remain faithful to him, Derrida must in some sense be unfaithful, since merely to give Levinas's work back to him in homage would be to deface its truth, and thereby perhaps to steal it from him. Simply to say yes to Levinas's work would in fact be to say no to it, to establish a relationship of pure subordination to its mastery. Again this problem seems in some sense to be relayed through Derrida's reading of Joyce. For the suggestion that *Finnegans Wake* might enact a movement of pure gift or expenditure is almost immediately countered by the argument that the very encyclopaedic scope of the novel, its 'hypermnesic' remembering-in-advance of the interconnectedness of all languages is what in fact condemns every reader to 'being in memory' of Joyce, produces a sense of enforced gratitude, unclearable debt (TWJ, 147). Derrida's reading of *Finnegans Wake* centres on a passage from the novel which evokes the disintegration of Babel and, in particular, on the two words, 'he war', in that passage.[51] These two words run together being, truth and violence (German 'war', third-person singular imperfect of 'sein' ('to be'), and 'wahr' ('true') and English 'war'). They represent, says Derrida, the voice of YAHWEH instituting the fall of Babel and thus 'the whole Babelian adventure of the book' (TWJ, 153). Spoken aloud, the translingual ambiguities disappear, and 'multiplicity remains controlled by a dominant language, English' (TWJ, 156). But, on the page, the multiplicity of languages embedded in the words 'he war' actually undermines the warring, centring force of God's authoritative utterance, in a 'contamination of the language of the master by the language he claims to subjugate, on which he has declared war' (ibid.).

This alternation between purity and contamination, unity and multeity, war and peace, serves as allegory for the form as a 'whole' of *Finnegans Wake*, that text which is simultaneously peaceful gift to the other and violent preoccupation of it. As such, *Finnegans Wake* is both a recapitulation and an exceeding of *Ulysses*. It is

> a little son, a little grandson of Western culture in its circular, encyclopedic, Ulyssean and more than Ulyssean totality. And then it is, simultaneously, much bigger than even this odyssey, it comprehends it, and this prevents it, dragging it outside itself in an entirely singular adventure, from closing in on itself and on this event. (TWJ, 149)

But, at the same 'moment' this radical exteriorization, and, as we might say, alteriorization of *Ulysses* in and through *Finnegans Wake*, the transvaluation of its warring totality into peaceful gift is itself precomprehended in a circle of gratitude to *Ulysses*, whose concluding female 'yes' already belongs to a differential economy of sameness and otherness, law and transgression. The tiny phrase 'he war', Derrida concludes, forms both a signature and a counter-signature: 'It says "we" and "yes" in the end to the Father or to the Lord who speaks loud, there is scarcely anyone but Him, but it leaves the last word to the woman who in her turn will have said "we" and "yes" ' (TWJ, 158). In a much longer piece about *Ulysses*, Derrida expands exponentially on the force of Molly's (and others') *yes* in the novel, detecting in the performative force of the word a disruption of the structure of economic reversion to plenitude that is otherwise so compelling in it, since the *yes* marks the opening of all discourse in responsibility to the other.[52] The point, however, is that no such pure giving is possible, least of all in the *yes* that Derrida says to Levinas's work, since such a pure giving would abolish the relationship of difference which establishes and makes inescapable the responsibility to the other from the beginning.

This anticipates the way in which, in 'At This Very Moment', the necessary entanglement of giving and egotistical reversion – of peace and war – is also related to the question of sexual difference. Drawing on, or perhaps in a certain way appropriating, the charge mounted by such theorists as Irigaray, that Levinas actually himself appropriates rather than authentically opening out to the female, Derrida apparently tries to protect against or reverse this effect by giving over the final pages of his essay to a female voice. This allows him simultaneously to articulate the critique of Levinas's appropriative ethics and to open his own text (in a gesture of ungrateful displacement that nevertheless aims to be essentially faithful to the self-distancing quality of Levinas's own work) to the voice of the other, as embodied in the female.

In this, of course, Derrida shadows Joyce's apparent surrender of

Ulysses to the female discourse of Molly Bloom, which both interrupts and completes the work, and, by unweaving it, gathers all its threads together. The gathering and ungathering force throughout 'At This Very Moment' of metaphors of rending, binding and knotting, which allow Derrida to evoke the relations, as Simon Critchley puts it, 'between binding and unbinding, between being bound to ontological or logocentric language while at the same moment being unbound to that language', and to see in that rhythm of binding and unbinding 'the absolute priority of ethical obligation',[53] may be the silent testimony to the presence of Molly/Penelope in the work. However, the strange, final words of Derrida's text, unlike those of *Ulysses*, are neither male nor female, but rather an interweaving or 'inter(el)acing' of male and female voices, producing a movement of utterance that is perhaps as much Beckettian as Joycean in the way in which the performative insistence of the words combines with a radical indeterminacy of form, and an uncertainty or multiplicity of origins:

> SHE DOESN'T SPEAK THE UNNAMEABLE YET YOU HEAR HER BETTER THAN ME AHEAD
> OF ME AT THIS VERY MOMENT WHERE NONETHELESS ON THE OTHER SIDE OF THE
> MONUMENTAL WORK I WEAVE MY VOICE SO AS TO BE EFFACED. (ATVM, 47)

I believe that Critchley mistakes the movement of Derrida's text in concluding his fine and vastly instructive essay on it with a celebration of the achievement or unambiguous maintaining of alterity.[54] Despite his acknowledgement of the irreducible difference of sexual difference for Derrida, Critchley is drawn, in describing the discursive asymmetry of 'At This Very Moment', into claiming an absolute separation between the logic of the same and the logic of the other in terms of a fixed differentiation of the sexual:

> The first moment of reading, performed by the voice of the Same (a masculine reader), engages in a repetition of the Levinasian text, where the reader produces a commentary which says the same as Levinas and shows how his work works. The second moment of reading, performed by the voice of the Other (a woman reader), of the Levinasian text, interrupts the intentions and shows how his work does not work.[55]

It is true that, a moment later, Critchley notes that 'these two readings and readers do not constitute an opposition or antinomy',[56] but this is not enough, I think, to protect his essay against the effects of a categorial division between the two performing 'moments' of the same and the other, which, by neglecting the difference of difference, along with

Derrida's own account of 'a performative without a present event, a performative whose essence cannot be resumed as to presence' (ATVM, 34–5), reverts to the maiming logic of the same. Critchley therefore restores to Levinas the dream of a pure and absolute alterity which, in intention and performance, Derrida's text both pays tribute to and shows to be impossible. As such, Critchley's account seems to be aligned with Levinas's work in its attempt to save the disintegrative ethical integrity of Saying against the recuperations of the Said, rather than with Derrida's insistence on their indivisibility and inter(el)acing. To maintain, as Levinas and, following him, Critchley do, a sense of the absolute value and force of ethical Saying over the value of the Said, along with a sense of the catastrophic and inescapable vulnerability of Saying to betrayal in being Said, is to be caught in the violent and paradoxical unhappiness of which Levinas accuses Derrida and deconstruction.[57] Derrida is no less aware than Levinas of the paradox of value involved in this inescapable vulnerability of ethical Saying to the thematizations of the Said, but where Levinas endlessly reproduces the paradox by the intensity of his struggles to escape it, Derrida inhabits the paradox in a different mode; not in a mode of acquiescence which would, after all, dissolve the paradox, but in a mode of determined tolerance, which is committed to think through and within the paradox of value, acknowledging the interdependence of gift and return, peace and war, ethics and ontology, the calculable and the incalculable, and therefore allowing ethical thought, in some sense, to regulate and possess its unstoppable movement of slippage and dispossession.

It is this determined tolerance which means that, in the end (though it is an ethical end that has yet to be begun), Derrida's thinking of the ethics of ethics, and the value of value, resists the pure suspension of value that, as we saw at the beginning of this chapter, has come to characterize a certain influential and powerful line of deconstructive theory. As such, it also resists the abstraction and asociality of Levinasian ethics and those ethics, such as Irigaray's, which reproduce these effects, and demands that the thinking of ethicity be made possible, actual, institutional, social.[58] Without simply restoring the *ethos* to ethics, or conjuring back into being the ethical character whose absence is mourned by Tobin Siebers, Derrida nevertheless seems increasingly to acknowledge that the site of the paradox of value, in which value is always caught between the desire for transcendence and the reversion to the same, is precisely the space of the social and the historical. The refusal to allow the thinking of ethics to proceed under the rubric of an absolute transcendence of the self, or of society, and a refusal to permit the abstract other to occupy the place of the social, is what makes deconstructive thinking of the question of value itself committedly and unmistakably political. The detour which, in order to return finally to questions of the ethical and political, Derrida takes through Joyce's *Ulysses*, itself one of this century's great exemplars of the power of ethical and aesthetic detour, also conducts Joyce's text toward that ethico-political destination. It does this not by achieving any simple identification between the aesthetic and the ethico-political or completed passage from one to the other, but by showing their mutual binding and unbinding. His deconstructive exploration of the imperative to rethink every ethical and political imperative, the value of suspending every value, indicates the irreducible value of detour itself, and the permanent ethico-political necessity for ethics and politics to be thought through and with the other-directed saying, responding and responsibility of other discourses such as the literary.

NOTES

1 Simon Critchley, 'The Chiasmus: Levinas, Derrida and the Ethical Demand for Deconstruction', *Textual Practice*, 3 (1989), p. 91.
2 Arkady Plotnitsky, 'Interpretation, Interminability, Evaluation: From Nietzsche toward a General Economy', in *Life after Postmodernism*, ed. Fekete, pp. 120–1.
3 Jacques Derrida, 'Afterword: Toward an Ethic of Discussion', in *Limited Inc*, p. 122.
4 Plotnitsky, 'Interpretation, Interminability, Evaluation', p. 137; Derrida, *Limited Inc*, p. 146.
5 Christopher Norris, *Deconstruction: Theory and Practice* (London: Methuen, 1982), pp. 79–84.
6 Derrida, *Limited Inc*, p. 124.
7 Barbara Johnson, *A World of Difference* (Baltimore and London: Johns Hopkins University Press, 1987), p. 2.
8 See, for example, Derrida's 'No Apocalypse, Not Now (full speed ahead, seven missiles, seven missives)', trans. Catherine Porter and Philip Lewis, *Diacritics*, 14 (1984), pp. 20–31, 'Racism's Last Word', trans. Peggy Kamuf, *Critical Inquiry*, 12 (1985), pp. 290–9 and 'But, Beyond ... Open Letter to Anne McClintock and Rob Nixon', trans. Peggy Kamuf, *Critical Inquiry*, 13 (1986), pp. 155–70. On the question of Paul de Man's wartime collaboration and the fierce debate it stimulated regarding the politics of deconstruction, see Derrida's 'Like the Sound of the Sea Deep within a Shell: Paul de Man's War', *Critical Inquiry*, 14 (1988), pp. 590–652, the replies gathered together in *Critical Inquiry*, 15 (1989), pp. 765–811, along with Derrida's rejoinder to the replies, 'Biodegradables: Seven Diary Fragments', ibid., pp. 812–73.

9 Plotnitsky, 'Interpretation, Interminability, Evaluation', pp. 125–6.
10 Alan Kennedy, *Reading Resistance Value: Deconstructive Practice and the Politics of Literary Critical Encounters* (Basingstoke: Macmillan, 1990), p. 77.
11 Ibid., p. 81.
12 Benjamin, 'Redemption of Value', p. 23.
13 Gregory S. Jay, 'Values and Deconstructions: Derrida, Saussure, Marx', *Cultural Critique*, 8 (1987–8), p. 156.
14 Ibid., p. 196.
15 Emmanuel Levinas, 'There is: Existence without Existents' (1946), repr. in *The Levinas Reader*, ed. Seán Hand (Oxford: Basil Blackwell, 1989), p. 32.
16 Levinas, 'Ethics as First Philosophy' (1984), ibid., p. 76.
17 Ibid., p. 78.
18 Ibid., p. 85.
19 ibid., p. 83.
20 Critchley, 'The Chiasmus', p. 103. Robert Bernasconi, who has been a most energetic and thoughtful commentator on Derrida's relationship to Levinas, is perhaps more attentive to Derrida's critique of the notion of ethics as first philosophy and has a more ambivalent sense of the relation between Derrida and Levinas: see 'Deconstruction and the Possibility of Ethics', in *Deconstruction and Philosophy: The Texts of Jacques Derrida*, ed. John Sallis (Chicago and London: University of Chicago Press, 1987), pp. 135–6. Nevertheless, Bernasconi sees deconstruction as the attempt to maintain the impossible question of the ethical relation without reducing it by the violence of conceptuality, an attempt which is the enactment of the ethical relation as set out by Levinas.
21 Kennedy, *Reading Resistance Value*, p. 41.
22 Martin Heidegger, 'Letter on Humanism' (1947), in *Basic Writings from 'Being and Time' (1927) to 'The Task of Thinking' (1964)*, ed. David Farrell Krell (London: Routledge & Kegan Paul, 1978), p. 228.
23 Ibid., p. 235.
24 Ibid., p. 236.
25 Jacques Derrida, *Of Grammatology*, trans. Gayatri Chakravorty Spivak (Baltimore and London: Johns Hopkins University Press, 1974). pp. 106–10.
26 Siebers, *Ethics of Criticism*, pp. 94–7.
27 Paul de Man, 'The Resistance to Theory', in *The Resistance to Theory* (Manchester: Manchester University Press, 1986), p. 19.
28 Ibid., pp. 104–5.
29 Ibid., p. 110.
30 Charles Peake, *James Joyce: The Citizen and the Artist* (London: Edward Arnold, 1977), p. 339; Patrick Parrinder, *James Joyce* (Cambridge: Cambridge University Press, 1984), pp. 123, 125–6.
31 One of the few deconstructive accounts of Joyce to articulate the question of ethical force alongside interpretative questions in *Ulysses* is Christina van Boheemen-Saaf's 'Joyce, Derrida, and the Discourse of "the Other"',

in *The Augmented Ninth: Proceedings of the Ninth International James Joyce Symposium, Frankfurt, 1984*, ed. Bernard Benstock (Syracuse, NY: Syracuse University Press, 1988). 'Instead of the traditional question, What does it mean?', she writes, 'the Joycean text (just as the Derridean one) suggests another query: What is the rationale of the otherness of this text? What makes it desirable, possible, or necessary to create texts which pervert the logos by a self-inscription of the Other?' (p. 93).

32   Peake, *Citizen and the Artist*, p. 273.

33   Terry Eagleton, 'Modernism, Myth and Monopoly Capitalism', *News from Nowhere*, 7 (1989), p. 21.

34   Booth, *Company We Keep*, p. 277.

35   Ibid., p. 345.

36   Simon Critchley has noted that Derrida seems here to be responding to Levinas's emphasis on the Abraham-like wandering rather than the Ulyssean homecoming of philosophy: '*The Work* thought radically is indeed a movement from the Same towards the other which never returns to the Same. To the myth of Ulysses returning to Ithaca, we would like to oppose the story of Abraham leaving his homeland forever for a still unknown land and even forbidding his son to be brought back to its point of departure' ('The Trace of the Other', trans. Alphonso Lingis, in *Deconstruction in Context*, ed. Mark Taylor (Chicago: University of Chicago Press, 1986), p. 348, quoted in Simon Critchley, ' "Bois" – Derrida's Final Word on Levinas', in *Re-reading Levinas*, ed. Robert Bernasconi and Simon Critchley (London: Athlone Press, 1991), pp. 163–4).

37   Bonnie Kime Scott, *Joyce and Feminism* (Brighton: Harvester Press, 1984), p. 207.

38   Boheemen-Saaf, 'Joyce, Derrida, and the Discourse of "the Other" ', pp. 102, 93–4.

39   Emmanuel Levinas, *Totality and Infinity: An Essay on Exteriority* (1961), trans. Alphonso Lingis (The Hague: Nijhoff, 1979), p. 195.

40   Levinas, 'Time and the Other', in *Levinas Reader*, p. 52.

41   Ibid., p. 49.

42   Sheldon Brivic, 'The Father in Joyce', in *The Seventh of Joyce*, ed. Bernard Benstock (Brighton: Harvester Press, 1982), p. 80.

43   Jean-Michel Rabaté, 'Paternity, Thy Name is Joy'; Ellen Carol Jones, ' "Writing the Mystery of Himself": Paternity in *Ulysses*', in *The Augmented Ninth*, ed. Benstock, pp. 220, 231.

44   Irigaray, 'The Fecundity of the Caress', p. 245.

45   Richard Kearney, 'Dialogue with Emmanuel Levinas', in *Face to Face with Levinas*, ed. Cohen, pp. 29–30.

46   Levinas, *Totality and Infinity*, p. 39.

47   Ibid., p. 195.

48   Kearney, 'Dialogue with Emmanuel Levinas', p. 19.

49   A recent attempt to claim a Judaic ethics for *Ulysses* is to be found in Ira B. Nadel's *Joyce and the Jews: Culture and Texts* (Basingstoke: Macmillan, 1989).

Nadel associates *Ulysses* and the Talmud on the grounds of their open-ended textuality; the ethical nature of the Talmud lies, he says, not in any body of moral law that it may contain so much as in its status as unfinished text, and the responsibility it transmits to continue interpreting its ethics (p. 117).

50 Emmanuel Levinas, 'Wholly Otherwise', trans. Simon Critchley, in *Re-reading Levinas*, ed. Bernasconi and Critchley, p. 7.

51 James Joyce, *Finnegans Wake* (London: Faber & Faber, 1939), p. 258, 1. 12.

52 Jacques Derrida, 'Ulysse gramophone: l'oui-dire de Joyce', in *Genèse de Babel: études présentés par Claude Jacquet* (Paris: CNRS, 1985), pp. 227–64.

53 Critchley, ' "Bois" ', p. 178.

54 Ibid., p. 186.

55 Ibid., pp. 171–2.

56 Ibid., p. 172.

57 Levinas, 'Wholly Otherwise', p. 7.

58 For a clear example of this commitment to the instituted value of the transvaluation of all values, one might turn to Derrida's essay on the role of the university, 'The Principle of Reason: The University in the Eyes of its Pupils', trans. Catherine Porter and Edward P. Morris, *Diacritics*, 13 (1983), pp. 3–20. In this essay, Derrida argues that the principal purpose of the university should be to 'interrogate the essence of reason and of the principle of reason, the value of the basic, of the principal, of radicality, of the *arkhe* in general, and it would attempt to draw out all the possible consequences of this questioning' (p. 16). If this seems to provide the ingredients for the traditional critique of the alleged asociality and denial of value in deconstruction, in the way it seems to put the question of value and ethical outcome on indefinite hold, allowing 'pure' or 'disinterested' research priority over applied or politically orientated research, the essay also concerns itself with the inescapability of practico-ethical outcomes for all intellectual work and the necessity of subjecting every claim to be disinterested to rigorous suspicion. What Derrida proposes here is an interested (and, in a transformed sense, institutional) thinking through of the opposition of the disinterested and the interested, the value-free and the utilitarian.

9

Beyond Cultural Value:
The Writing of the Other

Throughout this book I have maintained a certain strategic hesitation between what may be called the anthropological and the critical uses of the word 'culture' and consequently of the term 'cultural value'. If the anthropological use of the term names the entire ensemble of habits, beliefs and customs of an identifiable social group, then the critical use of the term implies a more restricted use of the word, to name collectively the most valued activities, traditions and monuments of such a group. In the first use of the term, there is no attempt to distinguish between, or evaluate, the different, interconnected forms that make up a culture, since anything that forms a part of a culture, from its marriage customs to its organization of labour, to its most typical aesthetic and representational practices, must be said to be 'cultural'. The second use of the term, sometimes signalled when Western cultures are being discussed by the phrase 'high culture', rests on a distinction between those forms and activities which merely characterize a culture and those forms and activities, typically in the sphere of art, religion and representation, which represent that culture's 'best self', or sense of its own best self.

Of course, this distinction is not merely methodological, since it also seems to mark a distinction between two fundamentally different forms of society, those advanced societies in which the process of economic specialization has brought about a division between artistic activity and the rest of socio-symbolic life, and those traditional societies in which such a distinction has little meaning. But in making such a broad distinction, we must retain a consciousness of the fact that the distinction between culture and high culture is the product of our own culture, and so must itself be partly the expression of our own cultural needs, values and anxieties, rather than any kind of 'value-free' representation of the really existing state of things. It is striking, for example, that the two competing senses of the word 'culture', which are held closely together in early-nineteenth-century accounts of culture, and especially in J. G. Herder's notion of the national or folk spirit of a people, crystallize out

within a couple of years of each other in the nineteenth century, in the
alternative definitions offered in Matthew Arnold's *Culture and Anarchy*
(1869) and E. B. Tylor's *Primitive Culture* (1871). For Arnold, culture is
defined as the 'disinterested pursuit of perfection ... simply trying to see
things as they are, in order to seize on the best and make it prevail'; and
again, as 'the enabling ourselves, whether by reading, observing, or
thinking, to come as near as we can to the firm intelligible law of things,
and thus to get a basis for a less confused action and a more complete
perfection than we have at present'.[1] The great innovation of E. B.
Tylor's *Primitive Culture*, on the other hand, is its inclusiveness, as
indicated in its opening affirmation that 'Culture or Civilization, taken
in its wide ethnographic sense, is that complex whole which includes
knowledge, belief, art morals, law custom, and any other capabilities and
habits acquired by man as a member of society.'[2] Against Arnold's
austere distinction between the 'machinery' or means of culture and its
disinterested, transcendent ends, Tylor assumes the broad synonymity of
the words 'culture' and 'civilization'.

But, different as they are, there is a level at which Arnold and Tylor
are articulating a shared experience. George Stocking has detailed the
ways in which Tylor's account of culture, though evidently intended as a
kind of rejoinder to Arnold's, in fact depends upon a similar teleological
privilege accorded to the ideal of advanced civilization, and a tendency to
measure savage and barbarian cultures in terms of their distance from
or proximity to this peak of cultural development.[3] For both of them,
as for many other nineteenth-century critics, the notion of culture also
embodies an ideal of development towards wholeness, an ideal asserted
in the face of an increasing awareness of cultural split or fragmentation.
Arnold's ideal of 'the harmonious perfection of our humanity' thus joins
with Tylor's methodological grasping of the unity of the process of
cultural development from primitive to advanced cultures. As James
Clifford has observed of Arnold and Tylor and their joint legacy to
anthropology, 'a powerful structure of feeling continues to see culture,
wherever it is found, as a coherent *body* that lives and dies. Culture is
enduring, traditional, structural rather than contingent, syncretic, historical. Culture is a process of ordering, not of disruption' (*PC*, 235).

This association between the aesthetic and the anthropological is to be
consolidated in the full-blown primitivism of much modernist theory,
which, by turning to the art and music of traditional or 'primitive'
cultures, will attempt an impossible synthesis between an ideal of pure
aesthetic autonomy and the ideal of an art which is at the centre rather
than at the margins of its society. The point with modernist as with

Arnoldian cultural theory is that the systematic linking of economic and symbolic realms in traditional or non-advanced societies is read according to an aesthetic ideology which is the reflex of the splitting of the two senses of culture from each other; thus, for example, complex connectedness or undifferentiation is read as 'wholeness', 'unity' and so on. The terminological problem of culture comes about just at the moment when culture itself has become visible as a problem for nineteenth-century society. The elaborate panoply of theories devised to measure the distance between those Western cultures in which 'culture' has been split between its inclusive (anthropological) and its specialized (aesthetics) senses, and those non-Western cultures where wholeness persists uncorrupted, is consequently itself the measure and expression of that split. As Pierre Bourdieu has warned, the extreme differentiation of the economic and artistic realms in advanced Western cultures produces the twin dangers of aesthetic ethnocentrism on the one hand, which allows the theorist to fantasize primitive or popular practices as purely aesthetic, and of economistic ethnocentrism on the other, which is blind to the complex and highly symbolic forms that economic behaviour may take in primitive societies. The ways in which Western cultures theorize the relationship between economic and symbolic activity in non-Western societies are liable either to collapse those relationships into narrow determination of the symbolic by economic interest, or to fanciful transcendence of the economic in the pure, playful excess of the symbolic.[4]

The idea of the split society, in which the specialization of economic activity brings about the autonomization of aesthetic or cultural experience, thus functions for anthropology and postanthropological culture as a kind of myth-producing machinery, the experience of loss or alienation regularly generating new back-formations of the prelapsarian state in which the economic and the aesthetic, society and culture, are at one with each other. If it is possible self-consciously to measure and take precautions against the primitivist myth which this state of alienation produces, we may also be struck by the recursive insistence of that myth. In Bourdieu's cautionary account just referred to, for example, the theory of the fragmented consciousness of the Western observer is fundamental to his account of the alienating or hallucinatory effects of that consciousness, the myth of the Fall remaining necessary therefore to the analysis of the mythical miscognitions resulting from that Fall.

The anthropological and the critical definitions of culture as embodied in the respective formulations of Tylor and Arnold involve in turn two distinct attitudes towards the question of value, though, in both cases, 'culture' must be said to be in a certain sense synonymous with 'value'. In the anthropological sense of the term, cultural activity represents the play of value, all the multiple and overlapping systems of equivalence and exchange which mediate between the different realms of economic and symbolic activity. By the beginning of the twentieth century, it is fair to say, the following had become the normative self-designation of the discipline of anthropology: 'The anthropological attitude is relativistic, in that in place of beginning with an inherited hierarchy of values, it assumes that every society through its culture seeks and in some measure finds values, and that the business of anthropology includes the determination of the range, variety, constancy, and interrelations of these innumerable values.'[5] But, in the critical and differential use of the term represented in one extreme form by Arnold's *Culture and Anarchy*, culture is defined as value at a certain distance from, or resisting measurement in terms of, other registers such as the economic; indeed, this definition of the value of high culture habitually gives to it the status of value as such. In the first definition, value is relative, dynamic and under transaction; in the second it is fixed, concentrated and affirmed as absolute. The anthropological account, which we have seen identifies culture with the play of value, makes no attempt to impose evaluative hierarchies on its material – though this is not to claim that such approaches, whether in anthropology or in sociology more generally, are themselves in any sense value-free. The critical definition of culture, on the other hand, is orientated towards evaluation, which is to say, around selection, preference and judgements of quality. If it is rare to find these two alternative accounts of culture in their pure or ideal form, it is also the case that there is a certain, residually stubborn opposition between them; an opposition exemplified, for example, in the tension between cultural studies and literary studies, the one drawing on what we have characterized as the anthropological definition of culture and the other still largely committed to the critical definition of culture. This is a version of the conflict or, rather, disconnection between interpretation and evaluation that we began in chapter 2 by diagnosing as the condition of the humanities.[6]

But in recent years this problem has been enacted most crucially not within the field of individual cultures, but across and between cultures. That is to say, the question of cultural value has been crossed with profound questions regarding the value of indigenous and local cultures as such, the nature of the value transactions between different cultures, and the relationship of universalist to particularist ways of modelling and regulating such value transactions. Ours is now a world in which it makes little sense to consider questions of art or aesthetics in purely national or even ethnic terms, or simply in the light of particular forms of cultural heritage or tradition. This is not merely to refer to such things as the growing spread and homogenization of (mainly Western) mass-cultural forms, the increasing co-ordination across national and even continental boundaries of the international art market and the widening of readerships and distribution networks in fiction publishing, all the factors that one might call the *globalization* of culture. It implies also the radical pluralizing of culture and cultures, the thick entanglement of culture in the evaluative-affirmative sense specified above with the heightened experience of cultural difference, a process which we might alternatively specify as *interculturation*.[7] It is not a matter any longer of Adorno's 'torn halves' of art and mass culture, which, while they do not form a whole, nevertheless present their discontinuity within what may still be experienced potentially as a single culture, even in its calamitous condition of cleavage. For now the rupture of the two senses of culture is part of a more general sundering and multiplication not only of cultural forms, but of definitions of what culture and cultural value may be: a proliferation, one should therefore say, not only of cultural values, but of the very economies of cultural value, a drawing into exchange of the very media of exchange by which cultural value is constituted. One of the most important effects, indeed, of this convolution of the economies of cultural value is to make newly visible the global or extracultural dimension at work even in the endogenous debates about cultural value in the nineteenth century; making it clear how tightly the value of culture as such in the Arnoldian sense is tied to a sense of national identity, which in turn comes into being in an anxious rebuttal of the alternative models of culture which ethnology was encountering. It is this which bonds Arnold's high and restrictive definition of culture so emphatically to Tylor's contrastingly expansionist definition.

A symptom of this new interinvolvement of cultural-aesthetic questions with questions of the newly complex relations between cultures is the recent two-way traffic between literary and cultural theory and the postmodern ethnography associated most particularly with Clifford Geertz and James Clifford. What brings the two realms of literary theory and ethnography together is a strengthened sense of the relationship between action and representation. On the literary side, this involves a new awareness of the ways in which literary texts and cultural representations in general do not merely represent the socio-political world, but in some primary way constitute or bring it about. On the ethnographic side, this is witnessed in an intensified interest in representational practices, and in customs and rituals considered as signification, or, in Nelson Goodman's phrase, 'ways of worldmaking', along with a heightened self-consciousness about the significative and rhetorical force of writing in all ethnographic knowledge.[8]

Clifford Geertz: Finding in Translation

In the work of Clifford Geertz, the attention to the forms and force of cultural signification comes close to an aestheticization of cultural life and the procedures used to interpret it, although it is important to note the very specific sense which Geertz gives to the term 'aesthetic'. He argues that it is necessary in considering artistic activity to avoid the two kinds of ethnocentric falsification, that either imply the fulfilment in primitive societies of the Schillerian vision of a totally aesthetic existence, or assume that the position of art in those societies is as highly specialized as in ours. Against the first falsification, it is necessary to acknowledge the relative degrees of specialization of artistic and aesthetic activity within different cultures, even as, against the second, one retains a sensitivity to the ways in which the particular quality or value of the aesthetic in any society has to do with its place in a general cultural outlook.

The most important function or value of artistic activity for Geertz is that it gives concrete form to experience. His famous essay 'Deep Play: Notes on the Balinese Cockfight' (1973) asserts that the purpose of the fight, considered as an artistic process, is to make various kinds of shared experience 'visible, tangible, graspable – "real," in an ideational sense. An image, fiction, a model, a metaphor, the cockfight is a means of expression; its function is neither to assuage social passions nor to heighten them ... but, in a medium of feathers, blood, crowds, and money, to display them' (DP, 444). In a later essay, on 'Art as a Cultural System' (1986), Geertz suggests that it is only the fact that 'certain activities everywhere seem specifically designed to demonstrate that ideas are visible, audible, and – one needs to make a word up here – tactible, that they can be cast in forms where the senses, and through the senses the emotions, can reflectively address them', which justifies the idea that art or aesthetic activity has any common nature across different cultures (LK, 118–19). Lest this be read as another kind of ethnocentrism, in its privileging of the value of aesthetic form over other aspects of artistic activity, Geertz warns us that the most important feature of this aesthetic objectification is not its fixing or reification of ideas, experiences or relations, but the fact that it makes these experiences in some way subsequently available for differential evaluation, among the group as a whole, in the light of differing experiences and values, and through the contingencies of time. He gives the example of a Bamileke chief who on taking office had his statue carved, a statue which, after his death, was slowly eroded by the weather just as his memory faded among his people. 'Where is the form here? In the shape of the statue, or the shape of its career?' enquires Geertz, going on to argue that 'no analysis of the statue that does not hold its fate in view, a fate as intended as is the arrangement of its volume or the gloss of its surface, is going to understand its meaning or catch its force' (*LK*, 119).

The purpose of this example is not, I think, to argue for any particular definition of art or its value, either in formal or processual terms – as it were, inverting the misrecognition of Balinese art as modernist by simply assimilating it to a postmodern paradigm of process and passage – but rather to establish for art a certain definitional liminality. Neither merely reflecting or being functionally reducible to custom and belief, nor standing mysteriously apart from their informing contexts and history, artistic practices seem to exist for Geertz at the hinge-point between these two dimensions, balanced between dependence and autonomy, immanence and transcendence. Such categorial indeterminacy is an important feature of an another example of non-Western art discussed in Geertz's 'Art as a Cultural System', the poetic discourse of Islam. Given the centrality within Islam of the notion of divine rhetoric, and the fact that the Koran is regarded not as the second-degree representation of sacredness, but as the embodiment of sacredness itself, the activity of worldly creation in words becomes highly ambivalent in Islamic societies. For poetry imitates, even as it seems to compromise, the sacredness of the divine word, instituting and inhabiting a threshold between the divine and the mortal: '[Poets] turn the tongue of God to ends of their own, which if not quite sacrilege, borders on it; but at the same time they display its incomparable power, which if not quite worship, approaches it' (*LK*, 111). Though Geertz does not put the matter explicitly in terms of value, it seems plain that the ambivalence of poetry indeed embodies an evaluative paradox: 'Poetry, rivaled only by architecture, became the cardinal fine art in Islamic civilization ... while treading the edge of the gravest form of blasphemy' (ibid.). Such a paradox is, one would have thought, scarcely tolerable for a culture founded since medieval times upon absolute distinctions, and distinctions of the absolute: a culture in which, as Geertz says, 'all statements were seen as either true or false ... [and] the sum of all true statements, a fixed corpus radiating from the Quran, which at least implicitly contained them all, was knowledge' (*LK*, 111–12). Geertz is not entirely clear about how to judge Islamic poetry in this respect. If at times he sees in it a smooth interfusion of the quotidian and the holy, a paradigmatic confirmation of the inseparability of earthly and heavenly affairs, he remains fascinated by the 'uncertain status and strange force' of this hybrid, dangerous 'para-Quran' (*LK*, 117). Islamic poetry, in this definition, hovers between integrative value and disintegrative force, marking a certain pause or hesitation in value itself.[9]

The most developed argument for the liminal function of the aesthetic is to be found in Geertz's earlier 'Deep Play' essay. The cockfight is at the heart of Balinese life, in its radically atomistic structure of alternating bursts of meaning and vacuity: as such, it is 'not an imitation of the punctuateness of Balinese social life, nor a depiction of it, nor even an expression of it; it is an example of it, carefully prepared' (DP, 446). But, at the same time, the cockfight is a disquieting negation of Balinese life and values, so different, in its 'flat-out, head-to-head (or spur-to-spur) aggressiveness', from the elaborate, ceremonial obliquity of Balinese manners and social behaviour. Here, 'a powerful rendering of social life as the Balinese most deeply do not want it ... is set in the context of a sample of it as they do in fact have it' (ibid.). In a similar way, Geertz claims that the cockfight brings into collision the Balinese value of *ramé*, or the busy plenitude of ordered social life and spatial relationships, and the disvalue of *paling*, or the vertiginous loss of the sense of relative social space; the cockfight, with the complex orderliness of its status structure and the scrambling confusion of the fighting cocks, 'is at once continuous with ordinary social life and a direct negation of it' (DP, 446).

Geertz's claim therefore is that the value of the aesthetic in Balinese life lies in a certain surpassing of the functional or the utilitarian, or a putting at stake of these values. In the case of the cockfight, the putting at stake is more than a metaphor, for the centrality in it of gambling makes for an interesting congruity between the aesthetic and the economic. The 'deep play' of the Balinese cockfight comes about precisely because the sums of money which are typically bet in the centre of the cockfight are so large as apparently to go beyond the rational calculation of mere gain and loss; for a man who bets half his entire fortune on the outcome of one fight, there is really little possibility of any positive financial outcome or simple dominion of the pleasure principle: for each side of the wager, 'the marginal utility of the pound he stands to win is clearly less than the marginal disutility of the one he stands to lose', such that 'having come together in search of pleasure they have entered into a relationship which will bring the participants, considered collectively, net gain rather than net pleasure' (DP, 433). The purpose of such 'deep play' is to raise the stakes on everything else that is symbolically in the ring during the cockfight – status, honour, pride and so on. The cockfight becomes a deeply 'appraisive drama', precisely because of its play with limits, with transgression, with disvalue. Of course, it is always possible to read this apparent transcending of cultural values back into a structure of economic exchange and profit, according to the principle of generalized positivity that I have examined in chapter 4, since, indeed, there must be, set against the apparent disutility of the cockfight, a measurable value or utility for the participants in terms other than the economic.[10] But the point about this particular instance of the aesthetic is that it institutionalizes a hiatus or hesitation between value and disvalue, which both belongs to and transcends (but then in its transcendence even more thoroughly belongs to) the field of value within Balinese culture.

Oddly, therefore, the value of the aesthetic seems to lie in its positing for evaluation the value of the aesthetic itself. The work of art or artistic process (and for Geertz, this is the most capacious of categories, which encompasses all of the organizing and form-giving activities of human culture, even, as we will see, the institution of the law) is lifted into a kind of intrinsic or autonomous value, in its foregrounding of its own formal substance, but this value is what makes it instantly and necessarily available for reabsorption back into the destructive element of relative estimations and judgements. Rather than being the mark of a fixed and formal distance from the concerns of ordinary life, the autonomous and apparently self-generating quality of art is the very thing that makes it able to become a bearer of the values and concerns of its society. Art is both extrinsic and intrinsic, at the heart of social life precisely by constituting a kind of parenthesis within it. The Balinese cockfight is therefore to be seen as 'a metasocial commentary' upon the social organization of status and value, a 'Balinese reading of Balinese experience, a story they tell themselves about themselves' (DP, 448).

This account of the value of art in non-Western cultures is very far from a certain Marxist paradise of precapitalist relations, in which fact and value are sweetly conjoined, and no structure of exchange exists to contaminate the pure incomparability of things in themselves. The fact that many of the institutions and activities of archaic societies may be described in the aesthetic terms which Geertz adopts is no warrant for assuming the Edenic oneness of social being and artistic practice in such societies. If Geertz is affirming the value of this mode of culture, it is on the grounds not of any unity between the two senses of culture we have been discussing (culture as whole way of life and culture as artistic excellence), but apparently of the particularly rich and complex transaction between these two dimensions of value that it seems to make possible.

One of the distinguishing features of Geertz's work is his sensitivity to the nature of the translation involved in this kind of commentary on the art practice of another culture. Translation is a productive metaphor for this process because of its embedded ambivalence. As all its practitioners and participants have sooner or later to acknowledge, translation is an impossible art. But that apprehension of the impossibility of translation cannot ever be merely theoretical, but must endlessly and variously be renewed through the particular difficulties encountered in the act of translation itself. In other words, only the necessary, irresistible act of translation can reveal its impossibility. For Geertz, the ambivalence of translation is an enactment of the problem of cultural relativism. For, if it is true in one sense that we can never fully know another culture as we know our own, then that knowledge must also by definition be partial and incomplete, because, if we truly *could* know nothing about another culture, then, *a fortiori*, we could never truly *know*, absolutely and for sure, that we could know nothing about them. Absolute forms of the doctrine of cultural relativism, in other words, need partly to concede what they deny, since the only way to measure the limitations of our understanding of another culture is by first attempting to go beyond them. To affirm the unknowability or untranslatability of other cultures, it is necessary in a sense to know what it is that one does not know, apprehend what in them resists translation into our terms. Being aware of one's limitations implies some (in itself limited) transcendence of them. If the most egregious form of ethnocentrism is the assumption, embodied through much of the history of Western anthropology, that other cultures can be subsumed without residue within our structures of knowledge, the countervailing assumption that nothing at all can be known about such cultures is itself another kind of ethnocentrism, and possibly of a more subtly reactionary kind.

The important point for Geertz is that the act of translation is more than the vehicle or procedure for understanding another culture, more than a set of preliminaries which might at a later stage lead to a full and translucent revelation of the truth of the culture we wish to understand. Ethnographic understanding is bound up in the process of translation, is 'found' as well as 'lost' in it. When we attempt to apprehend another culture, says Geertz, 'we do so not by looking *behind* the interfering glosses that connect us to it but *through* them' (*LK*, 44). In the essay 'Found in Translation: On the Social History of the Moral Imagination', Geertz takes as his example an account of the Balinese practice of suttee, or widow-burning, by the nineteenth-century Danish traveller L. V. Helms, and isolates the strange decentring and disordering of perceptions induced by the experience and its narration, which lurches between awestruck admiration at the dignity and splendour of the suttee spectacle, horror at its meaning and effects and reactionary justification of coercive imperial rule. Despite all the changes that have taken place since Helms's account, written in 1882, the Dutch suppression of suttee, the professionalization of the processes of ethnographic report and the steady penetration of Balinese life by missionaries, poets, photographers and tourists alike, the culture of Bali still has the capacity, says Geertz, to disorientate Western perceptions in a similar way, by bringing together the paradisal and the horrific.

In the twentieth century, this disorientation has principally affected Western notions of the social nature of art and what Geertz calls 'the moral status of artistic genius' (*LK*, 51). Bali has functioned simultaneously as 'a real-life image of a society in which the aesthetic impulse is allowed its true freedom, the unfettered expression of its inner nature' (ibid.), and as the origin of images of cruelty, hatred and brutality (and it is of course in the work of Artaud that these two aesthetic dimensions are brought together). The disordering effect of the conjoining of these opposites is to be understood neither entirely in terms of European ethnocentric projection, nor in terms of the absolute inaccessibility of Balinese aesthetic life, but in the very structure of hermeneutic convolution that connects and disconnects Balinese and European consciousness. Interpretation of Balinese festivity and cultural form must therefore be self-reflexive, working through and with the impediments to understanding and translation, rather than wishing them away or projecting oneself voluntaristically beyond them.

It has been possible for some commentators to suggest that this wary but still benign attitude towards the possibility of understanding between cultures conceals a form of interpretative domination. In a critical reading of the essay on the Balinese cockfight, Vincent Crapanzano complains that the interpretative self-consciousness later recommended by Geertz is very far from being present here. The dialogue of translation between cultures takes place in this essay in one direction only and for the benefit of the interpreting ethnographer and his readers. This effect is achieved, says Crapanzano, by a pronominal asymmetry, in which an undemonstrative, unselfconscious, but nevertheless hugely authoritative 'I' mediates the experience of an undifferentiated 'they' (the Balinese) who are not permitted to be dialogic co-partners in construing the meaning of the cockfight: 'There is never an I–you relationship, a dialogue, two people next to each other reading the same text and discussing it face-to-face, but only an I–they relationship' (HD, 74).

Crapanzano finds particularly unconvincing and forced Geertz's interpretation of the cockfight as an art form which can be discussed in the same terms as *King Lear* and *Crime and Punishment*. What is wrong with such an interpretation, Crapanzano believes, is that, in our culture, *King Lear* and *Crime and Punishment* are culturally and linguistically distinguished as certain kinds of artistic representation, whereas Geertz gives no evidence that the cockfight is so marked in Balinese culture. In the absence of such evidence, we must assume that 'cockfights are surely cockfights for the Balinese – and not images, fictions, models, and metaphors. They are not marked as such, though they can be read as such by a foreigner for whom "images, fictions, models, and metaphors" have interpretive value' (HD, 73). As is often the case, however, Crapanzano's dismissal of one ethnocentric assumption seems to rest upon another of an equally dubious nature. For, if it is illegitimate to assume that Balinese cultural forms are discussable in the same terms as Western works of art, it seems equally illegitimate to assume that the only Balinese cultural forms which were so discussable would be ones which were linguistically and culturally marked off in just the same way as Western art forms like tragedy and the novel. Perhaps the point here, and the point of much of what Geertz and others, such as Victor Turner and Richard Schechner, have written about the para-aesthetic nature of non-Western cultural forms and rituals, is that the clearly marked distinctions between art and experience, representation and actuality, of Western culture do not function in precisely the same ways in other cultures. But this is very far from saying that nothing distinguishes or frames off cultural forms such as the Balinese cockfight from what might in shorthand be seen as the sphere of immediate practicalities. Doubtless, Crapanzano is right to say that for the Balinese, a cockfight is indeed just a cockfight, rather than a tragic play; but what, after all, *is* a cockfight?

In criticizing Geertz's arrogation of interpretative authority and regretting the fact that 'Deep Play' offers only 'the constructed understanding of the constructed native's constructed point of view' (HD, 74), Crapanzano tends to assume the possibility of some pure understanding of the native from the native's point of view. It is not necessarily to undervalue the force of Crapanzano's criticism of Geertz's more outrageously (phall)Eurocentric characterizations of Balinese subjectivity, his attempt, for example, to assimilate the Balinese experience of the cockfight to the experience of the Western viewer of *Macbeth* or the spectator at the dogtrack, to feel that there is buried in Crapanzano's critique an inappropriate nostalgia for a 'real' as opposed to a 'constructed' native point of view. For, as we have seen, Geertz is claiming that what is happening in the cockfight is precisely the construction rather than the simple expression of a point of view. What Geertz means by the claim that the cockfight can be viewed as an art form is that it has the value not so much of an intense experience as of an intense and disquieting suspension of experience, a folding or framing of actuality, a kind of metacommentary, an evaluation of value. Crapanzano quotes Geertz's comment that 'enacted and re-enacted, so far without end the cockfight enables the Balinese, as, read and reread, *Macbeth* enables us, to see a dimension of his own subjectivity' (DP, 450), and objects, 'Who told Geertz? How can a whole people share a single subjectivity?' (HD, 74). This criticism goes home, for there is indeed something suspiciously neat in the way in which the ethnographer's allegorical reading of the cockfight, and his offering of it as an exemplary exercise in the reading of cultural data, is matched by the claim that the cockfight itself functions as a kind of self-conscious allegorizing for the Balinese participants of their own cultural values. And yet, again, there is something mistakenly insistent too about Crapanzano's objection to the idea that a whole people could be said to share 'a single subjectivity', since subjective singleness is precisely what, according to Geertz's argument, the experience of the cockfight makes doubtful, in yielding the forms and values of subjectivity for a certain kind of collective scrutiny.

If it is indeed the case that Geertz's reading in this instance can only in a rather specialized and abstract sense be called a dialogue, and must indeed be acknowledged rather as a kind of cultural appropriation, whose effect is to demonstrate the power of the ethnographer's allegorical command rather than to allow him really to reflect upon 'the tangle of hermeneutic involvements' (*LK*, 45) in which he is caught up, his work nevertheless has something important to say about the relationships between the distinctive, but complex value of cultural forms on the one hand, and the complex forms of evaluation effected by and between cultures on the other hand. In fact, not the least important of the implications of his work is that there is no clear or permanent distinction between the two dimensions. This is to say that the transactions of value within cultures, which are enabled to take place through para-aesthetic forms such as the cockfight, resemble and prefigure the transactions of value across and between cultures. Since a culture is never complete in itself, and occupies and defines itself in activities of self-exteriorization or auto-ethnography, such that the Western ethnographer's interpretative assault upon them is never a pure invasion of a self-identical totality from

an absolutely separated exterior; as Geertz puts it, in a sentence which
Crapanzano objects to for the way it apparently places the anthropologist
in a position of hidden authority over his narrative subjects (HD, 74),
'The culture of a people is an ensemble of texts, themselves ensembles,
which the anthropologist strains to read over the shoulders of those
to whom they properly belong' (DP, 452). Whether within or outside a
culture, value subsists paradoxically in the temporary suspension of
value, an enacted questioning of a culture's self which takes place on the
interior of a culture and on its exterior. The value of cross-cultural evaluation crosses in an emphatic way with those intracultural crossings of
value to be found in such activities as the cockfight.

It has to be acknowledged, however, that Geertz's earlier work constrains the implications of this interpretative multiplicity, by suggesting that the aesthetic activities of self-representation serve principally to
enable cultures to sustain and constitute themselves as self-recognizing
wholes. This reinstitutes a rather simpler structure of interiority and
exteriority than that suggested by Geertz's analysis of cultural overlayer-
ing, so that he can declare, in the closing sentences of *The Interpretation
of Cultures*, that 'societies, like lives, contain their own interpretations.
One has only to learn how to gain access to them' (DP, 453). It is this
which renders his earlier work vulnerable to the charges mounted by
Crapanzano and others, that he essentializes the workings of cultures
in order better to constitute his own authority over them, an authority
that is exercised not in a collective or participatory reading of that culture alongside its inhabitants, but in a sort of forcible hermeneutic
access.

However, Geertz's later work is informed by a rather different
consciousness of the inevitability of that process of cultural interference
which is represented *in petto* in the work of the ethnographer. Convinced
as he is that 'nobody is leaving anybody else alone and isn't ever again
going to' (*LK*, 234), Geertz is also optimistically unimpressed by
predictions of increasing global homogeneity or the universal rationalization of culture in the interests of multinational capitalism. His vision,
like that of the Lyotard whose assumptions he seems partly to share, is of
an increasing plurality and heterogeneity of cultural forms, and he
suggests that 'we are headed rather more toward the convulsions of alpha
than the resolutions of omega' (*LK*, 216). Like Lyotard, Geertz is guided
by Wittgenstein's notion of a world of separate and autonomous
language games, but he is much less driven than Lyotard by the need to
preserve the absolute singularity of such language games. For it is the
unavoidable collisions and interferences of globalized culture which

makes it impossible to keep language games, or local knowledges, entirely sequestered from each other (even if it is also this process which heightens the anxious awareness of their difference or imperfect commensurability). Where Lyotard counsels radical heterogeneity, Geertz affirms the need for hybridity, though of a kind that preserves and multiplies distinctions rather than attempting to synthesize them.

But for Geertz and for Lyotard both, the awareness of differences between cultures induces and accompanies an awareness of the interior differences within cultures, and the problem of cultural translation is one that moves in both syntaxes of difference. It is perhaps for this reason that, like some of the younger generation of postmodern ethnographers, Geertz has tended in more recent work to focus not merely on the problems of mediation between cultures, but on the problems of understanding 'our own', increasingly hybridized culture.[11] The concluding essay of the volume *Local Knowledge*, for example, focuses on a comparative analysis of legal systems and practice, with a view to establishing their quasi-aesthetic structure as 'part of a distinctive manner of imagining the real' (*LK*, 184). Geertz compares law to poetry, in the definition offered by Frank O'Hara, since law, rather than acting in a merely functional maintenance of social systems, 'makes life's nebulous events tangible and restores their detail' (*LK*, 182). Law proves to be a fertile subject for Geertz's particular brand of 'interpretive anthropology' and one that is close in its nature and effect to subjects such as the Balinese cockfight; for it is in law that cultures mediate between the realm of what in Western terms would be called practice and principle, fact and value, exploring the question of 'How, given what we believe, must we act; what, given how we act, must we believe' (*LK*, 180). If law is like art in not only embodying value, but also making visible and concrete the processes of its negotiation, then, as with the comparative interpretation of forms of art, the comparative analysis of law should lead not to a search for absolute and universal principles of good, but to a relativizing interchange between different forms of law, which is to say, different systems for relating fact and value.

Geertz remains clear that the purpose of such forms of interchange is not to throw into doubt all the beliefs and values that constitute and sustain Western systems of law. It is, rather, 'that one welds the processes of self-knowledge, self-perception, self-understanding to those of other-knowledge, other-perception, other-understanding; that identifies, or very nearly, sorting out who we are and sorting out whom we are among'. (*LK*, 181–2). In his most recent book, *Works and Lives: The Anthropologist as Author* (1988), Geertz makes open profession of his belief that this kind of comparative enquiry involves the ethnographer not only in attending to social forms considered as symbolic or quasi-aesthetic artefacts, but also in attending to the inescapability of artifice in his or her own discourse. The work that surveys the aesthetic instantiation of value in other cultures is itself just such an aesthetic instantiation:

> If there is any way to counter the conception of ethnography as an iniqui-tous act or an unplayable game, it would seem to involve owning up to the fact that, like quantum mechanics or the Italian opera, it is a work of the imagination, less extravagant than the first, less methodical than the second. The responsibility for ethnography, or the credit, can be placed at no other door than that of the romancers who have dreamt it up. (*WL*, 140)

For ethnography to continue and flourish, it must produce 'compar-able art' (*WL*, 139), participating in the Rortyan process of consolidating and extending a 'poeticized culture'. This means that ethnography must become aware of what, on the final page of *Works and Lives*, Geertz ambiguously refers to as 'the sources of its power' (*WL*, 149), meaning, evidently, its repertory of authority-giving rhetorical effects. For the younger generation of postmodern ethnographers, such a view leaves too much aside all the other 'sources of power', political and economic, which are always at the back of the ethnographer and his or her rhetoric. For, despite the strong influence and precedent provided for them by the work of Geertz, writers such as Talal Asad, James Clifford, Vincent Crapananzo, Kevin Dwyer and Stephen A. Tyler share a suspicion that the discursive asymmetries of the ethnographic encounter are not to be dissolved simply by the poeticization of ethnography when that poeticization remains in the service of the dominating Western self, no matter how leavened and relativized by its polite deference to the other who is its discursive object.[12]

James Clifford: Art-Value, Cultural Value

It is perhaps in the work of James Clifford that the negotiation of cultural value under the conditions of cultural interchange has been most cogently and influentially analysed, and the possibilities explored of a much more radically decentred or delegitimated ethnography. Such an ethnography would eschew the kinds of interpretative authority em-bodied in the figure of the detached exegete, penetrating the tangled mysteries of another culture in order to bring into the light a meaning hidden not just from the observer but from the participants in that culture themselves. This would require ethnography to give up the belief that any amount of saturation in another culture can obliterate the distance between observed and observed, along with the fiction of invisibility achieved by evaporating away from the eventual theoretical account all the ragged, uncomfortable, discursively tense conditions of research in the field. In coming to terms with the idea that other cultures are no more to be grasped single and whole than ours is, ethnographers would also be surrendering their aspirations to be the hermeneuts of cultural entirety. Clifford sets against the heroic 'ethnographic self-fashioning' of the early fieldwork tradition – as evidenced in the works of writers such as Bronislaw Malinowski, Edward Evans Evans-Pritchard and Margaret Mead – an alternative tradition, instanced principally in the work of French writers such as Marcel Griaule and Michel Leiris. This tradition resists the triumph of the final verdict, whether on another culture, or on the interpreting self. For Michel Leiris, especially, ethnography is indissolubly linked to the endlessly renewed but strictly interminable practice of autobiography, as the restlessly sceptical self refuses to subtract its own inconclusive experiences from the account it offers of the African other. Most importantly, Clifford resists the dangers of romantic appropriation evident in such work by looking forward to an ethnographic strategy of heteroglossia, 'a utopia of plural authorship that accords to collaborators not merely the status of independent enunciators but that of writers' (*PC*, 51).

For Clifford, as for Geertz, this alternative ethnographic tradition and possibility is bound up closely with cultural-aesthetic questions. Clifford also shares with Geertz an interest in the ways in which the encounter with other cultures might productively disorder the value distinctions between culture and high culture which has for so long defined the terms of such encounter. Clifford identifies in advanced societies of the West a system for the differentiation and relating of 'art' and 'culture', a system that enforces a disciplinary cleavage between the anthropological and sociological sciences on the one hand and the humanities on the other, while also accounting for the classification of cultural objects more generally. Art, Clifford suggests, is identified with the ideal form of authentic and enduring masterpieces, usually the work of original and singular artists. Culture, following the Arnold/Tylor split in the use of the term, signifies the realm of traditional or collective practice, though, as we have seen, according to the logic which Clifford himself has identified, singular artistic culture and culture in Tylor's sense of a whole way of life, are linked by the notion of 'authenticity'. Most cultural objects are classified according to one or other of these alternatives. Defined either as cultural artefacts or works of art, they are then exhibited in different ways in the different institutions of the ethnographic museum and the art museum – though this does not prohibit a 'controlled migration' at certain moments between the two zones (*PC*, 228).

Clifford is especially interested in the movement whereby cultural artefacts are given the status of art objects, since it is movement in this direction which reveals most clearly the differences in forms of value between collecting and collected cultures – differences, we may say, in the value of value. Clifford criticizes the tendency in Western collections of 'primitive art' to abstract objects from any explanatory context, and the tendency to measure the artistic value of an artefact in terms of how far it is possible to make this very abstraction. Primitive art is thus given aesthetic value in terms of a distinctively modernist aesthetic which stresses the entire, autotelic self-possession of works of art, relegating to a dependent and merely evidentiary status objects that seem to rely on their contexts to be understood. In fact, however, the distinction between aesthetic and cultural value (this latter in the post-Tylorian sense), is really a variation between cognates, since the collecting and display of aesthetic and cultural artefacts from other cultures share some fundamental characteristics. Drawing on the work of Susan Stewart and Jean Baudrillard, Clifford sees both artistic and ethnographic collection as governed by the psychology of gathering and accumulation, which depends upon the abrupt separation of the collected object from its original contexts and deployment within a secondary field of value which is rigorously demarcated from the first.[13] It would seem that there is an effect of complementarity built into this system, in which it is not only the purpose and effect of categorial distinctions between different sorts of value to maintain distinctions between objects, but also the reciprocal function of the exemplary objects to maintain the categorial distinctions of value. In turn, we may say that the value system thus set going maintains a permanent distinction between those who do the valuing and those whose cultures are subjected to evaluation. As Sally Price has recently argued, Western museums and collectors of primitive art tend to work with the assumption that since all archaic or tribal art is collective, anonymous and unselfconscious, it is meaningless to speak in terms of anything other than the merely functional value of such works for their originating cultures. The attribution of value can come about only as a result of its transplantation to a Western field of value (and in particular, the aesthetic authorization of the work under the individual signature of the collector or connoisseur), which comes to represent the possibility of value *as such*. 'According to the people who take this view', writes Price, 'the Western connoisseur does for African masks (to take but one example) what Marcel Duchamp did for urinals.'[14]

If this applies in intense and conspicuous fashion to the shearing of cultural objects away from their originating contexts for the purpose of establishing their aesthetic value, it nevertheless also applies to the collection of cultural artefacts for their illustrative or exemplary value for anthropological science. In both cases, objects are lifted clear of time, and installed in the imaginary eternal present of museum display. The 'Family of Art' suggested by syncretic exhibitions such as ' "Primitivism" in Twentieth-Century Art: Affinity of the Tribal and the Modern', held at the Museum of Modern Art in New York in 1984–5, thus keys cleanly into the notion of the universal history and essence of Man.

Clifford argues that, in both cases, we can discern a paradigm of salvage at work. According to this paradigm, cultural artefacts are always being rescued from cultures whose authentic being either lies lost in the ruined past or is on the point of vanishing. The act of collection rescues and redeems the products of this authentic culture, but in so doing participates in its destruction or denial. Perhaps we might see this as an intercultural dramatization of the paradox of aesthetic value as such in modernism, in which the aesthetic can substitute for the authentic value of undivided culture only as a result of the very exclusion of the aesthetic from culture as a whole, an exclusion which disproves its own claim to proleptic or retrieved authenticity. If the fascination with primitive art is an expression of 'the restless desire and power of the modern West to collect the world' (*PC*, 196), then it is also true that this fixation effects a self-division within Western culture, in an incapacity to conceive value except as a certain kind of self-collection, and a severing of aesthetic culture from culture in the largest sense. The value of Clifford's work lies in his diagnosis of this paradox as it is enacted across cultures and between the two categories installed by the term 'culture', the paradox that value can only exist in the fixated or fetishized forms which actually testify to the loss or suppression of value.

For Clifford, the most provocative scandal for this cultural-aesthetic system is the notion that tribal culture might not only belong to history (and therefore belong to those to whom history belongs) but also still possess and participate in a continuing history of its own. Clifford proposes as a model for this latter the kind of uncomfortably hybrid artistic and cultural activity that goes on among tribal or traditional cultures that have not simply vanished under the various stresses of imperialism, but have adapted in often surprisingly resourceful ways to them, borrowing and transforming materials and cultural styles from the 'outside' of their culture. This is a process which the salvage paradigm would judge as contamination, but which must be seen as merely an accelerated version of the kind of irregular adaptation which always anyway characterizes cultures on their 'inside'. Such a view of the continuing value of traditional art and culture stresses their animate inventiveness rather than the necessity for their redemption by the selective agencies of Western value. It stresses, in the words of Chinua Achebe which Clifford quotes, 'aesthetic value as *process* rather than *product*'. Achebe's vision of an Igbo art that is perpetually in composition (and also, given the 'formidable agencies of dissolution' of the tropical climate, decomposition) recalls Geertz's example of the processual art whose value emerges through its temporal career rather than being fixed atemporally in its form, and suggests for Clifford 'not the modernist allegory of redemption (a yearning to make things whole, to think archaeologically) but an acceptance of endless seriality, a desire to keep things apart, dynamic, and historical' (*PC*, 208–9).[15]

In breaking down the strict distinctions between modern and traditional culture, such models also break down, or at least compromise, the interior distinctions between the artistic and the anthropological senses of culture in the West. The point, however, is not to restore a more unified conception of culture, in which life and art, history and form, would commingle in Edenic oneness – for we have seen that this particular dream of unified culture is itself a by-product of the modernist system of value that is contested in Clifford's work. Instead, Clifford proposes as an analogy for the process of cultural adaptation he admires what is itself an effect of cultural hybridization, and the grotesque conjoining of disjunct spheres of value, namely, the Surrealist ethnography, or ethnographic Surrealism, associated with Georges Bataille, Michel Leiris and the Collège de Sociologie. Clifford focuses on an early, utopian period during the 1920s and early 1930s when the projects of Surrealism and ethnography had not hardened into their respective professionalisms, in which the pages of Bataille's *Documents* could be divided between articles on African sculpture and ethnographic practice and Surrealist subversions of the practices of everyday modern life (*PC*, 117–51). At this moment, the ethnographic impulse which 'provided a style of scientifically-validated cultural leveling, the redistribution of value-charged categories such as "music," "art," "beauty," "sophistication," "cleanliness," and so on' (*PC*, 131) was joined to an artistic practice and cultural critique devoted to an extreme defamiliarization of Western life and consciousness; both ethnography and art involving 'a radical questioning of norms, and an appeal to the exotic, the paradoxical, the *insolite*' (*PC*, 129). Again, we may detect in ethnographic Surrealism of this period a disruption of the economy of value relations within and between cultures: if it is impossible to be sure of the means of differentiating art from culture, this means it is impossible to maintain stable value distinctions between cultures.

By 1937, the effects of this utopian collision of spheres in France had been largely undone, with the growing specialization that restored Surrealism to the art world and made of ethnography and its subject a scientific profession; the symbol of this split is the institution of the Musée de l'Homme in 1937 and its definitive separation from the cultural order represented by the Musée d'Art Moderne (*PC*, 140). But, however briefly, ethnography and Surrealism had joined in the decade previously to form a 'science of cultural jeopardy', a 'theory and practice of juxtaposition' (*PC*, 147). In this kind of interchange, it is possible to read cultures and forms of culture with and against each other; possible, for example, to read Picasso's blending of African masks with European physiognomies in *Les Demoiselles d'Avignon* not, or not merely, as an invasion of the sacred unity of traditional culture, but as a parallel to the kind of outrageous carnivalizing of the game of cricket effected in the Trobriand Islands, which turns that most cerebral and abstract game into a crazy concoction of aggression, extravagance and paralogy (*PC*, 148).

Here, then, a later, dominant form of the conjoining of ethnography, the writing of culture, with the artistic production of culture, in which both culture and art are defined by forms of abstraction, distance and exteriority (the ethnographer who speaks on behalf of, but at a distance from, the culture he or she studies, the art object whose aesthetic value derives from its separation from its cultural context), is contested by an alternative conjuncture, which it is really the project of *The Predicament of Culture* to restore and renovate. Here, value as process and parody, consisting in the interior disruption of categories of art and culture, corresponds to a radically dialogic form of ethnographic writing, which takes place across and between cultures. It is a vision which does not abolish distinctions or collapse distances either between or within cultures, since such a collapse into unity is only the inverse product of the absolute fixations of value characteristic of the later model. Rather, it makes possible, under conditions that precede and surpass the hardening of the value of art and culture into the forms of fetish, the collective transaction of cultural value.

If the achievement of symmetry is not to be expected in such relationships of cultural adjustment, there are nevertheless differences between the two kinds of inventive cultural process, the Surrealist culture of the West and the creatively travestied cricket game of the Trobriand Islanders, which deserve attention. For, if it is true that Surrealism and the ethnography which accompanies it are to be seen as a reaching beyond the values of the known and knowable self into the realm of heterology, into the Kantian *Unform*, or the Bataillean *informe*, can be seen, in short, as an attempt 'to value – when it comes – the unclassified, unsought other' (*PC*, 147), it is nevertheless also the case that this desire for the dissolution of identity is a characteristically modernist desire, its embracing of the death of the ego always liable to swing into a heroically bracing encounter of the self with extremity. As such, it carries its own risks of appropriation and violent hallucination, requiring the other to function no longer as a prosthetically full or primally unified self, but to impersonate the ideal of postmodern dispersal. If the postmodern cultural project aims to invert the structure of the fetish which characterizes modernism, then in a certain sense, it reconstitutes it too, for one of the strangest characteristics of fetishistic projection is that to invert it is to repeat it. To encounter one's death through the imaginary intermediary of the other is in some profound sense part of the same process of substituting for that death by attributing to the other an idealized and compensatory fullness of life. Here, the death of the ego is the very means of its eager life, its dissolution of value the very grounds of value.[16] One of the most disturbing things about Clifford's claim, reworking the title of the 1985 MOMA exhibition, for the 'affinity of the tribal and the postmodern', and his programme for a renewed heterology of museum practice is precisely their programmatic nature, the fact that the 'unclassified, unsought other' is here so meticulously and knowingly pursued:

We need exhibitions that question the boundaries of art and the art world, and influx of truly indigestible 'outside' artifacts. The relations of power whereby one portion of humanity can select, value, and collect the pure products of others need to be criticized and transformed. This is no small task. In the meantime one can at least imagine shows that feature the impure, 'inauthentic' productions of past and present tribal life; exhibitions radically heterogeneous in their global mix of styles; exhibitions that locate themselves in specific multicultural junctures; exhibitions in which nature remains 'unnatural'; exhibitions whose principles of incorporation are openly questionable. (*PC*, 213)

Clifford's work in fact suffers from a certain displacement of the requirement of value. Although his position is to be distinguished clearly from that occupied by Lyotard, since for Clifford it is a question not of the multiplicity of singular language games, but of their determined crossings and mutative combinations, he in fact falls into the strange acquiescence characteristic of Lyotard's view of culture, an acquiescence which is the result of a certain will-to-unmaking which cannot acknowledge its own imperative authority. The ideal of an absolute dialogism of peoples, or, as it were, a pure interference of voices, is self-contradictory to the extent that it occludes the questions of agency, commitment and responsibility. Who holds to and assumes responsibility for realizing the ideal of the collective decentred writing of culture? Who sustains or justifies the absolute value of the dispersal of absolutes? If Clifford and those other writers associated with the project of a postmodern ethnography begin from a critique of the assumed invisibility of the processes of value-formation at work in the writing of other cultures by the West, their particular form of self-conscious relativism also runs the risk of depriving itself of an imperative language of value. The result of this might be to flatten the field of value back into an anthropological domain of purely functional relativities, in which values are observed from the outside from a position that can never grasp itself and its own imperatives.

This tendency is apparent in the scheme of cultural value offered in Clifford's work, a scheme worked out in terms of the four-point system of negations and contrasts of A. J. Greimas's semiotic square (the relationship between art and culture discussed above is only one part of this scheme). This scheme allows Clifford to relate art (defined as 'the zone of authentic masterpieces') not only to culture ('the zone of authentic artifacts'), but also to non-art ('the zone of inauthentic artifacts', such as tourist art) and non-culture ('the zone of inauthentic masterpieces', by which apparent oxymoron Clifford means such things as fakes, inventions and Dadaist anti-art (*PC*, 223–4)). These four positions are of course idealized forms of what in most cases exists in traffic between them.

Clifford's version of Greimas's square seems to draw heavily on the use made of it by Fredric Jameson in *The Political Unconscious* (1981) (*PU*, 46–9, 166–8, 254–5).[17] As we have seen, Jameson also uses the semiotic square to map out the thematization of the question of value in Conrad's *Lord Jim*. Clifford notes that the system of value he outlines actually works as much by excluding as by including cultural forms – it is not apparent, for example, where and how religious cultural forms would

The art-culture system: a machine for making authenticity (James Clifford, *The Predicament of Culture*, p. 224)

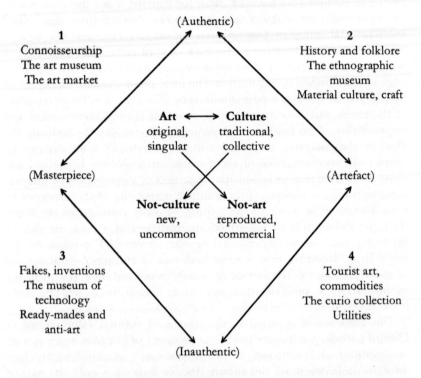

(Authentic)

1
Connoisseurship
The art museum
The art market

2
History and folklore
The ethnographic
museum
Material culture, craft

Art ⟵⟶ Culture
original,   traditional,
singular   collective

(Masterpiece)   (Artefact)

Not-culture   Not-art
new,   reproduced,
uncommon   commercial

3
Fakes, inventions
The museum of
technology
Ready-mades and
anti-art

4
Tourist art,
commodities
The curio collection
Utilities

(Inauthentic)

feature in it (*PC*, 226). But in both Jameson's and Clifford's mapping of the field of cultural value, the question of the evaluative force of the mapping itself does not and cannot figure in the scheme. For Jameson, this is because the system is produced out of the objective contradictions in which activity and value are seen as contradictory and irreconcilable; the map of value is therefore the sign of the absence or impossibility of 'real' value in an alienated world. The achievement of such real value could only ever come about as a result of the dialectical transcendence of the contradiction between activity and value which produces the textual dynamic in *Lord Jim*; there is thus no place for value as such in the semiotic square which maps the mutations and exchanges of value. Unlike Jameson, Clifford is not committed to any work of cultural synthesis or dialectical overcoming, but, in a similar way, a certain kind of real or imperative value cannot be included in the square, which, intended as it is to be 'a machine for making authenticity', is limited to the designation of purely functional relationships. But when Clifford writes of Claude Lévi-Strauss's struggle to gain recognition for the 'increasingly rare masterworks' of tribal artefacts (*PC*, 239), one wonders whether the unconditional assertion of value implied here could itself be assigned to its purely relative position on the semiotic square? More importantly, one wonders how the value of the breaching or hybridization of categories could be represented, if at all, except, as with Jameson's version of the value-problematic, with a dissolution of the system and the scheme which represents it.

This unrepresentability of value is what makes Clifford's postmodern ethnography in the end ethically underspecified, because unable to bring the imperatives which motivate it to evaluative visibility. This inability is not so much a failure to escape the paradox of value whereby it is necessary to affirm in absolute terms the contingency of all such absolutes, but a failure properly and fully to inhabit it, to acknowledge fully one's own necessary imperatives and value-investments. In this respect, Clifford's work may perhaps be vulnerable to the same charge that Geertz mounts against those ethnographers whose work is often held to exemplify the dialogically self-aware ethnographic writing that Clifford recommends. Geertz criticizes in the work of Vincent Crapanzano, Paul Rabinow and Kevin Dwyer a certain hyperinterpretative dissolution of the observing, recording self in structures of guilt. Of Kevin Dwyer's attempt to record the encounter of Western self and Moroccan other in *Moroccan Dialogues* (1982), for example, Geertz writes, 'as the aim in this case is to expose the unsolid ground upon which all such interaction inevitably rests, a tissue of careerism, deception, manipulation, and micro-imperialism, the self, rather than being rhetorically aggrandized is, no less rhetorically, undercut. Dwyer's "I" neither floats through his text nor engulfs it. It apologizes for being there at all' (*WL*, 95). The force of Geertz's critique against the generation he calls 'Malinowski's Children' is not directly at their 'sins of self-display', as Clifford seems to feel in his thin defence of them in *The Predicament of Culture* (*PC*, 113), but at a kind of irresponsible failure, despite all the saturated self-consciousness of their texts, to occupy the encounter, except in the mode of self-mutilating, but ultimately self-protective, malaise. The principal notes of their discourse are consequently those of 'estrangement, hypocrisy, helplessness, domination, disillusion. Being There is not just practically difficult. There is something corrupting about it altogether' (*WL*, 96). The continuation of the work of ethnography under the these conditions might seem to embody another version of the performative self-contradiction that we have detected everywhere in contemporary theory of cultural value, though in fact what is striking about it is precisely the tendency for this extreme of self-consciousness to cauterize itself against the hurt and responsibility of a more openly inhabited responsibility. When unremitting self-display produces invisibility and inviolability, then *qui s'excuse, s'accuse.*

Geertz is as convinced as any of those whose work he criticizes of the need for ethnography to help 'enlarge the possibility of intelligible discourse between people quite different from one another in interest, outlook, wealth and power, and yet contained in a world where, tumbled as they are into endless connection, it is increasingly difficult to get out of each other's way' (*WL*, 147), and, in the process, to remain highly self-conscious about its own discursive powers and effects. But, for Geertz, the ethical force and value of this is inseparable from an acknowledgement of one's own position and cultural identity, provisional and molested though it may be. The paradox of intercultural value for Geertz is how to engage with the voices, experiences and values of others without being tempted by forms of immunizing self-immolation; it is 'the double perception that ours is but one voice among many and that, as it is the only one we have, we must needs speak with it' (*LK*, 234). It is true that Geertz's rather genial self-possession is itself open to the objection that it is a means of immunizing the self against any form of violent or radical decentring. But his work usefully indicates the difficulty of mediating the question of value either from the viewpoint of the self completing itself in the detour of the other, or of the self grandiosely employing the other to celebrate its *manque à être*. As Derrida has observed of the anti-egological ethics of Levinas, it is not possible to avoid violence by an abolition of the violating self, since this constitutes a refusal of the ethical commitment of self to other which is itself a kind of violation; given this, the absolute non-violence of non-contact is a kind of war (VM, 146–7). For the ethical force and necessity of the encounter between cultures is concentrated neither around the value of self-identity or the self-identity of value, nor around the absolute dispersal and relativising of all value. Rather, it is governed by the irreducible necessity to impact these two dimensions of value, consolidating the value of dispersal, dispersing the value of consolidation. It is in this respect that the problems posed by the interculturation of cultural value curl into that complex helix of issues which have formed the recurrent object and destination of this enquiry into the nature of value and theories of it in our contemporary world. The quickening predicament that I have tried repeatedly to evoke here, and which our world must hereafter continue to encounter and explore, is that value cannot ever be wholly in the tenure of theory, since this is always illegitimately to arrest the transport of its absconding play; even though, more than ever, theory's vocation must be to resist the evacuation of value, must be in truth to instate and permanently to occupy the instances of its passage.

NOTES

1 Matthew Arnold, *Culture and Anarchy* (1869), ed. John Dover Wilson (Cambridge: Cambridge University Press, 1988), pp. 82, 163.

2 E. B. Tylor, *Primitive Culture*, 2 vols (London: John Murray, 1871), vol. 1, p. 1.

3 George Stocking, 'Arnold, Tylor, and the Uses of Invention', in *Race, Culture and Evolution: Essays in the History of Anthropology* (New York: Free Press, 1968), pp. 72–90.

4 Bourdieu, *Outline of a Theory of Practice*, pp. 177–8.

5 A. L. Kroeber and Clyde Kluckhohn, *Culture: A Critical Review of Concepts and Definitions* (Cambridge, Mass.: Peabody Museum of American Archeology and Ethnology, 1952), p. 150.

6 No one has done more to analyse the development and historical overlap of the two senses of culture than Raymond Williams, who gives useful social etymologies of the term throughout *Culture and Society* (London: Chatto & Windus, 1958), and in *Keywords: A Vocabulary of Culture and Society*, 2nd edn (London: Fontana, 1976), pp. 87–93. Williams's ambition for the sociology of culture inaugurated largely by his work, that it should operate at a point of convergence of the two senses, dealing both with the 'whole way of life' of a society, and with its most distinctive and valued artistic and intellectual products, has not, I think, been realized (see *Culture* (London: Fontana, 1981), pp. 10–14). This may be partly because the descriptive and evaluative commitments required of such a sociology cannot be reconciled in terms of the smooth 'convergence' that Williams imagines.

7 The conference on 'Cultural Value' at Birkbeck College in 1988, which marked the beginning of my interest in the question of value in contemporary theory, provided an interesting example of this entanglement. It soon became clear that the participants were dramatically divided in their understanding of the import of the conference theme. About half of the conference believed that 'cultural value' referred to the renewal of the question of the aesthetic in contemporary theory, while the other half assumed that what was at stake was precisely the competing political and ethical values of culture and cultures as such. What was striking and symptomatic was that these two dimensions, of postmodern aesthetics and postcolonial politics, of intracultural value and intercultural value, could no more be separated than they could be adequately brought together.

8 Nelson Goodman, *Ways of Worldmaking* (Indianapolis and Cambridge, Mass.: Hackett, 1978); *Writing Culture: The Poetics and Politics of Ethnography*, ed.

James Clifford and George E. Marcus. (Berkeley, Los Angeles and London: University of California Press, 1986).

9 Adopting a perspective such as this one makes it possible to read the orthodox Islamic condemnation of Salman Rushdie's *The Satanic Verses*, which is, in theme and substance, explicitly concerned with this issue of the entanglement of the sacred and the sacrilegious, scripture and blasphemy, as an (impossible) and violent attempt to exteriorize what exists as an interior complexity at the heart of Islamic culture, to protect and integrate sacred value and the value of the sacred by an act of disintegrative expulsion. Western defences of *The Satanic Verses* which rested on the alleged incapacity of Islamic readers to understand the status of fiction were therefore very wide of the mark. Rushdie's definition of the provisional sacredness of the work of literature in providing a space for the struggle or play of desacralization certainly in one sense mounts an exteriorizing and desacralizing critique of Islam (and other absolute value systems) from Islam's Western metropolitan outside. But, in another, more profound sense, it relies upon an insider's sense of the dangerous and inextricable proximity of truth to heresy in Islamic culture itself. See 'Is Nothing Sacred?', in *Imaginary Homelands: Essays and Criticism, 1981–1991* (London: Granta/Penguin, 1991), pp. 415–29.

10 See above, pp. 71–5.

11 Most importantly, this has joined Geertz's work to the postmodern project of anthropologizing anthropology itself: see his *Works and Lives: The Anthropologist as Author* (Cambridge: Polity Press, 1988).

12 See Talal Asad, *Anthropology and the Colonial Encounter* (London: Ithaca Press, 1973); Vincent Crapananzo, *Tuhani: Portrait of a Moroccan* (Chicago and London: University of Chicago Press, 1980); Kevin Dwyer, *Moroccan Dialogues: Anthropology in Question* (Baltimore and London: Johns Hopkins University Press, 1982); Stephen A. Tyler, *The Unspeakable: Discourse, Dialogue, and Rhetoric in the Postmodern World* (Madison: University of Wisconsin Press, 1987). A more pointed critique of the 'exclusively textual mode of ethnographic representation', which prevents a proper attention to the workings of power, and the material production and maintenance of symbolic systems, is offered by Bob Scholte in 'The Charmed Circle of Geertz's Hermeneutics: A Neo-Marxist Critique', *Critique of Anthropology*, 6 (1986), pp. 5–15 and extended to the work of those associated with the *Writing Culture* volume in 'The Literary Turn in Contemporary Anthropology', *Critique of Anthropology*, 7 (1987), pp. 33–47.

13 Clifford draws upon Jean Baudrillard's short-lived but immensely suggestive enquiry into the social semiotics of value attaching to objects in *Le Système des objets* (Paris: Gallimard, 1968) and Susan Stewart's analysis of the fetishism of the collecting impulse in *On Longing: Narratives of the Miniature, the Gigantic, the Souvenir, the Collection* (Baltimore and London: Johns Hopkins University Press, 1984).

14 Sally Price, 'Others' Art – Our Art', *Third Text*, 6 (1989), p. 70.

15 Clifford quotes from Chinua Achebe's 'Foreword' to *Igbo Arts: Community and Cosmos*, ed. H. M. Cole and C. C. Aniakor (Los Angeles: Museum of Cultural History, UCLA, 1984), p. ix.

16 I have attempted to examine a number of different forms of the 'perclusive' structure of postmodern theory, which evacuates its own authority in order the more effectively to reconstitute it, in my *Postmodernist Culture*.

17 See discussion above, pp. 150–3.

Works Cited

Adorno, Theodor and Horkheimer, Max. *Dialectic of Enlightenment* (1944). Trans. John Cumming. London: Verso, 1986.

Andolsen, Barbara Hilkert, Gudorf, Christine E. and Pellauer, Mary D. (eds). *Women's Consciousness, Women's Conscience: A Reader in Feminist Ethics.* San Francisco and London: Harper & Row, 1987.

Arnold, Matthew. *Culture and Anarchy* (1869). Ed. John Dover Wilson. Cambridge: Cambridge University Press, 1988.

Asad, Talal. *Anthropology and the Colonial Encounter.* London: Ithaca Press, 1973.

Barthes, Roland. *The Pleasure of the Text* (1973). Trans. Richard Miller. Oxford: Basil Blackwell, 1990.

Bataille, Georges. *Sur Nietzsche.* Paris: Gallimard, 1945.

—— 'Hegel, la mort et le sacrifice'. *Deucalion,* 5 (1955): 21–43.

—— *Eroticism* (1957). Trans. Mary Dalwood. London: John Calder, 1962.

—— 'La valeur d'usage de D. A. F. de Sade (lettre ouverte à mes camarades actuels). In *Oeuvres Complètes,* vol. 2 (Paris: Gallimard, 1970) pp. 54–69.

—— 'L'Economie à la mesure de l'univers'. In *Oeuvres Complètes,* vol. 7 (Paris: Gallimard, 1976), pp. 7–16.

—— *Literature and Evil* (1957). Trans. Alistair Hamilton. London: Marion Boyars, 1985.

—— *Visions of Excess: Selected Writings 1927–1939.* Trans. Allan Stoekl with C. R. Lovitt and D. M. Leslie. Manchester: Manchester University Press, 1985.

—— *The Accursed Share* (1949). Trans. Robert Hurley. New York: Zone Books, 1988.

—— *Inner Experience* (1943). Trans. Lesley Anne Boldt. Albany: State University of New York Press, 1988.

Battersby, Christine. *Gender and Genius: Towards a Feminist Aesthetics.* London: Women's Press, 1989.

Baudrillard, Jean. *Le Système des objets.* Paris: Gallimard, 1968.

—— *For a Critique of the Political Economy of the Sign* (1972). Trans. Charles Levin. St Louis: Telos Press, 1981.

—— *The Mirror of Production* (1973). Trans. Mark Poster. St Louis: Telos Press, 1975.

—— *L'échange symbolique et la mort.* Paris: Gallimard, 1976.

—— *Selected Writings*. Various translators. Ed. Mark Poster. Cambridge: Polity Press, 1988.

Beckett, Samuel. *Collected Poems in English and French*. London: John Calder, 1977.

—— *Disjecta: Miscellaneous Writings and a Dramatic Fragment*. Ed. Ruby Cohn. London: John Calder, 1983.

—— *Worstward Ho*. London: John Calder, 1983.

—— *Stirrings Still*. London and New York: John Calder and New Moon, 1989.

Benhabib, Seyla. *Critique, Norm, and Utopia: A Study of the Foundations of Critical Theory*. New York: Columbia University Press, 1986.

—— 'The Generalized and the Concrete Other: The Kohlberg–Gilligan Controversy and Feminist Theory'. In *Feminism as Critique*, ed. Benhabib and Cornell, pp. 77–95.

—— and Cornell, Drucilla (eds). *Feminism as Critique: Essays on the Politics of Gender in Late-Capitalist Societies*. Cambridge: Polity Press, 1987.

Benjamin, Andrew. 'The Redemption of Value: Laporte, Writing as Abkür-zung'. *Paragraph*, 12 (1989): 23–36.

Benstock, Bernard (ed.). *The Augmented Ninth: Proceedings of the Ninth International James Joyce Symposium, Frankfurt, 1984*. Syracuse, NY: Syracuse University Press, 1988.

Bernasconi, Robert. 'Deconstruction and the Possibility of Ethics'. In *Deconstruction and Philosophy: The Texts of Jacques Derrida*, ed. John Sallis (Chicago and London: University of Chicago Press, 1987), pp. 122–39.

—— and Critchley, Simon (eds). *Re-reading Levinas*. London: Athlone Press, 1991.

Bernstein, Jay M. 'Aesthetic Alienation: Heidegger, Adorno, and Truth at the End of Art'. In *Life after Postmodernism*, ed. Fekete, pp. 86–119.

Boheemen-Saaf, Christine van. 'Joyce, Derrida, and the Discourse of "the Other"'. In *The Augmented Ninth*, ed. Benstock, pp. 88–102.

Bond, E. J. *Reason and Value*. Cambridge: Cambridge University Press, 1983.

Booth, Wayne C. *The Company We Keep: An Ethics of Fiction*. Berkeley, Los Angeles and London: University of California Press, 1988.

Bourdieu, Pierre. *Outline of a Theory of Practice*. Trans. Richard Nice. Cambridge: Cambridge University Press, 1977.

—— *Distinction: A Social Critique of the Judgement of Taste* (1979). Trans. Richard Nice. London and New York: Routledge & Kegan Paul, 1984.

Brivic, Sheldon. 'The Father in Joyce'. In *The Seventh of Joyce*, ed. Bernard Benstock (Brighton: Harvester Press, 1982), pp. 74–80.

Burke, Carolyn. 'Irigaray through the Looking Glass'. *Feminist Studies*, 7 (1981): 288–306.

Cameron, Deborah. *Feminism and Linguistic Practice*. London: Macmillan, 1985.

Card, Claudia (ed.). *Feminist Ethics*. Kansas City: University of Kansas Press, 1991.

Clifford, James. *The Predicament of Culture: Twentieth-Century Ethnography, Literature, and Art*. Cambridge, Mass. and London: Harvard University Press, 1988.

—— and Marcus, George E. (eds). *Writing Culture: The Poetics and Politics of*

Ethnography. Berkeley, Los Angeles and London: University of California Press, 1986.

Cohen, Richard A. (ed.). *Face to Face with Levinas*. Albany: State University of New York Press, 1986.

Cole, H. M. and Aniakor, C. C. *Igbo Arts: Community and Cosmos*. Los Angeles: Museum of Cultural History, UCLA, 1984.

Connor, Steven. *Samuel Beckett: Repetition, Theory and Text*. Oxford: Basil Blackwell, 1988.

—— *Postmodernist Culture: An Introduction to Theories of the Contemporary*. Oxford: Basil Blackwell, 1989.

—— 'Between Earth and Air: Value, Culture and Futurity'. *Block* (forthcoming, 1992).

Corn, Tony. 'La Negativité sans emploi (Derrida, Bataille, Hegel)'. *Romanic Review*, 76 (1976): 65–75.

Cornell, Drucilla and Thurschwell, Adam. 'Feminism, Negativity, Inter-subjectivity'. In *Feminism as Critique*, ed. Benhabib and Cornell, pp. 143–62.

Crapanzano, Vincent. *Tuhani: Portrait of a Moroccan*. Chicago and London: University of Chicago Press, 1980.

—— 'Hermes' Dilemma: The Masking of Subversion in Ethnographic Description'. In *Writing Culture*, ed. Clifford and Marcus, pp. 51–76.

Critchley, Simon. 'The Chiasmus: Levinas, Derrida and the Ethical Demand for Deconstruction'. *Textual Practice*, 3 (1989): 91–106.

—— '"Bois" – Derrida's Final Word on Levinas'. In *Re-reading Levinas*, ed. Bernasconi and Critchley, pp. 162–89.

Culler, Jonathan. 'Communicative Competence and Normative Force'. *New German Critique*, 35 (1985): 133–44.

Daly, Mary. *Gyn/Ecology: The Metaethics of Radical Feminism*. London: Women's Press, 1979.

Davies, Lesley. *Caring: A Feminine Approach to Ethics*. Canterbury: University of Kent, 1990.

de Courtivron, Isabelle and Marks, Elaine (eds). *New French Feminisms*. New York: Schocken, 1981.

Delphy, Christine. 'Protofeminism and Antifeminism'. In *French Feminist Thought*, ed. Moi, pp. 80–109.

de Man, Paul. *The Resistance to Theory*. Manchester: Manchester University Press, 1986.

Derrida, Jacques. *Of Grammatology*. Trans. Gayatri Chakravorty Spivak. Baltimore and London: Johns Hopkins University Press, 1974.

—— *Writing and Difference*. Trans. Alan Bass, London: Routledge & Kegan Paul, 1978.

—— 'Violence and Metaphysics: An Essay on the Thought of Emmanuel Levinas'. Ibid., pp. 79–153.

—— *Margins of Philosophy*. Trans. Alan Bass. Brighton: Harvester Press, 1982.

—— 'The Principle of Reason: The University in the Eyes of its Pupils'. Trans. Catherine Porter and Edward P. Morris. *Diacritics*, 13 (1983): 3–20.

—— 'Two Words for Joyce'. Trans. Geoff Bennington. In *Post-structuralist Joyce: Essays from the French*, ed. Derek Attridge and Daniel Ferrer (Cambridge: Cambridge University Press, 1984), pp. 145–59.

—— 'No Apocalypse, Not Now (full speed ahead, seven missiles, seven missives)'. Trans. Catherine Porter and Philip Lewis. *Diacritics*, 14 (1984): 20–31.

—— 'Racism's Last Word'. Trans. Peggy Kamuf. *Critical Inquiry*, 12 (1985): 290–9.

—— 'Ulysse gramophone: l'oui-dire de Joyce'. In *Genèse de Babel: études présentés par Claude Jacquet* (Paris: CNRS, 1985), pp. 227–64.

—— 'But, Beyond ... Open Letter to Anne McClintock and Rob Nixon'. Trans. Peggy Kamuf. *Critical Inquiry*, 13 (1986): 155–70.

—— 'To Speculate – on "Freud" '. In *The Post-Card: From Socrates to Freud and Beyond*, trans. Alan Bass (Chicago and London: University of Chicago Press, 1987), pp. 259–409.

—— *Limited Inc*, 2nd edn, ed. Gerald Graff. Trans. Jeffrey Mehlman and Samuel Weber. Evanston, Ill.: Northwestern University Press, 1988.

—— 'Like the Sound of the Sea Deep within a Shell: Paul de Man's War'. *Critical Inquiry*, 14 (1988): 590–652.

—— 'Biodegradables: Seven Diary Fragments'. *Critical Inquiry*, 15 (1989): 812–73.

—— 'At This Very Moment in This Work Here I Am'. In *Re-reading Levinas*, ed. Bernasconi and Critchley, pp. 11–48.

Dewey, John. *Theory of Valuation*. In *John Dewey: The Later Works, 1925–1953*, ed. Jo Ann Boyditon and Barbara Levine (Carbondale and Edwardsville: Southern Illinois University Press, 1988), vol. 13, pp. 189–270.

Dwyer, Kevin. *Moroccan Dialogues: Anthropology in Question*. Baltimore and London: Johns Hopkins University Press, 1982.

Eagleton, Terry. *Criticism and Ideology: A Study in Marxist Literary Theory*. London: Verso, 1976.

—— *Literary Theory: An Introduction*. Oxford: Basil Blackwell, 1983.

—— 'Poetry, Pleasure and Politics'. In *Against the Grain: Selected Essssays 1975–1985* (London: Verso, 1986), pp. 173–80.

—— 'Modernism, Myth and Monopoly Capitalism'. *News from Nowhere*, 7 (1989): 19–24.

—— *The Ideology of the Aesthetic*. Oxford: Basil Blackwell, 1990.

Easthope, Antony. 'The Question of Literary Value'. *Textual Practice*, 4 (1990): 376–89.

Federman, Raymond and Graver, Lawrence (eds). *Samuel Beckett: The Critical Heritage*. London: Routledge & Kegan Paul, 1979.

Fekete, John (ed.). *Life after Postmodernism: Essays on Value and Culture*. Basingstoke and London: Macmillan, 1988.

Felski, Rita. *Beyond Feminist Aesthetics: Feminist Literature and Social Change*. London: Hutchinson Radius, 1989.

Flax, Jane. 'Postmodernism and Gender Relations in Feminist Theory'. *Signs: Journal of Women in Culture and Society*, 12 (1987): 621–43.

Foucault, Michel. 'Preface to Transgression'. In *Language, Counter-Memory, Practice: Selected Essays and Interviews*, ed. Donald F. Bouchard, trans. Donald F. Bouchard and Sherry Simon (Oxford: Basil Blackwell, 1977), pp. 29–52.

—— 'On the Genealogy of Ethics: An Overview of Work in Progress'. In *Michel Foucault: Beyond Structuralism and Hermeneutics*, ed. H. Dreyfus and Paul Rabinow (Chicago and London: University of Chicago Press, 1983), pp. 229–52.

Fraser, Nancy. 'Toward a Discourse Ethic of Solidarity'. *Praxis International*, 5 (1986): 425–9.

—— 'What's Critical about Critical Theory? The Case of Habermas and Gender'. In *Feminism as Critique*, ed. Benhabib and Cornell, pp. 31–56.

—— *Unruly Practices: Power, Discourse and Gender in Contemporary Social Theory*. Cambridge: Polity Press, 1989.

Freud, Sigmund. *Jenseits des Lustprinzips* (1920). In *Gesammelte Schriften* (Leipzig, Vienna and Zurich: Internationaler Psychoanalytischer Verlag, 1925), vol. 6, pp. 191–257.

—— *Aus der Anfängen der Psychoanalyse*. London: Imago, 1950.

—— *Beyond the Pleasure Principle* (1920). In *The Standard Edition of the Psychological Works of Sigmund Freud*, trans. James Strachey (London: Hogarth Press, 1953–73), vol. 18, pp. 1–64.

—— 'The Economic Problem of Masochism' (1924). Ibid., vol. 19, pp. 155–70.

Fry, Roger. 'An Essay in Aesthetics' (1909). Repr. in *Modern Art and Modernism: A Critical Anthology*, ed. Francis Frascina and Charles Harrison (London: Harper & Row, 1982), pp. 79–87.

Fullbrook, Kate. *Free Women: Ethics and Aesthetics in Twentieth-Century Women's Fiction*. Hemel Hempstead: Harvester Press, 1990.

Gallop, Jane. *Feminism and Psychoanalysis: The Daughter's Seduction*. London: Macmillan, 1982.

Geertz, Clifford. 'Deep Play: Notes on a Balinese Cockfight'. In *The Interpretation of Cultures* (New York: Basic Books, 1973), pp. 412–53.

—— *Local Knowledge: Further Essays in Interpretive Anthropology*. New York: Basic Books, 1986.

—— *Works and Lives: The Anthropologist as Author*. Cambridge: Polity Press, 1988.

Gench, Peter. *Mental Acts: Their Content and their Objects*. London: Routledge & Kegan Paul, 1957.

Gilligan, Carol. *In a Different Voice: Psychological Theory and Women's Development*. Cambridge, Mass.: Harvard University Press, 1982.

Goodman, Nelson. *Ways of Worldmaking*. Indianapolis and Cambridge, Mass.: Hackett, 1978.

Grimshaw, Jean. *Philosophy and Feminist Thinking*. Minneapolis: University of Minnesota Press, 1986.

Habermas, Jürgen. 'What is Universal Pragmatics?' (1976). In *Communication and the Evolution of Society*, trans. Thomas McCarthy (London: Heinemann, 1979), pp. 1–68.

—— 'Reply to my Critics'. In *Habermas: Critical Debates*, ed. J. Thompson and D. Held (Cambridge, Mass.: MIT Press, 1982), pp. 219–83.

—— 'Questions and Counter-Questions', *Praxis International*, 4 (1984): 229–50.

—— *The Theory of Communicative Action*. Vol. 1: *Reason and the Rationalization of Society*. Vol. 2: *Lifeworld and System: A Critique of Functionalist Reason*. Boston: Beacon Books; Cambridge: Polity Press, 1984, 1987.

—— *The Philosophical Discourse of Modernity: Twelve Lectures*. Trans. Frederick Lawrence. Cambridge: Polity Press, 1987.

Hanen, Marsha and Nelson, Kai (eds). *Science, Morality, and Feminist Theory*. Calgary: University of Calgary Press, 1987.

Hans, James S. *The Question of Value: Thinking through Nietzsche, Heidegger, and Freud*. Carbondale and Edwardsville: Southern Illinois University Press, 1989.

Harvey, David. *The Condition of Postmodernity: An Enquiry into the Origins of Social Change*. Oxford: Basil Blackwell, 1989.

Heath, Stephen. 'Difference'. *Screen*, 19 (1978–9): 50–112.

Heidegger, Martin. 'Letter on Humanism' (1947). In *Basic Writings from 'Being and Time' (1927) to 'The Task of Thinking' (1964)*, ed. David Farrell Krell (London: Routledge & Kegan Paul, 1978), pp. 193–242.

Irigaray, Luce. *Ethique de la différence sexuelle*. Paris: Editions de Minuit, 1984.

—— *This Sex which is Not One*. Trans. Carolyn Burke and Catherine Porter. Ithaca, NY: Cornell University Press, 1985.

—— 'The Fecundity of the Caress: A Reading of Levinas, *Totality and Infinity* section IV, B, "The Phenomenology of Eros"'. Trans. Carolyn Burke. In *Face to Face with Levinas*, ed. Cohen, pp. 231–56.

—— 'Women, the Sacred and Money'. Trans. Diana Knight and Margaret Whitford. *Paragraph*, 8 (1986): 6–17.

—— *Je, tu, nous: pour une culture de la différence*. Paris: Grasset, 1990.

Jameson, Fredric. *The Political Unconscious: Narrative as a Socially Symbolic Act*. London and New York: Methuen, 1981.

—— 'Pleasure: A Political Issue'. In Tony Bennett et al., *Formations of Pleasure* (London: Routledge & Kegan Paul, 1983), pp. 1–14.

Jay, Gregory S. 'Values and Deconstructions: Derrida, Saussure, Marx'. *Cultural Critique*, 8 (1987–8): 153–96.

Johnson, Barbara. *A World of Difference*. Baltimore and London: Johns Hopkins University Press, 1987.

Jones, Ellen Carol. ' "Writing the Mystery of Himself": Paternity in *Ulysses*'. In *The Augmented Ninth*, ed. Benstock, pp. 226–32.

Joyce, James. *Ulysses*. Ed. Hans Walter Gabler. Harmondsworth: Penguin, 1986.

—— *Finnegans Wake*. London: Faber & Faber, 1939.

Kant, Immanuel. *The Critique of Judgement* (1790). Trans. James Creed Meredith. Oxford: Clarendon Press, 1952.

Kaplan, Carey and Rose, Ellen Cronan. *The Canon and the Common Reader*. Knoxville: Tennessee University Press, 1990.

Kaplan, Cora. 'The Thorn Birds: Fiction, Fantasy, Femininity'. In *Sea Changes: Essays on Culture and Feminism* (London: Verso, 1986), pp. 117–46.

—— 'Wild Nights: Pleasure/Sexuality/Feminism'. Ibid., pp. 31–50.

Kearney, Richard. 'Dialogue with Emmanuel Levinas'. In *Face to Face with Levinas*, ed. Cohen, pp. 13–34.

Kellner, Douglas. *Jean Baudrillard: From Marxism to Postmodernism and Beyond.* Cambridge: Polity Press, 1989.

Kennedy, Alan. *Reading Resistance Value: Deconstructive Practice and the Politics of Literary Critical Encounters.* Basingstoke: Macmillan, 1990.

Kohlberg, Lawrence. *The Psychology of Moral Development: The Nature and Validity of Moral Stages.* San Francisco and London: Harper & Row, 1984.

Kristeva, Julia. 'The Ethics of Linguistics'. In *Desire in Language*, trans. Thomas Gora, Alice Jardine and Leon S. Roudiez (Oxford: Basil Blackwell, 1980), pp. 23–35.

—— 'Woman Can Never Be Defined'. In *New French Feminisms*, ed. de Courtivron and Marks pp. 137–41.

—— 'Psychoanalysis and the Polis'. Trans. Margaret Waller. In *The Politics of Interpretation*, ed. W. J. T. Mitchell (Chicago and London: University of Chicago Press, 1983), pp. 83–98.

Kroeber, A. L. and Kluckhohn, Clyde. *Culture: A Critical Review of Concepts and Definitions.* Cambridge, Mass.: Peabody Museum of American Archeology and Ethnology, 1952.

Lacan, Jacques. *Le séminaire livre xx: Encore.* Paris: Seuil, 1975.

—— 'On the Subject of Certainty'. In *The Four Fundamental Concepts of Psycho-Analysis*, trans. Alan Sheridan (Harmondsworth: Penguin, 1979), pp. 29–41.

Laplanche, J. and Pontalis, J.-B. *The Language of Psycho-Analysis.* London: Hogarth Press, 1983.

Leclerc, Annie. 'Parole de Femme' (1974). Extract reprinted in *French Feminist Thought*, ed. Moi, pp. 73–9.

le Doeuff, Michèle. *Hipparchia's Choice: An Essay concerning Women, Philosophy, Etc.* Trans. Trista Selous. Oxford: Basil Blackwell, 1991.

le Guin, Ursula. *Dancing at the Edge of the World: Thoughts on Words, Women, Places.* New York: Grove Press, 1989.

Levinas, Emmanuel. *Totality and Infinity: An Essay on Exteriority* (1961). Trans. Alphonso Lingis. The Hague: Nijhoff, 1979.

—— 'The Trace of the Other'. Trans. Alphonso Lingis. In *Deconstruction in Context*, ed. Mark Taylor (Chicago and London: University of Chicago Press, 1986), pp. 345–59.

—— *The Levinas Reader*, ed. Seán Hand. Oxford: Basil Blackwell, 1989.

—— 'Wholly Otherwise'. Trans. Simon Critchley. In *Re-reading Levinas*, ed. Bernasconi and Critchley, pp. 5–10.

Lovibond, Sabina. 'Feminism and Postmodernism'. *New Left Review*, 178 (1989): 5–28.

Lyotard, Jean-François. *Economie libidinale.* Paris: Editions de Minuit, 1974.

—— *The Postmodern Condition: A Report on Knowledge* (1979). Trans. Geoff Bennington and Brian Massumi. Manchester: Manchester University Press, 1984.

—— *Le Postmoderne expliqué aux enfants: Correspondance 1982–1985*. Paris: Galilée, 1986.

—— *The Differend: Phrases in Dispute*. Trans. Georges Van Den Abbeele. Manchester: Manchester University Press, 1988.

—— 'Time Today'. Trans. Geoff Bennington and Rachel Bowlby. *Oxford Literary Review*, 11 (1989): 3–20.

—— and Thébaud, Jean-Loup. *Just Gaming*. Trans. Brian Massumi. Manchester: Manchester University Press, 1985.

McCarthy, Thomas. *The Critical Theory of Jürgen Habermas*. Cambridge: Polity Press, 1984.

Macintyre, Alisdair. *After Virtue: A Study in Moral Theory*. London: Duckworth, 1981.

Mauss, Marcel. *The Gift: Forms and Functions of Exchange in Archaic Societies*. Trans. I. Cunnison. New York: Norton, 1967.

Meyer, Leonard B. 'Some Remarks on Value and Greatness in Music' (1959). Repr. in *Aesthetics Today*, ed. Morris Philipson and Paul J. Gudel, rev. edn (New York and Scarborough, Ont.: Meridian, 1980), pp. 267–86.

Middleton, Peter. 'Linguistic Turns', *Oxford Literary Review*, 11 (1989): 37–67.

Miller, J. Hillis. *The Ethics of Reading: Kant, de Man, Eliot, Trollope, James, and Benjamin*. New York: Columbia University Press, 1987.

Moi, Toril (ed.). *French Feminist Thought: A Reader*. Oxford: Basil Blackwell, 1989.

Mulvey, Laura. 'Visual Pleasure and Narrative Cinema', *Screen*, 16 (1975): 6–18.

Nadel, Ira B. *Joyce and the Jews: Culture and Texts*. Basingstoke: Macmillan, 1989.

Nicholson, Linda J. *Feminism/Postmodernism*. London: Routledge, 1990.

Norris, Christopher. *Deconstruction: Theory and Practice*. London: Methuen, 1982.

Nussbaum, Martha. 'Perceptive Equilibrium: Literary Theory and Ethical Theory'. In *The Future of Literary Theory*, ed. Ralph Cohen (New York and London: Routledge, 1989), pp. 58–85.

Oelmüller, Willi (ed.). *Normenbegrundung und Normendurchsetzung*. Paderborn: Schöningh, 1978.

Parker, Roszika and Pollock, Griselda. *Old Mistresses: Women, Art and Ideology*. London: Routledge, 1981.

Parrinder, Patrick. *James Joyce*. Cambridge: Cambridge University Press, 1984.

Peake, Charles. *James Joyce: The Citizen and the Artist*. London: Edward Arnold, 1977.

Plesu, Andrei. 'Elements for a Restoration of Ethics'. *Cahiers Roumains d'Etudes Littéraires: Revue Trimestrielle de Critique, d'Esthétique et d'Histoire Littéraires*, 1 (1987): 110–17.

Plotnitsky, Arkady. 'Interpretation, Interminability, Evaluation: From Nietzsche toward a General Economy'. In *Life after Postmodernism*, ed. Fekete, pp. 120–41.

Price, Sally. 'Others' Art – Our Art'. *Third Text*, 6 (1989): 65–71.

Prinz, Jessica. 'The Fine Art of Inexpression: Beckett and Duchamp'. In *Beckett Translating/Translating Beckett*, ed. Alan Warren Friedman, Charles

Rossman and Dina Sherzer (University Park and London: Pennsylvania State University Press, 1987), pp. 95–106.

Rabaté, Jean-Michel. 'Paternity, Thy Name is Joy'. In *The Augmented Ninth*, ed. Benstock, pp. 219–25.

Rajchman, John, 'Lacan and the Ethics of Modernity'. *Representations*, 15 (1986): 42–56.

—— 'Ethics after Foucault'. *Social Text*, 13/14 (1986): 165–83.

Richards, I. A. *Principles of Literary Criticism* (1924). Repr. London: Routledge & Kegan Paul, 1983.

Rorty, Richard. 'Le Cosmopolitisme sans émancipation: en réponse de Jean-François Lyotard'. *Critique*, 41 (1985): 570–83.

—— 'Habermas and Lyotard on Postmodernity'. In *Habermas and Modernity*, ed. Richard Bernstein (Cambridge, Mass.: MIT Press, 1986), pp. 161–76.

—— *Contingency, Irony, and Solidarity*. Cambridge: Cambridge University Press, 1989.

Rushdie, Salman. 'Is Nothing Sacred?' In *Imaginary Homelands: Essays and Criticism, 1981–1991* (London: Granta/Penguin, 1991), pp. 415–29.

Said, Edward. 'Opponents, Audiences, Constituencies, and Community'. In *The Politics of Interpretation*, ed. W. J. T. Mitchell (Chicago and London: University of Chicago Press, 1983), pp. 7–32.

Scholte, Bob. 'The Charmed Circle of Geertz's Harmeneutics: A Neo-Marxist Critique'. *Critique of Anthropology*, 6 (1986): 5–15.

—— 'The Literary Turn in Contemporary Anthropology'. *Critique of Anthropology*, 7 (1987): 33–47.

Scott, Bonnie Kime. *Joyce and Feminism*. Brighton: Hervester Press, 1984.

Siebers, Tobin. *The Ethics of Criticism*. Ithaca, NY and London: Cornell University Press, 1990.

Smith, Barbara Herrnstein. *Contingencies of Value: Alternative Perspectives for Critical Theory*. Cambridge, Mass. and London: Harvard University Press, 1988.

Soper, Kate. 'Postmodernism, Subjectivity and the Question of Value'. *New Left Review*, 186 (1991): 120–8.

Spivak, Gayatri Chakravorty. 'Scattered Speculations on the Question of Value'. In *In Other Worlds: Essays in Cultural Politics* (New York and London: Methuen, 1987), pp. 154–75.

Stewart, Susan. *On Longing: Narratives of the Miniature, the Gigantic, the Souvenir, the Collection*. Baltimore and London: Johns Hopkins University Press, 1984.

Stocking, George. 'Arnold, Tylor, and the Uses of Invention'. In *Race, Culture and Evolution: Essays in the History of Anthropology* (New York: Free Press, 1968), pp. 72–90.

Trilling, Lionel. 'The Fate of Pleasure' (1963). Reprinted in *Beyond Culture: Essays on Literature and Learning* (London: Secker & Warburg, 1966), pp. 27–87.

Tyler, Stephen A. *The Unspeakable: Discourse, Dialogue, and Rhetoric in the Postmodern World*. Madison: University of Wisconsin Press, 1987.

Tylor. E. B. *Primitive Culture*. 2 vols. London: John Murray, 1871.

White, Stephen K. *The Recent Work of Jürgen Habermas: Reason, Justice and Modernity*. Cambridge: Cambridge University Press, 1988.

Whitford, Margaret. *Luce Irigaray: Philosophy in the Feminine*. London and New York: Routledge, 1991.

Williams, Bernard. *Ethics and the Limits of Philosophy*. Cambridge, Mass.: Harvard University Press, 1985.

Williams, Raymond. *Culture and Society*. London: Chatto & Windus, 1958.

—— *Keywords: A Vocabulary of Culture and Society*. 2nd edn. London: Fontana, 1976.

—— *Culture*. London: Fontana, 1981.

Wolin, Richard. 'On Misunderstanding Habermas: A Response to John Rajchman'. *New German Critique*, 49 (1990): 139–54.

Index